Social Entrepreneurship and Social Enterprises
Nordic Perspectives

T0289732

Migrant women stepping into ethnic catering; homeless men employed to take care of bees producing honey for sale; young people on the edge getting microcredit funding to start social businesses; or former criminals joining forces to create social and economic structures for an honest lifestyle. These initiatives capture the transformative power of social enterprise and might indicate how social enterprises have the potential to make a difference for people and societies. The Nordic countries represent an interesting case. Social enterprises and co-operatives played a significant part in paving the way for the Nordic solidaristic welfare state.

As the welfare state grew, civil society organizations and co-operatives lost ground, to a certain extent. But in recent decades, the welfare state has been restructured and, simultaneously, the concepts of social entrepreneurship and social enterprises have gained attention. The Nordic context, with its extensive public welfare structures and a high degree of citizens' participation in public affairs, might affect the emergence of social entrepreneurship and social enterprises.

Linda Lundgaard Andersen is a Professor in Learning, Evaluation and Social Innovation at Roskilde University in Denmark.

Malin Gawell is an Associate Professor in Business Administration at Södertörn University in Sweden.

Roger Spear is a Professor of Social Entrepreneurship teaching organizational systems and research methods at the Open University, UK.

Routledge Studies in Social Enterprise & Social Innovation
Series Editors: Rocio Nogales, Lars Hulgård
and Jacques Defourny

A social enterprise seeks to achieve social, cultural, community economic or environmental outcomes while remaining a revenue-generating business. A social innovation is said to be a new idea or initiative for a social problem that is more effective, efficient, sustainable or just than the current process and that sees the society it is operating in receiving the primary value created rather than a private organization of firms.

Routledge Studies in Social Enterprise & Social Innovation looks to examine these increasingly important academic research themes as a central concept for social theories and policies. It looks to examine and explore the activities of social participation among civil society organizations, SMEs, governments and research institutions. The series will be publishing the breakthrough books of the new frontiers of the field as well as the books that define the state of the nation and that help advance the field.

Social Entrepreneurship and Social Enterprises
Nordic Perspectives
Edited by Linda Lundgaard Andersen,
Malin Gawell and Roger Spear

Social Entrepreneurship and Social Enterprises

Nordic Perspectives

Edited by
Linda Lundgaard Andersen,
Malin Gawell and Roger Spear

Routledge
Taylor & Francis Group

NEW YORK AND LONDON

First published 2016
by Routledge
711 Third Avenue, New York, NY 10017

and by Routledge
2 Park Square, Milton Park, Abingdon, Oxon OX14 4RN

First issued in paperback 2018

Routledge is an imprint of the Taylor & Francis Group, an informa business

Library of Congress Cataloging-in-Publication Data
Names: Lundgaard Andersen, Linda, editor. | Gawell, Malin, editor. |
   Spear, Roger, editor.
Title: Social entrepreneurship and social enterprises : Nordic
   perspectives / edited by Linda Lundgaard Andersen, Malin Gawell,
   and Roger Spear.
Description: First Edition. | New York : Routledge, 2016. | Series:
   Routledge studies in social enterprise & social innovation ; 1 |
   Includes bibliographical references and index.
Identifiers: LCCN 2016006817 | ISBN 9781138656260 (hardback :
   alk. paper) | ISBN 9781315621982 (ebook)
Subjects: LCSH: Social entrepreneurship—Scandinavia. |
   Scandinavia—Social policy. | Welfare state—Scandinavia.
Classification: LCC HD60 .S5922 2016 | DDC 361.7/650948—dc23
LC record available at http://lccn.loc.gov/2016006817

ISBN 13: 978-1-138-34009-1 (pbk)
ISBN 13: 978-1-138-65626-0 (hbk)
Typeset in Sabon
by Apex CoVantage, LLC

Contents

Tables and Figures

Tables

Figures

Foreword

Since the period of emergence in the 1990s, the social enterprise and social entrepreneurship field has rapidly become institutionalized to the extent that we find globally oriented interest organizations, policy programmes, markets and university degrees in all regions of the world. Thus, we have experienced its advancement as an organizational field, gradually closely connected to the more recent widespread interest in social innovation. Social enterprise and social innovation have convincingly made their entry in the international political arena as a sector for the production of welfare services combined with strong and often conflicting values with regard to social benefit, market value, franchising, participation and volunteerism. However, they remain contested and ambivalent notions or quasi-concepts (Defourny & Nyssens, 2012; Jenson & Harrisson, 2013) both in the academic and policy-making domains.

Regarding social entrepreneurship, the largest international compilation on the topic so far (Kickul, Gras, Bacq & Griffith, 2013) pointed out that the first publication on social entrepreneurship came out in 1991, whereas only six publications on the subject appeared globally between 1991 and 1996. Up until the end of the 1990s, social enterprise and social entrepreneurship were largely phenomena that aroused interest among practitioners and consultants. However, in Europe, specific interest in social enterprise had begun as soon as 1990, when the first academic journal on the topic was launched in Italy (*Impresa sociale*). In parallel, a group of researchers had begun to study the emergence of this new institutional arrangement balancing social, economic and participatory governance dimensions. In this context, 'social enterprises' began to be closely observed to understand how they originated and evolved in various national contexts, including Denmark and Finland (Borzaga & Defourny, 2001; Hulgård & Bisballe, 2004; Pättiniemi, 2004). Then things really took off, and in recent years, research examining social enterprise as a concept and comparing it with other types of entrepreneurship has continued to appear. It is only recently, however, that research in the Nordic region of the world has started to appear: this research examines the special characteristics that mark social enterprise and social innovation in the Nordic region and the Nordic countries (Hulgård, 2007; Pestoff, 2009;

Levander, 2011; Andersen & Hulgård, 2015). Moreover, a specialized network called the Social Entrepreneurship Research Network for the Nordic Countries was launched in 2011. Nevertheless, considering the special characteristics of the Nordic countries, there is still a shortage of publications on the interaction between social entrepreneurship, the public sector and the third sector in particular. The fact is that this interaction between the Nordic welfare state and change makers in the third sector probably played a key role as a midwife to more recent and wide-ranging examples of social enterprise and social innovation, for instance, in the large-scale cross-sectoral pilot programmes emerging in the late 1980s.

This volume will both help to establish a background for understanding the relation between the public welfare state in the so-called 'state-friendly societies' in the Nordic countries and to examine whether there is anything specifically Nordic in the field of social enterprise and social innovation. The universally oriented Nordic welfare model became one of the great mega innovations that attracted global attention in the post-war era. We may nevertheless need to ask if the Nordic model is a barrier or a platform for the making of resilient social enterprise and social innovation models aimed at building inclusive and socially just societies under the influence of demographic changes and profound globalization.

Professor Lars Hulgård
Founding member and president of the EMES
network, 2010–2015

References

Borzaga, C., & Defourny, J. (2001). *The Emergence of Social Enterprise*. London: Routledge.

Defourny, J., & Nyssens, M. (2012). Conceptions of Social Enterprise in Europe: A Comparative Perspective with the United States. In B. Gidron & Y. Hasenfeld (Eds.), *Social Enterprises* (pp. 71–90). Basingstoke, UK: Palgrave Macmillan.

Hulgård, L. (2007). *Sociale Entreprenører-en kritisk indføring*. København: Hans Reitzel.

Hulgård, L., & Bisballe, T. (2004). *Work Integration Social Enterprises in Denmark*. Working Papers Series no. 04/08. Liège: EMES European Research Network.

Jenson, J., & Harrisson, D. (2013). *Social Innovation Research in the European Union*. Brussels: European Commission, Directorate-General for Research and Innovation.

Kickul, J., Gras, D., Bacq, S., & Griffiths, M. (Eds.). (2013). *Social Entrepreneurship*. Cheltenham, UK and Northampton, MA: Edward Elgar Publishing.

Levander, U. (2011). *Utanförskap på entreprenad. Diskurser om sociala företag i Sverige*. Göteborg: Daidalos.

Lundgaard Andersen, L., & Hulgård, L. (2015). *Socialt entreprenørskab og social innovation. Sosialt entreprenørskap og sosial innovasjon: Kartlegging av innsatser for sosialt entreprenørskap og sosial innovasjon i Norden*. København: Nordic Council of Ministers.

Pättiniemi, P. (2004). *Work Integration Social Enterprises in Finland*. Working Papers Series no. 04/07. Liège: EMES European Research Network.

Pestoff, V. (2009). Towards a Paradigm of Democratic Governance: Citizen Participation and Co-Production of Personal Social Services in Sweden. *Annals of Public and Cooperative Economy*, 80(2), 197–224.

Preface

This book arose from a recognition that globally, we are seeing a substantial growth in social entrepreneurship, as the state withdraws from the classic Nordic system of welfare provision and transforms this into new forms of private-public-voluntary partnerships and hybrid organizational structures. Social entrepreneurship and social enterprise have emerged as important themes in the way that local and civic societies have responded to these challenging times by developing their social responsibilities into new, engaging forms of citizenship and social economies, whilst citizens have re-discovered self-help and participation as strategies for everyday life. However, as a field of public interest, research, knowledge sharing and teaching social entrepreneurship have reached varying degrees of institutional support in the Nordic countries and Baltic countries. Thus, an initiative was developed with the overall aim of establishing the Nordic, and also the Baltic region, as a leading area of comparative social entrepreneurship research by increasing the interaction between academics and the different actors in the field. SERNOC, a Nordic network, was established with support from NordForsk, and led by Professor Linda Lundgaard Andersen of the Centre for Social Entrepreneurship at Roskilde University.

Through a series of five two-day workshops and events, SERNOC was able to contrast experiences and knowledge in research as well as in teaching on social entrepreneurship in the participating countries: Denmark, Estonia, Finland, Norway and Sweden. Participants in these workshops contributed papers that were subjected to lively discussion and debate. An editorial group was established and made a selection of papers that expressed the rich diversity of experience and thinking in this rapidly developing field. There followed an extended process where the editors reviewed and helped develop these contributions through several drafts with the chapter authors. While this was a collective effort, the co-editors direct a special thank you to Malin Gawell of Södertörn University, who put a lot of insights and hours into the editorial work.

This book contributes to a distinctive regional perspective on the development of social entrepreneurship and social enterprise. It furthermore reveals narrative aspects of participatory approaches in which individuals and structures matter. We hope this makes an important and interesting contribution to the development of global research in the field of social entrepreneurship and social enterprise.

Acknowledgments

We would like to acknowledge with gratitude the financial support of Nord-Forsk in helping to establish the SERNOC network of meetings that led the production of this book.

We would also like to thank the support of the colleagues who took part in the SERNOC network workshops, those who contributed chapters and all those who supported the development of this intellectual contribution to the field over the course of several meetings and numerous exchanges.

1 Social Entrepreneurship and Social Enterprises in the Nordics

Narratives Emerging From Social Movements and Welfare Dynamics

Linda Lundgaard Andersen, Malin Gawell and Roger Spear

Migrant women gradually stepping into their new society and the labour market in their new countries via ethnic catering in the form of a social enterprise; homeless men employed to take care of bees producing honey for sale to the public; young people on the edge getting microcredit funding to start social businesses; men and women with long-term sickness/incapacity gradually developing labour market skills via co-operatives in gardening; or former criminals joining forces to create social and economic structures for an honest lifestyle.

These initiatives capture the transformative power of social entrepreneurship and might indicate how social enterprises have the potential to make a difference for people and societies. Social entrepreneurship has emerged strongly on the international scene and often serves as a vehicle for the provision of welfare services involving powerful and often-conflicting values of public utility, participation and volunteerism. We might picture social entrepreneurship as a generic term for initiatives that are innovative, cross cutting and often targeted at socially disadvantaged people. However, social entrepreneurship is also a phenomenon that contains considerable ambivalence stretched around the powerful dynamics of individualisation and collectivisation, between the social and the market, between marginality and mainstream and between neoliberalism and the solidarity economy.

The interest in social entrepreneurship and social enterprises has spread around the world like a driving wind during the last decades. There are several variations in the discourse—mostly focusing on ventures 'doing good' and/or acting as hybrid mediators of social, political and economic dimensions in society. The discourse is still, however, rather fragmented. The phenomena are furthermore to a great extent intertwined with local, regional and national as well as international characteristics. In this anthology, we try to capture these influences and ground them in empirically based explorations to reveal the role of social entrepreneurship and social enterprises in everyday life and in innovative transformations—and we do that in the setting of the Nordic countries—or 'the Nordics' as we used to frame it ourselves.

The Nordic countries represent an interesting case of the history and development of social entrepreneurship and social enterprises. In the early days of the welfare state, civil society and more specifically, so-called popular mass movements such as the labour movement and co-operatives played a significant part in paving the way for the Nordic solidaristic welfare state. As the welfare state grew, civil society organizations and co-operatives lost ground, to a certain extent. And during the recent decades, the welfare state has been re-assessed and restructured—and at the same time the concepts of social entrepreneurship and social enterprises have gained attention.

The Nordic context, with extensive public welfare structures and a high degree of citizens' participation in public affairs, might affect the emergence of social entrepreneurship and social enterprises slightly differently than countries with other types of social contracts. It further seems that the leading narratives and discourses that have shaped the Nordic societies also shape the narratives of social entrepreneurship and social enterprises in combination with the institutional structures and the ecosystem. Before we explore this hypothesis in this book comprising fifteen contributions (including this overview) from Denmark, Finland, Norway and Sweden, let us say a few more things about the global social entrepreneurship interest and 'the Nordics'.

A Global Interest in Social Entrepreneurship and Social Enterprises Meets 'the Nordics'

The meanings of social entrepreneurship and social enterprises are far from obvious and easy to specify. Conceptual discussions primarily stem from the 1980s and 1990s—even if the term social entrepreneurship was in writing already in the 1970s. These discussions have partly been held in parallel forums. Alex Nicholls (2010) argues that paradigm building actors such as the Ashoka Foundation (founded in 1980 by Bill Drayton), the Schwab Foundation (founded in 1998 by Klaus and Hilde Schwab) and the Skoll Foundation (founded in 1999 by Jeff Skoll) have, together with governments, particularly in the United Kingdom, played a vital role and in many ways influenced the development of the field of social entrepreneurship on a global scale. The early writings of Charles Leadbeater (1997) and Gregory Dees (1998) highlighted and promoted similar messages to an increasingly interested audience of politicians, businesspeople and in other spheres where 'social aims' were on the agenda. This 'stream' has influenced the emerging field of social entrepreneurship—but it is not the only influence.

During the same time, another 'stream' emerged with strong influences from the co-operative movement and particularly ideas about social co-operatives (Borzaga & Defourny, 2001; Defourny & Nyssens, 2012). This approach was grounded in European third-sector traditions, at times referred to as the *social economy*, which included co-operatives, associations, mutuals and foundations (Evers & Laville, 2004). The terms social co-operatives and later on, *social enterprises* (which included trading non-profits) were to dominate discussions. In 1996, the EMES international research network was founded and has been the node for the development of the influential EMES approach to social enterprises which highlight both economic dimensions defined as a continuous activity producing goods and/or services, a significant level of economic risk and a minimum amount of paid work (not only volunteers); social dimensions as an explicit aim to benefit the community, an initiative launched by a group of citizens and a decision-making power not based on capital ownership; and finally, participatory governance dimensions like a high degree of autonomy, a participatory nature, which involves the persons affected by the activity and limited profit distribution (Borzaga & Defourny, 2001; Defourny & Nyssens, 2012). Since then, the definitional criteria have been debated in the international research community and for instance, the question of the rigor by which these criteria have been applied has been discussed (Nyssen & Defourny, 2014; Pestoff & Hulgård, 2015).

There were also other alternative approaches already in the 1980s and 1990s. One particular concept that has had an influence on the development of the field in the Nordic countries is *societal entrepreneurship*, which originally was based on the interest in small business development in local communities (Johannisson & Nilsson, 1989; Johannisson, 1990). Societal entrepreneurship was at that time translated as *community entrepreneurship*, but later on referred to as *societal entrepreneurship* (Gawell, Johannisson & Lundqvist, 2009; Berglund, Johannisson & Schwartz, 2013). Even if the concept has another origin, there are large overlaps with both the *social economy* approach, especially through a rather collective approach, and also the interplay between economic and social/community/societal aims. Later on, *societal entrepreneurship* has partly also been used as an 'umbrella' term for entrepreneurship with community, social, cultural or ecological aims (Gawell, 2014a).

Nowadays, there is a wide variety of approaches related to *social entrepreneurship* and *social enterprises* as well as *social innovation*. As the chapters in this anthology reveal, there are strong similarities between the current international approaches and those found in the Nordic countries; thus, different versions co-exist but sometimes take slightly different forms depending on national contexts (Andersen, Bager & Hulgård, 2010; Hulgård, 2012; Gawell, 2014a, The Nordic Council of Ministers, 2015; Andersen, 2015b). But before we elaborate further on the characteristics of social entrepreneurship and social enterprises in the Nordic countries, let us elaborate a bit on 'the Nordics', which are sometimes referred to as 'the Scandinavians'.

One obvious feature is their shared geographical location on or close to the Scandinavian Peninsula in northern Europe—a location that without the warm Gulf Stream in the Atlantic Ocean would be very inhospitable especially during the long winters. There, approximately 27 million people live in the five main countries of Denmark, Finland, Iceland, Norway and Sweden (including also the self-governed Greenland, Faroe Islands and Åland). The population is concentrated in Denmark, the southern quarter of Sweden, and the capital regions of Finland and Norway. The majority of areas are, however, sparsely populated.

There is also a historical and cultural affinity. They share Viking and old Norse mythology (before year 1000 AD), similar languages (except for Finish), the Christianisation to Christianity and later, during the sixteenth century, the Protestant Reformation, all of which have been combined with different forms of collaboration as well as rivalry. They have endured several wars during seventeenth and eighteenth centuries that have contributed to different state constellations such as a Danish-Norwegian union and a Swedish-Finnish union in the sixteenth up to the eighteenth century, when Finland was engaged in war with Russia. During the nineteenth century, there was a Swedish-Norwegian union before the national states as we know them today took shape, and two countries (Denmark and Norway) shared the experience of German occupation during the Second World War.

Despite, or perhaps because of this somewhat turbulent history, the twentieth century has been characterized by a close collaboration manifested in the foundation of a Nordic Council in 1952, a Nordic passport union and labour market (1954) and a Nordic Council of Ministers (founded in 1971). All Nordic countries are members of the Schengen agreement but have taken different approach to the European Union (Denmark, Finland and Sweden are members). Norway, Denmark and Iceland are members of NATO. Only Finland uses the euro.

Last, but not least, there is yet another common feature for the Nordic countries: the transformation from countries in which the majority of the population was rather poor and governed by legislation restricting social and political freedom to the extent that one million people emigrated from Sweden to America between 1850–1910 (Statistics Sweden, 2015), to modern societies based on individual rights and a high standard of living with developed public welfare services. This transformation has permeated socioeconomic development during the last century. In many ways, it resembles the patterns of industrialization and democratization in other Western countries. However, the development of mixed economies with a relatively high degree of international trade has been combined with the development of a tax-based public system of provision for, among other things, education, health care and social care. There have been variations of timing and detail implementation between the Nordic countries, but the strong pattern of similarities has been referred to as 'the Nordic way' or as 'social democratic welfare regimes' in Esping-Andersen's typology.

A Social and Entrepreneurial Welfare State

There were several forces driving the development of the welfare state. Equality, democracy, social development and industry's economic interest in good support for the workforce are often mentioned. The development was influenced strongly by social democracy as well as social liberal ideas. Co-operatives and other membership-based associations were common in the creation of the welfare states even though these social democratic welfare regimes (Esping-Andersen, 1990) came to be dominated by public service provision.

Salamon and Anheier (1998) adopted a similar approach in their social origins theory of the development of the non-profit sector in different types of countries. They argued that in the social democratic model:

> State-sponsored and state-delivered social welfare protections are quite extensive and the room left for service-providing non-profit organiza-tions quite constrained. This type of model is most likely where working class elements are able to exert effective political power, albeit typi-cally in alliance with other social classes. While the upshot is a limited service-providing non-profit sector, however, it is not necessarily a lim-ited non-profit sector overall, as some accounts would suggest. To the contrary, given the political battles likely to be involved in the extension of state-provided welfare protections, we can expect non-profit organi-zations to still be quite active in such societies, but with a significantly different role, a role not as service providers but as vehicles for the expression of political, social, or even recreational interests. (p. 229)

The welfare state in the Nordic countries has played, and continues to play, a significant role in framing and undergirding the development of not only the non-profit sector, but also social entrepreneurship and social enterprises through funding and infrastructure, educational support, knowledge shar-ing and research—even though this has also been the pushed forward by individual entrepreneurial agents as well as more collective entrepreneurial activities. Mariana Mazzucato has argued that the entrepreneurial state as a more general phenomenon largely is underestimated in international lit-erature on social entrepreneurship and social enterprises. She accentuates the three factors that arose from her analysis: the necessity of building and paying attention to how institutions and organizations in government are able to create long-run growth strategies, the ability to engage in the world of uncertainty, winning and losing and developing a better understanding of the different roles played in the 'ecosystem' of innovation (Mazzucato, 2013, p. 198ff). This approach is largely consistent with Nordic scholars conceptualising the contemporary welfare state on the one hand as being transformed into the 'competition state' (Pedersen, 2013) supported by the 'social-economic conception' of reforming welfare institutions and govern-ance by regulation, neoliberal individualism and persuasion of the value of flexible labour markets. This position is well aligned to the critics of social entrepreneurship and social enterprises claiming this to be driven by market forces and the individual neoliberal entrepreneurial approach to social prob-lems (Hulgård, 2011). On the other hand, an opposing conceptualisation makes a case for the 'social and innovative welfare state' still guided by equality, solidarity and inclusion but simultaneously strongly focused on the creation of a strong and innovative state economy that actively invests in welfare and modifies imbalances and insufficiencies generated by the free market (Sirovátka & Greve, 2014; Greve, 2015). This approach likewise mirrors well the notion that social entrepreneurship and social enterprises might be forming a new solidarity economy and a people-centred development (Hulgård & Shajahan, 2012).

Structural Changes Challenge the Nordic Welfare Model

The strong structures supporting a market-based economy as well as a tax-funded (social) public sector have been exposed to challenges during the latter part of twentieth century. Traditional industry has had to cope with increased global competition. New businesses have benefited from growing global markets. The Nordic countries have all been through economic reforms, including the de- or re-regulation of former public domains. Again, the timing has varied between countries. So has the severity of these challenges as well as the political approach used to cope with them. Still, we can talk about a common development that partly is shared with many other countries; however, with the Nordic welfare model as a point of departure and not radically questioned as such, the situation in the Nordic countries still is characterized by varieties of capitalism with relatively strong labour market unions and tax-funded public welfare services—a co-ordinated market economy in the 'varieties of capitalism' typology (Hall & Soskice, 2001).

The last decades' transformations have provided the context for the emergence of discussions on social entrepreneurship and social enterprises. On the one hand, these discussions have many similarities to international discourses and the same types of social entrepreneurship and social enterprises can be seen as in other parts of the world. On the other hand, there are differences. There is already public support for services that often are provided by third-sector organizations including social enterprises—even though policy for such services is currently under reconstruction. There is also a strong tradition of rights to equal and democratic influence both in terms of advocacy as well as in the distribution of tax-funded activities.

Social Entrepreneurship and Social Enterprises in the Nordic Countries

A Nordic perspective on social entrepreneurship and social enterprises is based on and inspired by international currents, but it is also inspired by researchers and practitioners embedding social entrepreneurship and social enterprises in the national, cultural and historical contexts. This book does not have ambitions for a comparative analysis across different countries, but an exploration of research within an international region, namely, the

Nordic region. It offers the possibility of drawing some conclusions about the nature of research in the region and how it may be understood within its context. And through its detailed study of a set of apparently similar countries, it provides interesting insights into patterns of development of social entrepreneurship and social enterprises at this supra-national regional level.

We have, in this anthology, had an inclusive approach in which researchers have been invited to participate in the Nordic network on research in social entrepreneurship (SERNOC) to discuss social entrepreneurship and social enterprises. Instead of establishing a unanimous definition as a point of departure, the different researchers in the network and in this anthology bring in slightly different approaches, which brings out the richness of perspectives and approaches to social entrepreneurship in the Nordic region. Some specific streams in the field of social entrepreneurship and social enterprises can, however, be identified. These streams can be noticed in practice, public debate and in research. They are not clearly demarcated from each other, even though particular characteristics can be identified.

Firstly, with roots in co-operative and popular mass movement traditions, participatory approaches and democratic governance structures are common. These types of ventures can be found both in established forms and among new initiatives. This stream of influence relates to the EMES approach to social enterprises and social economy, but also to discussions about non-profit organizations or civil society organizations.

Secondly, there is a stream that derives from the field of entrepreneurship that historically has been and still to a large extent is embedded in a business/economic discourse. This particular stream has, however, 'broadened' the understanding of entrepreneurship to include and even focus on different types of social aims rather than prioritizing financial and/or self-interest aims. This stream can be referred to as community entrepreneurship or in Sweden, as societal entrepreneurship.

Thirdly, issues of experimental laboratories, of developing welfare services and participatory governance structures, of forming collaborations with the civic society as well as private and public partnerships are at the centre of this development as well. This promotes features of hybridity referring to the multifaceted profiles: multiple stakeholders, multiple objectives and multiple resources. Victor Pestoff points out that the Nordic countries, due to their specific welfare state origins and developments, are very likely to develop hybrid organizations as they enter the era of social entrepreneurship and social enterprises (Pestoff, 2014).

Social entrepreneurship is about social engagement combined with some kind of entrepreneurial action (Gawell, 2008), and social enterprises are basically about the creation and running of ventures with social aims (Gawell, 2014a). In the following chapters, a rich display will provide insights on how different specifications of these basic definitions and studies of social entrepreneurship and social enterprises aim to understand how new socio-economic dynamics are reshaping crucial aspects of life and the societies we live in.

Major Approaches to Social Entrepreneurship and Social Enterprises

From a Nordic perspective, a historical framework is important for fully understanding their experience of social entrepreneurship and social enterprises. In Nordic research from Denmark, Sweden, Finland and Norway, there is evidence that early forms of social enterprises and co-operatives acted as important drivers for innovation in the development of industry, agriculture and local communities, but then subsequently, the establishment and expansion of the welfare state led to a weakening of these phenomena because of the government taking over some of their socio-economic activities. More recently in the 2000s, we are seeing a new wave of interest in social entrepreneurship and social enterprises. This has been inspired by developments in Europe and the USA, but also driven by a process to transform the Nordic welfare state through new forms of co-operation and partnership with civil society organizations.

From a Danish perspective, Hulgård and Andersen (2009) point out that social entrepreneurship and social enterprises represent an interesting special case in the international development of this field. Social entrepreneurship and social enterprises reached Denmark from outside, partly via a European socio-economic tradition, particularly from countries such as Belgium, France and Italy, and partly via a more market-oriented approach to the provision of social services from countries such as the USA and United Kingdom. Historically, Denmark occupied a very strong position in the first socio-economic wave that swept across the world from the mid-1800s onwards with the development of the co-operative movement. The second socio-economic wave arose internationally through the development of the voluntary sector from the mid-1980s onwards. In this instance, Denmark experienced a high degree of project organization in the social area at the expense of organization and business development, whereas the country was slightly slower in responding to the third socio-economic wave, in which the emphasis was on the development of coherent welfare strategies and policies (Hulgård & Andersen, 2009). In addition, the modernisation of the welfare state that has been in progress since the 1980s represents yet another brick in the complex picture. Danish modernisation has taken the form of a long series of focused political and administrative programmes and can be understood as a development of social entrepreneurial dimensions in welfare services and organizations, with the introduction of 'quasi-market-based' welfare services, self-management and greater emphasis on user influence being among the focus areas (Andersen, 2014). Danish social enterprises are examined in configurations such as 'corporate sustainability strategies and institutional theory' (Hockerts & Wünstenhagen, 2010; Agrawal & Hockerts, 2013; Hockerts, 2014), and identifying the contribution of design thinking to social enterprises' value creation (Krull, 2013), social value creation and financial interests in social entrepreneurship as an innovation field between cooperation and governance (Fæster, 2013), and studies of the source of social entrepreneurship through explorative case studies of Danish and British social enterprises (Kulothungan, 2014).

In Sweden, there is no legal structure or official regulations defining social entrepreneurship or social enterprises. There are, however, different 'versions' of social entrepreneurship and social enterprises that can rather be seen as subcultures with slightly different approaches to these elusive phenomena (Gawell, 2014a). One 'version' draws heavily on co-operative principles and influences from European social co-operatives/social enterprises and the social economy (Stryjan, 1996, 2006; Pestoff, 1998, 2008; Levander, 2011; Gawell, 2014a, 2015). Their role in integrating long-term unemployed people is commonly highlighted. Another in many ways overlapping 'version' stems from non-profit popular mass movement participatory principles (Gawell, 2006, 2014a). A third 'version' is primarily grounded in (small) business and local community development and is often referred to as *societal entrepreneurship* (Johannisson & Nilsson, 1989; Johannisson, 1990; Gawell, Johannisson & Lundqvist, 2009; Berglund et al., 2013; Gawell, Pierre & von Friedrichs, 2014), whereas a fourth 'version' is characterized by a more 'conventional' business approach and can therefore be referred to as *social purpose businesses* (Gawell, 2014a). There are furthermore contributions focusing on public entrepreneurship (Bjerke & Karlsson, 2013), on policy and institutional aspects of social entrepreneurship (Lundström & Zhou, 2014) or viewing entrepreneurship more generally as social change (Steyaert & Hjorth, 2006).

From a Finnish perspective, Harri Kostilainen and Pekka Pättiniemi point to how social enterprises are being formed against the background of international research and practice, with experiences being taken in particular from Italy, with its type A and type B model definitions of social co-operatives, and from the United Kingdom's reform of public services. Social enterprises can be identified specifically through two particular roles as change agents and as contract partners for the delivery of public services. They outline a brief historical perspective, which, as far as Finland is concerned, shows that before the expansion and establishment of the welfare state, social enterprises and co-operative forms played an important and innovative role in the development of industrial society and local communities (Kostilainen & Pättiniemi, 2013). Finland therefore has a long history in which 'citizenship organizations' played a role as producers of services and new forms of co-operatives has emerged (Moilanen, 2010; Pellervo, 2012). The development of social enterprises has, however, been modest in Finland in recent years, and in decline compared with ordinary private enterprises.

From a Norwegian perspective, a mapping report indicates increased attention towards social entrepreneurship in recent years through the setting up of organizations, the publication of literature and the establishment of Internet resources, blogs, forums and networks giving social entrepreneurs exposure. Examples of this include *The Pilot*, a network of social entrepreneurs and philanthropists who in 2012 published an action plan for social innovation and social entrepreneurship, and books suggesting action to promote social entrepreneurship (Schei & Rønning, 2009; Gustavsen & Kobro, 2012). An earlier Norwegian report based on interviews with 20 social entrepreneurs and a documentary analysis proposes three types of actors shaping the development of social entrepreneurship and social enterprises: the concept developer, the specialist and the idealist (Utredning om sosialt entreprenørskap, 2011).

Policies and Emerging Institutional Structures

It is well established that the initiation, development and consolidation of social entrepreneurship and social enterprises demands support frameworks and incentive structures that combine financial, legal, business and social dimensions. A number of international research reports have documented this and developed the concept of an ecosystem of support (ICF Consultant Services, 2014), just as a number of European policy initiatives in recent years have established related measures (European Commission, 2011). Likewise, research, development and knowledge sharing as well as education represent dimensions in the development of a multi-faceted ecosystem of support. Since social entrepreneurship and social enterprises in the Nordic countries tends to be a more recent phenomenon, the development of policies for ecosystems of support is still in progress.

The ecosystems of support for social entrepreneurship and social enterprises can be based on different dimensions. Andersen (2014) argues that four dimensions, practice, policy, education and research, are significant elements in how to stimulate and consolidate. The ecosystem developed by ICF Consulting Services focuses on entrepreneurial-related issues like legal frameworks, social impact markets and measurements, networks and mutual support structures and mechanisms as well as specialist business development (ICF Consulting Services, 2014, p. 6). However, the Nordic case illustrates that we need to widen the ecosystem to include education and research as drivers for developing social entrepreneurship and social enterprises. The pivotal point to accentuate is that the four-dimensional model shapes a dynamic, interrelated and interacting system that can both hinder and increase the development and consolidation. An educational system permeated by social entrepreneurial thinking and acting generates knowledge, social and cultural forms of capital that increase action potential, which in turn would affect practice in many different ways (Hulgård & Andersen, 2014, p. 59).

The four dimensions highlighted by Andersen are all well-established features of the Nordic countries' societal infrastructure, state capacity and the subject of public- and private-driven development, albeit with different national degrees of implementation. The political dimension consisting of legal framework for social enterprises, venture capital and support structures is well developed in Finland, but less so in the other Nordic countries. Denmark has just implanted a legal definition for social enterprises and launched a certificate procedure.

The biggest influence on the development of social entrepreneurship and social enterprises is, however, the more general shift in welfare policies such as the labour market, health care and social care policies that have been implemented during the last decades. Private service providers in welfare-related sectors have been promoted through public procurements and/or client choice models (Gawell, 2014b; Gawell & Westlund, 2014; Andersen, 2015a). This shift is elaborated on further in many of the chapters in this anthology. There are furthermore hubs, advice and support forums, incubators and network groups representing significant strategic and up-skilling elements in social entrepreneurship and social enterprise spheres—and the Nordic countries display a rich variety of such initiatives.

The educational dimension has been particularly important in developing the ecosystem of support in a number of Nordic countries. In principle, this covers elementary school, youth training, but bachelor/master programmes and doctorates related to social entrepreneurship and social enterprises are probably the most established and consolidated in Denmark, although educational initiatives are also gaining ground in the other Nordic countries. Two centres, the *Centre for Social Entrepreneurship* and the *Danish Centre for Social Economy*, have been set up with large grants from a special socio-political government committee (Satspuljen) aimed at developing, researching and establishing education and capacity development in social entrepreneurship, social enterprises and civil society organizations over a period of eight years. The *Centre for Social Entrepreneurship* has a special task to research how and whether social entrepreneurship and social enterprises might adapt in relation to disadvantaged citizens and groups (Hulgård, Andersen, Bisballe & Spear, 2008; Andersen & Hulgård, 2010; Andersen, 2015b). In Sweden, support for start-up counselling for co-operative ventures has been given to *Coompanion* (former LKU/FKU) for the last 30 years, and this has contributed to, among other things, the development of parent co-operative nursery schools and work-integration social enterprises.

In general, the Nordic countries have been developing university studies within social entrepreneurship and in social enterprises. In brief, Roskilde University in Denmark offers two master's programmes: a part-time master's programme in social entrepreneurship and a full-time international master's programme in social entrepreneurship and management. Corresponding to this, a large number of Nordic universities offer courses in social entrepreneurship, such as the Copenhagen Business School and the Centre for Entreprenørskap at Oslo University and in Sweden, there have been individual courses at different levels for several years at Chalmers, Gothenburg University, MidSweden University, the Stockholm School of Entrepreneurship (collaboration between the Karolinska Institute, Konstfack, the Royal Institute of Technology, Stockholm School of Economics, Stockholm University) and Södertörn University. Other universities have now followed to develop different courses, but there are currently no other full, coherent programmes.

And there are several different courses and other initiatives throughout the established system of folk high school and other popular education institutes (studieförbund). Social entrepreneurial learning seems to vary between formal, instructor-initiated learning and non-formal learner-led forms of interactions (Levinsohn, 2015).

A Few Words on Scope and Scale

One might hypothesise that social entrepreneurship and social enterprises follow a similar pattern of development to that of non-profits. Janelle Kerlin's analysis of the development of social enterprise globally (2010) takes a similar approach to the social origins theory developed by Salamon and Anheier (1998) and argues that the origins of social enterprise derived from four factors: civil society, state capacity, market functioning and international aid. But her analysis is at a quite an aggregate level—seven regions, with Europe being one of them. And as indicated in the analysis of Salamon, Sokolowski, and Anheier (2000), it is possible to have quite different levels of non-profit activity within Europe depending on the third-sector regime.

But we make an important contribution by complementing this structural institutional approach with the analysis of discourses influencing the shape of social enterprise development. Thus, it is important to look at the role of global and national discourses in framing possible pathways for social enterprise development. We have already referred to global influences. On the European level, there are a number of initiatives influencing development: firstly, the influence of the European Social Fund in placing the social economy on the agenda; secondly, the Social Business Initiative, which has opened the field to social enterprises; and thirdly, social innovation initiatives (BEPA, FP7) with their emphasis on inclusive growth also provide legitimacy to social entrepreneurship and the development of social enterprises.

The above two approaches (Kerlin and Salamon et al., respectively) offer some explanations for the way in which social enterprise has emerged in the Nordic countries; from a common starting point, the role of the third sector has been crowded out as far as service provision is concerned, and there has been more focus on advocacy. The social origins approach has also informed our analysis by emphasising the importance of historical institutional arrangements that shape the development of a sector.

It is difficult to give a precise account of the scale of social entrepreneurship and social enterprises. The processes referred to as social entrepreneurship are highly varied and elusive, and the ventures referred to as social enterprises vary substantially depending on definition; most existing definitions of social enterprises are not easy to match with experiences on the ground, as the definitions lack equivalence with legal forms in the Nordic countries, with some exceptions. In Finland, there is a law on social enterprises with a focus on work integration (see Kostilainen and Pättiniemi in this volume). In Denmark, a registration for social enterprises has just been implemented, but recent surveys point to a limited number of approximately 300 social enterprises that consequently often are positioned as laboratories for welfare development, work integration, urban development and green, sustainable products (Jacobsen, 2013; Thuesen, Bach, Albæk, Jensen, Hansen & Weibel, 2013).

In Sweden, the Swedish Agency for Growth and Regional Development manages a register of ventures that want to be included on the register and that are deemed to meet the following criteria: firstly, a primary goal of providing work integration for people with difficulties entering the ordinary labour market; secondly, creating participation through co-ownership or other well-developed forms of engagement; thirdly, re-investing profits in their own or similar activities; and finally, they should be privately owned and governed.[1] There are currently 350 ventures listed in this register. Demarcation lines between these social ventures referred to as social enterprises and other social ventures that are simply registered as 'ordinary' business or 'ordinary' non-profit associations and could for different reasons also be referred to as social enterprises of some sort are very vague and therefore this list can only be seen as a partial indicator.

Since the numbers of social enterprises in the Nordic countries are currently quite limited, social entrepreneurship and social enterprises tend to be regarded as kinds of micro experimental laboratories for renewal of welfare services typically dedicated to disadvantaged groups of citizens gaining better capabilities through up-skilling, democracy and citizenship. We argue, however, that different forms of social entrepreneurship and social enterprises have played significant roles in the transformation of the Nordic countries from places providing rather poor and harsh livelihoods for the majority of the people to places enjoying relatively secure and prosperous conditions during the last century or so. In addition, this social entrepreneurial wave strengthens the democratically governed public governance structures in which social, political and economic aspects have been addressed. It has furthermore influenced private for- and non-profit actors to recognize the importance of good working and living conditions as well as social security for the workers and others in society. These developments have not, however, always been automatic or even smooth. The processes have faced both protests and continual challenges.

This anthology breaks new ground theoretically and empirically. It takes a pioneering approach by defining a field of interest: a supra-national region that shares a similar welfare system, has a variety of capitalism and which to a large extent has faced similar challenges in recent years. Previous studies (e.g., Kerlin, 2010) have chosen larger and much more diverse regions as a focus of analysis. Secondly, our approach broadens from institutional theoretic analyses, and recognises the importance of discourses in framing discussions and shaping policy, and thus it argues that the forms that social entrepreneurship and social enterprise take have to be seen in the context of the historical evolution of both institutions and discourses. Consequently, the choice of field and the broad analytical framework provide a theoretical perspective that goes beyond the Nordics, and hopefully will inform research activity in many other parts of the world.

From an Introduction to Multiple Contributions

Following this editorial introduction to this anthology, there are four groups of chapters. The first, examines social entrepreneurship in national contexts, and, comprises four chapters (2–5). In "Social Entrepreneurship: Demolition of the Welfare State or an Arena for Solidarity?", Linda Lundgaard Andersen and Lars Hulgård characterize the 'new' discourse of social entrepreneurship as coming to Denmark from the international scene, but they also trace significant historical links to the traditions of the co-operative movement, the experimental tradition and to decades of welfare modernisation in Denmark. The chapter demonstrates its present relevance to the current situation in Denmark through five current platforms for social entrepreneurship; it concludes by pointing to how social entrepreneurship appeals to fundamentally different strategies for the future of modern welfare society, and by arguing that these potentials and expectations seem to be pushing and pulling the articulation of social enterprise in several different directions.

In "Social Entrepreneurship and Social Enterprises: Chameleons Through Times and Values", Malin Gawell explores some of the aspects that social entrepreneurship in Sweden 'stir up'. The chapter discusses developments in the emerging field of social entrepreneurship in Sweden, and Gawell points to how it is obvious at first glance that social entrepreneurship, in any form in which it appears, is part of an intertextual vision of 'good development' in which social aims are ascribed to solve social problems in a smooth way. However, social entrepreneurship addresses vital aspects of social life in society, and it is important to note that these are filled with tensions—especially in times when social contracts are renegotiated.

The "Evolution of the Social Enterprise Concept in Finland" is addressed by Harri Kostilainen and Pekka Pättiniemi, who point to how Finland accommodates a rich and established sector of social economy organizations playing legitimate roles as a part of the welfare state. These organizations have had a particular importance in service delivery for specific special needs and for disadvantaged areas in the country. The chapter analyses the evolution of the Finnish concept of social enterprise and the institutionalization of this phenomenon. Finnish social enterprises in recent times are expected to effectively combine the business skills of private enterprises with a strong social mission.

And finally, Hans Abraham Hauge and Tora Mathea Waswik introduce "Social Enterprise as a Contested Terrain for Definitions and Practice: The

Case of Norway", in which they highlight how the meaning of 'social enterprise' currently is contested in public discourse by social entrepreneurs and actors representing dominant political and economic interests in public, business and voluntary organizations. The concept is used rhetorically to promote divergent perspectives on how commercial strategies should be used to address social problems. The chapter discusses the possibility of social enterprise being co-opted by powerful actors' interests, or on the other hand, whether social enterprise can contribute to citizens' freedom from dependency on the welfare state's social services.

This is followed by a second group of three chapters (6–8) examining social entrepreneurship, social innovation, and cultural processes. The first is "Practicing Entrepreneuring and Citizenship: Social Venturing as a Learning Context for University Students", in which Bengt Johannisson unfolds a training, teaching and practicing enactive research project for developing social, economic and value entrepreneurship aimed at students from a Swedish business school. Students experienced collaborating with practitioners in three social ventures in the regional context, and experienced the challenges of social entrepreneuring as a collective endeavour. Their overall lessons learned were that learning for and through social entrepreneuring are not just about acquiring instrumental knowledge, but are also an existential challenge.

In "Employees as Social Intrapreneurs: Active Employee Participation in Social Innovation", Catharina Juul Kristensen begins by recognising hat employees form an important but less explored and utilized resource for social innovation in public or third-sector welfare organizations. The chapter contributes by conceptualising active employees as social intrapreneurs that participate in social innovation and thereby elucidate its potential and multiplicity. Employees draw on their important knowledge of the everyday challenges of the organizations and the wishes and needs of their users and customers and of the local communities in order to inspire and refine innovations.

Brita Fladvad Nielsen and Jonas Asheim explore in "The Added Value of Social Entrepreneurship in Contemporary Social Design in Norway" the differences and similarities between Norwegian social designers and social entrepreneurs. They find that although these actors share the common goal of improving life quality through products and services, they are to a large extent separated. Based on six open-ended interviews and a selection of the social entrepreneurship literature, their findings are that social designers are trained to emphasise empathy and environmentally sustainable solutions, whereas social entrepreneurs strengthen the economic sustainability as well as leadership and risk-taking roles.

The third group of chapters (9–12) examines social entrepreneurship and the mobilisation of local resources, beginning with "Social Entrepreneurship: Between Odysseus's Scar and Abraham's Sacrifice". Here, Daniel Ericsson, based on a narrative turn, brings the City of Malmö into focus, where social entrepreneurship initiatives are being proposed to reduce health inequalities among citizens. This chapter suggests that social entrepreneurship in theory and practice is shaped by the narrative styles of Homer and the Old Testament, and that building the legitimacy of social entrepreneurship apparently entails not only aligning biased interests with neoliberal and managerial discourses, but also narrating the reality of social entrepreneurship by means of enchanting digressions and tacit truth claims.

In "Social Entrepreneurship as Collaborative Processes in Rural Sweden", Yvonne von Friedrichs and Anders Lundström discuss social entrepreneurship as a collective force for local communities to address structural changes in society. They draw upon five examples of how small Swedish communities have developed various collaborative models of social entrepreneurship by engaging with different stakeholders in order to keep or develop prosperity and well-being for local residents. The results shows that there are no quick fixes, that community-based entrepreneurship is a long-term activity that has to be worked on in each local context and that decisions on how to make the work successful must be made locally.

Unni Beate Sekkesæter analyses "Microfinance as a Case Study of Social Entrepreneurship in Norway" in the context of the Nordics as a social capital building process and arena for learning and exchange of experience among self-employed and small business owners in Norway. The chapter draws on data from fieldwork in Norway, Hordaland County and the author's involvement in building a microfinance organization in Norway. The benefit for those who managed to start their own enterprise and for society overall may be very substantial as can be seen in Hordaland, where the financial turnover achieved by members of the 21 network groups has been substantial, allowing women to continue to live and work in rural areas.

Anders Edvik and Fredrik Björk in "Social Change Through Temporary, Short-Term Interventions: The Role of Legitimacy in Organizing Social Innovations" focus on a neglected dimension of social innovation, arguing that organizational aspects of social innovation deserve more attention. Using institutional theory, more specifically, the concept of legitimacy, the chapter looks at why project grants have become an important way of organizing social innovation processes, especially those that are structured around cross-sector collaboration. The argument is illustrated by five examples from the regional ecosystem of social innovation and social entrepreneurship in the Skåne Region in Sweden.

The final group of chapters (13–15) addresses social entrepreneurship in policy-informed sectors. It begins with a chapter by Malin Gawell, Elisabeth Sundin and Malin Tillmar, who explore and discuss "Entrepreneurship Invited Into the (Social) Welfare Arena" and how this invitation is handled by different actors and what conditions favour entrepreneurship. Departing from a variety of empirical cases from the private, public and non-profit sectors, the chapter illustrates expressions of social entrepreneurship in current welfare society. Neither social considerations nor entrepreneurship are new phenomena in any sector, so what is described and discussed is current changes and new expressions, not something entirely new.

In "Narratives of Social Enterprises: Their Construction, Contradictions and Implications in the Swedish Debate", Ulrika Levander explores the construction of Swedish work-integration social enterprises and their internal contradictions and implications. Work-integration social enterprises stand out as an important remedy for social challenges, such as mass unemployment and social marginalization, but what does this imply for their capabilities of simultaneously embracing ideals of democratic grassroot participation of marginalized groups?

Finally, in "Democratic Innovations: Exploring Synergies Between Three Key Post-New Public Management Concepts", Victor Pestoff points to how the concepts of democratic governance share much in common with those of social enterprise, social innovation and co-production, which are highly complex phenomena involving multiple dimensions and requiring a multidisciplinary approach. Yet, the academic debate normally oversimplifies them, often from the perspective of a single discipline, whereas this chapter identifies the multi-dimensional and multi-disciplinary nature of these concepts.

These chapters develop a rich analytical tapestry of experiences of social entrepreneurship and social enterprise in a distinctive supra-national region of Europe: the Nordics. These four Nordic countries face similar issues of reshaping their traditional social democratic welfare regimes and engaging with global capitalism. And our thematic examination of how these Nordic countries are framing these concepts of social entrepreneurship and social enterprise and developing their practices reveals important similarities, but at the same time, an interesting diversity. We argue that the form that social entrepeneurship takes can only be understood in terms of both the institutional context and the discourses emerging from the historical interplay between civil society movements, new and old economic actors, and evolving state policies. The anthology provides researchers and policy makers with important insights on how this new wave of socio-economic change is playing a key role in transforming the way in which a supra-national region engages with current issues of our times.

Note

1. Swedish Agency for Growth and Regional Development register of social ventures, www.sofisam.se.

References

Agrawal, A. & Hockerts, K. (2013). Institutional Theory as a Framework for Practitioners of Social Entrepreneurship. In T. Osburg & R. Schmidpeter (Eds.), *Social Innovation: Solutions for a Sustainable Future*. Heidelberg: Springer Science.

18　*Linda Lundgaard Andersen, Malin Gawell and Roger Spear*

Andersen, L. L. (2014). *Concepts in Social Entrepreneurship and Social Innovation: Nordic Council Workgroup on Social Entrepreneurship and Social Innovation.* Keynote speech, 3 February, Nordic Council Meeting, Malmö University.

Andersen, L. L. (2015a). Micro-Processes of Collaborative Innovation in Danish Welfare Settings: A Psychosocial Approach to Learning and Performance. In A. Agger, B. Damgaard, A. H. Krogh & E. Sørensen (Eds.), *Collaborative Innovation in the Public Sector: Northern European Experiences.* Sharjah: Bentham EBooks.

Andersen, L. L. (2015b). Social Entrepreneurship and Social Innovation: Human Economy, Governance and Volunteerism Revisited. In N. R. Jensen (Ed.), *CURSIV#15: Voluntary Work and Youth Unemployment.* Aarhus: Aarhus University Press.

Andersen, L. L. & Hulgård, L. (2010). Socialt entreprenørskab—fyrtårne og kuldsejlede projekter. In L. L. Andersen, L. Hulgård & T. Bager (Eds.), *Socialt entreprenørskab.* Odense: University Press of Southern Denmark.

Andersen, L. L., Hulgård, L. & Bager, T. (2010). *Socialt entreprenørskab.* Odense: University Press of Southern Denmark.

Berglund, K., Johannisson, B. & Schwartz, B. (2013). *Societal Entrepreneurship: Positioning, Penetrating, Promoting.* Cheltenham, UK & Northampton, MA: Edward Elgar.

Bjerke, B. & Karlsson, M. (2013). *Social Entrepreneurship: To Act as If and Make a Difference.* Cheltenham: Edward Elgar.

Borzaga, C. & Defourny, J. (2001). *The Emergence of Social Enterprise.* London: Routledge.

Dees, J. Gregory. (1998). Enterprising nonprofits. *Harvard Business Review*, 76, 54–69.

Defourny, J. & Nyssens, M. (2012). *The EMES Approach of Social Enterprise in a Comparative Perspective.* EMES Working Papers Series 12/03.

Defourny, J. & Nyssens, M. (2014). The EMES Approach of Social Enterprise in a Comparative Perspective. In J. Defourny, L. Hulgård & V. Pestoff (Eds.), *Social Enterprise and the Third Sector: Changing European Landscape in a Comparative Perspective.* London: Routledge.

Esping-Andersen, G. (1990). *The Three Worlds of Welfare Capitalism.* Princeton: Princeton University Press.

European Commission. (2011). *Social Business Initiative: Creating a Favourable Climate for Social Enterprises, Key Stakeholders in the Social Economy and Innovation.* Available at http://ec.europa.eu/internal_market/social_business/docs/COM2011_682_en.pdf.

Evers, A. & Laville, J. L. (2004). *The Third Sector in Europe.* Cheltenham: Edward Elgar.

Fæster, M. (2013). *Innovationsfeltet mellem samarbejde og styring: En feltanalyse om social værdiskabelse og økonomiske interesser i socialt.* Roskilde: Center for Social Entrepreneurship, Roskilde University.

Gawell, M. (2006). *Activist Entrepreneurship: Attac'ing Norms and Articulating Disclosive Stories.* Stockholm: Stockholm University.

Gawell, M. (2008). Socialt entreprenörskap—en kombination av socialt engagemang och entreprenöriellt handlande. In *En ljudbok om ungt entreprenörskap.* Luleå University.

Gawell, M. (2014a). Soci(et)al Entrepreneurship and Different Forms of Social Enterprises. In A. Lundström, C. Zhou, Y. von Friedrichs & E. Sundin (Eds.),

Social Entrepreneurship: Leveraging Economic, Political, and Cultural Dimensions. Heidelberg, New York, & London: Springer.

Gawell, M. (2014b). Social Entrepreneurship and the Negotiation of Emerging Social Enterprise Markets. *International Journal of Public Sector Management*, 27(3), 251–266.

Gawell, M. (2015). *Social Enterprise in Sweden: Intertextual Consensus and Hidden Paradoxes*. ICSEM Working Papers No 8. Available at www.iap-socent.be/sites/default/files/Sweden%20-%20Gawell.pdf, accessed 10 November 2015.

Gawell, M., Johannisson, B. & Lundqvist, M. (2009). *Entrepreneurship in the Name of Society: A Reader's Digest of a Swedish Research Anthology*. Stockholm: KK-Stiftelsen.

Gawell, M., Pierre, A. & von Friedrichs, Y. (2014). Societal Entrepreneurship—A Cross-Boundary Force for Regional and Local Development Cherished for Multiple Reasons. *Scandinavian Journal for Public Administration*, 18(4), 109–130.

Gawell, M. & Westlund, H. (2014). Social Entrepreneurship as a Construct of a Liberal Welfare Regime? In H. Douglas & S. Grant (Eds.), *Social Innovation, Entrepreneurship and Enterprise: Context and Theories*. Prahran: Tilde University Press.

Greve, B. (2015). *Den sociale og innovative velfærdsstat*. Copenhagen: Hans Reitzel Forlag.

Gustavsen, K. & Kobro, U. L. (2012). Sosialt entreprenørskap som ledd i innsatsen mot fattigdom. Telemarksforskning, TF-rapport nr. 305.

Hall, P. A. & Soskice, D. (2001). *Varieties of Capitalism: The Institutional Foundations of Comparative Advantage*. Oxford: Oxford University Press.

Hockerts, K. (2014). How Hybrid Organizations Turn Antagonistic Assets into Complementarities. *California Management Review*, 57(3), 83–106.

Hockerts, K. & Wünstenhagen, T. (2010). Greening Goliaths Versus Emerging Davids—Theorizing About the Role of Incumbents and New Entrants in Sustainable Entrepreneurship. *Journal of Business Venturing*, 25(5), 481–492.

Hulgård, L. (2011). Social Economy and Social Enterprise: An Emerging Alternative to Mainstream Market Economy? *China Journal of Social Work*, 4(3), 123–138.

Hulgård, L. & Andersen, L. L. (2009). *Socialt entreprenørskab i Danmark—status*. CSE Publications 06:09. Roskilde: Center for Socialt Entreprenørskab, Roskilde University.

Hulgård, L., Andersen, L. L., Bisballe, L. & Spear, R. (2008). *Alternativ beskæftigelse og integration af socialt udsatte grupper*. CSE Publications 02:08. Center for Socialt Entreprenørskab, Roskilde University.

Hulgård, L. & Shajahan, P. K. (2012). Social Innovation for People-Centered Development. In F. Moulaert, D. MacCallum, A. Mehmood & A. Hamdouch (Eds.), *Handbook on Social Innovation: Collective Action, Social Learning and Transdisciplinary Research*. Southampton: Edward Elgar.

ICF Consulting Services. (2014). *Map of Social Enterprises and Their Eco-Systems in Europe: European Commission Employment, Social Affairs & Inclusion*. Available at http://ec.europa.eu/social/main.jsp?langId=en&catId=89&newsId=2149, accessed 15 November 2015.

Jacobsen, H. R. (2013). *Virksomheder med udvidet socialt ansvar*. Centre for Economic and Business Research (CEBR), Copenhagen Business School.

Johannisson, B. (1990). Community Entrepreneurship—Cases and Conceptualization. *Entrepreneurship and Regional Development*, 2(1), 71–88.

Johannisson, B. & Nilsson, A. (1989). Community Entrepreneurship—Networking for Local Development. *Journal of Entrepreneurship and Regional Development*, 1(1), 1–19.

Kerlin, J. A. (2010). A Comparative Analysis of the Global Emergence of Social Enterprise. *Voluntas: International Journal of Voluntary and Nonprofit Organizations*, 21(2), 162–179.

Kostilainen, H. & Pättiniemi, P. (2013). Evolution of Social Enterprise Concept in Finland. In H. Kostilainen & P. Pättiniemi (Eds.), *Avauksia yhteiskunnallisen yritystoiminnan tutkimukseen*. Helsinki: FinSERN.

Krull, P. (2013). *Designtænknings bidrag til sociale virksomheders værdiskabelse—et casestudie*. Aarhus: Aarhus University.

Kulothungan, G. (2014). *Genesis of Social Entrepreneurship: An Exploration Through Case Studies*. Roskilde: Centre for Social Entrepreneurship, Roskilde University.

Levander, U. (2011). *Utanförskap på entreprenad: Diskurser om sociala företag i Sverige*. Göteborg: Daidalos.

Levinsohn, D. (2015). *No Entrepreneur Is an Island: An Exploration of Social Entrepreneurial Learning in Accelerators*. Jönköping: Jönköping University.

Lundström, L. & Zhou, C. (2014). Rethinking Social Entrepreneurship and Social Enterprises: A Three Dimensional Perspective. In A. Lundström, C. Zhou, Y. von Friedrichs, E. Sundin (Eds.), *Social Entrepreneurship: Leveraging Economic, Political, and Cultural Dimensions*. Heidelberg, New York, & London: Springer.

Mazzucato, M. (2013). *The Entrepreneurial State: Debunking Public vs. Private Sector Myths*. London: Anthem Press.

Moilanen, H. (2010). *Työosuuskunnat ja työosuuskuntien kautta työllistyminen Suomessa—alustavia tuloksia tutkimusmatkan varrelta*. Presentation at "Työllisyys ja osuuskunnat", Eduskunta, Helsinki, Finland.

Nicholls, A. (2010). The Legitimacy of Social Entrepreneurship: Reflexive Isomorphism in a Pre-paradigmatic Field. *Entrepreneurship Theory & Practice*, 34(4), 611–633.

The Nordic Council of Ministers. (2015). *Sosialt entreprenørskap og sosial innovasjon: Kartlegging av innsatser for sosialt entreprenørskap og sosial innovasjon i Norden*. Tema Nord 502. Available at http://norden.diva-portal.org/smash/get/diva2:789262/FULLTEXT01.pdf, accessed 1 March 2015.

Pedersen, O. K. (2013). Political Globalization and the Competition State. In B. Brincker (Ed.), *Introduction to Political Sociology*. Copenhagen: Hans Reitzel.

Pellervo. (2012). *Osuustoiminta-lehti 4/12 Teemasivut 15.8.2012*. Available at www.pellervo.fi/otlehti/ot4_12/osuustoimintayritykset.pdf.

Pestoff, V. (1998). *Beyond the Market and State: Social Enterprises and Civil Democracy in a Welfare Society*. Aldershot: Ashgate.

Pestoff, V. (2008). *A Democratic Architecture for the Welfare State*. London: Routledge.

Pestoff, V. (2014). Hybridity, Innovation and the Third Sector. In J. Defourny, L. Hulgård & V. Pestoff (Eds.), *Social Enterprise and the Third Sector: Changing European Landscape in a Comparative Perspective*. London: Routledge.

Pestoff, V. & Hulgård, L. (2015). *Participatory Governance in Social Enterprise*. Paper presented at the EMES International Conference on Social Enterprise, Helsinki, Finland.

Salamon, L., Sokolowski, S. W. & Anheier, H. K. (2000). *Social Origins of Civil Society: An Overview.* Working Paper of the Johns Hopkins comparative non-profit sector project no. 38. The Johns Hopkins Center for Civil Society Studies.

Salamon, L. M. & Anheier, H. K. (1998). Social Origins of Civil Society: Explaining the Nonprofit Sector Cross-nationally. *Voluntas: International Journal of Voluntary and Non-Profit Organizations*, 9(3), 213–248.

Schei, B. & Rønnevig, E. (2009). *Vilje til endring—Sosialt Entreprenørskap på norsk.* Available at www.mothercourage.no/sosialt_entreprenoerskap/vilje_til_endring/frontpage/schei_roennevig_vilje_til_endring.pdf, accessed 13 June 2015.

Sirovátka, T. & Greve, B. (2014). *Innovation in Social Services: The Public-Private Mix in Service Provision, Fiscal Policy and Employment.* Aldershot: Ashgate.

Statistics Sweden. (2015). *Historical Statistics.* Available at www.scb.se/sv_/Hitta-statistik/Artiklar/Massutvandring-till-Amerika-slag-mot-befolkningen/, accessed 10 December 2015.

Steyaert, C. & Hjorth, D. (2006). *Entrepreneurship as Social Change.* Cheltenham: Edward Elgar.

Stryjan, Y. (1996). Sweden: The Emergence of Work-integration Social Enterprises. In C. Borzaga & J. Defourny (Eds.), *The Emergence of Social Enterprise.* London & New York: Routledge.

Stryjan, Y. (2006). The Practice of Social Entrepreneurship: Notes Toward a Resource-perspective. In C. Steyaert & D. Hjorth (Eds.), *Entrepreneurship as Social Change.* Cheltenham: Edward Elgar.

Thuesen, T., Bach, H. B., Albæk, K., Jensen, S., Hansen, N. L. & Weibel, K. (2013). *Socialøkonomiske virksomheder i Danmark: Når udsatte bliver ansatte.* Copenhagen: SFI: The National Research Centre on Welfare.

Utredning om sosialt entreprenørskap. (2011). *Utarbeidet av DAMVAD for Nærings- og Handelsdepartementet.* Available at www.regjeringen.no/no/dokumenter/utredning-om-sosialt-entreprenorskap/id675776/, accessed 15 June 2015.

2 Social Entrepreneurship

Demolition of the Welfare State or an Arena for Solidarity?

Linda Lundgaard Andersen and Lars Hulgård

The most striking slogans that characterize the 'new' discourse of social entrepreneurship have come to Denmark from the international scene, but we can nevertheless trace a significant historical equivalent in Denmark connecting the tradition for social economy to the co-operative movement and to decades of welfare modernisation incorporating people's participation through cultural, political and economic objectives. In this chapter, we first give a brief introduction to social entrepreneurship and position it in relation to social enterprise. We then demonstrate its present relevance in Denmark through five current platforms for social entrepreneurship, showing how these are influenced both by international trends and the roots of the Danish experimental tradition. We conclude with a discussion of how social entrepreneurship appeals to fundamentally different strategies for the future of modern welfare society, pointing to how these potentials and expectations seem to be pushing and pulling the articulation of social enterprise from all sides.

Social Entrepreneurship as a Vehicle for Powerful and Conflicting Values

Social entrepreneurship has emerged strongly on the international political scene as a vehicle for the provision of welfare services involving powerful and often conflicting values of public utility, franchising, corporate social responsibility, participation and volunteerism. Both in supra-national organizations such as the European Union and in national and local contexts, policies and other significant measures are being formulated with the aim of promoting social enterprises, social entrepreneurship and the social economy. However, social entrepreneurship is a phenomenon that contains considerable ambivalence. The phenomenon unfolds between the powerful dynamics of individualisation and collectivisation that are rooted in national and international developments in the welfare sector over the past 30 years. In the Danish case, social entrepreneurship has arrived from abroad, partly by way of a European social economy tradition primarily from, for instance, Belgium, France and Italy, and partly through a more market-consistent approach to social services from e.g., the USA and United Kingdom. While the most striking slogans that characterize this 'new' discourse have come to Denmark from the international scene, we can nevertheless trace a significant historical equivalent in Denmark that connects the Danish tradition for social economy in the form of co-operatives and in general the co-operative movement, as well as people's participation and movements targeting an integrated framework of cultural, political and economic participation. Another equivalent to the social entrepreneurship and social enterprise agenda was the experimental and developmental tradition of the mid-1980s to the mid-1990s that strongly influenced such important welfare areas as social services, social and labour market integration of ethnic minorities, lifelong learning and the development of local cultural institutions.

Social Entrepreneurship: Its Roots and Horizon

Social entrepreneurship is defined as the creation of social value through innovation with a high degree of participation, often involving civil society and often of economic importance. In social entrepreneurship, the innovations are often blurring the boundaries between the three sectors: state, market and civil society. Social value and innovation are present in most definitions (Dees, Emerson & Economy, 2002; Austin, Stevenson & Wei-Skillern 2006; Nicholls, 2006; Light, 2008), whereas the three other aspects are also often emphasised but with varying emphasis. Participation and civil society are crucial categories because they indicate that social entrepreneurship is not just about achieving social outcomes, but also about the processes and relationships that create social values. This approach is in line with current thinking in the field of social innovation theory, with its emphasis on social innovation as precisely the integration of process and outcome (BEPA, 2010; Moulaert, Jessop, Hulgård & Hamdouch, 2013). This means that social innovation is concerned with change in the social relations that produce innovation just as much as with the product of innovation (Moulaert, 2005). Furthermore, it is an empirical fact that actors from civil society are the most sought-after partners in social entrepreneurship in the form of voluntary organizations or concerned and responsible groups of citizens who want to make a difference (Hulgård, 2007; Andersen, Bager & Hulgård, 2010). The economic component is important to demonstrate the entrepreneurial nature. Schumpeter (1934) emphasises that it is not the invention itself that can be called entrepreneurship, but rather, its subsequent practical implementation. Therein lies the innovation: "[economic] leadership in particular must hence be distinguished from 'invention'. As long as they are not carried out into practice, inventions are economically irrelevant" (Schumpeter, 1934, p. 66). It is the practical implementation that generates the innovation, and such innovations are often of economic importance, not only in economic entrepreneurship, but also in social entrepreneurship. For the entrepreneur, this might be taking a financial risk, and for the social entrepreneur, a social risk to involve the participants and socially disadvantaged citizens in the innovation. Finally, it is empirically known that practical examples of social entrepreneurship often take place across more than one sector (Nyssens, 2006). Kerlin (2009) has also demonstrated how social entrepreneurship in the USA typically takes the form of partnerships between actors from civil society and private companies, whereas similar activities in Europe often imply collaboration between the public sector and civil society and increasingly also involve companies' practice of corporate social responsibility. Civil society seems generally to be the common denominator in social entrepreneurship, whereas other partners will vary according to world region and local institutional context.

Many Forms of Entrepreneurship

Social entrepreneurship represents one of several developments in the understanding of entrepreneurship and innovation from an original focus on agents of economic change (Schumpeter, 1934) to the inclusion also of public entrepreneurs (Ostrom, 1965), moral entrepreneurs (Becker, 1963; Hunter & Fessenden, 1994) and civic entrepreneurs (Henton, Melville & Walesh, 1997). Whereas the moral entrepreneur is concerned with creating new binding moral standards (the struggle for smoke-free public spaces is often highlighted as a result of the efforts of moral entrepreneurs), public and social entrepreneurs are engaged in creating binding innovations to enhance local, social action and coordination (Ostrom, 1965; Svendsen & Svendsen, 2004). But who are the social entrepreneurs, and what is their role in innovation in the private and public institutions of the welfare society?

Both public entrepreneurs and social entrepreneurs are concerned with producing sustainable, collective goods through innovation and collaboration. Elinor Ostrom, who in 2009 became the first and so far only female recipient of the prestigious Nobel Prize in economics, asked as early as 1965 in her dissertation whether there is a parallel to private sector entrepreneurship among actors who "provide public goods and services in the public sector", stating that, if such is the case, it must be characterized as "public entrepreneurship" (Ostrom, 1965, p. 24). In her dissertation, Ostrom focused on how public entrepreneurs realise a vision for collective action to coordinate the various production factors in order to create public goods and services. It was precisely her understanding of citizens' roles as innovators and entrepreneurs that inspired the Nobel Committee to nominate Ostrom in 2009 for her work on citizen governance of common pool resources. Ostrom demonstrated that the management of common goods by groups and associations of citizens often gives much better results than those typically presented in economic theory. Her research into how ordinary citizens become public entrepreneurs also makes her a key figure in the development of research-based knowledge of social entrepreneurship, which would otherwise suffer from a lack of systematic theoretical and empirical research.

Ostrom is also a good example of how social and public entrepreneurship until recently have been under-researched in both sociology and political science. It is interesting that political or public entrepreneurship (public innovation) right up to 2009 was not acknowledged as an essential element of modern political theory. Ostrom's studies of the importance of collective action in the creation and management of goods and services represent an alternative to the view that people are always looking to maximise their own individual benefit because they are generally "interested in very narrow selfish goals" (Tullock, 1970, p. 33, quoted from Nannestad 2009, p. 842), or because their goal is to make an individual entrepreneurial profit (Schneider, Teske & Mintrom, 1995). In this way, Ostrom's research and other collectivistic approaches to public and social entrepreneurship represent knowledge that may prove crucial for finding new ways out of today's economic and multi-dimensional crisis.

In research into both public and social entrepreneurship, we see a dividing line between the importance given to the individual entrepreneur on the one side and to collectives and organizations on the other. Whereas Schneider, Teske and Mintrom emphasise that it is "alert individuals" motivated by the possibility of "personal gain" (Schneider et al., 1995, p. 56) who become public entrepreneurs, Ostrom highlights the importance of collective action. We see a similar dividing line in social entrepreneurship, where especially American analyses (Dees, 1998; Dees et al., 2002) and interest organizations such as Ashoka and the Skoll Foundation attach great importance to the individual entrepreneur, whereas European researchers more often relate to the creation of community associations in the third sector (Defourny, 2010) and the historical importance of the social economy in the development of the European welfare states (Pestoff, 2009).

Until the late 1990s, social entrepreneurship was primarily a phenomenon that attracted interest from practitioners and consultants who, like Douglas Henton and his colleagues from "Collaborative Economics" (a consulting organization), began to think of themselves as civil and social entrepreneurs who worked to create arenas for cooperation between businesspeople, government officials and leaders of civil society in order to enhance local cohesion and prosperity (Leadbeater, 1996; Henton et al., 1997; Hulgård, 2007). But from then on, the idea gained momentum. As early as 2006, an account of the situation demonstrated that activities that can be characterized as social entrepreneurship take place more often than other forms of entrepreneurship, which led to a considerable increase in publishing activity in research and education (Steyart & Hjorth, 2006). Social entrepreneurship is still a poorly developed field of research and is strongly influenced by the fact that some of the most important references in the field were written by journalists (Bornstein, 2004) and consultants and social entrepreneurs (Leadbeater, 1997; Elkington & Hartigan, 2008; Mawson, 2008), and that the early research publications in the field are brief and sporadic (Dees, 1998; Austin et al., 2006). In recent years, however, more research has been undertaken in this area, elucidating social entrepreneurship conceptually and in relation to other types of entrepreneurship (Mair, 2006; Steyart & Hjorth, 2006; Hulgård, 2007; Light, 2008; Nicholls, 2008; Andersen, Bager & Hulgård, 2010; Defourny, 2010; Fayolle & Matlay, 2010; Hulgård, 2011).

But also, the conventional private market economy has become interested in social entrepreneurship and the third sector as an access point to exploit the market at the bottom of the pyramid (BoP). According to Elkington and Hartigan, two of the social enterprise field's most successful lobbyists, the BoP market represents about four billion low-income consumers. The BoP is just waiting for successful social entrepreneurs to address these "government or market failures and bring much-needed benefits to poor people or, in the case of the more commercially minded, to make money in unlikely circumstances" (Elkington & Hartigan, 2008, p. 42). The study of movements and tensions in the social enterprise field is also inspired by international development discourses linked both to social work (Desai, Monteiro & Narayan, 1998; Ho & Yen, 2010; Hulgård & Shajahan, 2012; Andersen, 2014) and to an approach to social innovation based on a strong process perspective (Moulaert et al., 2012; Moulaert, Jessop, Hulgård & Hamdouch, 2012).

Two Positions Within Social Entrepreneurship and Social Enterprise

Social entrepreneurship, however, is not merely a phenomenon that has arisen in parallel with other forms of entrepreneurship. It is also a phenomenon closely related to what we may call the SE field, which mainly consists of 'social enterprise' and 'social entrepreneurship', and also draws on the experiences of the 'social and solidarity economy' (Hart, Laville & Cattani, 2010). Here, we will focus on the relationship between social entrepreneurship and social enterprise. Muhammad Yunus, economist, social entrepreneur and winner of the 2006 Nobel Peace Prize for his work with microcredit and poverty reduction, has provided an interesting distinction between social enterprise and social entrepreneurship. In his view, any innovative initiative that has a social value may be described as social entrepreneurship, and on that basis, he states, "All those who design and run social businesses are social entrepreneurs. But not all social entrepreneurs are engaged in social businesses" (Yunus, 2007, p. 32). We share the view that social entrepreneurship is a broader phenomenon than social enterprise. Both phenomena occur on the basis of certain developmental processes in the welfare state and the third sector (as further discussed in the final section). Whereas social entrepreneurs first and foremost are agents of change, the social value creation in social enterprises takes place through business creation and resources derived substantially from market-based income (Borzaga & Defourny, 2001; Nyssens, 2006; Kerlin, 2009; Ridley-Duff & Bull, 2011; Defourny, Hulgård & Pestoff, 2014). Ridley-Duff and

Bull (2011) point out that there are two clear positions within social enterprise. The first position is rooted in European research on the third sector and social economy, whereas the other is grounded in American research into social entrepreneurship (Ridley-Duff & Bull, 2011, p. 31).

The first position sees social enterprise as part of the development history of the third sector from the 1980s. In the European context, the research network EMES, which took its name from its first research project from the mid-1990s (the Emergence of Social Enterprise in Europe), has produced research on how a new kind of hybrid called 'social enterprise' gradually began to emerge among voluntary organizations, non-governmental organizations and other third-sector organizations from the 1980s onwards. Such social enterprises are characterized in part by basing their operations on a wide variety of material and non-material resources and pursuing various notable but often potentially conflicting objectives, including advocacy, local activism and market-based income (Borzaga & Defourny, 2001; Nyssens, 2006). The EMES network thus documented how voluntary and other organizations in civil society at the European level began to develop from the 1980s on the basis of certain dynamics that brought them closer to the market (Borzaga & Defourny, 2001; Hulgård & Bisballe, 2004). According to the EMES, social enterprises can be identified by three kinds of criteria. The first is a set of *economic criteria*, one being the production and sale of goods or services, while another is that the organization is not entirely run by volunteers, but also involves some paid employment. Secondly, there is a set of *social criteria*, such as a strong desire to be of benefit to the local community or to the particular users targeted by the enterprise, and the fact that local citizens, users or associations have initiated the enterprise. Thirdly, there is a set of *governance criteria*, which imply that the social enterprise has a high degree of autonomy and is therefore not directly subject to public authority, and also that it has a participatory nature that permeates its management and the choices made concerning, for instance, work procedures.

The definition by the EMES network has had a major impact on other researchers in the third sector, social economy and social entrepreneurship in Europe, and notably also in Asia and Latin America (Nicholls, 2006; Kerlin, 2009; Fayolle & Matley, 2010), and on the development of political initiatives and legislation in Europe and Asia. In Europe, social enterprise and social entrepreneurship are closely linked to the budgetary pressure on the welfare state and the highly articulated need for innovation, especially in social services. Social enterprises and other organizations in the social economy are important for several reasons. Firstly, they create both service provision and employment aimed at socially vulnerable citizens who would otherwise have no chance in the labour market (Nyssens, 2006; Hulgård, Andersen, Spear & Bisballe, 2008). Secondly, they have historically been strong innovators in the general development of social services in health, education and personal care (Borzaga, 2011). Thirdly, people who are active in third-sector organizations are 'trained' to take responsibility not just for themselves, but also for other people's needs and opportunities (Putnam, 2000; Hulgård & Spear, 2006; Andersen, Hulgård & Bager, 2010). In this way, participation in social enterprises and other third-sector organizations does not only have the potential to develop social capital, but such organizations may also serve as schools of democracy, as highlighted by the former President of the European Commission, Romano Prodi, in a speech to the European Co-operative Convention (Prodi, 2002).

The second position sees social enterprise as a subset of social entrepreneurship and has its roots in the focus of American researchers and consultants on understanding SE as a new social sector in addition to or traversing the three traditional sectors in the welfare triangle: state, market and civil society. According to this position, social enterprise is "the institutional form created by social entrepreneurs" (Ridley-Duff & Bull, 2011, p. 31). This model is more individualistic, focusing on alliances between commercial and social entrepreneurs, including the possibility to learn from management and business models developed in the private sector. This approach is often highly critical of any form of public welfare state, whether it is the type of criticism by management guru Peter F. Drucker that "the megastate . . . has not delivered on a single one of its promises" (Drucker, 1994, p. 78), or the claim by the British consultant and journalist Charles Leadbeater that the social entrepreneur is an alternative to the welfare state, which is "ill-equipped to deal with many of the modern social problems it has to confront" (Leadbeater, 1997, p. 85), which is why social entrepreneurs prefer to learn from successful private commercial entrepreneurs (Mawson, 2008). The perception of a contradiction between innovative social entrepreneurs and the cumbersome, bureaucratic welfare state has come to be shared by many of the main actors in the field. It is therefore a major priority to develop leadership skills among social entrepreneurs. Such competence will enable social entrepreneurs to build the necessary alliances with the business world. Such alliances can provide capital, expertise and insight into managemen for the benefit of marginalized and poor communities. It is ultimately a matter of creating "a fit between investor values and community needs" (Dees, 2001, p. 5) and thus this approach to social entrepreneurship confirms rather than challenges the conventional perceptions of phenomena such as 'enterprise', 'market' and 'entrepreneur'.

Social Entrepreneurship in Denmark: Social Enterprise in Numbers

Until now, we have focused on outlining the international and national traditions of social entrepreneurship and social enterprises followed by the sketching of two historic and conceptual positions of social enterprises. We now turn in more detail to the current landscape in Denmark. In the following, we look at the numbers of social enterprises as well as identify five dominant platforms of social entrepreneurship and social enterprise in Denmark in order to provide a snapshot of current discourses.

If we look at the numbers of social enterprises in Denmark, we can conclude that these organizations are still a niche phenomenon. Three studies recently tried to document the numbers based on different definitions, and found the following. Two studies from 2013 shared the same definition of social enterprises as not-for-profit companies with a social, health or environmental goal, with sales of products or services, and reinvesting profits in the company and being independent from the public sector; this resulted in the same findings of numbers: 300 social enterprises with an employment and job creation purpose being identified (Jensen, 2013; Thuesen, 2013). A third study defined social enterprises as having social and/or employment-related purposes, with sales of market-based services and/or products, with profits reinvested in company purpose, being registered for taxes and employing disadvantaged people; this study found 129 different social enterprises "working with inclusion of vulnerable groups to the labor market" (Jacobsen, 2013). Finally, the Danish Governmental Committee on Social Enterprises in 2013 provided a 'snapshot' of existing social enterprises, drawing upon the existing data as above, defined as having a social purpose, with significant commercial activity, being independent from the public sector, allocating profit to a social purpose and having responsible and inclusive corporate governance; this reaffirmed the number close to 300 social enterprises (Danish Governmental Committee on Social Enterprises, 2013).

Based on these reviews, it is clear that research into the numbers of social enterprises is a fairly new field of research and has not yet been established as a continuously clearly defined survey activity; rather, it has so far been implemented as single and somewhat random studies performed by a number of different actors and institutions. The fact that these surveys display a variety of statistics about social enterprises weakens their validity and points to the necessity of further research (from 129 to 300 social enterprises). In addition, the data points to social enterprises in Denmark still being a niche phenomenon.

Social Entrepreneurship in Denmark: Five Platforms

In Denmark, five significant platforms can be identified, pointing to how social entrepreneurship as a concept and practice is shaped and developed by various actors who seek to influence concepts and the SE field by developing definitions and development strategic practices. In Table 2.1, we present five current platforms from the Danish arena of social entrepreneurship and social enterprise: 1) The Centre for Social Economy [Center for Socialøkonomi], a consultancy and knowledge centre supported by governmental social funding; 2) The think tank Monday Morning, which has promoted social entrepreneurship through analyses and reports to enhance documentation and policy making; 3) The Centre for Social Development [Center for

Table 2.1 Social Entrepreneurship in Denmark: Five Platforms

	Centre for Social Economy	The Think Tank Monday Morning	Social + Centre for Social Development	Copenhagen City Council Strategy	The Social Capital Fund
Terminology	Social economic enterprises and social innovation, user involvement	Entrepreneurs with social objectives Enthusiastic individuals as innovators	Social inventions = social innovation with particular characteristics that reveal methodology and level of inventiveness	Social economic entrepreneurs and enterprises are supported for improved welfare and welfare solutions	Social change through social business Investments in close cooperation with the 'social first' venture fund
Activity	Consultancy, guidance and knowledge centre	Strategy and policy development	Social experimentation: implementation of social inventions	Initiate and create a framework for social (economic) enterprises	Loans and dialogue for social enterprises
Market	Sales of products and services, reinvestment of profits from fundraising to business activity	Growth, professionalisation and efficiency based on market conditions. Social entrepreneurs = private suppliers to the public market	Involved in partnerships, consortia, cooperatives, social franchising. Private and public online platforms for communication	Market orientation Focus on fundraising and networks	DKK 4 million applied to 4–5 investments until 2013 Create growth in successful social enterprises and return on investment
Civil Society	Cross-sector partnerships User involvement Involvement of several actors across branches and sectors	Commitment from three sectors, history, proximity potential, legitimacy and advocacy from civil society	Can be developed in civil society based on values of inclusion, funding for public welfare, vulnerable citizens	Weak representation, but cross-sectoral emphasis Annual conference for actors from the three sectors to increase cooperation	Weak representation Improve life and social capital of vulnerable groups, priority to social rather than financial results
Relation to the State	Organizationally independent of the state, hybrid enterprises with public service procurement and contracts and independent income	New corporate form, public procurement and investment funds State is both a prerequisite and a hindrance	Public scaling and spread schemes based on policy, best practice, standards and 'artificial' demand incentives	Operate across sectors and create framework conditions Reduction of bureaucracy Establishment of task force	Weak representation Solve social problems by doing business

Social Udvikling], which initiated and launched an initiative called 'social inventions'; 4) Social enterprises as part of the development of a local government strategy initiating social enterprise as a tool for reintegrating marginal citizens here exemplified by the Copenhagen City Council; and 5) The Social Capital Fund [Den Sociale Kapitalfond], which is the first Danish social venture fund for the financial support of newly established social enterprises. This is not an exhaustive list, but presents the key actors in the Danish scene, although the Centre for Social Economy has been closed down recently. Our approach here is to present the actors' own representations of their objectives, activities and strategies as disseminated on their websites, in mission statements or from presentation materials and reports. We aim at a textual analysis focusing on intentions, purposes and goals, as the present chapter does not allow for a deeper analysis of practices and results.

Overview: Five Platforms for Social Entrepreneurship in Denmark

This overview is interesting in many ways. *Firstly*, it reveals that social entrepreneurship is a rather new phenomenon in Denmark, as four of the five initiatives have emerged since 2010, while the oldest one, The Centre for Social Economy, was established in 2007 and ceased to exist in 2014. There is some variation in resources between the different platforms. The Centre for Social Economy was mainly funded by governmental subsidies as well as their own profits from advisory, consultancy and reporting services. The Centre for Social Development is a large consulting firm with social inventions as a sub-field staffed by two consultants with separate funding from two Danish foundations, VELUX and VILLUM. The Social Capital Fund has received funding from the Danish foundations TrygFonden and Velux Foundation; it funds a number of social enterprises with up to DKK 4 million ($\approx$ € 535 000) and requires a seat on the board of the social enterprises it invests in. The Social Capital Fund has grown rapidly since it was founded in 2011 and has a management team of eight consultants.

Secondly, the five initiatives reveal a high degree of pluralism and diversity in views and definitions of social entrepreneurship and the social enterprise field, similar to the variety in the international discourses on SE. We see that the actors use different terminology in Danish, which may be translated as 'social economic enterprises', 'social inventions' and 'social entrepreneurship', all of which have become part of the Danish public discourse. Many favour the Danish term 'social economic enterprise' used by the Centre for Social Economy and the Copenhagen City Council. On the other hand, Monday Morning's analytical and policy work refers to social enterprises. Monday Morning has indicated in its analyses that it uses the Danish translations of social entrepreneurship and the social entrepreneur: 'social iværksætter' (Monday Morning, 2010). Finally, the Centre for Social

Development has developed its own label using Social+, where, inspired by
Stuart Conger and James Mark Baldwin, they unfold and develop those
authors' 'social inventions' using the equivalent Danish term (Sørensen &
Frederiksen, 2010, p. 5). This is thus "a term to describe social innovation
with some specific characteristics, and by identifying the specific characteristics of social inventions, we can enhance the lens through which we will
be able to find and develop social inventions" (Sørensen & Frederiksen,
2010, p. 3). They further state that "a social invention is a ground-breaking
initiative that changes the ways in which people relate to themselves and
each other. A social invention solves or prevents a social problem—or facilitates social progress. A social invention may be a notable new method,
organizational form, procedure, technological solution, legislation, etc."
(Sørensen & Frederiksen, 2010, p. 6). Consequently, Social+ is a social initiative seeking to identify a specific methodology that leads to an invention
and may result in new welfare solutions through best practices and civil
society involvement.

Thirdly, in Denmark, social entrepreneurship has very rapidly achieved
a considerable institutional anchoring in terms of support structures, representation of interests, access to resources and knowledge production. Thus,
for example, the Centre for Social Economy was targeting social enterprises,
but in practice, its activities were aimed more broadly at social entrepreneurs through networking, mentoring, advice and policy development in
relation to the relevant political level (Social Economy: A Mission Statement
for the Centre for Social Economy). Several local community councils are
creating support structures in the form of specific 'consultancy and start-up
teams', the establishment of relatively small pools of funding for the start up
of new social enterprises and the production and implementation of strategic plans and documents, which often position social enterprises and social
entrepreneurship as significant key initiatives for the development of new
welfare strategies (Copenhagen City Council's policy for social enterprises
in 2009 and Aarhus City Council's strategy for so-called social economic
entrepreneurs in 2012).

Fourthly, all the platform initiatives are concerned with acting and positioning themselves according to trends in the market and in civil society.
All actors view the market as probably *the* most central arena for entrepreneurship, and if there is a common denominator in the five initiatives, it
would seem to be the considerable attention given to faith in the market as
the primary arena for social entrepreneurs. The market represents sales and
growth, economic value, incentive, motivation, efficiency, professionalism
and return on investment. On the other hand, most (but not all) initiatives
are concerned with involving civil society in their activities and strategies. In
this perspective, civil society means partnerships, user involvement, commitment, legitimacy, advocacy and vulnerable citizens; however, two platforms,
the City Council strategy and the Social Capital Fund, provide a weaker
representation of civil society involvement.

Fifthly, several actors have relations with the (welfare) state, and this leads to hybrid enterprises that are dependent on the state in terms of, for instance, public procurement, subsidies, contracts and funding as well as the development of relevant policies and best practices. For these actors, social entrepreneurship cannot start up and evolve without governmental frameworks and interaction, since these provide a certain means of survival, but also bring with them certain obstacles. State regulation of social entrepreneurship has further expanded from 2013 with the adoption of a budget and a legislation that for the first time commits the state to developing a framework for social enterprises. Monday Morning, for example, describes the state as both a prerequisite and a hindrance and the City Council strategy identifies public bureaucracy as a difficulty that must be eliminated in order for social entrepreneurship and social enterprises to be realised. The Social Capital Fund downplays the role of the state, which it regards as unimportant for venture activity.

Social Entrepreneurship Forming Part of Welfare Discourse

There is no doubt that social entrepreneurship both in Denmark and internationally forms part of the discourse on the future of the welfare state. It is a rapidly growing subject, marked by a dynamism that can be difficult to capture, since the organizations and actors who shaped the field initially tend to be replaced by new institutions. Since 2014, the Danish parliament and government has devoted some attention and resources to the expansion of the SE field. Thus, in June 2014, the parliament adopted a new law on the registration of social enterprises (Social Enterprise Law nr. 148). According to the law, a social enterprise has to be centred on a social mission, be independent of the government, participatory and responsible in its governance, reinvest in social purposes and accept only limited distribution of profits, if any at all. Simultaneously with the implementation of the law, the government appointed a new National Centre for Social Enterprises and a National Council on Social Enterprise (both closed in 2016). Whereas the former was the government centre for implementing the new law on social enterprise, the latter was an independent council, served by the National Centre, to give advice to the government on social enterprise, social entrepreneurship and social economy.

Another interesting initiative is the organization 'Social Entrepreneurs in Denmark', which started out in 2010 as an alumni initiative by former students at the part-time master's programme in Social Entrepreneurship from Roskilde University, but which is emerging as a more general interest organization for social entrepreneurs in Denmark. This organization has managed to scale its activities and grow organically with network meetings in the various Danish regions and a number of sub-committees engaged in giving advice to start-ups, monitoring social entrepreneurship and social enterprise performance, developing international activities and providing locally based network meetings. Similarly, a group of students from all Danish universities in 2012 founded the DANSIC organization. DANSIC is an acronym for Danish Students' Social Innovation Club, and its key activity is organizing an annual event with 400 participants on social innovation and social entrepreneurship each year. DANSIC is run by a new batch of volunteers who every year define and organize the following year's activities from scratch, including fundraising and sustaining the multiple bottom lines of the organization.

Similarly, internationally we have seen social entrepreneurs being highly active in forming interest organizations, policy initiatives and practical initiatives. Interest organizations are scaling their activities and at all political levels strategies are being developed to promote the contribution of social entrepreneurs to addressing the problem of providing and developing social services at a time of cost pressures arising from demographic change, cultural diversity, greater expectations and increasing global competition (BEPA, 2010).

Demolition of the Welfare State or an Arena for Solidarity?

The above-mentioned social entrepreneurship activities in Denmark harmonise nicely with two major movements that have influenced the current perceptions of welfare and social services. The first movement is characterized by marketization and privatization of public responsibility for welfare (Gilbert, 2002; Borzaga & Santuari, 2003; Pestoff, 2009; Hulgård, 2010b). The second trend has arisen from both social movements and public programmes concerned with experimentation with new forms of collective responsibility, solidarity and civil society-based input into political developments (Andersen & Hulgård, 2008; Hart, Laville & Cattani, 2010; Hulgård & Shajahan, 2012; Andersen, 2015). Both in the marketization/privatization trend and the civil society trend, social entrepreneurship is perceived as an appropriate response to the social challenges the world faces. We also find both trends in Denmark, but they contribute actively to achieving the potential of social entrepreneurship in two quite distinct ways.

Across national differences and types of welfare regimes, the past 30 years have seen a global re-orientation of welfare states towards increased privatization and individualisation, and thereby a restructuring of the classic welfare state as conceived in the aftermath of World War II (Titmuss, 1977). This trend has had an extensive impact internationally and creates a new framework for welfare state renewal processes. Social entrepreneurship, as a tool for innovative social initiatives in the welfare society, fits almost perfectly into this new frame. Although the development of modern welfare states started early in the twentieth century, it was only in the late 1940s that politicians and experts began to envisage developments within a *universal* welfare state framework (Borzaga & Santuari, 2003, p. 36). From then until about 1970, policy development in welfare was underpinned by the vision of a comprehensive welfare state. The welfare state was a prime mover for modern society, without which it could not function. The universal welfare state was an asset in every corner of the high-speed society that quickly developed in the post-war period. The British social policy expert and welfare theorist Richard M. Titmuss has documented the importance of the universal orientation with his concept of an institutional and redistributive welfare model. For Titmuss, the development of a universal welfare state represented not only the horizon for European societies, or in a more limited manner, for Scandinavia; it was a dynamic global welfare policy horizon for all countries to aspire to (Titmuss, 1987, 1977). With this perception, he laid an important foundation for the understanding of modern welfare in the post-war period (Esping-Andersen, 1990).

From the 1970s, however, the social policy orientation started to change not only in the USA but internationally: "[the] European welfare state systems began to crumble" (Borzaga & Santuari, 2003, p. 38) under the financial burden, which at the same time gave rise to major organizational challenges in heightening social responsibility. The new trend in welfare state orientation is to downplay public responsibility for dealing with social problems. A combination of changes in the high-level political power relations and increasing dissatisfaction with the welfare state from both right and left sowed the seed for change, which included the rapid progress of the New Right's approach to welfare (Taylor, 2003, p. 3). From the 1970s, the modern welfare states with their emphasis on individual responsibility and participation at the expense of public responsibility began to be oriented towards a different vision from the universal and institutional welfare model. Social policy paradigms such as activation and self-help gained in importance, as did the combination of individual responsibility and participation, which made its mark on developments in pensions, the total amount of preventative health care and housing. These areas all contribute to a polarisation that is far removed from the universal welfare model that revolves around universalism and redistribution.

The changes in the welfare state towards privatization at the expense of citizenship not only underscore the importance of individual responsibility, but also seem to facilitate social enterprise and social entrepreneurship as a meeting point for innovative actors from the three sectors. But economic globalisation and the changed welfare state have not merely led to increased individualisation and marketization. These changes have also helped to create a new platform for civil society, social solidarity and new forms of collective responsibility for the development of the welfare society. Thus, we see a paradox in that social enterprise and social entrepreneurship can be crucial elements both in a privatization strategy and in a strategy that seeks to extend the terrain of civil society as a third principle for the organization of society, based on collective responsibility and reciprocity. The second scenario in the direction of solidarity and new forms of collectivity is as fundamental as the first scenario for an understanding of the current enthusiasm for everything pertaining to the field of SE. Already in the year 2000, Michael Woolcock welcomed the interest in social capital and civil society, since it facilitated the return of sociology to the political scene (Woolcock, 2000), and Marilyn Taylor (2003) saw the same trend as a shift from a belief in the pre-eminence of the market towards a responsiveness to invest in social enterprises as an important way of helping to ensure local sustainability.

Conclusion

In summary, we have outlined the field of social entrepreneurship and social enterprise in Denmark, pointing to how the 'new' discourse of social entrepreneurship came to Denmark from the international scene, but also linking to a historical Danish equivalent connecting the tradition for social economy to the co-operative movement and to decades of welfare modernisation. In this tradition, people's participation through cultural, political and economic objectives has been incorporated and developed. We have then touched upon the number of social enterprises in Denmark, concluding that this is a fairly new and not yet validated monitoring practice and that the numbers of social enterprises point to social enterprises still being a niche phenomenon. Five current SE platforms have been identified and analysed as both influenced by international trends as well as the roots of the Danish experimental tradition.

Finally, we might consider how we should understand the expectations and the notable initiatives in social entrepreneurship and social enterprises that we have seen unfold in Denmark. Is this a sign of the increasing influence of civil society as a sphere of solidarity and reciprocity, or is this the liberal market forces entering the civil spheres? Is social entrepreneurship then primarily an expression of the effective and innovative creation of social services based on existing market premises, or does it offer a utopian horizon for the development of more participatory and inclusive practices linked to the social movements and the possibility of a more sustainable and inclusive society? It is still too early to conclude how the Danish actors in this paradigm—and the numbers of this phenomenon—will unfold and develop social entrepreneurship. The activities involved are too new and have not yet delivered on long-term sustainability, but the coming years will reveal more clearly how Danish social entrepreneurship and social enterprises will develop—and following these developments could be rather interesting.

References

Andersen, L. L. (2014). Micro-Processes of Collaborative Innovation in Danish Welfare Settings: A Psychosocial Approach to Learning and Performance. In E. Sørensen & E. Agger (Ed.), *Collaborative Innovation in the Public Sector: European Experiences and Lessons*. Bentham EBooks.

Andersen, L. L. (2015). *Social Entrepreneurship and Social Innovation: Human Economy, Governance and Voluntarism Revisited. CURSIV*, No.15. Aarhus University Press.

Andersen, L. L. & Hulgård, L. (2008). *Workplaces with an Inclusive Profile—and Their Everyday Strategies: Social Enterprises and Work Integration in Denmark.* Paper for International Workshop on Ethnographies of the Social Economy, 14–15, University of Durham.

Andersen, L. L., Hulgård, L. & Bager, T. (2010). Socialt entreprenørskab. In L. L. Andersen, L. Hulgård & T. Bager (Eds.), *Socialt entreprenørskab.* Odense: University Press Southern Denmark.

Austin, J., Stevenson, H. & Wei-Skillern, J. (2006). Social and Commercial Entrepreneurship: Same, Different, or Both? *Entrepreneurship: Theory and Practice,* 30(1), 1–22.

Becker, H. S. (1963). *Outsiders: Studies in the Sociology of Deviance.* New York: The Free Press.

BEPA (Bureau of European Policy Advisers). (2010). *Empowering People, Driving Change: Social Innovation in the European Union.* Brussels: European Commission.

Bornstein, D. (2004). *How to change the world: Social entrepreneurship and the power of ideas.*

Borzaga, C. & Santuari, A. (2003). New Trends in the Non-Profit Sector in Europe: The Emergence of Social Entrepreneurship. In *The Non-Profit Sector in a Changing Economy.* Paris: OECD.

Centre for Social Development. www.sus.dk/.

Centre for Social Entrepreneurship, Roskilde University. Available at www.ruc.dk/forskning/forskningscentre/cse/.

Copenhagen City Council: Policy for Social Economic Enterprises in 2009. www.kk.dk/eDoc/Socialudvalget/29–04–2009%2016.15.00/Referat/30–04–2009%2014.12.58/4500194.PDF and www.kk.dk/eDoc/Borgerrepr%C3%A6sent ationen/03–06–2010%2017.30.00/Referat/15–06–2010%2012.00.37/5495127. PDF.

Copenhagen City Council: Proposed Strategy for Social Economic Enterprises. Available at www.kk.dk/eDoc/%C3%98konomiudvalget/25–05–2010%2015.15.00/Dagsorden/19–05–2010%2016.02.23/5451624.PDF.

Danish Governmental Committee on Social Enterprises. (2012). *Recommendation Report.* Published by Committee on Social Enterprises. Available at http://socialvirksomhed.dk/en/files/recommendationreport.pdf, accessed 10 April 2015.

DANSIC—Danish Social Innovation Club. Available at www.facebook.com/danishsocialinnovationclub.

Dees, J. G. (2001). *The Meaning of Social Entrepreneurship.* Duke University, Fuqua School of Business, accessed 10 April 2015.

Dees, J. G., Emerson, J. & Economy, P. (2002). *Strategic Tools for Social Entrepreneurs: Enhancing the Performance of Your Enterprising Nonprofit.* New York: John Wiley & Sons.

Defourny, J. & Borzaga, C. (2001). *The Emergence of Social Enterprise.* London & New York: Routledge.

Defourny, J., Hulgård, L. & Pestoff, V. (2014). *Social Enterprise and the Third Sector—Changing European Landscapes in a Comparative Perspective.* London & New York: Routledge.

Defourny, J. & Nyssens, M. (2010). Conceptions of Social Enterprise and Social Entrepreneurship in Europe and the United States: Convergences and Divergences. *Journal of Social Entrepreneurship*, 1(1), 32–53.

Drucker, P. F. (1994). The theory of the business. *Harvard Business Review*, 72(5), 95–104.

Elkington, J. & Hartigan, P. (2008). *The Power of Unreasonable People*. Boston: Harvard Business Press.

Esping-Andersen, G. (1990). *The Three Worlds of Welfare Capitalism*. Cambridge: Polity Press.

Evers, A. & Laville, J.-L. (2004). *The Third Sector in Europe*. Cheltenham & Northampton: Edward Elgar.

Fayolle, A. & Matley, H. (Ed.) (2010). *Handbook of Research on Social Entrepreneurship*. Cheltenham: Edward Elgar

Gilbert, N. (2002). *Transformation of the Welfare State: The Silent Surrender of Public Responsibility*. Oxford: Oxford University Press.

Hart, K., Laville, J.-L. & Cattani, A. D. (2010). *The Human Economy*. London: Polity Press.

Henton, D., Melville, J. & Walesh, K. (1997). *Grassroots Leaders for a New Economy—How Civic Entrepreneurs Are Building Prosperous Communities*. San Francisco: Jossey Bass Publishers.

Hulgård, L. (2007). *Sociale entreprenører—en kritisk indføring*. Copenhagen: Hans Reitzels Forlag.

Hulgård, L. (2010a). Discourses of Social Entrepreneurship: Variations of the Same Theme? In J. Defourny, L. Hulgård & V. Pestoff (Eds.), *Social Enterprise, Social Entrepreneurship, Social Economy, Solidarity Economy: An EMES Reader on the "SE Field"*. Liège: EMES European Research Network.

Hulgård, L. (2010b). Public and Social Entrepreneurship. In K. Hart, J.-L. Laville & C. Cattani (Eds.), *The Human Economy*. London: Polity Press.

Hulgård, L. (2011). Social Economy and Social Enterprise: An Emerging Alternative to Mainstream Market Economy? *China Journal of Social Work*, 4(3), 201–215.

Hulgård, L., Andersen, L. L., Spear, R. & Bisballe, L. (2008). *Alternativ beskæftigelse og integration af socialt udsatte grupper: Erfaringer fra Danmark og Europa*. CSE Publications 02:08. Roskilde: Roskilde University.

Hulgård, L., and Bisballe, T. (2004). *Work integration social enterprises in Denmark*. No. 04/08. Working Papers Series.

Hulgård, L. & Shajahan, P. K. (2012). Social Innovation for People-Centered Development. In F. Moulaert, D. MacCallum, A. Mehmood & A. Hamdouch (Eds.), *Handbook on Social Innovation: Collective Action, Social Learning and Transdisciplinary Research*. Southampton: Edward Elgar.

Hulgård, L., & Spear, R. (2006). Social entrepreneurship and the mobilization of social capital in European social enterprises. Social enterprises: At the crossroads of market, public policies and civil society, 85–108.

Hunter, J. D. & Fessenden, T. (1994). The New Class as Capitalist Class: The Rise of the Moral Entrepreneur in America. In H. Kellner & F. Heuberger (Eds.), *Hidden Technocrats: The New Class and New Capitalism*. New Brunswick & London: Transaction Publishers.

Jacobsen, H. R. (2013). *Virksomheder med udvidet socialt ansvar*. Centre for Economic and Business Research (CEBR) Copenhagen Business School.

Jensen, E. (2012). *Fokus på socialøkonomiske virksomheder.* Notat om social-økonomiske virksomheder med beskæftigelsesfremmende og jobskabende formål. Århus: CABI.

Kerlin, J. A. (2009). *Social Enterprise: A Global Comparison.* Lebanon: Tufts University Press.

Leadbeater, C. (1997). *The Rise of the Social Entrepreneur.* London: Demos.

Light, P. (2008). *The Search for Social Entrepreneurship.* Washington, DC: Brookings Institution Press.

Mawson, A. (2008). *The Social Entrepreneur—Making Communities Work.* London: Atlantic Books.

Mandag Morgen. (2010). Velfærdens iværksættere—en dansk strategi for socialt iværksætteri. First edition. www.mm.dk/velfærdens-iværksættere, accessed 15 April 2014.

Moulaert, F., Jessop, B., Hulgård, L. & Hamdouch, A. (2013). Social Innovation: A New Stage in Innovation Process Analysis? In F. Moulaert, D. MacCallum, A. Mehmood & A. Hamdouch (Eds.), *The International Handbook on Social Innovation: Collective Action, Social Learning and Transdisciplinary Research.* Southampton: Edward Elgar.

Moulaert, F., MacCallum, D., Mehmood, A. & Hamdouch, A. (2012). *The International Handbook on Social Innovation: Collective Action, Social Learning and Transdisciplinary Research.* Southampton: Edward Elgar.

Nicholls, A. (2008). *Social Entrepreneurship: New Models of Sustainable Social Change.* Oxford: Oxford University Press.

Nyssens, M. (2006). *Social Enterprise: At the Crossroads of Market, Public Policies and Civil Society.* London: Routledge.

Ostrom, E. (1965). *Public Entrepreneurship: A Case Study in Ground Water Basin Management.* Dissertation. Los Angeles: University of California.

Pestoff, V. (2009). *A Democratic Architecture for the Welfare State.* London: Routledge.

Putnam, Robert D. (2001). *Bowling alone: The collapse and revival of American community.* Simon and Schuster.

Ridley-Duff, R. & Bull, M. (2011). *Understanding Social Enterprise: Theory and Practice.* London: Sage Publications.

Schneider, M., Teske, P. & Mintrom, M. (1995). Public entrepreneurs. *Princeton University Press,* 17(2), 30–45.

Schumpeter, J. A. (1934). *The Theory of Economic Development.* Cambridge: Harvard University Press.

Social Capital Fund. Available at www.densocialekapitalfond.dk/.

Social Economic Enterprises—a Mission Statement for the Centre for Social Economy. Available at www.socialokonomi.dk/sites/default/files/mediafiles/Socialoekonomisk_idegrundlag.pdf.

Social Enterprise Law on Registered Social Enterprises No. 148. Available at www.retsinformation.dk/Forms/R0710.aspx?id=161853, accessed 9 November 2015.

Social Entrepreneurs in Denmark—an Alumni Association. Available at www.sociale-entreprenører.dk/.

Sørensen, A. & Fredriksen, A. H. (2010). *Sociale opfindelser.* Copenhagen: Centre for Social Development.

Steyart, C. & Hjorth, D. (2006). *Entrepreneurship as Social Change.* Cheltenham: Edward Elgar.

Svendsen, G. L. H. & Svendsen, G. T. (2004). *The Creation and Destruction of Social Capital—Entrepreneurship, Co-operative Movements and Institutions.* Cheltenham: Edward Elgar.

Taylor, M. (2003). *Public Policy in the Community.* Houndsmills: Palgrave Macmillan.

Thuesen, T., Bach, H. B., Albæk, K., Jensen, S., Hansen, N. L. and Weibel, K. (2013). *Socialøkonomiske virksomheder i Danmark: Når udsatte bliver ansatte.* The National Research Centre on Welfare, 13:23. Copenhagen: SFI.

Yunus, M. (2007). *Creating a World without Poverty.* New York: Public Affairs.

3 Social Entrepreneurship and Social Enterprises
Chameleons Through Times and Values

Malin Gawell

In this chapter, the development in the emerging field of social entrepreneurship in Sweden will be presented and elaborated. In the current discussion, it is obvious at first glance that social entrepreneurship, in any form in which it appears, is part of an intertextual vision of a 'good development' in which social aims are ascribed to solve social problems in a smooth way. However, social entrepreneurship addresses vital aspects of social life in society, which is filled with tensions—especially in times when social contracts are renegotiated. The aim of this chapter is to explore some of these aspects that social entrepreneurship in Sweden 'stir up'.

An Old Phenomenon and New Terminology

There is not yet a universal definition of social entrepreneurship (Borzaga & Defourny, 2001; Dees, 2001; Hjorth & Bjerke, 2006; Mair, Robinson & Hockerts, 2006; Nicholls, 2006; Steyaert & Hjorth, 2006; Borzaga, Galera & Nogales, 2008; Gawell, Johannisson & Lundqvist, 2009; Berglund, Johannisson & Schwartz, 2013; Pierre, von Friedrichs & Wincent, 2014). From a basic view, social entrepreneurship is social engagement combined with some type of entrepreneurial action. It refers to social beings, interaction and care. It furthermore refers to entrepreneurship: actions that contribute to dynamics in all spheres of society, despite being embedded in the economic discourse for many years (Schumpeter, 1934; Swedberg, 2000, 2008; Steyaert & Katz, 2004). This means that social entrepreneurship can take many different forms. As a matter of fact, there are currently different versions of social entrepreneurship in Sweden and in many other countries (Gawell, 2014). There are entrepreneurial initiatives that take on characteristics of the non-profit sector or adopt co-operative traditions as they emerge. There are also initiatives that take on business traditions, including practices combining profit aims with social missions. Most commonly, social entrepreneurship is associated with private initiatives and is differentiated from the initiatives of public authorities. This can, however, be questioned based on the understanding of entrepreneurship as a process in which people create something new in *mind*, *speech* and *action* (Johannisson, 2005) or, in Schumpeter's terms, introducing new types of resources, new ways of producing and new products and finding new markets for consumption or application or new ways of organizing. Entrepreneurial initiatives can thereby also take on the form of a public sector organization as they emerge. As a matter of fact, social entrepreneurship often—and maybe even most of the time—evolves in the dynamic interplay between sectors and spheres in society (Berglund et al., 2013). This phenomenon is not new, even though at least some of the terminology has emerged during the last several decades. Therefore, before going into the current discussion related to the term *social entrepreneurship* and other closely related terms, such as *societal entrepreneurship* and *social enterprises*, let us look into some historical phases that have influenced the Swedish history of and the current view on social entrepreneurship, for history has, as we will see, something to tell us about current practice.

Three Historical Phases Colouring Social Entrepreneurship in Sweden

History and context are always complex; there are a number of interpretations and competing narratives. The presentation in this chapter is simplified, and there are several dimensions that can be discussed and interpreted differently. One such dimension is the emancipatory effect of the so-called Swedish model, which, it is rather safe to say, has been emancipatory for many people—even the majority. However, it is also important to remember that norms and practices have also been enforced on groups that have not been able to make their voices heard in Sweden. In spite of these cautions, let us review some historical phases that have affected Swedish society and the current debate on and practices of social entrepreneurship in three steps.

Protests and Joint Social Mobilization

In the nineteenth century, Sweden was a relatively poor country in which the majority lived in rural areas as farmers, defying harsh climates, or as workers, defying harsh working conditions. It was a time of tension, even subversive uprisings. Food riots occurred in combination with protests against forced conscription to wars with no public support and with protests against the state monopoly on preaching. At this time, there was also an emerging middle class that, together with a traditional upper class, gained access to socio-economic resources that could be used for more than one's own livelihood. These resourceful groups partly interacted with the subversive social movements mentioned above, but took a slightly more moderate position. Needs, combined with social concerns partly influenced by international humanistic fashion, and available resources facilitated initiatives that we would currently refer to as social entrepreneurship initiatives. Many of these initiatives had a focus on basic health care, working conditions and civil rights.

The nineteenth century, characterized by subversive social movements for basic human rights and decent conditions combined with the more moderate, humanistic and engaged middle class with resources to organize promoted the specific form of civil society organization called '*Folkrörelse*', which, directly translated, means 'people's movements', but is commonly termed 'popular mass movements' in English (Lundström & Wijkström, 1997; Wijkström & Lundström, 2002). However, this century did not solely deal with combined interests or humanistic values. Ideas of equality were promoted, for example, by the labour movement, and several types of organizations promoted ideas of democracy for both political representation and grassroots practices. These 'popular mass movements' came to be characterized by a broad, open membership base, democratic organizational structures and a combined role advocating for better conditions and delivering services to those in need (Amnå, 2005). Different organizations were 'clustered' in relation to the labour movement, women's movements, temperance movement and religious revivalist movements, among others (Arne, 1994; Wijkström & Lundström, 2002).

The Construction of the Swedish Model

The discussions prevalent in the nineteenth century continued into the twentieth century, taking a more institutionalized form. The political support for social democrats increased. Sweden was headed by a social democratic government for 44 consecutive years (1932–1976). During this time, the vision for a 'good home' for everyone was made explicit, with reference to a 'people's home' or '*Folkhem*' in Swedish (Larsson, 2008). It was part of the development of a welfare state with a relatively large public sector providing health care, education, etc. Socialist ideas were combined with capitalism in what has been referred to as the 'Swedish model' or the 'third way'.

During this time, many of the topics advocated for by popular mass movements and other types of organizations were adopted by the public sector, which also took over many of the social services run by civil society organizations. The Red Cross' mobile dental clinics for children became the basis for public dental clinics all over the country, and the temperance movement's reading groups' book-lending system became the basis for public libraries run by municipalities, just to mention a few examples. In historical narratives, popular mass movements are ascribed a successful innovative role in the development of the welfare state and the scope of the public sector, with reference to the latter part of the nineteenth century and first part of the twentieth century.

In this way, the large public sector has dominated social and other public services in Sweden. Health care, child care, elder care, social services, education, infrastructure and, partly, housing were provided by or co-produced with the public sector during most of the twentieth century. This illustrates, together with similar models in neighbouring Nordic countries, what

Esping-Andersen (1990) refers to as a socio-democratic welfare regime. Because of their aim and scope, the initiation and development of the public sector can be seen as a social entrepreneurial initiative—maybe even the largest entrepreneurial initiative in Sweden during this time (Gawell, 2014). Popular mass movements and other types of civil society organizations achieved a limited complementary role as service providers but continued as advocates (Svedberg, 2005). These characteristics were noted in the John Hopkins comparative study on non-profit sectors (Lundström & Wijkström, 1997; Wijkström & Lundström, 2002).

During the last decades of the twentieth century, the size and role of the public sector were increasingly debated (Trägårdh, 2007). As in many other countries, the influences of market-based economies and even neoliberal views grew stronger in Sweden. Entrepreneurship became a key concept and the concept of social entrepreneurship entered the field (for further discussion, see Gawell & Westlund, 2014).

Reconsidering the Swedish Model and New Concepts Entering the Field

The new era that emerged during the latter part of twentieth century and flourished in the early twenty-first century meant the deregulation of several branches that were previously dominated by the public sector. Economic policies aiming for financial growth dominated 'development', and balanced public expenditures were prioritized. Deregulations of the financial and transportation sectors were followed by school reform in 1992, in which conditions for private alternatives improved. During the first decade of the twenty-first century, health care, child care, and elder care provided by the public sector were subject to competition through procurements and/or client choice models (Munkhammar, 2009). These services were still under public control through financial terms and contracts; they were not really a matter of de-regulation, but rather of re-regulation influenced by new public management (Ivarsson Westerberg & Forsell, 2014; Jacobsson, Pierre & Sundström, 2015).

Non-profit organizations hoped for increased resources. However, they had to compete with both other non-profit organizations and for-profit businesses (see the further discussion in Gawell, Sundin and Tillmar in this volume). This was also the time when references to *social entrepreneurship*, *social enterprises* and the term *societal entrepreneurship* became increasingly popular in Sweden and internationally. This can be seen as an expression of a renewed interest in the social aspects of society that might have been caused by the sharp focus on economic aspects in policy and the societal discourse in general during the last several decades. It can be partly seen as an increased interest in change, highlighting entrepreneurial dynamics and innovation rather than bureaucracy and organizational stability, which had been key concepts for a period of time. It can also be seen as part of the renegotiation of social contracts in society in Sweden as well as elsewhere, in which social entrepreneurship seems to be cherished for several different reasons (see also Gawell, Pierre & von Friedrichs, 2014).

There is great overlap in the use of the terms *social entrepreneurship*, *societal entrepreneurship* and *social enterprises*. Some even use the concepts more or less synonymously even though there seem to be preferences for one or the other among different groups (Gawell et al. 2009). The term *social enterprise* is very popular among people belonging to or influenced by the European co-operative and social economy discourse (Stryjan, 2001). More specifically, the term social enterprise rather focuses on the ventures than on the dynamic entrepreneurial process of emergence or change. The term *societal entrepreneurship* is popular among groups that relate specifically to dynamics and change or, in a broad sense, to social aims. Social entrepreneurship could, for example, be the development of a rural community or cultural initiatives explicitly emphasizing cross-sectorial interaction (see, e.g., Gawell et al, 2009; Berglund et al, 2013; von Friedrichs, Gawell & Wincent, 2014). This concept is not often used when entrepreneurship is related to addressing social problems or the needs of specific target groups, such as people with disabilities. In these cases, the concept *social entrepreneurship* seems to be preferred. Societal entrepreneurship is sometimes translated to community-based entrepreneurship in English. These conceptualisations overlap, but there are also significant differences that need attention and accurate use, especially in some types of discussions. However, it is not currently possible to understand the state of one of these concepts without including the others. Politicians and other policy makers also use all of these concepts in speeches and have begun to include them in policy documents (e.g., SOU, 2007; Prop, 2009/10, p. 55; Ministry of Enterprise, 2012). However, there are still no clear definitions of or legal grounds for these new terms.

With this somewhat sketchy background on which important keystones of Swedish society are described, we will now elaborate more specifically on the current status of social entrepreneurship in Sweden.

Current Expressions of Social Entrepreneurship

Because there are no specific legal structures of social entrepreneurship or social enterprises or specific certifications or other markers, it is not possible to quantify or categorize this phenomenon in Sweden today. Different versions of social entrepreneurship and social enterprises have, however, been identified (Gawell, 2014). These versions are rather based on sub-cultures in which initiatives largely take on norms and practices already established in the non-profit sector or the business sector or by co-operative organizations. The ventures created through entrepreneurial processes are therefore referred to as non-profit social enterprises, co-operative social enterprises that often focus on work and integration and social purpose businesses

(Gawell, 2014, 2015). However, categorizations of different versions, ideas, methods and arguments are borrowed from the different spheres—often in a rather scrambled way.

Engagement and Ideals Combined With Pragmatism

In studies of over 200 social entrepreneurial initiatives during the 2002–2014 period, great variation is noticeable.[1] However, all refer to social engagement as a common denominator. It is expressed in slightly different terms but clearly highlighted through their aims or mission statements. In some cases, there are also references to specific ideas such as help-to-self-help, empowerment and equality. This is particularly noticeable among initiatives that can be characterized as non-profit or co-operative initiatives. However, through the deconstruction of mission statements and project plans, other ideals can be noticed. Among social purpose businesses, the notion of private enterprise and a demarcation from public sector initiatives are highlighted. Let us examine three examples for illustration. An initiative presenting what I would categorize as a social purpose business argues that its initiative will support unemployed people to start their own businesses and thereby enable them to fulfil their dreams and to independently make a living. Another initiative is heavily influenced by the co-operative tradition and relates to the long-time unemployed and start-ups. However, yet another initiative highlights the need to include processes supporting empowerment as important for target groups that have been out of work for a long time as well as work as a tool not only for social well-being, but also for economic independence. The third example relates to an initiative that presents itself as a non-profit organization, highlighting the need to reach target groups that others either have difficulties reaching or refrain from engaging due to a lack of profitability or financial constraints.

Alongside the engagement and ideals expressed by current social entrepreneurship initiatives, the studied ventures present different models of organization, again inspired by non-profit, co-operative or for-profit traditions. Initiatives influenced by the co-operative tradition often refer to the concept of social enterprise, which, without formally adopting that structure, is most commonly understood as work-integrating social enterprises in the international discourse. Initiatives based on non-profit traditions sometimes hesitate to refer to social entrepreneurship, arguing that they do not want to commercialize the field of social work. However, they do not seem to hesitate to apply the dynamic innovative aspect of the concept in other ways. The third version of social entrepreneurship elaborated on in this chapter, initiatives that can be characterized as social purpose businesses, present their business-like model(s) as obvious in the sense of being efficient and successful. Comparisons or reflective analysis behind the choices of models are conspicuous as a result of their absence; instead, it is common to use the model with which those involved have the most experience.

With regard to engagement, ideals and experience-based skills, there is a great deal of pragmatism characterizing these ventures. Although they do not compromise on specific aspects, they seem to prioritize the possibility to act as they pragmatically adjust to the terms and conditions of public authorities, market-based resources and/or the support of individuals.

Traditional Values and New Ventures

In newer social entrepreneurship initiatives and social enterprises, traditional values are mixed with new practices. The investigation and identification of needs are at least a part of the entrepreneurial process. Later on, this identification is re-constructed through organizational narratives of social enterprises. Although in most cases, it is not possible to clearly define the total population due to the informal characteristics of the field, beneficiaries are engaged or even become the drivers behind the identification of needs, especially in the development of activities through which these needs are to be met. The development of new activities is commonly characterized by learning-by-doing to see what works rather than analytically deciding on optimal strategies. Therefore, the development process can seem crooked and often dependent on different types of project funding. Many social entrepreneurs and social enterprises, however, develop skills to address changes and to include fragmentation in longer time perspectives.

More closely examining four cases that initiated their activities during the last decades, we note that all focus on and include beneficiaries. In one case, the beneficiaries, former drug abusers and/or criminals, initiated and currently run the organization through a democratic membership-based association. Full membership is only possible for those who share this background. Others are welcome to be supporting members. In another case targeting young people and especially young 'troublemakers', beneficiaries participate in forming activities through a 'trial-and-error' approach. The organization is, however, run as a foundation without formal membership governance structures. Nevertheless, the people in this organization refer to traditional *folkhem* values when asked what guides their practices.

In two other cases, both with a strong focus on the work integration of long-unemployed people, beneficiaries participate in the planning and development of activities as well as gradually in decision-making and ownership. In both these cases, different types of consortium models are used to facilitate manageable units for people without experience and often with the need for adjusted and supportive structures in which to work. The empowerment process and participants' striving towards independence are emphasised.

While these ventures all provide services, they also associate with people with an interest in changing conditions for people with difficulties. In some cases, this association is based on informal structures. However, in many cases, it is based on formal membership and/or ownership structures. These cases furthermore practice a voice role, advocating for different solutions that they consider to be related to their particular target groups. The youth organization working primarily with 'troublemakers' served the roles of a 'non-fighting fight club' as well as a 'player in the welfare system'.

Policy Makers' Approach to Social Entrepreneurship

The fragmented and occasionally confusing practices of social entrepreneurship and social enterprises are also reflected in policy discussions. The clearest stream is related to initiatives aiming for integrating the long unemployed. Policy interest in this stream has largely adopted co-operative-based principles of work-integrating social enterprises, such as the importance of participative working methods and empowerment for target groups. Networks of practitioners, civil servants and policy makers have played an active role in the development of this field, sometimes with funds from the European Social Fund. Two of these projects (2004–2007 and 2009–2014) have nationally promoted the development of work-integrating social enterprises. A collaborative policy platform has emerged during the last decade in which the Ministry of Enterprise and the Ministry of Labour, together with national agencies with a focus on enterprises, labour markets and social insurance, collaborate with the autonomous Association for Local Authorities and Regions to coordinate public policies to support the development of work-integrating social enterprises, as they consider these types of activities to be in line with the aims of labour market policies, specifically with the more overarching aims of newer types of welfare policies.

The policy initiatives in this stream of social entrepreneurship have primarily attempted to raise awareness and knowledge about these types of ventures, specifically among people working on different levels in public authorities (Ministry of Enterprise, 2010). References to the term 'work-integrating social enterprises' have been incorporated in policy documents and official instructions as possible collaborators within labour market programmes. Specific favourable conditions for these ventures have not, however, been granted, as the principle of 'competitive neutrality' has characterized policies during the last several decades by letting private actors compete for public contracts. Differentiations between for-profit or non-profit and large or small actors have thereby not been achieved.

Policy initiatives towards the other versions of social entrepreneurship are more vague. On one hand, there are policies with a focus on entrepreneurship and enterprises in general that begin to 'open up' for social entrepreneurship and for the concept of societal entrepreneurship used in Sweden. On the other hand, there are policies with a focus on non-profit organizations and different aspects related to civil society. In both these fields of policies, social entrepreneurship has been noted and referred to rhetorically, but no specific programmes, regulations or legal actions have been taken. Policy attention has been expressed, for example, in the governmental proposition with a focus on policy for civil society launched by the

Ministry of Democracy and Equality in 2009 (Prop, 2009/10:55) and the national strategy for innovation launched by the Ministry of Enterprise in 2012 (Ministry of Enterprise, 2012).

These examples of policies including social entrepreneurship have different aims, which makes the policy interest in social entrepreneurship rather fragmented. On one hand, it is recognised for its social engagement and social cohesion in society. On the other hand, it fits into a more neoliberal discourse of private enterprises, business and growth. Even if the terminology of social entrepreneurship—including societal entrepreneurship and social enterprises—is common, there are differences in the narratives in which it is used.

Social Entrepreneurship: Part of a Search and Different Claims for Solutions

As already stated, social entrepreneurship is a relatively new concept but an old phenomenon. The current expressions are in many ways coloured by the historical trajectory of a civil society characterized by participation in a democratically governed public welfare society. This specific context of social entrepreneurship is shared largely with the other Nordic countries and, to a certain extent, with other countries with strong welfare structures in addition to other types of social contracts and ways to organize these issues. This context differs from those of other countries where public initiatives in these fields are scarce and even more from contexts where catastrophes and conflicts make public initiatives absent, for example.

In spite of these differences, there are, however, similarities that seem universal. Neither the engagement of suffering or less fortunate people as well as people who are vulnerable or exposed to violence, nor the notion that people act upon 'perceived necessities' or in other words, what they perceive as necessary to do something about (see Gawell, 2013), are limited to specific cultures or countries. It seems that the interest in social entrepreneurship is more widely part of searching for new or renewed ways to cope with and handle different types of social problems on a human-to-human level, in communities, in national or regional societies or on a global level. It thereby relates to needs, ideas and resources in a rather complex way. The findings on the roles of social entrepreneurship in the Swedish context can hopefully contribute to the understanding of roles and of what is at stake in social entrepreneurship discussions elsewhere.

At Least Five Roles of Social Entrepreneurship

In the international literature, social entrepreneurship is commonly related to a value-creating and/or an innovative role in society. This is the case in Sweden. The value creation role has been highlighted either from a single social bottom line or a double or *triple bottom line* where social as well as ecological and economic aspects are valued (Blombäck & Wigren, 2009; Tillmar, 2009). It is, however, argued that even though value creation is an important aspect of social entrepreneurship, it can be difficult to measure all significant aspects, such as innovative outcomes that might challenge the established value system. Such initiatives might only be valued from another standpoint (Gawell et al., 2009).

This innovative role highlights the role of social or societal entrepreneurship in dynamics of different levels of society (Frankelius, 2009; Lundqvist, 2009; Sundin, 2009). This role is more developed in some initiatives, but more modest in others (Gawell, 2013). As shown in the historical overview, this innovative role is not new. Civil society and some civil society initiatives have been ascribed significant roles in innovative phases of the development of Swedish welfare society.

Another role of social entrepreneurship has been identified in Swedish studies. Especially related to community development, a mobilizing role of social entrepreneurship has been highlighted in which people as well as other resources work together towards common aims that are more or less public (Johannisson & Nilsson, 1989; Asplund, 2009; Lindhult, 2009). This mobilizing role is further observed in relation to initiatives targeting long-time unemployed people and work training through work-integrating social enterprises (Gawell, 2014).

In continued studies of social entrepreneurship in Sweden, two more roles appear. The first is the development of social activities and thereby the provision of social services in society—specifically, in Swedish welfare society. Social entrepreneurship functions in arenas of associations in which funds can be raised from grants and donations as well as arenas of more business-like conditions, such as bidding, contracts and more transactional relations. Both forms are characterized largely by public funding, as is the common practice in Sweden. This type of 'mixed market' is not, however, new to ventures engaging in social activities. Many established non-profit organizations have developed hybrid organizational formations including membership-based associations, foundations and limited companies depending on the types of activities they run. This helps them handle the different relations and different conditions of the 'mixed market'. In Sweden, different types of ventures in these organizational groups are traditionally owned by a membership-based association.

The other additional role of social entrepreneurship is to contribute to the debate on what needs should be addressed, how to address these needs and how these needs should be regarded by other actors in society. Again, there is a historical parallel to the time when civil society organizations advocated for specific social issues. In some current studies on social entrepreneurship in Sweden, this role is significant, at least as it relates to some of the aspects of ventures. In some studied cases, this role is less apparent. There is a range of cases, from those that hardly raise their voice at all to those that can be characterized as almost exclusively voice organizations, political entrepreneurs (von Bergmann-Winberg, 2014) or activist entrepreneurs (Gawell, 2006).

Social entrepreneurship can thus be seen as an intermediary actor at the centre of the negotiation of roles in society. Due to the positive discourse and lack of critical discussions of social entrepreneurship in society, this deliberative role is generally, however, not explicitly discussed, even if social entrepreneurship claims to resolve challenges in society.

Different Views on Development and Competing Claims for Solutions

There is not much open critique against social entrepreneurship in Sweden, even though some people argue that it is leading to the commercialization of social initiatives and is a threat to public solutions that they argue are preferable. Basically, there is a consensus in support of a democratic and sustainable welfare society in economic, social and environmental terms (Ekengren Oscarsson & Bergström, 2013). Behind this common positive positioning, there are, however, different views on how to build such a society. The confidence in the capacity of individual and market-based solutions to resolve so-called *wicked problems* that are difficult to recognise and to solve due to incomplete or even contradictory requirements (Churchman, 1967; Rittel & Webber, 1973) is the most obvious difference; however, this difference does not appear in black and white terminology. Representatives of different initiatives and experts in the field argue for a combination of market-based and public solutions. However, there are differences in what traits market-based businesses, non-profits and public sector initiatives are ascribed; they are not always based on systematic evaluations, but rather are mixed with stakeholder ideologies, interests and occasionally simply a rationalization of one's own practice.

Based on the interest in social entrepreneurship combined with the development of Swedish society in the last two or three decades, social entrepreneurship can be seen as a part of the shift towards what Esping-Andersen (1990) would call a liberal welfare society in which market solutions play a fundamental role. In contrast earlier, the twentieth century, social entrepreneurship played a role in the construction of the Swedish socio-democratic welfare model (Gawell & Westlund, 2014). Social entrepreneurship is thus not biased towards certain societal models in general, even though it is biased towards current movements in society.

In the ventures that highlight market-based solutions, business-like skills and conditions for operation are emphasised. However, no matter what type of venture is advocated, very few actors argue that these social activities should be exclusively privately funded in Sweden. In fact, many seem to take public funding more or less for granted, at least as a fundamental condition for operation, even though the need for alternative funding is emphasised to decrease dependency. Some actors argue the need to improve income generation by sales, even if it minimally decreases the dependency on public funding in Sweden because public authorities procure social services either through direct contracts or through different types of client choice models.

Social Entrepreneurship and Social Enterprises: Chameleons Through Times and Values

Like chameleons, ventures in the fields of social entrepreneurship and social enterprises move among a colourful shrubbery of human needs, perceptions and actions, as well as institutional settings. Entrepreneurial initiatives tune in, adjust to and occasionally stand out in and push or even prey on the environment. We can recognise a historical trajectory and observe renewed combinations and new expressions of social entrepreneurship. Social entrepreneurship becomes a lens through which to study different aspects of social life and the organization of societies.

By definition, social entrepreneurship entails emphasis on dynamics rather than on the scope of describing sectors as such, even if changes can only be understood properly in relation to established practices and structures. This means that apart from analysing social entrepreneurial initiatives as such, it is of interest to unfold critical aspects hidden by the social entrepreneurship discourse, which is influenced by what Nicholls (2010) identified as paradigm-building actors who promote individual heroes as a point of departure, adopt business-like practices as ideal, a link with global community of social entrepreneurs among (commercial) entrepreneurs and, finally, establish the role of social entrepreneurs as voice and advocacy agents bringing social justice to practice. This version of social entrepreneurship is visible in Sweden, especially among what has been referred to earlier as social purpose businesses. However, the other versions of social entrepreneurship highlight aspects beyond this internationally dominating discourse on social entrepreneurship. These aspects are highly interwoven with the debate and negotiation of Swedish society throughout several centuries. They are not limited to the Swedish context, but they appear explicitly in this particular context—throughout history as well as in current debates. These aspects include the relation between **needs and resources,** the relation between **opportunities and responsibilities** and the relation between **dependence and the question of equality.**

Even though Sweden is a rich nation with a high standard of living and a developed welfare system, not everyone shares this sense of prosperous lifestyles. Physical and mental illnesses as well as different types of disabilities affect people as elsewhere in the world. Drugs and violence lead to abuse, and exclusion leads to marginalization. Even if conditions are milder in Sweden than in many other countries in the world, repressive forces are not absent—in spite of historical initiatives to limit or even eliminate them and structures that explicitly include elements of social security. However, these aspects are eternal rather than finite and have to be handled and potentially defended throughout time, which means that the need for social entrepreneurship is indefinite. Studies from the Swedish context highlight social entrepreneurship not as isolated initiatives but as a part of health care, education and labour market functions, to mention a few examples.

Behind the more general assumption that social entrepreneurs respond to needs in society, the studies on which this chapter is based reveal differences regarding *who* should identify what needs to address and *how* to address these needs. This discussion on representation has been on-going at least throughout the historical phases referred to in this chapter. Social entrepreneurship is often ascribed a bottom-up approach. Social entrepreneurship is commonly a more bottom-up approach than activities initiated from a hierarchical top, such as state or other public authorities. However, in the many studied cases, few actually had a bottom-up approach in the sense that the initiative is actually initiated, developed and driven by people who themselves make up the primary target group. The majority of cases studied or reviewed in the social entrepreneurship literature come 'from the side', that is, from people who are affected, who perceive it is necessary to act and who possess at least some economic, social or political capital to mobilize means for action. There are exceptions where, for example, former drug abusers and people with criminal backgrounds engage in creating a venture 'for me and people like me'. More often, there are combinations in which beneficiaries are highly involved in articulating the scope and working methods with the support of more resourceful people.

In spite of generally good living conditions, 'needs seek resources'. Unfortunately, resources do not automatically match them. Needs create a demand, but not necessary a demand in economic terms. Demand in economic terms is a conceptualisation of the willingness to pay combined with an ability to pay. Illness, disabilities and marginalization often decrease the ability to pay. Resources are therefore often raised elsewhere. In the case of Sweden, the tax-funded public finance dominates either in the form of grants, through procurements or client choice models. In addition, donations, foundation grants, membership fees and different types of fundraising activities exist, but public funding dominates. Social entrepreneurship and social enterprises are thus a part of the welfare society rather than an alternative to it. This also means that social services such as work rehabilitation are fundamental to and occasionally dominate social enterprise income.

The resources controlled by the welfare state have, with the transformed system in which private actors are invited as service providers, become opportunities for social entrepreneurs and different types of enterprises. In some cases, businesses have made substantial profits. However, in most of the fields in which meeting needs requires substantial effort, financial pressure equates to rather poor conditions—at least in the mid- or long term. Different types of investments and short-term project grants make funding easier initially or for the time being, as many social entrepreneurship initiatives have become skilled at applying for funds.

The increased financial opportunities that the reallocation of financial resources bring lead to considerations of allocation of responsibilities. Public responsibility has not formally decreased. There have, however, been difficulties in accountability, especially related to qualitative aspects. Additionally, aspects such as participation and influence have occasionally even been left out of contracts and instead been arbitrarily provided. Earlier on, social entrepreneurship initiatives and social enterprises had been able to provide services as a complement to the public sector and thereby were only held accountable for their own ventures. As they, together with for-profit ventures, become partners in the public welfare system, they are also held responsible for the system in the beneficiaries' eyes. They are, so to speak, not necessarily in opposition any longer, even though some initiatives still have a strong advocating voice.

Last but not least, dependency and the question of equality have characterized Swedish society for centuries. Dependency and equality are generally not addressed explicitly in the business-influenced social entrepreneurship discourse; thus, the entrepreneur, the ventures as such and potential impacts are in focus. In some parts of the social entrepreneurship discourse, even traditional charity models dominate. The discussion on dependency and equality is, however, often related primarily to cooperatives or traditional association. Here, the earlier arguments related to the Swedish model—that is, that individuals, regardless of income, should have the same right to care when needed—remain in some parts of the social enterprise and social entrepreneurship discourse, as do arguments that no individual should have to rely on arbitrary charity from wealthy people. Individuals should also have the right to represent themselves or to choose who they want to represent them as much as possible.

To conclude, studies of social entrepreneurship, societal entrepreneurship and social enterprises in Sweden show many similarities with the recent international discourse. However, they emphasise some aspects that are not as commonly addressed elsewhere. The two most pivotal aspects are the close relation to a strong welfare state with extensive responsibilities in social matters and, second, the right to representation and influence by individuals targeted by social activities. This calls for a critical analysis of social entrepreneurship beyond the current dominant discourse. Does social entrepreneurship lead to the emancipation and empowerment of individuals, does it consolidate power structures or does it contribute to increasing inequalities? Studies of over 200 cases in the Swedish system show that different versions of social entrepreneurship can produce all of the above; depending on how they work, they bring one or another into practice. Social entrepreneurship is thereby a motley phenomenon in a variegated colourful shrubbery that calls for thorough reflection in relation to potential beneficiaries as well as the system in which common goods are produced, that is, the types of social contracts set into practice by the current social entrepreneurship trend. Social entrepreneurship is thus highly political, not necessarily in politically partisan terms or limited to authoritarian governance, but rather in the sense that it affects people's everyday live and the relations between people when vulnerability undermines one's potential.

Note

1. Gawell 2006, 2011a, 2011b, 2012, 2013a, 2013b, 2014.

References

Ahrne, G. (1994). *Social Organizations: Interaction Inside, Outside and Between Organizations.* London: Sage Publications.
Amnå, E. (2005). Scenöppning, scenvridning, scenförändring. In E. Amnå (Ed.), *Civilsamhället: Några forskningsfrågor.* Stockholm: Riksbankens Jubileumsfond in collaboration with Gidlunds förlag.
Asplund, C. (2009). Societal Entrepreneurs for Local and Regional Development. In M. Gawell, B. Johannisson & M. Lundqvist (Eds.), *Entrepreneurship in the Name of Society.* Stockholm: KK-stiftelsen.
Berglund, K., Johannisson, B. & Schwartz, B. (2013). *Societal Entrepreneurship: Positioning, Penetrating, Promoting.* Cheltenham, UK and Northampton, MA: Edward Elgar.
von Bergmann-Winberg, M.-L. (2014). Att skapa ett kommunalt varumärke—en jämförande nordisk studie. In Y. von Friedrichs, M. Gawell & J. Wincent (Eds.), *Samhällsentreprenörskap—samverkande för local utveckling.* Östersund: Mid Sweden University Press.
Blombäck, A. & Wigren, C. (2009). The Firm as Societal Entrepreneur. In M. Gawell, B. Johannisson & M. Lundqvist (Eds.), *Entrepreneurship in the Name of Society.* Stockholm: KK-stiftelsen.
Borzaga, C. & Defourny, J. (2001). *The Emergence of Social Enterprises.* New York: Routledge.
Borzaga, C., Galera, G. & Nogales, R. (2008). *Social Enterprises: A New Model for Poverty Reduction and Employment Generation.* EMES / UNDP.
Churchman, W. (1967). Guest Editorial. *Management Science,* 14, 4.
Dees, G, (2001, first published 1998). *The Meaning of 'Social Entrepreneurship'.* FEDF Partners. Available at www.redf.org, accessed 12 May 2015.
Ekengren Oscarsson, H. & Bergström, A. (2013). *Svenska Trender 1986–2013.* SOM Institute, Gothenburg University.
Esping-Andersen, G. (1990). *The Three Worlds of Welfare Capitalism.* Cambridge: Polity Press.
Frankelius, P. (2009). Societal Entrepreneurship for the Wealth of Nations. In M. Gawell, B. Johannisson & M. Lundqvist (Eds.), *Entrepreneurship in the Name of Society.* Stockholm: KK-stiftelsen.
von Friedrichs, Y., Gawell, M. & Wincent, J. (2014). *Samhällsentreprenörskap.* Östersund: Midsweden University.
Gawell, M. (2006). *Activist Entrepreneurship: Attac'ing Norms and Articulating Disclosive Stories.* Stockholm: Stockholm University Press.
Gawell, M. (2011a). *Inte vilket entreprenörskap och företagande som helst: En fältstudie av 7 projekt med finansiering från den Europeiska socialfonden.* Stockholm: Tillväxtverket rapport 90.

Gawell, M. (2011b). *Entreprenörskap och företagande i projekt finansierade av Europeiska socialfonden: Rapport från en kartläggning av projekt som beviljats medel 2008–2009.* Stockholm: Tillväxtverket.

Gawell, M. (2012). *Kreativa Hederliga Företagare—det krävs både mod och tålamod: Analys av ett KRIS-projekt finansierat av Europeiska socialfonden.* Stockholm: KRIS.

Gawell, M. (2013a). *Socialt företagande och försöken att finna fungerande sätt.* Stockholm: Arvsfonden.

Gawell, M. (2013b). Social Entrepreneurship: Action Grounded in Needs, Opportunities and/or Perceived Necessities? *Voluntas: International Journal of Voluntary and Nonprofit Organizations*, 24(4), 1071–1090.

Gawell, M. (2014). Soci(et)al Entrepreneurship and Different Forms of Social Enterprises. In A. Lundström, C. Zhou, Y. von Friedrichs & E. Sundin (Eds.), *Social Entrepreneurship Levering Economic, Political and Cultural Dimensions.* Berlin, Heidelberg, & New York: Springer.

Gawell, M. (2015). Social Enterprise in Sweden: Intertextual Consensus and Hidden Paradoxes. ICSEM Working Paper No. 08. Liege: The International Comparative Social Enterprise Models (ICSEM) Project. Available at www.iap-socent.be/sites/default/files/Sweden%20-%20Gawell.pdf, accessed 14 December 2015.

Gawell, M., Johannisson, B. & Lundqvist, M. (2009). *Entrepreneurship in the Name of Society.* Stockholm: KK-stiftelsen.

Gawell, M., Pierre, A. & von Friedrichs, Y. (2014). Societal Entrepreneurship— A Cross-Boundary Force for Regional and Local Development Cherished for Multiple Reasons. *Scandinavian Journal for Public Administration*, 18(4), 109–130.

Gawell, M. & Westlund, H. (2014). Social Entrepreneurship as a Construct of a Liberal Welfare Regime? In H. Douglas & S. Grant (Eds.), *Social Innovation, Entrepreneurship and Enterprise: Context and Theories.* Prahran: Tilde University Press.

Hjorth, D. & Bjerke, B. (2006). Public Entrepreneurship: Moving from Social Consumer to Public Citizen. In C. Steyaert & D. Hjorth (Eds.), *Entrepreneurship as Social Change.* Cheltenham: Edward Elgar.

Ivarsson Westerberg, A. & Forsell, A. (2014). New Public Management och administrationssamhället. *Organisation & Samhälle: Svensk företagsekonomisk tidskrift*, 2, 40–44.

Jacobsson, B., Pierre, J. & Sundström, G. (2015). *Overing the Embedded State: The Organizational Dimension of Governance.* Oxford: Oxford University Press.

Johannisson, B. (2005). *Entreprenörskapets väsen.* Lund: Studentlitteratur.

Johannisson, B. & Nilsson, A. (1989). Community Entrepreneurship. Networking for Local Development. *Journal of Entrepreneurship & Regional Development*, 1(1), 1–19.

Larsson, J. (2008). *Folkhemmet och det europeiska huset: Svensk välfärdsstat i omvandling.* Stockholm: Hjalmarsson & Högberg förlag.

Lindhult, E. (2009). Development Partnership as Societal Entrepreneurship. In M. Gawell, B. Johannisson & M. Lundqvist (Eds.), *Entrepreneurship in the Name of Society.* Stockholm: KK-stiftelsen.

Lundqvist, M. (2009). The University of Technology in the Societal Entrepreneurship Arena. In M. Gawell, B. Johannisson & M. Lundqvist (Eds.), *Entrepreneurship in the Name of Society.* Stockholm: KK-stiftelsen.

Lundström, T. & Wijkström, F. (1997). *The Nonprofit Sector in Sweden.* Manchester: Manchester University Press.

Mair, J., Robinson, J. & Hockerts, K. (2006). *Social Entrepreneurship*. Hampshire: Palgrave.

Ministry of Enterprise. (2010). *Handlingsplan för arbetsintegrerande sociala företag*. Ministry of Enterprise *N2010/1894/ENT*.

Ministry of Enterprise. (2012). *Den nationella innovationsstrategi*. Stockholm: Regeringskansliet.

Munkhammar, J. (2009). *Försäljning av statliga bolag under tre decennier*. Stockholm: Timbro.

Nicholls, A. (2006). *Social Entrepreneurship: New Models of Sustainable Social Change*. New York: Oxford University Press.

Nicholls, A. (2010). The Legitimacy of Social Entrepreneurship: Reflexive Isomorphism in a Pre-paradigmatic Field. *Entrepreneurship Theory & Practice*, 34(1), 1042–2587.

Pierre, A., von Friedrichs, Y. & Wincent, J. (2014). Entrepreneurship in Society: A Review and Definition of Community-Based Entrepreneurship Research. In A. Lundström, C. Zhou, Y. von Friedrichs & E. Sundin (Eds.), *Social Entrepreneurship: Leveraging Economic and Political and Cultural Dimensions*. Heidelberg, New York, & London: Springer.

Prop (2009/10:55). *En politik för det civila samhället*. Stockholm: Ministry of gender equality and integration.

Rittel, H. & Webber, M. (1973). Dilemmas in General Theory of Planning. *Policy sciences* 4.2 (1973): 155–169.

Schumpeter, J. (1934). *The Theory of Economic Development*. Cambridge: Harvard University Press.

SOU 2007:66. *Rörelser i tiden*. Stockholm: Statens offentliga utredningar.

Steyaert, C. & Hjorth, D. (2006). *Entrepreneurship as Social Change*. Cheltenham: Edward Elgar.

Steyaert, C. & Katz, J. (2004). Reclaiming the Space of Entrepreneurship in Society: Geographical Discursive and Social Dimensions. *Entrepreneurship & Regional Development*, 16(3), 179–196.

Stryjan, Y. (2001). The Emergence of Work-Integration Social Enterprises in Sweden. In C. Borzaga & J. Defrouny (Eds.), *The Emergence of Social Enterprise*. London: Routledge.

Sundin, E. (2009). Care in SMEs—The Hidden Social Entrepreneurship. In M. Gawell, B. Johannisson & M. Lundqvist (Eds.), *Entrepreneurship in the Name of Society*. Stockholm: KK-stiftelsen.

Svedberg, L. (2005). Det civila samähllet och välfärden—ideologiska önskedrömmar och sociala realiteter. In E. Amnå (Ed.), *Civilsamhället—några forskningsfrågor*. Stockholm: Riksbankens Jubileumsfond i samarbete med Gidlunds förlag.

Swedberg, R. (2000). *Entrepreneurship: The Social Science View*. Oxford: Oxford University Press.

Swedberg, R. (2008). *Schumpeter: Om skapande förstörelse och entreprenörskap*. Stockholm: Nordstedts akademiska förlag.

Tillmar, M. (2009). Societal Entrepreneurs in the Health Sector: Frontier Crossing Combiners. In M. Gawell, B. Johannisson & M. Lundqvist (Eds.), *Entrepreneurship in the Name of Society*. Stockholm: KK-stiftelsen.

Trägårdh, L. (2007). *State and Civil Society in Northern Europe: The Swedish Model Reconsidered*. New York: Barghahn Books.

Wijkström, F. & Lundström, T. (2002). *Den ideella sektorn: Organisationerna i det civila samhället*. Stockholm: Sober Förlag.

4 Evolution of the Social Enterprise Concept in Finland

Harri Kostilainen and Pekka Pättiniemi

In Finland, there is a rich and established sector of social economy organizations. It has had a legitimate role as a part of the welfare state. These organizations have had an important role in the service delivery for specific special needs and areas. Within this sector, with influences also from other sectors, what is referred to as *social enterprises* has emerged. In this chapter, the evolution of the Finnish concept of social enterprise and the institutionalization of the phenomenon is analysed.

In the recent Finnish debate, social enterprises are expected to combine the business skills of private enterprises with a strong social mission. Public administration expects social innovations from the private sector that might have an important role in delivering (welfare) services and labour market integration. The European Social Fund has been a major player in developing different forms of social enterprises.

Explaining the Evolution of the Social Enterprise Concept in Finland

We have witnessed a dramatic change in the delivery of public services in Finland during the last decades. According to the National Institute of Health and Welfare (THL 25/2011), the number of private operational units providing social services grew from 741 in 1990 to 4,350 in 2010. Of these 4,350 units, 35 per cent were maintained by social economy organizations and social enterprises. In 2010, different types of private social service providers including social enterprises employed 61,800 people, more than half of them in different types of social economy organizations and social enterprises. The growth of employment in social services from 1990 to 2008 was 67,800 employees; of this growth, 64 per cent occurred in private operational units that provide social services, and 36 per cent occurred in public service units. According to a study (Laiho, 2011), public procurement from private actors is estimated to increase due to several issues: municipal strategies, customer's choice approach and the expansion of the service voucher experiment, as well as tax exemptions for household services and some homecare services.

In this chapter, we analyse the institutional change that has taken place in delivering welfare services as well as the evolution of social enterprises in Finland. We apply the theory of explanatory modes of institutional change (Mahoney & Thelen, 2009a) for describing the political context, the characteristics of institutions, the types of dominant change agents and the types of institutional changes in delivering welfare services. To understand the evolution of social enterprises, we use the concept of *niche* to represent the position or function of an entity, such as a social enterprise within a larger community or environment, such as welfare service delivery (Popielarz & Neal, 2007). The concept of niche allows us to understand the changes of social enterprises under different environmental conditions and how social enterprises interact in the competitive conditions induced by a finite environment.

In the following section, we analyse the changing nature of the Finnish welfare state and how this change has shaped the possibilities for social enterprises. In the third section, we try to position the Finnish experience in relation to general trends in the Nordic countries. In the fourth section, we analyse the recent phases of the development of the social enterprise concept in Finland. We identify the developmental phases of social enterprises as: 1) A new social movement, 2) A labour market measure, 3) A vehicle renewing welfare state service provisions and 4) The institutionalization of the Finnish social enterprise concept. Finally, we draw our conclusions and sketch future developments and the role of social enterprises in Finland.

The research approach on which this chapter is based includes a content analysis of recent research and other relevant literature. In addition, our research data includes European Social Fund Single Programming Documents from the structural fund periods 1995–1999, 2000–2006, 2007–2013 and 2014–2020, as well as EQUAL programme documents, evaluation reports of these programmes and personal field work notes from diverse development projects under these programmes. We have also used other relevant literature, official reports and data on different segments of social enterprises.

Social Economy Organizations in the Finnish Welfare State

In Finland, the traditional expression of social enterprises is based on social economy organizations: co-operatives, mutual societies, associations and foundations practicing economic activities. The role of these traditional social economy organizations has been strong and recognised: for example, there are legal frameworks: the Co-operative law (Co-operatives Act 22/1901), the Law on Association (Associations Act 1/1919) and the Foundation law (Foundations Act 109/1930). Mutual (insurance and financial) companies apply both co-operative legislation and insurance company legislation (Insurance Companies Act 174/1933). They all share the following goals: 1) Independence from the state, 2) Ownership based on people, not on capital, 3) The principle of one member, one vote and 4) Achieving social goals and sustainable economic results. (Defourny & Delvetere, 1999; Pättiniemi, 2007). There are also dedicated financial instruments such as Finland's Slot Machine Association, which was established in 1938 to finance voluntary actions and the development of social and health care associations.

The traditional forms of social enterprises have counteracted inequality and fostered social and economic development in Finland. During the shift from an agricultural to an industrial society, from the 1880s to the late 1950s, traditional forms of social enterprises represented self-help and self-defence (Laurinkari, 2007). Social economy organizations emerged where there was a lack of vital services and where resources were scarce. Social policy measures, aims and practices were central innovations and drivers of the diffusion of consumer co-operatives around the country (Inkinen, 2001). A vital sector, namely that of volunteer associations, has established an important role, especially in furthering the interests of the most vulnerable groups and in developing and organizing services for them. Foundations are an important financier and maintainer of many welfare services that require specialized expertise. Sectors where foundations a play major role can be found, for example, in the area of work integration and social housing. Mutual societies still make a significant impact in the field of non-life insurance.

The role of social economy organizations changed when the welfare state emerged. Some social innovations by traditional social enterprises were transferred to the handling of the public sector when the welfare state was developed and when it matured from the 1940s to the 1980s. Municipalities took over the responsibility of organizing and financing universal welfare service functions, doing so via fairly high taxation. In addition to social and health care, widespread welfare policies extended to cover education, employment, housing and leisure (e.g., Niiranen, Seppänen-Järvelä, Sinkkonen & Vartiainen, 2010). The traditional social economy organizations acquired a new role in delivering services to various specific needs of different vulnerable groups, e.g., those with hearing and speaking disturbances, the visually impaired, disabled war veterans, people with respiratory problems and several other groups.

A great change in providing welfare services has been taking place in the Finnish welfare state since the early 1990s. This is a result of a number of simultaneous changes in the needs and demands for services. Such changes have been brought about by, e.g., an aging population, legislation, funding, education and public commitment to different social policy measures and programmes. There have also been changes in the values and motivations of Finnish citizens.

The increasing need for more and different types of individualised welfare services, the difficulties in recruiting new staff and the need for motivating the existing staff in the field of welfare services mean challenges to the financing and delivering of services. Finland's sparsely populated areas are facing extreme challenges and yet, at the same time, investments from municipalities and the public sector are becoming scarce (Pihlaja, 2010). The consequence is increased competition and (quasi)markets for financing and delivering public services. The shift in social service provision from public to private service provision (including different types of social economy organizations and social enterprises) during the past two decades is clear.

New types of social enterprises, activities and tasks have been evolving in the welfare state since the beginning of the 1990s. A part of the growth of large private companies in the social services sector can be explained by the fact that social enterprises are, in general, very vulnerable as economic units due to their size, limited resources and other reasons such as staff business and managerial skills. In Finland, only a few major cities have been able to develop market-driven welfare services. They lack markets that could interest profit-seeking enterprises. Therefore, the answer might be found in establishing social enterprises in one way or another (Pihlaja, 2010).

Finnish Social Enterprise Development in the Nordic Context

The European Commissions comprehensive study "A map of social enterprises and their eco-systems in Europe" argues that social enterprises and their ecosystems in the Nordic countries have common development trajectories (European Commission, 2014), but a Nordic Council study (Nordic Council of Ministers, 2015) found differing practices and paths.

It has been argued (Hulgård & Lundgaard Andersen, 2015) that there are four characteristics common to social enterprises in the Nordic countries: 1) The Nordic welfare state is an innovative and active partner to social enterprises; 2) Social enterprises co-operate and interface with the public, private and third sector; 3) Social enterprises reach beyond work integration; and 4) Social enterprises function as arenas for citizens' participation, learning and provision of (welfare) services.

The Nordic countries have been known for their universalistic welfare states for decades. The model has aimed to guarantee equal opportunities for citizens and competitive advantages for private and public economies. However, the Nordic countries are now facing challenges that are very alike as they work to maintain their proven welfare model. There is an urgent and common need for new, sustainable solutions with which to maintain and further develop the Nordic welfare models. Social enterprises might be vehicles for developing and implementing new solutions to diverse societal challenges. In Finland as well as in the other Nordic countries, the welfare state was an innovative and active partner for traditional social enterprises. Today, the state is more like a contract partner, with many kinds of private service providers competing on the growing welfare markets. This applies to traditional welfare associations and foundations that are trying to find their way in a changed environment. A common obstacle to the development of social enterprises and related innovations in the Nordic countries is the lack of cross-sectorial cooperation, also dubbed the 'silo mentality' in administration (Nordic Council of Ministers, 2015). The silo mentality applies to Finnish social enterprises, hindering collaboration between different actors and sectors.

Despite the similarity of challenges, the countries differ in their methods of responding to their challenges. Finland has drifted to exclusive dual-labour markets, considering them to be the way to maintain economic growth. For example, Denmark has invested more in active labour market policy measures than has Finland (Kostilainen & Nieminen, 2011).

The structure of Finnish society has been inclusive throughout the stages of growth and the maturing of the welfare state. The aim of the welfare state has been to enable it to improve poor living conditions and citizens' social and economic well-being in order to foster economic growth. The push for improving living conditions and welfare services often comes from traditional forms of social enterprises that still play a role in delivering welfare services. The recent debate on how to foster competitiveness has meant a transition towards a more exclusive welfare state in which institutions do not work for the benefit of the most vulnerable groups. Therefore, a deficit in morale has risen that is now becoming apparent and is seen especially in the growth of individuality that lessens the feeling of togetherness (Hiilamo, 2011; Niiranen et al., 2011). At the same time, however, there are initiatives and efforts targeting inclusive, collective actions mobilized by various social enterprises and social movements.

Entrepreneurial activities with weighty social goals can be connected to policies that aim to bring back the inclusiveness of the enabling welfare state. One of the key ideas of the Finnish welfare state concept was to invest in human capital in order to enhance equal opportunities and to thereby advance the economic and social development of all citizens. In this universal welfare state concept, all citizens have equal access to free and good-quality public services supported by taxation. The concept still exists, but it has been at least partly replaced by the distribution of the policies of the strongest interest groups in our society. As a result, those groups who do not have a strong voice in our society are almost neglected. Income inequality has grown, and citizens' equal opportunities to improve their economic and social conditions have been weakened. Recent research estimates that the Finnish welfare system is good if not excellent for 80 per cent of Finnish citizens, but for the most vulnerable 20 per cent, it is one of the worst in Europe (Saari, 2015; THL, 2015). This 20 per cent are people who for various reasons are excluded from the labour market; the Finnish welfare system is strongly based on labour market participation. Recently, we have again seen efforts by the public sector to invest resources in human capital, not merely in direct payments of passive social benefits. The aim of these efforts is to keep the welfare state viable (Hiilamo & Saari, 2010).

The role of the state providing services for its citizens has changed in Finland. Finnish governments have based some of their social enterprise policies on the experiences of the United Kingdom. In the United Kingdom, the state has withdrawn from delivering various (welfare) services and at the same time, it has launched a policy framework, various support structures and different instruments in order to develop a viable social enterprise sector. Despite the development of certain institutional practices and experiments in social enterprises, Finland does not have any specific policy frameworks for the role of social enterprises in the welfare society; therefore, it is challenging to develop a viable social enterprise ecosystem.

Development Phases of Social Enterprises in Finland

In recent discussions, social enterprises have been expected to combine the business skills of the private sector with a strong social mission. Various stakeholders expect social innovations from the private sector that might play an important role in delivering public (welfare) services and in labour market integration. These expectations are seen in the programmes, documents and operation guidelines of the European Social Fund as well as in the economic resources made available by that organization. The European Social Fund has been a major player in the development of the social enterprise concept in Finland.

Next, we present four phases of recent Finnish social enterprise development.

Emergence of New Generations of Social Enterprises

In the early 1990s, worker co-operatives and other types of self-help groups were established by unemployed people. They stemmed directly from the needs of their participants during times of deep recession and heavy unemployment. The Ministry of Labour struggled with the persistent hard core of structural unemployment consisting of 180,000 people and almost 90,000 disabled job seekers. Worker co-operatives and other self-help groups became '*rapid action forces*' to partly resolve the severe unemployment and the structural changes in the Finnish society. In that period, all new initiatives were welcomed to solve the crisis. The self-help model also became one of the measures and an object of (European) political control.

One explanation for the emergence of new labour co-operatives is that the Finnish labour market changed dramatically. The shift from an inclusive full-employment system to the dual division of the labour market took place rapidly. The dual-labour market contains those in the core labour market who have steady incomes and careers and those who are strapped in the intermediated labour market and precarious jobs. The markets for hiring temporary workforces in Finland were marginal and new labour co-operatives emerged at least partly to fulfil this market niche.

During Finland's first structural fund period in the European Union from 1995–1999, a new Finnish model of co-operatives was developed mainly through European Social Fund projects. Hundreds of new co-operatives were established. Research and studies on new co-operatives were lively. Various development measures were set up, including, for example, the development of the regional concept 'how to start up co-operative enterprises'. For the same purpose, study groups were set up for consultants and civil servants. Managers of the new co-operatives were trained in co-operative entrepreneurship and participative management.

The model of the new Finnish co-operatives was benchmarked from other European countries, mainly Spain, the United Kingdom and Italy. The labour co-operative model was a Finnish social innovation that enabled combining a wage income and unemployment benefits, thus offering a flexible way for the individual to maintain his or her social security. The Ministry of Employment and the Economy decided that it was possible to combine unemployment benefits more flexibly with salary incomes in cases in which there are at least seven members in an established worker co-operative. The aim was to lower the barrier between entrepreneurship and paid work. On the other hand, these co-operatives were seen as a measure to produce welfare services with the help of decentralised ownership and to integrate into the labour market the unemployed and those who found it difficult to find work, as the Italian social co-operatives had done.

Worker co-operatives based on self-help have reached a credible and established position in the business information and education system in Finland. For example, a number of universities of applied sciences have established student co-operatives for 'learning-by-doing' entrepreneurial education. New co-operatives are well known even though their relative share of the established enterprises is marginal. Approximately 200 new co-operatives are established annually (Pellervo, 2012).

A study (Moilanen, 2010) on new co-operatives identified five categories that we consider parts of the new social enterprise movement that emerged in the early 1990s: 1) Employee-owned co-operatives characterized by a common business idea and stable work relations, 2) Co-operatives of self-employed persons in which the co-operative is seen as a vehicle for administrative and marketing functions, 3) Labour co-operatives with the aim of finding employment opportunities for their unemployed members, 4) Incubators in the co-operative form and 5) Co-operatives that attract people who wish to gain extra income from their hobbies.

According to the co-operative register (Osuuskuntarekisteri, 2015), there currently are about 1,600 worker and labour co-operatives in Finland. It is (Moilanen, 2010) estimated that they have approximately 12,600 members and employ approximately 6,650 people; of those, 1,590 persons are employed full time, 1,960 persons part-time and 3,100 people temporarily. Most members of these co-operatives earn a part of their daily income from other sources as well. The smallest co-operatives have three members and the largest 188; the average size is 10 members.

Social Enterprises as a Labour Market Measure

Parliamentary discussion on the need for social enterprise regulation started in Finland in the late 1990s. Parliamentary propositions were put forth in the late 1990s and certain public sector committees and working groups were established, with their work resulting in a common conclusion: there was no need for specialized legislation on social enterprises.

However, the discussion on the need for work-integration social enterprises and their possible role had raised interest and fallen on the fertile ground of developing intermediate labour markets. The idea of work-integration social enterprises as means for employing people with disabilities and those inside the hard core of unemployment was further developed by various interest groups inspired by projects funded through the European Social Fund.

Encouraged by the impressive results of certain experimental projects funded through the European Social Fund and after a short parliamentary debate, the Act on Social Enterprises (Act 1351/2003) entered into force in 2004. The act limits "social enterprises" to only the field of work integration. The ownerships and backgrounds of these organizations can be categorized as follows: 1) Work-integration social enterprises that are re-organized from sheltered workshops owned by municipalities and/or by foundations and volunteer associations, 2) Social enterprises that are established as co-operatives and owned by self-help groups and local organizations, 3) Volunteer associations for the unemployed and community associations and 4) Entrepreneurial initiatives (see also Pättiniemi, 2006).

The aim of the act was supported by European Structural Fund programmes (2000–2006), which were also used for developing an operational model for the new social economy and social enterprises in Finland. The National Equal Theme Network on social enterprises co-ordinated and integrated development projects relating to social enterprises. The networking groups collected and mainstreamed good practices that had been created throughout the country in order to improve the growth of social enterprises. This high-level forum for social enterprises gathered interest groups to discuss the Finnish model for social enterprises. The Italian type of consortiums was rooted in the regions of Satakunta and Lapland. The Ministry of Trade and Industry funded the Tampere Region Cooperative Centre for the national task of promoting co-operative entrepreneurship through counselling, education and information dissemination. In 2005, a university network was established for multi-disciplinary studies and research into co-operative and social economy.

The situation of registered work-integration social enterprises (WISE) (Act 1351/2003) is problematic. During the preparation and the introduction of the new legislation, politicians and civil servants were highly aware of the possible problems relating to the freedom of competition and public procurement legislation. Because of these concerns, the act does not genuinely provide any special support or incentives to establish work-integration social enterprises (Pättiniemi, 2004). Registered work-integration social enterprises have the right to use the 'Butterfly Mark' dedicated to them. The Butterfly Mark is not well known and its use is rare.

Work-integration social enterprises are basically in a position similar to any other business as far as obtaining private or public funding is concerned. However, a work-integration social enterprise may be granted certain public subsidies on special terms and conditions as compensation for employing people with impaired work ability and as compensation for the resulting reduced productivity. Pay subsidies, employment policy assistance and investment support are the forms of support that may be granted to work-integration social enterprises on exceptional terms and conditions.

Incentives to register as a work-integration social enterprise have not been compelling enough for many organizations. Only a few labour co-operatives and other social economy organizations active in the field of work integration have registered themselves as work-integration social enterprises. The expected results have not been met. At the end of 2009, 212 work-integration social enterprises employed a total of 1,316 employees, of whom 380 were disabled and 385 were long-term unemployed (Grönberg & Kostilainen, 2012). We have also argued that these modest results come about because the law does not suit or serve properly either one of the two mainstream groups of work integration, namely the long-term unemployed and the disabled (Kostilainen & Pättiniemi, 2013b). By August 2015, the number of registered work-integration social enterprises had decreased to 55 (TEM, 2015).

Social Enterprises as a Vehicle for Renewing Welfare State Service Provision

As in the other Nordic countries, the public sectors in Finland, especially the municipalities, have carried the responsibility for welfare services. As we described in the introduction, during the past two decades, a rearrangement and also privatization have taken place concerning, for instance, social and health care services. There has also been a need for new kinds of services and approaches. More than one third (35 per cent) of the private social and welfare service deliverers are social economy organizations and social enterprises (THL, 2011). It is not clear at the moment how, with whom and with which resources Finnish municipalities will organize their social and welfare services in the future. The current policy messages are not clear.

Trading in the welfare markets has increased and this has caused the traditional funder of non-profit welfare associations (see Table 4.2), the Finnish Slot Machine Association (RAY), to re-orient. The profits from RAY's games are used for promoting health and social welfare in Finland. RAY supports approximately 780 organizations in Finland annually. In 2013 the RAY support was, in total, € 413.3 million (RAY, 2014). RAY provides funding only in areas in which there is no fear of distorting competition. The Finnish tax authority has also assumed a more stringent view of what activities it considers to be of general interest (and thus tax free) and which activities constitute trading. At the same time, a trend for increased professionalisation is found in third-sector organizations and difficulties in recruiting volunteers are becoming more common (Pessi & Oravasaari, 2010). The main reasons for a non-profit welfare association to establish a social enterprise include the need to respond to the changes in the operational environment as well as the need to react in order to hold a market share in the growing welfare ser vice markets. There is an emerging trend for non-profit welfare associations to establish trading enterprises. These organizations seem to develop towards more commercialization in all their tasks, especially in those relating to their management. The new concept includes, for example, the *branding* of social enterprises in order to distinguish them from conventional enterprises and traditional non-profit welfare associations.

The Social Enterprise as a Distinctive Business Model

During the European Social Fund period from 2007–2013, several projects and initiatives developed forms of assistance to encourage innovations and the development and growth of social enterprises. For example, civil servants and enterprise advisors were advised and educated in a project carried out by Tampere Region Co-operative Centre, commissioned and steered by the Ministry of Employment and the Economy. At that time, research into social enterprise activities took organized forms, and international connections and interaction were brought about. There has been a growing interest in social enterprises in Finland.

There was a political interest to broaden the concept of the social enterprise. A comparative study (Pöyhönen et al., 2010) was carried out on the different experiences of social enterprises in Europe and a report was published about social enterprises in the United Kingdom (Bland, 2010). According to a working group appointed by the Ministry of Employment and the Economy, the social enterprise concept is a business model for reinforcing and diversifying forms of entrepreneurship, renewing public service delivery and organizing non-governmental organizations so that they may apply market-based service functions and integrate into the labour market (Laiho, Grönberg, Hämäläinen, Stenman, & Tykkyläinen, 2011). The Ministry of Employment and the Economy also steered a national development project (Lilja & Mankki, 2010) for work-integration social enterprises. The project produced policy recommendations that aim to improve the operational preconditions of work-integration social enterprises and to offer guidance and support for the establishment, development and growth of work-integration social enterprises (Grönberg & Kostilainen, 2012). These recent developments and the public debate in Finland show a general expectation that social enterprises should combine the business skills of the private sector with a strong social mission.

One of the most important outcomes, and perhaps the only tangible one, from the above-mentioned working group appointed by the Ministry of Employment and the Economy was the launch of the 'Finnish Social Enterprise Mark'. The 'Finnish Social Enterprise Mark' is meant for businesses that aim to address social or ecological problems and that promote social goals. The vision and mission of social enterprises, independent of the enterprise form, must be to invest the majority, at least 50 per cent, of their profits for a common good. The business model also requires openness and transparency (Suomalaisen Työn Liitto, 2015). These three primary criteria should be met before applying for the Mark, which is granted by the Committee of Social Enterprises, comprised of representatives of various stakeholders and managed by the Association for Finnish Work. Other characteristics of social enterprises are also taken into consideration (see the in-depth analysis of the 'Finnish Social Enterprise Mark' by Kostilainen & Tykkyläinen, 2015). The 'Finnish Social Enterprise Mark' aims to serve as a concrete tool for social enterprises to develop and communicate their business model.

The 'Finnish Social Enterprise Mark' has been granted (Suomalaisen Työn Liitto, 2015) to 73 enterprises. However, there is still work ahead before the Mark is more widely known and used. Currently, the future of the Mark's administration is fragile due to its dependency on state aid.

Considering the evolution of the different forms of Finnish social enterprises, the following table (Table 4.1.) presents in four categories the different social enterprise types, grouping them according to their outcomes and numbers.

Institutionalization of the Finnish Social Enterprise Concept

In Finland, as elsewhere, social enterprises are expected to improve the quality of public services, generate innovations, improve productivity and have a preventive effect on harmful social, environmental and health problems among the population. Finnish social enterprises are modelled on international examples, experiences and research. Significant inputs and influences for the development of Finnish work-integration social enterprises have come from Italian type A and type B social co-operatives and the United Kingdom public sector service reform, through enabling social enterprises.

The European Structural Fund programmes and their priorities have also played a role in facilitating and governing this trend (Kostilainen & Pättiniemi, 2013b). Due to the needs of the Finnish society and the priorities of the funding available, the focus of development has been on work-integration social enterprises and social enterprises providing welfare services.

Table 4.1 Social Enterprises in Finland Per Category

Type of SE	Outcome	Number of SEs
Not-for-profit organizations delivering mainly social services (social economy organizations)	Not for profit, services for general interest, community development and empowerment	~ 3,150
Businesses owned by social economy organizations (clear social mission statement)	For profit, services for general interest, financing of services of third-sector organizations	~ 50
Worker co-operatives (incl. labour co-operatives)	For profit, empowerment of members, employment opportunities for the unemployed, services for members	~ 1,500
WISEs (Act (1351/2003) on social enterprises)	For profit, employment for those in a weak labour market position	~ 55
Social Enterprise Mark holders	Social value with solid business model	~ 73
TOTAL		**~ 4,828**

Source: adjusted (8/2015) from (Lilja & Mankki 2010, p. 18); (Merenmies & Pättiniemi 2010, p. 187)

Numerous projects have formed the breeding ground for a nascent support environment and an ecosystem for social enterprises, dealing with business support for start-up social enterprises, research and development and training, dedicated financial instruments and promotional activities.

Business and start-up guidance and services are organized in Finland by the Ministry of Employment and the Economy in accordance with the guidance concept 'Enterprise Finland' (Enterprise Finland, 2015). The guidance services for social enterprises are integrated into Enterprise Finland. There are no guidance units or services dedicated specifically to social enterprises. However, there have been projects to train business advisors on the distinct characteristics of different social enterprise types, and there also is a handbook on social enterprises for business advisors.

There have been projects to develop social enterprise training and education, but currently, there are no university programmes or other programmes (e.g., MBAs or master's programmes) dedicated to social enterprises or social enterprise management. Some universities and educational institutions have integrated certain aspects of social enterprises into their conventional enterprise and management training curricula. However, there is a growing interest among university students to do their master's and PhD theses on social enterprises. The research community FinSERN, established in 2010, brings together Finnish researchers and organizations that need to apply research knowledge and are interested in social enterprises (www.finsern.fi). FinSERN organizes conferences and annual thesis competitions and it also publishes news on topics related to social enterprise research.

Social enterprises do not yet have any special financial instruments. They are entitled to use the same instruments as all businesses. Social enterprises may be caught between 'too commercial' for RAY funding and 'too social' for actors providing business funding (Pöyhönen, 2009). Some attempts have been made to map and organize dedicated financial instruments for social enterprises (Rove, Floman & Malmivirta, 2011). There are also various crowdfunding initiatives, e.g., Pankki 2.0, mesenaatti.me and Invesdor and, for the moment, the Finnish Innovation Fund Sitra (www.sitra.fi) is studying and initiating impact investment in Finland. The lack of dedicated financing and support structures for social enterprises may be caused by the fact that the phenomenon is still marginal, the concept of social enterprises is blurred and contested, the majority of social enterprises are fragile and the enterprises are not well organized. The traditional social economy organization co-operatives (www.pellervo.fi) and welfare associations (www. soste.fi) have established their lobbying and other support structures. Their attitudes towards social enterprises are mixed. Social enterprises might be seen as rivals or as an important and vital business model for their member organizations.

There have been several attempts to organize the evolving social enterprise sector to give a voice to it. In autumn 2014, the Finnish Social Enterprise Coalition "Arvo-liitto ry" (www.arvoliitto.fi) was launched. The 30 current members, all social enterprises, are owned primarily by traditional welfare associations and foundations. The aim of the coalition is to enhance the Finnish social enterprise business model and its viability.

The social enterprise business model and the 'Finnish Social Enterprise Mark' have some promising elements but might still be in danger of dilution because of the following factors: 1) Competition neutrality, a view raised mainly by certain interest groups and federations of employers and businesses, and 2) The fear that there may be a qualitative deterioration in working conditions, a view raised by trade unions.

The described developments and the institutionalization process of social enterprises and their ecosystem have also influenced the role of social enterprises in relation to the welfare state. Social enterprises have had at least two roles: 1) Change agents and 2) Contract partners in the production of public services. The following table (Table 4.2) summarizes the recent development and the roles of Finnish social enterprises.

Simultaneously with the described social enterprise concepts, new types of organizing and working emerge in settings promoting social entrepreneurship. Our examples include HUB Helsinki (www.hub13.fi) and the establishing of smartups. Smartups are defined as start-ups that help free their users from the inefficient use of resources (for more, see SmartUp Manifesto, 2014).

Table 4.2 Development Phases of 'New' Social Enterprises in Finland

'SEs as a new social movement 1995–1999'	Self-help, labour co-operatives, the Italian model, bottom-up development approach. SEs as change agents.
'SEs as a labour market measure 2000–2006'	Act 1351/2003 on SEs, misinterpretation of the SE concept, in reality WISEs, mix of different European influences, top-down development approach. SEs develop from change agents to contract partners.
'SEs as a vehicle renewing welfare state service provision 2007–2013'	Extended approach towards SEs, SEs as a part of a welfare-mix provision of welfare services, high impact from the United Kingdom model, intense top-down development approach but also some bottom-up initiatives. The traditional associations and foundations are the main contract partners of employment services in the field of work integration. Launch of the Finnish Social Enterprise Mark (criteria for SEs). SEs as contract partners
Forms of institutionalized SE concept in Finland	Act 1351/2003 on work-integration social enterprises Social Enterprise Mark Social Enterprise Ecosystem beginning to take shape Arvo-liitto (Finnish Social Enterprise Coalition)

According to the Global Entrepreneurship Monitor (GEM) (Stenholm, Heinonen, Kovalainen, & Pukkinen, 2010), social entrepreneurial activity in Finland is relatively high compared to the other Nordic countries, Europe and even globally. According to the GEM study, almost half (43 per cent) of Finnish early-stage social entrepreneurial activity is not-for-profit social entrepreneurship that emphasises social and/or environmental goals and has an earned income strategy. In innovation-driven and wealthy economies, such as Finland, social entrepreneurship may partially replace other forms of entrepreneurial activity. This emerging social entrepreneurial activism is seen in the development of sole proprietor entrepreneurship that includes a strong ethical and social dimension.

Conclusions

The theory explaining the modes of institutional change is useful in understanding the change of welfare service delivery and the evolution of social enterprises in Finland. Reviewing the evolution of the social enterprises, we found that the concept of niche allowed us to understand better the changes and interaction of social enterprises under different environmental conditions.

The development and conditions for social enterprises follow similar paths in the Nordic countries. The Nordic welfare model is contested by the changing operational environment explained earlier and by changing political ideologies. In the Nordic countries, the private provision of welfare services has increased rapidly. The Nordic countries have moved from full employment to more flexible and insecure labour markets. These changes have created opportunities in all the Nordic countries for various social enterprise initiatives. Work-integration social enterprises have been innovative but, in the Nordic countries, they form only a marginal way to enhance the employment opportunities of the disabled. Social enterprises in the field of welfare service provision may be seen at least partly as a counterforce to the increasing international commercial competition in the open welfare market. Simultaneously, social entrepreneurial activities are diversifying and finding new grounds while the younger generation is establishing 'smartups'.

The social democratic ideology and parties have been the main promoters of the development of the Nordic welfare state and its model. In Finland, social democrats have dramatically lost ground and support during the past decades. In addition at this time, labour market organizations seem to be unable to renew their behaviour and policies. These changes have influenced the current welfare and employment policies.

The lack of a national vision and any strategic approach to social enterprises and their role in the Finnish society has led to an ineffective use of different social enterprise development measures and activities during the past decades. Furthermore, the programme approaches adopted by recent Finnish governments pose the potential risk that social enterprises with their own missions and goals will become subordinated to the tasks that the administration has thrown to them: to further employ those in weak labour market positions and to take care of the marginalized people through measures such as the provision of welfare services in remote areas. Dependency on programme-based monetary resources may result in well-functioning markets for social enterprises not developing and in certain social entrepreneurial initiatives perhaps closing down when the current programmes end. The development of social enterprises in Finland is also hindered by the currently nascent ecosystem that does not support the special characteristics of the social enterprise business model. For example, business opportunities are prioritized instead of social needs, and user participation is seldom included.

In the Nordic countries, social enterprises can organize socially and economically sustainable services. Social enterprises whose cultures and ways of operating are put on economically and socially sustainable grounds will continue and develop as problem solvers for social problems and as hubs for social innovations. Sustainable, organized social enterprises are based on and legitimized by quality, user-driven innovations, cost-effectiveness and humane and preventive work. This could, at its best, reduce the moral deficit in society and increase its positive social capital. The position of Finnish social enterprises is heavily dependent on how the future governments take care of this business model. Where there is political will, recognition and a social enterprise policy, a viable social enterprise sector is made possible.

References

Act on Social Enterprises. (1351/2003). Finnish law.
Associations Act. (1/1919). Finnish law. Last amended 26.5.1989/503.
Bland, J. (2010). *Yhteiskunnallinen yritys—ratkaisuja 2000- luvun haasteisiin Ison-Britannian malli ja sen kokemukset.* Työ- ja elinkeinoministeriö. Toukokuu 2010. Strategiset hankkeet 22/2010.
Co-operatives Act (22/1901). Last amended 14.6.2013/421.
Defourny, J. & Develtere, P. (1999). *The Social Economy: The Worldwide Making of a Third Sector.* In J. Defourny, P. Delveltere & B. Fonteneau (Eds.), *L'économie Sociale au Nord at au Sud.* Paris & Bruxelles: De Boeck Université.
Enterprise Finland. (2015). *Information and Assistance on Running Business in Finland.* Available at www.yrityssuomi.fi/en/home.
European Commission. (2014). *A Map of Social Enterprises and Their Eco-Systems in Europe: Country Reports: Denmark, Finland and Sweden.* Brussels: European Commission Directorate-General for Employment, Social Affairs and Inclusion. Available at http://ec.europa.eu/social/keyDocuments.jsp?advSearchKey=socentc ntryrepts&mode=advancedSubmit&langId=en&policyArea=&type=0&country= 0&year=0&orderBy=docOrder, accessed 18 May 2015.
Foundations Act. (109/1930). Finish law. Last amended 24.4.2015/487.
Grönberg, V. & Kostilainen, H. (2012). *Sosiaalisten yritysten tila ja tulevaisuus.* Työ- ja elinkeinoministeriön julkaisuja 12/2012. Helsinki: Edita Publishing Ltd.
Hiilamo, H. (2011). *Uusi hyvinvointivaltio.* Helsinki: Into Kustannus.
Hiilamo, H. & Saari, J. (2010). *Hyvinvoinnin uusi politiikka—johdatus sosiaalisiin mahdollisuuksiin.* Helsinki: Diakonia-ammattikorkeakoulu.
Hub13. (2015). *Startup Space in Helsinki.* Available at www.hub13.fi.
Hulgård, L. & Lundgaard Andersen, L. (2015). Social Entrepreneurship and Social Innovation. In Nordic Council of Ministers (Eds.), *Social Entrepreneurship and Social Innovation Initiatives to Promote Social Entrepreneurship and Social Innovation in the Nordic Countries.* Copenhagen: TemaNord 2015:562.
Inkinen, K. (2001). *Diffuusio ja fuusio osuuskauppainnovaation levinneisyys ja sen dynamiikka 1901–1998l.* Helsinki: Acta Universitas Oeconomicae Helsingiensis.
Insurance Companies Act. (174/1933). Finish law. Last amended 20.3.2015/303.
Invesdor. (2015). www.invesdor.com/finland/en.
Kostilainen, H. & Pättiniemi, P. (2013a). *Avauksia yhteiskunnallisen yritystoiminnan tutkimukseen.* Riika: Yhteiskunnallisen yritystoiminnan tutkimusverkosto ry FinSERN.
Kostilainen, H. & Pättiniemi, P. (2013b). Evolution of Social Enterprise Concept in Finland. In H. Kostilainen & P. Pättiniemi (Eds.), *Avauksia yhteiskunnallisen*

74   Harri Kostilainen and Pekka Pättiniemi

yritystoiminnan tutkimukseen. Riika: Yhteiskunnallisen yritystoiminnan tutkimusverkosto ry FinSERN.

Kostilainen, H. & Tykkyläinen, S. (2015). The Characteristics of Finnish Social Enterprise. In H. Kostilainen & P. Pättiniemi (Eds.), *Yhteiskunnallisen yritystoiminnan monet kasvot*. Helsinki: Diakonia-ammattikorkeakoulu

Laiho, U.-M. (2011). HYVÄ 2009–2011. *Toiminta ja tulokset: Sosiaali- ja terveyspalvelujen markkinat*. Työ- ja elinkeinoministeriön julkaisuja Konserni 8/2011. Helsinki: Edita Publishing Ltd.

Laiho, U.-M., Grönberg, V., Hämäläinen, P., Stenman, J. & Tykkyläinen, S. (2011). *Yhteiskunnallisen yrityksen toimintamallin kehittäminen*. Työ- ja elinkeinoministeriön julkaisuja Konserni 4/2011. Helsinki: Edita Publishing Ltd.

Laurinkari, J. (2007). *Yhteisötalous—johdatusperusteisiin*. Helsinki: Gaudeamus.

Lilja, I. & Mankki, J. (2010). *Yhteiskunnallinen yritys—luova ja yhdistävä toimintatapa*. Helsinki: HP Paino.

Mahoney, J. & Thelen, K. (2009a). *Explaining Institutional Change. Ambiguity, Agency, and Power*. Cambridge: Cambridge University Press.

Mahoney, J. & Thelen, K. (2009b). A Theory of Gradual Institutional Change. In J. Mahoney & K. Thelen (Eds.), *Explaining Institutional Change. Ambiguity, Agency, and Power*. Cambridge: Cambridge University Press.

Merenmies, J. & Pättiniemi, P. (2010). Yhteisötalous ja yhteiskunnalliset yritykset. In H. Hiilamo & J. Saari (Eds.), *Hyvinvoinnin uusi politiikka—johdatus sosiaalisiin mahdollisuuksiin*. Helsinki: Diakonia-ammattikorkeakoulu.

Mesenaatti.me. (2015). http://mesenaatti.me/en/.

Moilanen, H. (2010). *Työosuuskunnat ja työosuuskuntien kautta työllistyminen Suomessa—alustavia tuloksia tutkimusmatkan varrelta*. Presentation at "Työllisyys ja osuuskunnat", Eduskunta, Helsinki, Finland.

Nieminen, A. & Kostilainen, H. (2011). *Työllisyysjärjestelmien inklusiivisuus—Tanskan ja Suomen vertailua*. s. 141–157. Tampere: Tampereen yliopisto, Yhteiskunta- ja kulttuuritieteiden yksikkö, Työelämän tutkimuskeskus. Available at www.uta.fi/tyoelamantutkimuspaiva.

Niiranen, V., Seppänen-Järvelä, R., Sinkkonen, M. & Vartiainen, P. (2011). *Johtaminen sosiaalialalla*. Helsinki: Gaudeamus.

Nordic Council of Ministers. (2015). *Social Entrepreneurship and Social Innovation Initiatives to Promote Social Entrepreneurship and Social Innovation in the Nordic Countries*. Copenhagen: TemaNord 2015:562.

Osuuskuntarekisteri. (2015). *Pellervo Register of Co-operatives in Finland*. Available at Osuuskuntarekisteri.pellervo.fi.

Pankki2.0. (2015). http://pankki2.fi/english-0.

Pättiniemi, P. (2004). La nuova legge sulle imprese sociali in Finlandia. *Impressa Sociale*, 73(4), 160–168. Brescia: Italy.

Pättiniemi, P. (2006). *Social Enterprises as Labour Market Measure*. Kuopio: Kuopio University Publications E. Social Sciences 130, University of Kuopio.

Pellervo. (2012). *Osuustoiminta-lehti 4/12 Teemasivut 15.8.2012*. Available at www.pellervo.fi/otlehti/ot4_12/osuustoimintayritykset.pdf.

Pellervo. (2015). *Service Organization for Finnish Co-operatives*. Available at http://pellervo.fi/kielet/english/.

Pessi, A.-B. & Oravasaari, T. (2010). *Kansalaisjärjestötoiminnan ytimessä. Tutkimus RAY:n avustamien sosiaali- ja terveysjärjestöjen vapaaehtoistoiminnasta*. Avustoiminnan raportteja 23. Helsinki: Yliopistopaino.

Popielarz, P-A. & Neal, Z-P. (2007). The Niche as a Theoretical Tool. *Annual Review of Sociology*, 33, 65–84.

Pöyhönen, E. (2009). *Analysis Finland: Better Future for Social Economy Network.* Unpublished Working Paper.

Pöyhönen, E., Hänninen, E., Merenmies, J., Lilja, I., Kostilainen, H. & Mankki, J. (2010). *Sosiaaliset ja yhteiskunnalliset yritykset: Uuden talouden edelläkävijöitä?* Helsinki: Yhteinen yritys-hanke. Available at www.tem.fi/files/26291/YY-raportti_110210.pdf.

RAY. (2014). www.ray.fi/en/beneficiaries.

Rove, K., Floman, E. & Malmivirta, M. (2011). *Yhteiskunnallisen yrittämisen rahastomalli.* Eera Oy.

Saari, J. (2015). *Huono-osaiset: Elämän edellytykset yhteiskunnan pohjalla.* Helsinki: Gaudeamus.

Sitra. (2015). *The Finnish Innovation Fund Sitra on Impact Investments.* Available at www.sitra.fi/artikkelit/liiketoiminnan-kehitys/impact-investing-sijoita-ja-vaikuta, accessed 20 August 2015.

SmartUp Manifesto. (2014). Available at www.demoshelsinki.fi/wp-content/uploads/2014/11/Smartup-Manifesto-Demos-Helsinki.pdf, accessed 25 September 2015.

SOSTE. (2015). *The Finnish Federation for Social Affairs and Health.* Available at www.soste.fi/soste/soste-in-english.html, accessed 1 October 2015.

Stenholm, P., Heinonen, J., Kovalainen, A. & Pukkinen, T. (2010). *Global Entrepreneurship Monitor: Finnish 2009 Report.* Series A Research Report A 1/2010. TSE Centre for Research and Education, Turku School of Economics.

Suomalaisen Työn Liitto. (2015). *Finnish Social Enterprise Mark 9.10.2015.* Available at http://suomalainentyo.fi/tietoa-meista/jasenyritykset/#merkki/yhteiskunnallinen-yritys, accessed 9 October 2015.

TEM. (2015). Ministry of Employment and the Economy. *Social Enterprises Register.* Available at www.tem.fi/index.phtml?s=2567, accessed 9 October 2015.

THL. (2011/25). *Statistical Report.* Helsinki: National Institute of Health and Welfare.

THL. (2015). *Perusturvan riittävyyden arviointiraportti 2011–2015.* Perusturvan riittävyyden II arviointiryhmä. Terveyden ja hyvinvoinnin laitos. Working Paper 1/2015. Helsinki: National Institute of Health and Welfare (THL).

5 Social Enterprise as a Contested Terrain for Definitions and Practice

The Case of Norway

Hans Abraham Hauge and Tora Mathea Wasvik

The meaning of 'social enterprise' in Norway is currently contested in public discourse between actors identifying themselves as social entrepreneurs and actors representing dominant political and economic interests in public, business and voluntary organizations. The concept is used rhetorically to promote divergent perspectives on how commercial strategies should be used to address social problems. We describe precursors to social enterprise in Norway, with emphasis on the dominant position of the state in provision of social services in the post-World War II period and recent trends that to some extent blur traditional distinctions between public, business and voluntary organizations. The meanings attributed to social enterprise by various actors in public discourse are presented. We conclude with a discussion on the possibility of social enterprise being co-opted by powerful actors' interests, or alternatively, whether social enterprise can contribute to citizens' freedom from dependency on the welfare state's social services.

What Meanings Are Attributed to 'Social Enterprise' in Public Discourse?

In a similar way to the other Nordic countries, Norway has a welfare state developed in close collaboration between the state and voluntary organizations (Selle, 1992). Business entrepreneurs also contributed substantially to the creation of social value in the communities where they operated (Barth, 1963). From the 1940s onwards, the state took a dominant role as responsible for providing solutions to social problems, and this development was supported by most voluntary organizations (Lorentzen, 2007). There was, and continues to be, widespread agreement that state responsibility is the preferred approach to secure citizens' autonomy, specifically their independence from for-profit market conditions, family and charity when they are unable to provide for themselves (Vike, 2012).

The Norwegian welfare state provides universal benefits and services to all its citizens (in principle). The state is by no means immune to long-term challenges of demographic changes and economic recession, but substantial oil and gas revenues in the past two decades have enabled the implementation of less invasive austerity measures in Norway than in most European countries. Although there is probably not the same sense of urgency in Norway as in the other Nordic countries, a dominant issue in political discourse is how to mobilize resources and decrease demand in order to be able to maintain universal social services. The same types of initiatives have been taken as in the other Nordic countries: continuous reforms in the public sector, creating social service markets open to for-profit businesses and measures to stimulate contributions by voluntary organizations.

In conjunction with these developments, there has been an increased interest in social entrepreneurship, social entrepreneurs and social enterprise. These concepts are attributed various meanings, and there is no widely used definition either in research, practice or policy making in Norway. In general terms, however, as noted by Gawell (2014, p. 257), "work on both social entrepreneurship and social enterprises addresses expressions of social engagement combined with entrepreneurial action and the constructs of enterprises as means for operation". Following this assertion, a 'social enterprise' can be seen as a means for 'social entrepreneurship' undertaken by 'social entrepreneurs'. Although highly rudimentary, this delimitation would probably make 'common sense' to the various actors engaged in the public discourse on social enterprise in Norway. It is also consistent with how these constructs are used in relation to each other in this chapter.

The research issue highlighted in this chapter is how the meanings attributed to social enterprise—in the wide sense of being a means used by social entrepreneurs for the purpose of social entrepreneurship—are developed in discourse by those engaged in or facilitating social enterprises. In addition to actors identifying themselves as social entrepreneurs, actors representing public, political, voluntary and for-profit business organizations contribute to this discourse. Actors in such organizations participate in, collaborate with or compete with social enterprises. They also constitute the context in which social enterprises develop and strongly influence the meanings attributed to such enterprises.

The approach taken here is social constructionist, in the sense that the emphasis is on actors' construction of social reality as they perceive it (Hacking, 2000). Such construction is ongoing and dynamic and does not necessarily produce realistic accounts of the phenomenon itself. The discourse on social enterprise reflects how social problems traditionally have been addressed and how these problems should be addressed in the future. Social enterprise is a concept used by different actors to promote different interests, and it is likely that "[over] the longer term, social enterprise will be determined not by theorists but by social practices and institutions that are associated with, and labelled as, social enterprises" (Ridley-Duff & Bull, 2011, p. 79). It is likely that how social enterprise is understood and talked about will influence how it becomes manifest in a particular context.

In order to empirically investigate the public discourse on social enterprise in Norway, texts were searched for predominantly on the Internet and in databases of newspapers, concrete texts easily available to those taking an interest in social enterprise. The concepts used separately or in combination when conducting the searches were 'sosialt entreprenørskap' (social entrepreneurship), 'sosial entreprenør' (social entrepreneur) and 'sosial virksomhet' (social enterprise). The majority of texts identified have been written to inform and generate interest for specific enterprises and were as such only indirectly relevant to the research issue. The texts highlighted in the analysis present the views or policies of actors taking a more general interest, such as presenting arguments on what social enterprise is, who should do it, how it should be carried out or facilitated and what it should aim to accomplish. These texts are normative and in varying degrees, prescriptive.

When examining the data, two interesting features could be noted at an early stage of analysis. The number of texts was small, and they also represented the views of distinctly different actors. These actors could be identified respectively as social entrepreneurs (people starting social enterprises themselves), an umbrella organization for voluntary organizations, one public and one private provider of seed funding for social enterprises and representatives of the administrative and political levels in local councils. Taken together, the texts present the views and policies of actors with considerable power to define how social enterprise should be understood in the Norwegian context.

Firstly, however, it is necessary to relate the analysis in this chapter to what has already been established through research on social enterprise in Norway. Secondly, the precursors for the development of social enterprise in Norway are highlighted in order to clarify the context in which the analysed texts have been written. Then the meanings attributed to social enterprise by entrepreneurs, voluntary organizations, seed funding institutions and local authorities are presented and analysed. In conclusion, some tentative implications of this research are discussed, with emphasis on future challenges for social enterprise practice and research.

Research on Social Enterprise in Norway

Internationally, the academic field of social enterprise has become less dominated by confusion and a lack of conceptual clarity (Defourny, Hulgård & Pestoff, 2014). Social enterprise has been determined as "a hybrid phenomenon based upon multiple resources from market income, redistribution allocated through the state and reciprocity often originating in the civil society" (Hulgård, 2014, pp. 77–78). Social enterprise can emanate from within or outside of either the public, private or third sectors (Ridley-Duff & Bull, 2011). Social enterprise is both independent from and intertwined in the three sectors, allowing a multitude of manifestations of the phenomenon in practice. These manifestations are not arbitrary, but "deeply rooted in the social, economic, political and cultural contexts" (Defourny & Nyssens,

2014, p. 60) in which they emerge, suggesting that academic research should emphasise comparisons between contexts such as countries.

To date, there has been a limited number of contributions to research on social enterprise in the Norwegian context. These contributions have all addressed the question of how many social enterprises there are, emphasising the challenges in the lack of an authoritative definition for deciding what should and should not be determined as a 'social enterprise' (Damvad, 2012; Gustavsen & Kobro, 2012; Kaupang, 2014; Nordic Council of Ministers, 2015). Criteria for defining the phenomenon are suggested by the researchers, with references to international academic discourse and national policies addressing social problems. The suggestions differ markedly and are not based on extensive empirical investigations.

In the survey undertaken by the consultancy company Damvad (2012) on commission for the Norwegian Ministry of Trade and Industry, social enterprises were defined as organizations selling goods and/or services on a commercial basis to realise social objectives, aiming for profit and being independent of the state. Damvad was not able to establish or tentatively suggest how many such enterprises there are in Norway. They conducted qualitative interviews with representatives from 15 organizations meeting their criteria, but provided no information about why these organizations were selected or if, and if so how, the organizations were representative of social enterprises. Damvad noted considerable variation in choice of formal organization, in types of commercial activities and in motivation for doing social enterprise, but their main focus was to develop recommendations on how the state can contribute to social enterprise as a means to address social problems. Implications of differences in understandings of social enterprise in the Norwegian context were not discussed.

Gustavsen and Kobro (2012) made a short reference to the Damvad survey, dismissing it as irrelevant to their study of how social entrepreneurship can alleviate poverty among children. Instead, they suggested a 'pragmatic perspective' based on a detailed examination of entrepreneurial intentions, actions and the consequences thereof. They did not apply this perspective to concrete examples, such as case studies of social enterprises. Instead, they made a number of recommendations to public policy makers, based on academic literature and national policy objectives in relation to poverty.

The consultancy company Kaupang (2014) juxtaposed voluntary engagement and social enterprise as external resources that local authorities can benefit from in their provision of social services. They defined social enterprises as private businesses seeking to promote social goals through their activities and earnings, and identified only six such enterprises in their survey of 90 of Norway's 428 local authorities. As in the other surveys, Kaupang highlighted policy recommendations for the public sector.

The Nordic Council of Ministers commissioned a survey of social entrepreneurship and social innovation in the Nordic countries, focusing primarily on the potential for work integration of vulnerable groups (Nordic

Council of Ministers, 2015). In their definition of social entrepreneurship, a cross-national group of experts emphasised innovation, involvement of intended recipients and inter-sector collaboration in addition to the application of sustainable commercial strategies to target social problems. A survey was carried out among 193 organizations identified as social entrepreneurs by the experts, based on their knowledge of each Nordic country. A total of 37 of 52 organizations from the Norwegian sample responded, a majority of which did practice in accordance with the expert group's definition. The survey made several recommendations for Nordic collaboration on practice, research and policy making.

Particularly relevant to the approach taken in this chapter is the fact that no research has analysed the various meanings attributed to social enterprise by actors engaged in Norwegian public discourse or what interests these actors can be seen as representing. In order to analyse this issue, it is necessary to take account of the particular characteristics of the Norwegian context.

Precursors of the Emergence of Social Enterprise in Norway

The meaning of social enterprise is contingent on the characteristics of the context in which it unfolds. Formative historical experiences and current trends are both relevant to an understanding of the emergence of social enterprise in Norway. There are in particular two relevant contextual features: the dominant position of the state in the provision of social services in the post-World War II period, and recent trends that to some extent blur traditional distinctions between public, business and voluntary organizations.

Voluntary organizations were crucial to the development of the welfare state in all the Nordic countries (Selle, 2012; Rothstein, 2001; Hulgård, 2007). They channelled citizen engagement on a variety of social issues. They were instrumental not only in setting social problems on the agenda, but also in initiating entrepreneurial activities to address such problems (Defourny & Nyssens, 2013). In the period from 1900 to the late 1940s, the Norwegian state was liberal, in the sense that it welcomed and supported most initiatives from civil society. However, the relationship between the state and voluntary organizations changed from the 1940s onwards. In a synthesis of historical events, Lorentzen (2007) sees the dominant social democratic Labour Party as a driving force behind these changes. The Labour Party was sceptical to charity and other forms of philanthropic civic engagement, and systematically undermined such initiatives in favour of public services. The ideal was that vulnerable groups and individuals should not have to rely on generosity, but have their social needs defined as rights guaranteed by a strong state. The services should be delivered by professionals and not by amateur volunteers. Voluntary organizations were seen as conveying interests of vulnerable groups, not as representing counter-voices to be stimulated in political discourse.

For the most part, these changes were welcomed by voluntary organizations, many of which had advocated state responsibility for social problems. Although criticized for a variety of reasons, the welfare state has continued to enjoy strong popular support in Norway, so much so that no elected representatives in the parliament want to replace it or reduce it substantially. In recent years, the Nordic welfare state model has also attracted positive interest for a number of reasons. The comparatively speaking equal distribution of resources and life chances has favourable consequences for public health in all social strata of a population (Wilkinson & Pickett, 2009), as well as for human development (UNDP, 2014), and possibly also for democratic stability (Piketty, 2014). Recently, an active and strong state has been asserted as a precursor for entrepreneurship in general (Mazzucato, 2013).

Kuhnle and Selle (1992) characterize Norway as a state-friendly country, with ideological compatibility between civil society and the state. A benign consequence of this characteristic is a high level of trust between citizens and the state (Skirbekk & Grimen, 2012; Staksrud et al., 2014). This societal feature is also evident in the high level of consensus among citizens—expressed over decades in parliamentary elections—that the state must take primary responsibility for addressing social problems. Private business organizations have contributed only marginally. For instance, in the mid-1980s, voluntary organizations still owned and operated 15,7 per cent of all social services, compared with 0,8 per cent owned and operated by for-profit businesses (NOU 1988:17). Collaboration between the public sector and voluntary organizations is still extensive across the whole spectrum of services (Selle & Strømsnes, 2012). Voluntary organizations are routinely invited to participate in developing state-level public policy on all social issues. They are often initiators of innovation in public service organizations (Andreassen, 2011), and they are recognised as proficient in delivering services to vulnerable groups, for instance, those living in poverty (Sivesind, 2008).

Nevertheless, there have been major changes in citizens' motivation for civil engagement, especially from the 1980s onwards. These changes have been summarized as a change from social movements to philanthropy, from donation of time to donation of money, from society-wide to high social status engagement, from membership in voluntary organizations to individual contributions and from collectivistic to individualistic projects (Wollebekk & Sivesind, 2010). These features are not particular to Norway, and they have had greater impact on the type of activities citizens engage in than on their level of engagement, meaning more activities motivated by personal interest and fewer motivated by collective objectives. The size of the voluntary sector in Norway has remained fairly high and stable, contributing approximately two per cent of GDP and 3,5 per cent of the labour force (Statistics Norway, 2014).

In parallel with the state attaining increased control over social services, there has, however, been a development that has seemed to blur the distinctions between public, business and voluntary organizations. Voluntary organizations providing social services have become professionalised and more similar to public service organizations. They have also become more similar to business organizations as their weakened membership base has stimulated more commercial activities, like selling services at market prices and applying marketing strategies to raise funds through donations. Businesses have become more interested in contributing to social and environmental goals, often referred to as the *triple bottom line* of profit, people and planet (Elkington & Robins, 1994). The public sector has privatized more social services and has implemented strategies from business organizations.

Norway has followed the global trend of continuous reforms in public services, attempting to realise better services at a lower cost (Lynn, 2006). Responsibility for a wide array of services has been decentralised from the state to the local level. Provision of services has been customized to meet the requirements of the 'New Public Management' philosophy of budget control being more important than professional autonomy (Vike, 2004; Lynn, 2006; ; Endresen, 2014). Public services have become more exposed to competition with private for-profit businesses (Herning, 2015), and also exposed to what has been called 'privatization from within' with benchmark strategies and a range of other approaches associated with 'New Public Management' (Ramsdal & Skorstad, 2004).

The intensity in change initiatives is manifest, for instance, in reorganizations, which public sector employees experience more frequently than their colleagues in the private sector (Christensen & Lægreid, 2000; Messel, 2013; Endresen, 2014). Research has documented that the combination of more responsibility and limited resources, particularly at the local council level, is experienced by employees as delegation of dilemmas (Vike, 2004; Damsgaard & Eide 2012) and as a surplus of expectations leading to work stress (Hauge, 2011; Klemsdal, 2013). There is growing concern about the costs of auditing and controlling services, both in terms of money spent on administration and in terms of reduced social capital as a consequence of the lack of trust in professional discretion (Health Services Campaign/ Helsetjenesteaksjonen, 2015). On the other hand, these developments have also stimulated public innovation and more emphasis on participation and co-production with the users of services.

The context in which social enterprise emerges in Norway is thus one characterized by a strong welfare state struggling to adjust its provision of services to increased demands, numerous well-established voluntary organizations more or less integrated in the welfare state, an increasing number of businesses wanting to sell their products and services to the state or alternatively engage in some form of corporate philanthropy, and an increased demand for voluntary engagement by a population on average more motivated by individual than collective projects. It is a context welcoming social innovation and entrepreneurship, but how social enterprise will be understood in this context is not a foregone conclusion.

Social Entrepreneurs on the Meaning of Social Enterprise

What meanings do people identifying themselves as social entrepreneurs establishing social enterprises in Norway attribute to their activities? The definitions presented in brief previously in this chapter suggest a multitude of possible meanings. Consistent with a social constructionist approach, it is more reasonable to see these definitions as sensitizing concepts suggesting features to look for, rather than seeing them as conclusive. The emphasis here is on documenting and analysing how 'social enterprise' directly or indirectly is contested in discourse between actors attributing various meanings to the concept. In the following, these actors are identified as social entrepreneurs, voluntary organizations, funding institutions and local authorities. Their perspectives are presented consecutively, starting with the social entrepreneurs.

People identifying themselves as social entrepreneurs have not engaged much in public discourse in Norway on the meanings of social enterprise. The majority has prioritized informing about their individual enterprises and activities in order to generate interest. However, an important initiative was taken in 2008 when the Network for Social Entrepreneurship was established, resulting in the publication of a book the following year (Schei & Rønnevig, 2009). Some of the contributors to the network and the book subsequently participated in establishing a centre for social entrepreneurship and innovation, which is now engaged in political processes at local and national levels.

The book by Schei and Rønnevig (2009) presents coherent narratives from ten social entrepreneurs. They are engaged in a variety of activities related to literacy, education, child abuse, domestic violence, sports, work integration of vulnerable groups, vocational training for young people, social business, aid to developing countries and microcredit. They all describe their motivations, ambitions, practices, learning experiences and achievements. Despite their differences, the narratives reveal several similarities. For instance, all the social enterprises were originally started by one or two people with innovative ideas on how to address a specific social problem. Although their focuses differ, they are all relevant to one of two broad categories of social problems: work integration for vulnerable groups, or enhancing health, learning and integration among young people. The majority of the social enterprises offer consultancy services, although some combine such services with selling products they develop. All but two enterprises predominantly approach the public sector, asserting that their activities will cut public costs for social services.

A recurring theme in the book is the personal qualities of social entrepreneurs. They appear as highly motivated citizens willing to take the personal risk associated with setting up a business for the purpose of generating social value. The editors make a summary statement of what they learned from working with the book:

> We have travelled through a landscape where we have met people with unique social engagement—the social entrepreneurs. What characterizes

a social entrepreneur is that he or she has a vision and an inner need to accomplish change for vulnerable groups. Their passion and belief in their cause make them persevere and be creative in order to succeed [. . .] [they can] 'change the world by having the courage to realise their dreams for the common good' [. . .] [and experience] 'a need for a different and higher consciousness of community, empathy, belonging and reciprocity'.

(Shei & Rønnevig 2009, p. 5–6, author's translation)

Social entrepreneurs are thus presented as part of a movement of individuals disenchanted with the lack of solutions for social problems in the world; their unifying feature is perseverance fuelled by ideological and normative motivation, more or less in opposition to state and for-profit market economies. They are motivated by facilitating the empowerment of vulnerable individuals and groups, enabling them to utilize their resources in the best interest of themselves and the community. Their social enterprises are not, however, initiated or owned by vulnerable groups themselves. What is highlighted as central to the meaning of social enterprise is the opportunity for motivated individuals to realise social value on the outside of public, business and voluntary organizations, for the benefit of, but not organized by, certain groups in civil society. The extent to which such an understanding of social enterprise is representative of most social entrepreneurs is difficult to assess, because many do not engage in public discourse.

Voluntary Organizations on the Meaning of Social Enterprise

As mentioned earlier in this chapter, traditionally not-for-profit voluntary organizations have taken up commercial strategies to fund their activities. Whether or not such strategies and activities are characterized as social enterprise is important to the meaning of this concept in the Norwegian context. Almost 300 voluntary organizations with more than 50,000 local units are members of the Association of NGOs in Norway (Frivillighet Norge). This association seeks to promote the interests of its members and engage in policy making on various issues. For instance, the association is promoting a public register for voluntary organizations, established on the initiative of the voluntary organizations themselves in 2009. The association is thus engaged in defining the criteria for recognition as a voluntary organization.

In 2012, the Association of NGOs in Norway participated in a public hearing on the Damvad (2012) survey of social entrepreneurship in Norway. In its response, the association stressed the importance of clearly distinguishing between social enterprises and voluntary organizations. The meaning attributed to social enterprises was that they are for-profit businesses and should be approached as such by the state. Public funding designated for voluntary organizations should therefore not be used for social enterprises

(Association of NGOs in Norway, 2015). Hence, the association defined social enterprise as different from and potentially in conflict with voluntary organizations, and mobilized to defend the interests of its members.

The response by the Association of NGOs in Norway is probably representative of scepticism towards 'social enterprise' in the voluntary sector, even though several voluntary organizations engage in commercial activities to generate funds for their work. Some such activities are carried out within separate organizational entities that could reasonably be understood as social enterprises. As will become evident below, other actors have different perspectives on the relationship between voluntary organizations and social enterprises.

Seed Funding Institutions on the Meaning of Social Enterprise

Among those providing seed funding, two actors stand out because of the amount of funding they offer. They are both highly specific on the criteria they use for acknowledging an applicant as a social enterprise relevant for funding. One of the two is a private business engaged in corporate philanthropy (Ferd), and the other is the state-owned Norwegian Labour and Welfare Organization (NAV).

Ferd presents itself on its homepage as "a family-owned Norwegian investment-company committed to value-creating ownership of businesses and investments in financial assets" (Ferd, 2013). Ferd has had 'social entrepreneurs' as an independent business area since 2009, providing funding for social enterprises in the region of NOK 25 million (€ 2,7 million) annually. In comparison, Ferd's value-adjusted equity was close to NOK 25 billion (€ 2,7 billion) in 2014. In addition to funding, Ferd provides business training, consultancy and access to its business networks for the social enterprises it includes in its portfolio.

Ferd's primary owner has written extensively on the subject of social entrepreneurship in the mass media, and detailed his views on the matter in a magazine article. He emphasised the ambition to get maximum social impact in return for investments and the importance of developing sustainable business that can be scaled up to the benefit of as many people as possible (Andresen, 2010).

A different approach to seed funding of social enterprises is taken by the state-owned Norwegian Labour and Welfare Organization (NAV). Annually since 2011, NAV has provided seed funding for social enterprises generating new solutions to combating poverty and social exclusion. In 2015, NAV provided almost NOK 9 million. The criteria applied by Ferd and NAV respectively can be summarized as follows:

When comparing Ferd and NAV as seed funding institutions, some interesting similarities and differences can be noted. They both prioritize funding in the start-up phase, emphasise competent leadership and sustainable

Table 5.1 NAV's and Ferd's Criteria for Funding Social Enterprises

	NAV's criteria for seed funding (NAV, 2015, translation by authors)	Ferd's criteria for seed funding (Ferd, 2013, translation by authors)
Goals	The goal of the social enterprise is to solve social problems innovatively The enterprise is motivated by social outcomes	The target group has to be children and adolescents in Norway Outcomes of activities must be measurable and beneficial to society
Business criteria	The enterprise cannot pay dividends to its owners The enterprise has a business model that can make it sustainable The enterprise is included in the public register for voluntary organizations Innovative, competent leaders and employees	There has to be a sustainable business model There has to be an ambition to scale up production The social enterprise has to be in an early stage of development The management of the enterprise has to be credible and experienced A series of milestones has to be agreed upon Business idea has to be innovative, realistic and explained in detail
Other criteria	Applicants must define themselves as 'social entrepreneurs' should be locally supported	Ferd must be included as an active owner contributing not only funds but also competence and access to networks
Period of funding	A maximum period of three years	3–7 years

business models for addressing social problems, and neither of them have criteria for ownership or participation. Among notable differences are NAV's emphasis on local support whereas Ferd emphasises up-scaling and measurability; NAV does not allow a dividend for owners whereas Ferd does; NAV requires the social enterprise to be qualified for inclusion in the public register for voluntary organizations (meaning it has to be not for profit), whereas Ferd has no such requirement; NAV's support is limited to funding, whereas Ferd requires part ownership in return for a combination of funding, business training and access to networks.

In Ferd's approach, the meaning of social enterprise is compatible with venture capitalism, which is an approach to developing enterprises Ferd is highly familiar with and competent in. In NAV's approach, the meaning of social enterprise is compatible with project funding of voluntary organizations' initiatives to improve social services, which is an approach NAV is highly familiar with and competent in—and is in opposition to the understanding of social enterprises presented by the Association of NGOs in Norway.

Local Councils on the Meaning of Social Enterprise

The present Norwegian government included facilitating the use of social enterprise in the provision of social services in its political platform (Regjeringen, 2013), but has yet to detail how this will be carried out. The majority of social services are commissioned at the level of local government. Until now, there have been only a few initiatives within local government, and the overall situation is one of uncertainty as to what meanings local councils will attribute to social enterprises.

Two relevant initiatives in this context have been taken by the Norwegian Association of Local and Regional Authorities (KS), the only employer association for local authorities, and by the Oslo City Council (by far the most populous local authority area). KS represents the administrative level in all local government organizations, whereas the Oslo City Council represents the political (owner) level of that particular local authority.

KS anticipates a future in which social enterprises have an important role to play in provision of services, and has recently commissioned a research and development project to survey this issue. The survey will investigate how local authorities can benefit from social enterprises, what social enterprises need in order to contribute to local authority services, how such a development can be facilitated by changes in laws and regulations and what could be learned from similar experiences in other countries (KS, 2015).

In 2014, the political representatives on the Oslo City Council voted unanimously for a proposition positioning social enterprise in a much wider context than public services. They want to be long-term partners, participants in research projects, advocates for funding, advocates for a national competence centre, and facilitators of entrepreneurship in the city council and in schools (Johansen, 2015).

The meanings attributed to social enterprise by the Association for Local and Regional Authorities and the Oslo City Council are markedly different. KS sees social enterprise as an approach for improving social services, meaning higher quality at a lower cost. The Oslo City Council recognises social enterprise as a phenomenon in its own right and sees itself as a potential partner and facilitator, thereby not emphasising a purchaser-provider relationship.

Discussion: Social Enterprise as a Means to Freedom From Dependency?

A variety of perspectives on the meaning of social enterprise have been suggested by social entrepreneurs, voluntary organizations, public and private seed funding institutions and local authorities. Social enterprise is put forward as: 1) An opportunity for motivated individuals to realise social value on the outside of public, business and voluntary organizations, 2) A for-profit business different from voluntary organizations, 3) A voluntary organization aimed at improving social services using commercial strategies,

4) A for-profit business approach similar to venture capitalist approaches, 5) A means of provision of local authority social services and 6) A potential partner for local authorities. Although few actors voice their opinions, those who do so represent considerable economic and political power. There are no indications of convergence between their perspectives. Whether and how the tensions between them will be resolved is not possible to determine at present. There are, however, some other implications of this research that are relevant to discuss.

The results indicate that the concept of social enterprise is used mostly as a rhetorical device to promote specific ideological and economic interests. Furthermore, it is used both to indicate the emergence of a new social phenomenon and as a new term for existing practices. Several activities that could reasonably be thought of as social enterprise, such as cooperatives or commercial activities in voluntary organizations, are not included in the discourse. Conversely, some of the organizations branding their activities as social enterprise could probably just as well be characterized as voluntary organizations or for-profit business enterprises tapping into positive interest and funding opportunities associated with social enterprise. In order to make scientific progress, it is necessary to investigate the relationships between rhetoric and practice, and between traditional and potentially new practices aimed at creating social value.

Earlier in this chapter, there was mention of how public, business and voluntary organizations contributed to solving social problems in the past, and how the current trend blurs the distinctions between such organizations. In theory, social enterprise can combine the best from each sector in concerted efforts to maximise social value. It is still too early to determine whether social enterprise will bridge resources in such a way, or if it will be more or less co-opted by strong interests in one of the sectors. At this point in time, however, the co-optation scenario seems most likely, as several powerful actors highlight sector interests. Put bluntly and highly tentatively, the public sector is most interested in how social enterprise can lead to better and less expensive social services, the voluntary sector is distancing itself from expectations to engage more in commercial activities and the business sector is interested in social enterprise as a means for corporate philanthropy. Several of the social entrepreneurs who describe social enterprise as an opportunity for motivated individuals to realise social value on the outside of public, business and voluntary organizations in the book by Schei and Rønnevig (2009) have subsequently adjusted their activities to conform with Ferd's or NAV's criteria for seed funding, making their enterprises more similar to for-profit business organizations or voluntary organizations, respectively. A similar development in the relationship between social enterprises and the state has been noted in Sweden (Gawell, 2014).

Lundgaard Andersen and Hulgård (in this volume) discuss, with reference to Denmark, whether initiatives related to social entrepreneurship are a sign of increasing influence of civil society or a sign of conventional private market economy becoming interested in market opportunities associated with people at the bottom of the (socio-economic) pyramid. Interestingly, neither of these tendencies is prominent in Norway. The social entrepreneurs are predominantly individuals not motivated by monetary success, and voluntary organizations distance themselves from social enterprise. There are few for-profit social business initiatives, and established businesses seem more interested in social enterprise as a means to contribute to the creation of social value than to profit from it. Possibly, interest in social enterprise in Norway can be seen as an extension of continued interest in citizens' freedom from dependency on others, characterized by a long cultural tradition of emphasis on autonomy as described by Vike (2012). If social enterprises, by means of applying bottom up approaches to participation and co-production in commercially sustainable activities, can contribute to the autonomy of vulnerable individuals and groups, they will be a viable alternative to dependency on welfare state social services. This is certainly the ambition of many of the social entrepreneurs themselves, but the extent to which such a development will manifest itself is difficult to predict.

An interesting avenue for future research is to analyse in depth the practices of those engaged in or facilitating what they understand as social enterprise. It is reasonable to assume that the meanings attributed to social enterprise will continue to develop in interaction between social entrepreneurs, vulnerable groups and contributors from the three sectors. From a policy perspective, it is to be expected that social enterprise will be regulated by law at some time in the future, as this has occurred in many countries already. Lawmakers should carefully assess what interests and future scenarios they are promoting when they regulate what should and should not be acknowledged as social enterprise.

References

Andreassen, T. A. (2011). Innovasjoner som kjempes fram: Fra politisk nytenking til institusjonell nyskaping'. In H. C. G. Johnsen & Ø. Pålshaugen (Eds.), *Hva er innovasjon? Perspektiver på innovasjonsforskning*. Kristiansand: Høyskoleforlaget.

Andresen, J. H., Jr. (2010). Det nye velferdssamfunnet; hvordan entreprenørens initiativ løser sosiale problemer'. *Samtiden*, 4, 26–37.

Association of NGOs in Norway. (2015). *Høringssvar—Utredning om sosialt entreprenørskap og innspill til Nærings- og handelsdepartementets videre arbeid*. Available at www.frivillighetnorge.no/no/frivillighetspolitikk/samhandling_mellom_staten_og_frivillig_sektor/H%C3%B8ringssvar+-+Utredning+om+sosialt+entrepren%C3%B8rskap+og+innspill+til+N%C3%A6rings-+og+handelsdepartementets.b7C_wlfU4_.ips, accessed 20 June 2015.

Barth, F. (1963). *The Role of the Entrepreneur in Social Change in Northern Norway*. Oslo: Universitetsforlaget.

Christensen, T. & Lægreid, P. (2000). *New Public Management: Design, Resistance, or Transformation? A Study of How Modern Reforms Are Received in a Civil*

Service System. Bergen: LOS-senteret. Available at www.nb.no/nbsok/nb/6b448b 8a79cef8ba7738fe7451332784.nbdigital?lang=no#5, accessed 10 June 2015.

Damsgaard, H. L. & Eide, K. (2012). Utfordringer i velferdsstatens yrker—slik nyutdannede profesjonsutøvere ser det. *Fontene forskning*, 1, 9–80.

Damvad. (2012). *Utredning om sosialt entreprenørskap—Utarbeidet av DAM-VAD for Nærings- og Handelsdepartementet.* Available at www.regjeringen. no/globalassets/upload/nhd/vedlegg/rapporter_2012/sosialt_entreprenorskap_mars2012.pdf, accessed 2 March 2015.

Defourny, J., Hulgård, L. & Pestoff, V. (2014). Introduction to the "SE Field"'. In J. Defourny, L. Hulgård & V. Pestoff (Eds.), *Social Enterprise and the Third Sector: Changing European Landscapes in a Comparative Perspective.* New York: Routledge.

Defourny, J. & Nyssens, M. (2013). Social Innovation, Social Economy and Social Enterprise: What Can the European Debate Tell Us? In F. Moulart, D. MacCallum, A. Mehmood & A. Hamdouch (Eds.), *The International Handbook on Social Innovation: Collective Action, Social Learning and Transdisciplinary Research.* Cheltenham: Edward Elgar Publishing.

Defourny, J. & Nyssens, M. (2014). The EMES Approach to Social Enterprise in a Comparative Perspective. In J. Defourny, L. Hulgård & V. Pestoff (Eds.), *Social Enterprise and the Third Sector: Changing European Landscapes in a Comparative Perspective.* New York: Routledge.

Elkington, J. & Robins, N. (1994). *Company Environmental Reporting: A Measure of the Progress of Business and Industry Towards Sustainable Development.* Nairobi: UNEP IE Technical Report.

Endresen, A. (2014). Virksomhetens sosiale kapital—et analytisk perspektiv for å studere tverrfaglig og tverrprofesjonelt samarbeid i organisasjoner. In E. Willumsen & A. Ødegård (Eds.), *Tverrprofesjonelt samarbeid: et samfunnsoppdrag.* Oslo: Universitetsforlaget.

Ferd. (2013). *Om Ferd sosiale entreprenører.* Available at http://ferd.no/sosiale_entreprenorer/sosiale_entreprenorer_1, accessed 8 June 2015.

Gawell, M. (2014). Social Entrepreneurship and the Negotiation of Emerging Social Enterprise Markets. Re-considerations in Swedish Policy and Practice. *International Journal of Public Sector Management*, 27(4), 251–266.

Gustavsen, K. & Kobro, L. (2012). *Sosialt entreprenørskap som ledd i innsatsen mot fattigdom.* Telemarksforskning No. 305. Available at www.telemarksforsking.no/publikasjoner/filer/2114.pdf, accessed 8 August 2015.

Hacking, I. (2000). *The Social Construction of What?* Oxford: Oxford University Press.

Hauge, H. A. (2011). *How Can Employee Empowerment Be MadeConducive to Both Employee Health and Organisation Performance? An Empirical Investigation of a Tailor-Made Approach to Organisation Learning in a Municipal Public Service Organisation.* Bergen: University of Bergen.

Health Services Campaign/Helsetjenesteaksjonen. (2015). Available at http://helsetjenesteaksjonen.no/V01/, accessed 18 June 2015.

Herning, L. (2015). *Velferdsprofitørene: Om penger, makt og propaganda i de norske velferdstjenestene.* Oslo: Forlaget Manifest.

Hulgård, L. (2007). *Sociale entreprenører—en kritisk indføring.* Copenhagen: Hans Reitzel.

Hulgård, L. (2014). Social Enterprise and the Third Sector—Innovative Service Delivery or a Non-Capitalist Economy? In J. Defourny, L. Hulgård & V. Pestoff (Eds.), *Social Enterprise and the Third Sector: Changing European Landscapes in a Comparative Perspective*. New York: Routledge.

Johansen, I. (2015). *Oslo bør være en foregangskommune i sosialt entreprenørskap.* Available at www.ivarjohansen.no/temaer/annet/4848-entreprenor06072014.html, accessed 21 June 2015.

Kaupang. (2014). *Velferd i nytt terreng—Hvordan kan kommunen som arbeidsgiver samarbeide med frivillig sektor og sosiale entreprenører innen pleie- og omsorgstjenestene.* Vol. R7940. Available at www.ks.no/globalassets/blokker-til-hvert-fagomrade/arbeidsgiver/arbeidsgiverpolitikk/rapport_velferd-i-nytt-terreng_ ks_agenda-kaupang.pdf, accessed 6 June 2015.

Klemsdal, L. (2013). *Hva trenger vi ledere til? Organisering og ledelse i komplekse arbeidssituasjoner.* Oslo: Gyldendal forlag.

KS/the Norwegian Association of Local and Regional Authorities. (2015). *Forespørsel om tilbud på KS FoU-prosjekt nr. 154027: «Sosiale entreprenører—kommunale endringsagenter».* Available at www.ks.no/contentassets/005cd1e668614f8b9123 2f0b172676d9/tilbudsforesporsel-ks-fou-prosjekt-nr-154027sosiale-entreprenore rkommunaleendringsagenter.pdf, accessed 20 June 2015.

Kuhnle, S. & Selle, P. (1992). *Government and Voluntary Organizations: A Relational Perspective.* Aldershot: Avebury.

Lorentzen, H. (2007). *Moraldannende Kretsløp—Stat, samfunn og sivilt engasjement.* Oslo: Abstrakt Forlag.

Lynn, L. J. (2006). *Public Management: Old and New.* Oxford: Routledge. Available at http://bem.fisip.unsri.ac.id/userfiles/file/Bahan%20Teori%20Pembangunan. pdf, accessed 5 June 2015.

Mazzucato, M. (2013). *The Entrepreneurial State: Debunking Public vs. Private Sector Myths.* London & New York: Anthem Press.

Messel, J. (2013). *I velferdsstatens frontlinje: barnevernspedagogers, sosionomers og vernepleieres historie*, 252–283. Oslo: Universitetsforlaget.

Mothercourage. (2014). *Nettverk for Sosialt Entreprenørskap.* Available at www. mothercourage.no/sosialt_entreprenoerskap/1303884474, accessed 12 June 2015.

NAV/the Norwegian Labour and Welfare Administration. (2015). *Tilskudd til sosialt entreprenørskap—bekjempelse av fattigdom.* Available at www.nav.no/no/ NAV+og+samfunn/Samarbeid/Tilskudd+gjennom+NAV/Tilskudd+til+frivillig+arb eid+mot+fattigdom/Tilskudd+til+sosialt+entreprenorskap, accessed 13 June 2015.

The Nordic Council of Ministers. (2015). *Sosialt entreprenørskap og sosial innovasjon: Kartlegging av innsatser for sosialt entreprenørskap og sosial innovasjon i Norden.* Vol. TemaNord 2015:502. Available at http://norden.diva-portal.org/ smash/get/diva2:789262/FULLTEXT01.pdf, accessed 1 March 2015.

NOU/Norwegian Official Report. 1988:17. *Frivillige Organisasjoner.* Oslo: Ministry of Finance.

Piketty, T. (2014). *Capital in the Twenty-First Century.* Cambridge, MA: Belknap Press.

Ramsdal, H. & Skorstad, E. (2004). *Privatisering fra innsiden: om sammensmeltingen av offentlig og privat organisering.* Bergen: Fagbokforlaget.

Regjeringen/the Norwegian Government. (2013). *Politisk plattform—Sundvoldenplattformen.* Available at www.regjeringen.no/nb/dokumenter/politisk-plattform/ id743014/, accessed 8 June 2015.

Ridley-Duff, R. & Bull, M. (2011). Defining Social Enterprise. In R. Ridley-Duff & M. Bull (Eds.), *Understanding Social Enterprise—Theory and Practice*. London: Sage Publications.

Rothstein, B. (2001). Social Capital in the Social Democratic Welfare State. *Politics & Society*, 29(2), 207–241.

Schei, B. & Rønnevig, E. (2009). *Vilje til endring—Sosialt Entreprenørskap på norsk*. Available at www.mothercourage.no/sosialt_entreprenoerskap/vilje_til_endring/frontpage/schei_roennevig_vilje_til_endring.pdf, accessed 13 June 2015.

Selle, P. (1992). Voluntary Organisations and the Welfare State: The Case of Norway. *Voluntas: International Journal of Voluntary and Nonprofit Organizations*, 14(1), 1–15.

Selle, P. & Strømsnes, K. (2012). *Organisasjonene og det offentlige: har vi fått en ny frivillighetspolitikk?* Senter for forskning på sivilsamfunn og frivillig sektor/Norwegian Centre for Research on Civil Society and the Voluntary Sector, 6.

Sivesind, K. H. (2008). *Halvveis til Soria Moria—ikke-kommersielle velferdstjenester, politikkens blinde flekk?* Oslo: Institutt for samfunnsforskning/Institute for Social Research.

Skirbekk, H. & Grimen, H. (2012). *Tillit i Norge*. Oslo: Res Publica.

Staksrud, E., Steen-Johnsen, K., Bernard, E., Gustafsson, M. H., Ihlebæk, K. A., Midtbøen, A., Sætrang, S., Trygstad, S. & Utheim, M. (2014). *Ytringsfrihet i Norge: Holdninger og erfaringer i befolkningen*. Oslo: Fritt Ord, ISF, IMK, FAFO.

Statistics Norway. (2014). *Satellittregnskap for ideelle og frivillige organisasjoner, 2012*. Available at www.ssb.no/orgsat/, accessed 7 June 2015.

UNDP. (2014). *The 2014 Human Development Report—Sustaining Human Progress: Reducing Vulnerabilities and Building Resilience*. Available at http://hdr.undp.org/sites/default/files/hdr14-report-en-1.pdf, accessed 6 June 2015.

Vike, H. (2004). *Velferd uten grenser: den norske velferdsstaten ved veiskillet*. Oslo: Akribe forlag.

Vike, H. (2012). Varianter av vest-europeiske statsformasjoner. Utkast til en historisk antropologi'. *Norsk Antropologisk Tidsskrift*, 3, 126–142.

Wilkinson, R. & Pickett, K. (2009). *The Spirit Level: Why More Equal Societies Almost Always Do Better*. London: Allen Lane.

Wollebæk, D. & Sivesind, K. H. (2010). *Fra folkebevegelse til filantropi? Frivillig innsats i Norge 1997–2009*. Available at www.sivilsamfunn.no/Ressurser/Publikasjoner/Rapporter/2010/2010–003, accessed 2 June 2015.

6 Practicing Entrepreneuring and Citizenship

Social Venturing as a Learning Context for University Students

Bengt Johannisson

Training university students for entrepreneurship that concerns social as well as economic value creation benefits from a learning context that integrates individual, organizational and territorial development. This chapter reports the experiences from practicing such an approach addressing students in a business school at a Swedish university. Practicing enactive research, the author as a researcher and teacher designed, initiated and realised a project aiming at adding a social dimension to the region's innovation strategy. Collaborating with practitioners in the three social ventures making the core of the project and with institutions in the regional context, the students experienced the challenges of social entrepreneuring as a collective effort. The students' overall lesson is that learning for and through social entrepreneuring is not just about acquiring instrumental knowledge. It is also an existential challenge, meaning being thrown between anxiety and boredom that only active personal involvement can turn into a constructive experience.

Broadening the Scope of Entrepreneurial Learning

Alert entrepreneurship and responsible citizenship combine in work-integrating social enterprises where profits are reinvested in the operations. The need for entrepreneurship as creative organizing is especially strong in such enterprises in highly institutionalized welfare economies like the Nordic ones where New Public Management (NPM) ideals (Christensen & Laegreid, 2002; Gawell in this volume) have to be counteracted in order to open up for creative processes, for entrepreneur*ing* (Steyaert, 2007; Johannisson, 2014a). In such economies, social ventures usually draw upon resources from all three sectors in society—the private, the public as well as the non-profit sector—that in a regional setting are closely intertwined. Social enterprises with dual goals thus have to manage a broad repertoire of resources provided by stakeholders who are guided by different logics (Berglund, Johannisson & Schwartz, 2012).

Knowledge creation in the context of social entrepreneuring may concern the individual agent, the social organization and/or its spatial local/regional context. Individual training usually addresses either practicing social entrepreneurs or marginalized people who are empowered to build a new identity as employed by the social enterprise or coached by it to become self-employed. Organizational learning for a more effective production of social value may be achieved by intra-organizational measures but also through inter-organizational collaboration in the local/regional setting. The latter approach will as well increase the innovative potential of the territory at large. Less discussed, though, is the training for and learning through social entrepreneurship of university students in order to make them experience not just what entrepreneuring generally calls for, but also how they may contribute to society by practicing it.

Lessons from recently published research on individual education/training/learning in social-entrepreneurship contexts include the importance, almost the necessity, of an experiential learning approach; see, for example, Smith, Barr, Barbosa and Kickul (2008) and Chang, Benamraoui and Rieple (2014). It is then crucial to recognise the greater complexity and ambiguity that characterize social entrepreneuring in comparison with for-profit venturing. Social enterprises have to deal with several institutional logics and negotiate with a broad set of stakeholders (Smith et al., 2008; Berglund et al., 2012; Pache & Chowdhury, 2012;). Lourenco, Jones and Jayawarna (2012) state "that there is a value in introducing learning content related to sustainable entrepreneurship to nascent entrepreneurs with a profit-first mentality" (p. 855). Contemporary research thus seems to justify the furthering the students' insight into social entrepreneuring as a road to insights into entrepreneuring in general.

The purpose of this chapter is to enquire into the implications of intertwining individual, organizational and regional venturing activities for university students' learning for and through social entrepreneuring, that is, venturing that is socially as well as financially sustainable.

The empirical setting for the research reported here is Linnaeus University and its Växjö campus in southern Sweden. There, education about and for entrepreneuring has long traditions. Already in the 1970s, a forerunner of this university offered a unique business program including internships in entrepreneurial small firms in the region. In those days, the students were taught to become administrators supporting the business entrepreneur rather than to become nascent entrepreneurs themselves (Johannisson, 1991). This programme became a national role model and it also got international attention (Vesper & Gartner, 1997). However, in the mid-1990s, an attempt was made to inspire the students to also launch their own (commercial) ventures. In those days, there was a global pressure for such entrepreneurship. This effort, however, failed, and the programme was terminated by me, as I was its director. A few years later, it reappeared as the present Enterprising and Business Development (EBD) programme. This educates the students to become project leaders in established business firms, a kind of organizational entrepreneurship (Hjorth, 2012). (Social) venturing in a designed setting therefore appeared as appropriate when trying to broaden their perspective.

Usually, technology rather than social concerns is used to energize economies. The Triple Helix framework, then, is a widely spread model that links the innovative potential of a territory to its economic-technical assets and the interaction between universities as research institutions, the business community and government (Etzkowitz & Leydesdorff, 2000). This model has to be completed/adjusted in two respects in order to provide an appropriate (conceptual) take-off point for the present research challenge. To begin with, a social dimension that recognises the contributions of the non-profit sector has to be added—it has to be turned into a *Quadruple Helix*. It also has to be taken into consideration that universities are involved in education as much as in research. The potential contributions by students as nascent professionals also have to be considered.

The chapter is organized as follows. In the next section, I, within a practice-theoretical framework, provide the conceptual points of departure for the empirical enquiry into social entrepreneuring and how its lessons may be adopted by individuals, organizations and regions. Then, the project *SORIS*, as the enactment of a *SOcial Regional Innovation System*, its antecedents, initiation, emergence and outcome, is introduced. The following section delivers a more detailed report on how the involved university students experienced SORIS as a learning context for social entrepreneuring. In a separate section, I then reflect upon the relations between the students and the project management. In the final section, the lessons taught are summarized and reflected upon with respect to their implications for entrepreneurial learning.

Social Entrepreneuring and Learning as a Practice

Since an entrepreneurial attitude means considering change as a natural state, entrepreneuring and learning are closely associated (Cope, 2005; Hjorth & Johannisson, 2007). Recognising that entrepreneuring is about 'getting things done' (Schumpeter, 1943/1987, p. 132), it is appropriate to consider it as a practice (Drucker, 1985; Johannisson, 2011). The process features that are ascribed entrepreneuring invite an ontology of becoming (Chia & Holt, 2006). This recognises that the world is constantly on the move, unknowable and (therefore) unforeseeable. The corresponding epistemology tells that knowledge is created experientially, but also that the environment is enactable through concerted hands-on (inter)action (Weick, 1969/79, 1995; Smircich & Morgan, 1982).

General scholarly discourses on education, training and learning concerning entrepreneurship differentiate between advancing knowledge about, for or through entrepreneurship. Where *education about* entrepreneurship is a typical academic activity where theoretical ideas about entrepreneurship are communicated, *training for* entrepreneuring aims at providing a set of practical tools for the enactment of a venture. *Learning through* entrepreneuring means that an ongoing dialogue between curious, experimenting and reflecting individuals provides them with an own, personal identity that embodies capabilities and responsibilities. The literature usually focuses on the differences between learning about and for entrepreneurship; see, for example, Pache and Chowdhury (2012). Learning through entrepreneuring, however, seems to be especially relevant in the context of social entrepreneuring considering that it aims at turning the students into also more conscientious citizens.

Adopting a process perspective on entrepreneurship that presents it as a practice brings learning for and through entrepreneuring closer together. For example, learning through entrepreneuring shares with training for entrepreneuring the importance of learning-by-doing (see Chang et al. (2014)). Learning then appears an incessant embodied activity in any kind of venturing, whether studied from the perspective of the individual, the social venture or the spatial context, here, the region. *Individual* training for and learning through entrepreneuring concerns both the existential drama associated with immersing into the identity of an entrepreneur and the practical challenges that the enactment of a venture entails. This presents learning as a social and situated activity, as an outcome of continual embodied interactivity, a practice indeed (Gherardi, Nicolini & Odella, 1998; Howorth, Smith & Parkinson, 2012), rather than just a cognitive process where knowledge is diffused from an expert to a novice. Social learning as a practice also turns the individual into an agent for collective learning, whether in a functional/organizational or territorial context.

Learning as a social (inter)activity thus provides the foundations for a bridge between individual and *organizational learning*. Most explicitly, this image is caught by the notion 'community of practice'; see, for example, Wenger (1998). This suggests that individual learning usually takes place in formal or informal organized settings. Argyris and Schön (1974) have as well systematically inquired into the interface between individual and organizational learning, presenting employees as agents for and/or major contributors to organizational learning.

The literature on *regional learning* usually downplays the role of the individual as an agent of change and instead focuses on structures of interrelated formal organizations and institutions. In a recent review of theories about learning regions, Asheim (2012) presents the development of the field in a phase model. His discourse, though, is saturated with a belief in the instrumentality, manageability and cumulative feature of regional learning processes. Grabher (2001) is instead critical to such assumptions and argues that territorial development benefits from diversity as much as it stimulates self-organizing.

SORIS: A Multi-Level Social-Entrepreneurship Venture

It is a challenge indeed to track the emergence of creative processes such as entrepreneuring. Each such process is unique and therefore it has to be tracked and reported in detail in order to be properly interpreted. That calls for what I address as 'enactive' research (Johannisson, 2014b). This approach is here used to inquire into the emergence of a social regional innovation system framing training for social entrepreneuring.

Disclosing Social Processes: The Need for Enactive Research

Academic discourses on regional development do not pay much attention to individuals who intentionally take on the role of creative organizers in regional settings. Some models, though, recognise that individual entrepreneurs may orchestrate the enactment of a learning region; compare with (Ylinenpää 2012). The concern here is even more challenging. Can and, if so, should the means for regional change be designed and actualized also by the academic community as an institution or individual researchers and teachers? Answers to the 'should' question call for ethical considerations; see, for example, Van de Ven (2007), whereas answers to the 'can' question also call for what I address as 'enactive research'.

Enactive research into entrepreneuring means that the scholar her-/himself initiates and immerses cognitively, emotionally and practically into an entrepreneurial process (Johannisson, 2011, 2014b). Since the emergence of such processes is sensitively dependent upon their initial conditions, it can only be made intelligible by the researcher her-/himself. Enactive research as a methodology obviously challenges received conceptions of social research. When applied to social entrepreneuring, it easily brings her/him into the mined field where academia and activism meet; compare with Flood et al. (2013).

The need for situated knowledge implies that familiarity with the context is crucial in enactive research (Johannisson, 2014b). Only such insight makes it possible for the researcher to properly 'read' the potentialities of unique initiatives. Before launching the project SORIS, I for several years had been involved in one of the local work-integrating social enterprises (Macken) as a researcher as well as a mentor at its school of entrepreneurship (see Johannisson (2012)). As the chairman of the board of Macken's Friends, an organization supporting Macken, I was also well acquainted with further social enterprises and organizations in the region. Being a member of the university staff for several decades and the director of the forerunner to EBD, I was also well up in both the academic and the regional business communities.

In Sweden, all universities are either public institutions or publically subsidized private ones. Therefore, they are expected to fulfil three major tasks: research, education and involvement in a dialogue with the wider society. As Figure 6.1 indicates, SORIS did not only contribute to the accomplishment of all three tasks: the project also integrated them. Through SORIS, contemporary research about social entrepreneurship was 'translated' into enactable social ventures that offered both students and teachers/researchers opportunities to practice entrepreneuring and thereby contribute to sustainable regional development.

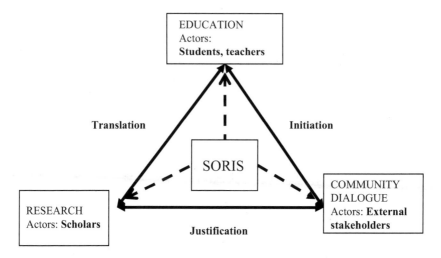

Figure 6.1 Positioning SORIS in the Academic Task Context

The Enactment of SORIS

In late 2013, Linnaeus University hosted a regional conference that heralded SORIS. The conference addressed practitioners in the social economy and concerned the feasibility of and need for measuring the means for and effects of social venturing. The conference's conclusion was that the impact of social innovations must be possible to measure in order to provide legitimacy—qualitative judgements were considered to be not good enough. The additional lessons from the conference were summed up by us in a call for the creation of a social regional innovation system in order to make visible the collective potential of the social economy.

Conveniently, the Swedish Agency for Economic and Regional Growth just after the conference invited applications for the funding of minor projects aiming at promoting social innovations. An application for funding of the project SORIS was formally filed by a non-profit association: Macken's Friends (cf. above). Once the application was supported also by the regional authorities and Linnaeus University, it was promptly accepted by the state agency. The proposed project was also backed up by a loosely coupled network encompassing the majority of the (mainly non-profit) organizations making the regional social economy. I established a steering committee for the project, including resourceful representatives of the private, public and non-profit sectors, also members of my personal network. I as the project leader and a project assistant were employed on a part-time basis. We orchestrated SORIS's everyday operations, governing the three social ventures and supervising two bachelor theses. Figure 6.2 provides an overview of SORIS's organization.

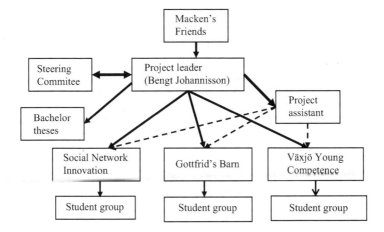

Figure 6.2 SORIS's Organization

SORIS's ventures were staffed with the freshmen on the bachelor pro-gramme EDP at Linnaeus University. The students' involvement lasted for four months during the 2014 spring semester, their second one. SORIS's challenge thus was to motivate the business students to join a learning pro-cess that would turn them into not just more entrepreneurial professionals, but into reflecting and responsible citizen as well. Before their involvement in SORIS, the students' acquaintance with entrepreneuring was limited to education *about* entrepreneurship in business contexts. SORIS's ambition instead was to provide *training for* and *learning through* social entrepre-neuring. Accordingly, the freshmen were invited to choose one of three ventures to engage in and were organize into groups accordingly. The two bachelor theses by third-year students in the same programme were as well designed and completed during the spring semester. One thesis reviewed the regional (social) innovation concept and carried out an empirical study in collaboration with one of the freshmen groups. The other thesis reported an independent course evaluation of the freshmen's participation in SORIS.

The three social ventures were enacted sequentially from March to May 2014 and in an order that reflected their increasing distance from the program's focus on organizational entrepreneurship. The ventures lasted a month each and were reported publically at an Innovation Forum at the university on the last Friday of the month concerned. Then, the process leader(s) and student representatives jointly presented proposed measures to enact the venture. A panel of (regional) experts scrutinized their social busi-ness concept and the associated discussion was moderated by me. About a week after the forum, the students were individually examined by brief written reports where they were asked to reflect upon their personal experiences gained while involved in SORIS and also to position their professional experiences against contrasting images of entrepreneuring.[1]

The lessons learnt from the students' venturing as well as the findings presented in the two bachelor theses were presented at a regional conference in September 2014. It was announced as an 'opening space' event with the ambition to mobilize further ideas for the enactment of a social regional innovation system. The conference explicitly addressed representatives of all three societal sectors as well as the university staff, although the participants from the non-profit sector dominated the audience. Including the experiences from that conference, the overall lessons from SORIS were summarized by me to be delivered to the authorities as an invited review of the proposed new regional innovation strategy. Before its submission, an outline of that review was discussed in public at a 'closing space' event staged by the SORIS project in December 2014. The participants at the September event as well as all panel members from the three spring forums were invited to this final gathering organized by SORIS. In early January 2015, the revised review was submitted to the regional authorities. This report concluded that the SORIS project was a joint venture across societal sectors and integrated the three generic functions of the university: education, research and community dialogue (see Figure 6.1).

SORIS as a Situated Learning Context for (Social) Entrepreneuring

When, as in the SORIS case, educating students have more elaborate ambitions than just communicating cognitive lessons, the way of staging experiential learning is crucial. Only in perspective of the design of the students' learning platform will it be possible to make sense of the emergence of the concrete social ventures.

Setting the Stage

SORIS as a training arena for social entrepreneuring stands out in three respects: how it was instigated, how it was staged and its ambition to make the students aware of their responsibilities as citizens. First, SORIS was not the outcome of an altogether planned and designed effort, but came into existence by linking three independent events in the autumn of 2013: a vision stated at a regional conference, an invitation by a national authority to apply for funding of projects concerning social innovation and the request by the coordinator of the EBD program to offer the students action-based practice in entrepreneuring. Second, SORIS rather appeared as a kind of organizational/regional entrepreneurship than as three independent (social) ventures. These remained tightly controlled by SORIS as a project organization aiming at providing a concerted contribution to regional development.

Third, the design of SORIS as an arena for students' learning was inspired by what Paolo Freire addresses as 'conscientization', that is developing a 'critical self-consciousness' (Freire, 2001, p. 18; compare also Berglund & Johansson, 2007). Conscientization as a generic learning approach was adopted in order to bridge between SORIS as an interactive research inquiry and as an educational journey. Since SORIS was realised within an entrepreneuring framework, it was evident to present the enactment as an experiential and existential challenge that aimed at changing the mindset of the students and enforce their entrepreneurial selves and engagement as citizens. From a research and education perspective, this implies that *how* the enactment of SORIS was accomplished was as crucial—to both its participants and the readers of this chapter—as *what* came out of the process.

At the outset of SORIS in February 2014, I informed the students about entrepreneuring as a practice, in general and as applied to SORIS in particular. The first venture being enacted—*Social Network Innovation*—aimed at establishing a tighter network between the work-integrating social enterprises in the region. An experienced consultant, also the chairperson of the board in one of these social enterprises, became Social Network Innovation's process leader. The second venture—*Gottfrid's Barn*—was about energizing an emerging social venture in the tourism industry. SORIS took on the role as a temporary incubator for the venture and mentored the nascent social entrepreneurs. Themselves excluded from the labour market, they stayed as formal leaders and collaborated with the students in a feasibility study. The third venture aimed at creating a staffing company offering young people's competences to private- and public-sector employers. A former hard-core economist who had converted into a social activist and also brought up the venture idea became the process leader of *Växjö Young Competence*.

The SORIS Venturing Activities as Experienced by the Students

Here, the venturing processes of the three SORIS ventures are briefly summarized as evolving, yet organized, events from the perspective of the students and with a focus on their experiences of the venturing as not only a learning experience, but also an existential challenge. Since these experiences are dependent upon the interplay between the individual ventures and the shared SORIS arrangements, further reflecting on the shared context is needed.

The SNI Network of Social Enterprises

The task force Social Network Innovation, or SNI, was established in order to investigate how the (then) eight work-integrating social enterprises in the region could develop, individually as well as collectively, by way of collaboration. An experienced consultant, also chairperson on the board of one of the involved social enterprises, became the process leader. She, together with two third-year students writing their bachelor theses within SORIS, designed a study of the broader informal network that arranged monthly meetings for all social ventures in the region. The freshmen then interviewed representatives for these social ventures on issues and in a format that was planned by their older programme mates. The freshmen also put together a statistical report that was delivered at the first Innovation Forum (end of March 2014). In their reflections, the students brought up concerns, which mainly were associated with how the SNI venture was organized and managed and the limited action frame that the students were offered. Some students' voices illustrate what learning experiences this design has (not) created:

> Although we collaborate a lot with [commercial] firms on our program it has been a very interesting experience to visit these social ventures which are so different. It has been exciting to meet these real enthusiasts who fight to improve the living conditions for other people although their very limited financial resources put a spoke in their wheel . . . In the beginning it was a bit messy and fuzzy with respect to who was going to do what but that was only to be expected considering the size of our group. There were some misunderstandings but these were eventually sorted out. However, my personal contribution could have been larger. It is always like that. I still have the feeling that I am at the beginning of becoming an entrepreneur. It is difficult to take own initiatives while still a beginner and all the time having the feeling that you have to check with somebody else because you yourself do not know what should be done. Many of us do not dare to let ourselves go even if that was the very idea. (Female student)
>
> As a student you are expected to remain seated, raise your hand and ask or answer questions. That is why I experienced SORIS, where decisive steps forward were taken, as a bit of a clash. Instead of doing what I was told I was expected to find solutions and tasks on my own. On jobs outside the academic world I have taken own initiatives but somehow it is easy to take on the role as a student and not oneself look for solutions to problems . . . During this project I have got many new ideas about entrepreneurship—which probably was the intention. There have been many question marks down the road but as Bengt Johannisson has explained that is a considerable part of entrepreneurship. Find/create solutions where there are question marks rather than asking new questions. I am considering what to create. (Male student)
>
> I experienced that we as students mainly were used as a resource for carrying out interviews. Contributing with constructive criticism I think it would have been more relevant if we ourselves had been made responsible for how to bring about the creation of [an] SNI for social enterprises, how to identify and contact such enterprises in the Växjö locality, how to put together a relevant questionnaire. To really plan and implement a project. Instead we visited the enterprises with

interview agendas we had not created ourselves and therefore could not really stand up for when the interviewee raised questions. It does not appear as very entrepreneurial to allocate a questionnaire and telephone numbers to call [for arranging a meeting] and make no own contribution. Then it is difficult to get committed to a venture. (Female student).

Obviously, the students felt that their real competences had not been acknowledged, blaming both themselves and the project/process leaders. Yet the oscillation in the venturing process between tight control and ambiguity seems to have triggered considerable reflection. The SNI venture itself successfully ran its operations throughout the project period (2014) with regular monthly member meetings. Two applications for continued innovative activities were filed and were both approved by a publically financed organization supporting cooperatives. One of the grants concerned the development of the SNI inter-organizational network, while the other one was awarded to one of its members for creating a shared outlet for products from local social enterprises. These development projects were successfully realised in 2015.

Gottfrid's Barn: An Emerging Social Enterprise

Gottfrid's Barn, named after an empty farm building in the countryside about 20 kilometres from Växjö, was a venture idea that was born before SORIS was launched. The two nascent entrepreneurs and process leaders, a man and a woman in their fifties, had already in quite a lot of detail planned how to convert the barn into a tourism facility, for example, by including a showroom for local firms and by offering accommodation to visitors to the region. Their intention was to run the operations as a social enterprise. The entrepreneurs' main concern was how to finance the venture, and they had at the start of SORIS already approached a number of public organizations, including the university, for advice on that matter.

Soon enough, SORIS's management and the student group concerned diagnosed an urgent need for a hands-on feasibility study. A market investigation among the other local tourism firms in the vicinity therefore was outlined by the entrepreneurs and after a revision, was carried out by the students. Some of them with experience from similar projects completed the general study with research in their special fields. The major concern of the student task force was the limited learning and 'absorptive capacity' of the process leaders. The students' disappointment with them as process leaders very clearly came through in their reflection reports. The statements, however, also reveal that the students, when about to close their involvement in the venture, pulled themselves together, took action and made profound learning experiences:

As students we potentially represented a huge resource in the project but due to bad management that resource was not fully used . . . [It was unacceptable] that we as students with only a few days' notice on some occasions were instructed to participate in a meeting. My problem was that we on one hand were expected to do 'nonsensical' tasks in the project, on the other were assumed to re-orient our everyday life in order to support it. This was too much for me, usually a very energetic and positive person . . . [However,] life is not always fair—some will get more laborious and others simpler tasks. The sooner you realize this the sooner you will understand that you should not sulk because of that. (Male student)

However, towards the end of the project (a few days before the innovation forum) I found a prime mover, the motivation that was needed to finish the project. I was not at all motivated when considering it as an assigned task that had to be accomplished . . . Then I experienced a kind of revelation that made me think something like: *Although I for long have considered this to be an unrealizable venture that is very laborious I do not want to do a bad job. Not for my own or the university's sake but because it is about Mary's and Paul's lives. Even if I am not fully committed to the venture and perhaps think that what they say about it is ridiculous it remains incredibly important to them. I am not going to do a half-hearted job just because I do not see what they see in Gottfrid's Barn.* (Female student, italics in original, assumed names of the social entrepreneurs)

Another student with his own experience from organizing different kinds of events was worried about Mary and Paul's limited entrepreneurial competences and contacted a former employer, an entrepreneur, for advice. The student closes his reflections as follows:

I have learnt a lot when it comes to launching a venture, for example the need for preparations and importance of personal networking . . . By activating my contact with the entrepreneur while being involved in Gottfrid's Barn I vitalized my relation to him. I am convinced that if I maintain that contact we will collaborate in the future. Additional contacts of this kind will dramatically increase my possibilities to start a business or carry out innovative projects. (Male student)

On one hand, the students thus experienced their involvement in Gottfrid's Barn as exploitive, boring and hopeless. On the other hand, the students' voices tell that they tried to deal with the situation they were put in in the best possible way, considering it as an instrumental, moral and existential learning opportunity. The venture Gottfrid's Barn never actualized.

VYC: A Boundary-Spanning Youth Cooperative

The third venture—Växjö Young Competence (VYC)— offered this student group more freedom of action than the two other two groups. The venture was already envisioned by a young immigrant economist ('Bernard', assumed name) who at the time of SORIS worked as a volunteer in a social enterprise located in Växjö. He and the students together established VYC as a staffing venture. With the young and *democratic* social entrepreneur as their process leader, the student group intended to organize a trade show where unemployed young people would present their competences to potential employers. For practical reasons, the enactment of the venture had been postponed from March to May. The students did not, though, use the extra available time for negotiating with stakeholders. Valuable time needed for organizing the trade show in detail was lost and finally, the show had to be cancelled altogether as a spring event. This caused a lot of frustration among the students. Nevertheless, the staffing business was later (during the summer 2014) formalized as a cooperative that also included students as board members.

> [I]t has not been clear who pulls the strings. Rather than having a process leader who assigns tasks several persons have taken on the role as the leader which has made the students suffer . . . The ambiguous leadership made that we on one hand were told that we were free to create and be innovative, to work in an entrepreneurial way, on the other were given instructions to follow. This in my mind does not stimulate creativity. Instead it caused much confusion, inefficiency and a lot of duplication of work. (Male student)
>
> I did not feel comfortable with correcting information given because then it would not appear as a serious project which would make it more difficult to attract the firms . . . For sure we have participated in and developed a process and even if VYC's objective has remained the same—and appreciated by many as interesting and excellent—the ambiguous invitation [of potential employers] may make the venture uninteresting after all. My philosophy is to nurture my contacts and I do not want to confuse people with new information. (Female student)
>
> My main lesson from the project is that plans [are] not always realized. Our first intended project was cancelled all together and then Bengt tried to [make] the best of the situation and contacted Bernard. When neither the trade show realized we had to accept that . . . The most disappointing experience [however] is that not all students have been as inspired and motivated as Liam and myself. I have tried to energize the others but experienced quite a lot of negativism during the project. It is sad because VYC contributes to society, it is launched for a good cause. (Female student)

These reflections reveal that the emergent character of the VYC created a number of problems for the students. These included vague (democratic!) leadership and felt insecurity when approaching (commercial) enterprises with information concerning the intended trade show. However, as the third quote communicates, some students also realised that not just the management of SORIS and the venture was to blame for the situation that had emerged. They themselves were also responsible.

When formalized as a cooperative, VYC's board included the social entrepreneur (as the chairperson), another young immigrant academic as well as two students from the EDP programme and myself. In the autumn of 2014, VYC mediated a number of assignments but on a far smaller scale than planned. Instead, the EDP students themselves arranged an event that was detached from SORIS and targeted the local/regional business community. During spring 2015, the student representatives informed the VYC's board that they were going to leave it. Later that year, VYC was put on ice.

SORIS's Venturing as an Experience Shared Between Students and Staff

The accounts of the three ventures—summarized in Table 6.1 below—signal that the road to increased insight into entrepreneuring in general and social entrepreneuring in particular was more demanding than expected by both the students and me as the project leader. The student group involved in SNI felt like exploited workers, the students contributing to Gottfrid's Barn like

Table 6.1 SORIS's Social Ventures: An Overview

Venture feature	SNI	Gottfrid's Barn	VYC
Objective	Intensify collaboration between work-integrating social enterprises	Feasibility study of social enterprise	Establish a staffing enterprise, offering the competences of young people
Origin	Regional network of social organizations	Nascent social entrepreneurs	Converted young immigrant economist
Number of students	15	12	10
Venture leadership	Authoritative	Irresolute	Democratic
Student identity	Worker	Consultant	Entrepreneur
Process characteristic	Expediency	Ambivalence	Dialogue
Activities	Regular meetings, words as deeds	Market research	Feasibility study, enactment of cooperative
Immediate student experience	Shut-in feeling	Frustration	Insufficiency
Venture outcome (as for May 2015)	Institutionalized and granted innovation support	Not enacted, regionally recognised though	A registered cooperative with limited activities

mismanaged consultants and the student group engaged in VYC like failed entrepreneurs. Obviously, we underestimated the institutionalizing forces that already during their first semester had made the students into reluctant followers rather than would-be entrepreneurs. There seems to have been a need for unlearning such attitudes before deliberating their entrepreneurial selves through the SORIS project. However, the time needed for such a 'deconstruction' was simply not available.

The successful enactment of SORIS's three ventures was conditioned by the ability of the students concerned to produce concrete results by collaborating with both fellow students and practitioners under time pressure. The project management expected that the students' parallel internships in local businesses would have provided both practical experience and social skills. However, the students were only trained to work in teams of two and not ten or more. It thus turned out that horizontal interaction between students in and between the venture groups as well as the vertical ties to older and more experienced program mates were very limited.

SORIS's project management had to adapt its actions and interactions to both changing external conditions and the students' hesitant attitudes towards SORIS. Practically, this meant that the project assistant and I had to spend a lot of time either on facilitating for the students or simply doing what we originally considered to be their job. An attempt by me to trigger the students involved in Gottfrid's Barn to become more active by appealing to the objectives of their bachelor programme failed completely. The students considered my emailed exhortation as an insult, which reduced their commitment to the venture even more. Neither was the greater freedom offered the VYC students successful. Only a few students took any initiative and those who did were not very persistent. Although the student group developed several innovative ideas about how to get along, they never mobilized either the skills or the energy needed to implement them, partly due to competing activities both in their programme and outside the university.

The main reason for SORIS's limited success seems to have been unfulfilled expectations regarding both myself as its initiator and the students. I as the project leader, teacher and researcher had just experienced that several of the members of an older cohort of EDP students, then in their second year of the programme, had volunteered as mentors in the business start-up programme run by a local social enterprise. Thus, and with good reason, I imagined alert students ready to take action. They as freshmen in the programme on their part had expected a project that would have given them the opportunity and freedom to enact, at least initiate, (individual) own ventures reflecting their own interests. In high school, many of the students had explored commercial venturing in programmes such as Junior Achievement. Now the students were looking forward to the opportunity to unleash their creativity by venturing in a new context, the university. Although the students throughout the venturing processes were explicitly welcomed to take own initiatives, they failed to come. Several of the students combined their full-time studies with part-time work, but they seemed to keep the experiences gained there apart from their role as university students. Few of them, for example, mobilized the further resources that their personal connections outside the university might have brought to their venture.

SORIS's ventures as innovative ways of enacting social enterprises also had a difficult journey. This meant that goals had to be changed and ambitions reduced. As regards the SNI network, the social enterprises did not discuss specializing individually in order to collectively become more effective or tender jointly. Instead, SNI organized joint information, education and marketing activities that retained the individual enterprises. The two would-be entrepreneurs at Gottfrid's Barn attracted public attention, although the realisation of the venture remained hampered for financial and private reasons. The VYC venture barely survived the winter of 2014–15.

Conclusions: Social Entrepreneuring as an Existential Challenge

The enactment of SORIS addressed a double challenge. The main one was to identify the potential/benefits of training for and learning through social entrepreneuring by integrating individual, organizational and regional measures. The other challenge, conditioning the main one, was to build concrete bridges between the three generic tasks of all Swedish universities— 'research', 'education' and 'community dialogue'(cf. Figure 6.1). The students' individual and the university's organizational hardships tell that the enactment of SORIS obviously was a very demanding and arduous learning exercise. Did the ambition to make SORIS cover all three university tasks while adopting a regional perspective create more problems than support in our search for insight into social venturing as a road to enhancing university students' entrepreneurial capabilities?

There are at least five possible answers to this question. The first one is that experiential learning also includes gaining insight from mistakes (compare with Pittaway and Thorpe (2012, p. 852–853)). Nevertheless, some of the mistakes may have been avoided if the freshmen had been invited to an appreciative inquiry exercise during their first semester and accordingly been given the opportunity to contribute to both the contents and the design of SORIS, cf. Busche (1999). Such involvement might have made them more committed to the venturing exercise—and feel more responsible for mistakes made down the road (cf. Smith et al. (2008)). At least this might have made the students experience SORIS as an organized effort to create space for own initiatives and not as a reformatory, if not a prison (compare with Morgan (1998)).

A second possible answer is that the attempt to integrate the three university tasks through the enactment of SORIS was over-ambitious and drew attention from the objective to advance the students' learning in general and entrepreneurial capabilities in particular. However, it is an argument that does not hold considering that all valid university education must be based on rigorous research which in turn is expected to be relevant to society. Whatever the short-term effects, the relationships between the three tasks have to be nurtured in order to provide academic quality. The SORIS project suggests that such quality also should include measures taken by universities to enact a better world.

A third potential answer is that the regional/societal dimension of SORIS and implication in terms of involvement of multiple stakeholders simply made the whole exercise too complex for the students. The real-life conditions that were brought in by SORIS, such as institutional and/or organizational restrictions as well as need for systematic networking in order to amplify own resources, had not been experienced, let alone reflected upon, by the great majority of the students.

A fourth interpretation of the students' frustration in the context of SORIS is that it forced them to join a social venture that was alien to them as business school students. Gibb (2002) even argues that such students are so influenced by management thinking that it is difficult to turn them into entrepreneurial learners even in a commercial context, let alone in a social one.

Finally, a fifth possible explanation is that SORIS as a 'real' project with public financiers and further stakeholders had to be tightly governed in order to meet expectations, even obligations, and time restrictions. I did not take into consideration that there may be a trade-off between on one hand offering a learning context for students that pays due attention to their needs and gaining insight into entrepreneurial processes and meeting external expectations on the other.

None of these explanations is however satisfactory, separately or jointly. The students' reflections, as illustrated in the quotes above, show that they recognised the importance of becoming familiar also with social entrepreneuring and the value of the lessons learnt through that involvement. Accordingly, if entrepreneurial learning is recognised as an existential experience where the individual's self-identity is put at stake, a much more generative interpretation of the students' experiences in SORIS is accomplished. While participating in SORIS, the students went through a cognitive, emotional and conative catharsis that brought them out of their comfort zone (compare with (Snow, Corno & Jackson, 1996)). This breakout may have produced a pioneering and 'second-order' learning experience, suggesting that you have to challenge yourself in order to gain new insights. Csikszentmihalyi and Csikszentmihalyi (1988) and their notion of 'flow' supports this interpretation. Ideally, flow in any kind of practice appears as a 'corridor' of learning where challenges and competences balance, or rather are brought to balance, by increasing either the challenge or the competences. The original model of flow then suggests that when the challenge being encountered is perceived as overwhelming considering the own competences, a state of anxiety arises, whereas boredom characterizes

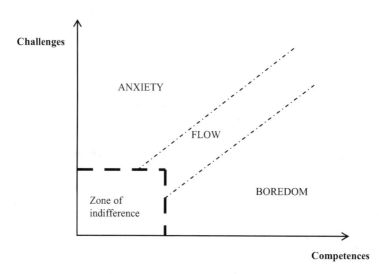

Figure 6.3 Balancing Challenges and Competences as a Trigger of Learning Processes
Source: Csikszentmihalyi and Csikszentmihalyi 1988.

a situation where the individual perceives her/himself as too competent for a task (see Figure 6.3).

The lesson taught by SORIS is that the balancing act only is effectuated if perceived own competences as well as experienced challenges both have moved beyond a minimum level. Below that level, a state of indifference or impassiveness rules. Lack of group dynamics seems to have kept the majority of the students in SORIS within this *zone of indifference*. To be successful, an entrepreneurial learning project thus must bring the students out of both their comfort zone and their indifference zone. This calls for engaged teachers as well as students who practice solidarity and mutual concern both within and beyond their own group.

Note

1. These contrasting images were represented by (Shane & Venkataraman 2000) and (Sarasvathy 2001). This part of the examination will not be discussed here.

References

Argyris, C. & Schön, D. A. (1974). *Theory in Practice: Increasing Professional Effectiveness*. San Francisco: Jossey-Bass.
Asheim, B. (2012). The Changing Role of Learning Regions in the Globalizing Knowledge Economy: A Theoretical Re-Examination. *Regional Studies*, 46(8), 993–1004.

Berglund, K., Johannisson, B. & Schwartz, B. (2012). *Societal Entrepreneurship—Positioning, Penetrating, Promoting*. Cheltenham: Edward Elgar.

Berglund, K. & Johansson, A. W. (2007). Entrepreneurship, Discourses and Conscientization in Processes of Regional Development. *Entrepreneurship & Regional Development*, 19(6), 499–525.

Busche, G. R. (1999). Advances in Appreciative Inquiry as an Organizational Development Intervention. *Organization Development Journal*, 17(2), 61–68.

Chang, J., Benamraoui, A. & Rieple, A. (2014). Learning-by-Doing as an Approach to Teaching Social Entrepreneurship. *Innovations in Education and Teaching International*, 51(5), 459–471.

Chia, R. & Holt, R. (2006). Strategy as Practical Coping: A Heideggerian Perspective. *Organization Studies*, 27, 635–655.

Christensen, T. & Laegreid, P. (2002). *New Public Management: The Transformation of Ideas and Practice*. Aldershot: Ashgate.

Cope, J. (2005). Toward a Dynamic Learning Perspective of Entrepreneurship. *Entrepreneurship Theory & Practice*, 29(4), 373–397.

Csikszentmihalyi, M. & Csikszentmihalyi, I. S. (1988). *Optimal Experience-Psychological Studies of Flow in Consciousness*. Cambridge, MA: Cambridge University Press.

Drucker, P. (1985). *Innovation and Entrepreneurship*. New York: Harper & Row.

Etzkowitz, H. & Leydesdorff, L. (2000). The Dynamics of Innovation: From National System and 'Mode 2' to a Triple Helix of University-Industry-Government Relations. *Research Policy*, 29(2), 109–123.

Flood, M., Martin, B. & Dreher, T. (2013). Combining Academia and Activism. *Australian Universities Review*, 55(1), 17–26.

Freire, P. (2001). *Pedagogy of Freedom: Ethics, Democracy, and Civic Courage*. Lanham, MA: Rowman & Littlefield.

Gherardi, S., Nicolini, D. & Odella, F. (1998). Toward a Social Understanding of How People Learn in Organizations: The Notion of Situated Curriculum. *Management Learning*, 29(3), 273–297.

Gibb, A. (2002). In Pursuit of a New 'Enterprise' and 'Entrepreneurship' Paradigm for Learning: Creative Destruction, New Ways of Doing Things and New Combinations of Knowledge. *International Journal of Management Reviews*, 4(3), 223–269.

Grabher, G. (2001). Ecologies of Creativity: The Village, the Group, and the Heterarchic Organisation of the British Advertising Industry. *Environment and Planning*, 33, 351–374.

Hjorth, D. (2012). *Handbook of Organizational Entrepreneurship*. Cheltenham: Edward Elgar.

Hjorth, D. & Johannisson, B. (2007). Learning as an Entrepreneurial Process. In A. Fayolle (Ed.), *Handbook of Research in Entrepreneurship Education, Volume 1. A General Perspective*. Cheltenham: Edward Elgar.

Howorth, C., Smith, S. M. & Parkinson, C. (2012). Social Learning and Social Entrepreneurship Education. *Academy of Management Learning & Education*, 11(3), 371–389.

Johannisson, B. (1991). University Training for Entrepreneurship: Swedish Approaches. *Entrepreneurship and Regional Development*, 3(1), 67–82.

Johannisson, B. (2011). Towards a Practice Theory of Entrepreneuring. *Small Business Economics*, 36, 135–150.

Johannisson, B. (2012). Tracking the Everyday Practices of Societal Entrepreneuring'. In K. Berglund, B. Johannisson & B. Schwartz (Eds.), *Societal*

Entrepreneurship—Positioning, Penetrating, Promoting. Cheltenham: Edward Elgar.

Johannisson, B. (2014a). Entrepreneurship: The Practice of Cunning Intelligence. In P. Braunerhjelm (Ed.), *20 Years of Entrepreneurship Research—From Small Business Dynamics to Entrepreneurial Growth and Societal Prosperity.* Stockholm: Swedish Entrepreneurship Forum.

Johannisson, B. (2014b). The Practice Approach and Interactive Research in Entrepreneurship and Small-Scale Venturing. In A. Carsrud & M. Brännback (Eds.), *Handbook of Research Methods and Applications in Entrepreneurship and Small Business.* Cheltenham, UK & Northampton, MA: Edward Elgar Publishing.

Lourenco, F., Jones, O. & Jayawarna, D. (2012). Promoting Sustainable Development: The Role of Entrepreneurship Education. *International Small Business Journal,* 3(8), 841–865.

Morgan, G. (1998). *Images of Organization.* Thousand Oaks, CA: Sage.

Pache, A. C. & Chowdhury, I. (2012). Social Entrepreneurs as Institutionally Embedded Entrepreneurs: Toward a New Model of Social Entrepreneurship Education. *Academy of Management Learning & Education,* 11(3), 494–510.

Pittaway, L. & Thorpe, R. (2012). A Framework for Entrepreneurial Learning: A Tribute to Jason Cope. *Entrepreneurship & Regional Development,* 24(9–10), 837–859.

Sarasvathy, S. D. (2001). Causation and Effectuation: Toward a Theoretical Shift from Economic Inevitability to Entrepreneurial Contingency. *Academy of Management Review,* 26(2), 243–263.

Schumpeter, J. A. (1943/1987). *Capitalism, Socialism and Democracy.* Sixth edition. London: Unwin.

Shane, S. & Venkataraman, S. (2000). The Promise of Entrepreneurship as a Field of Research. *Academy of Management Review,* 25(1), 217–226.

Smircich, L. & Morgan, G. (1982). Leadership: The Management of Meaning. *Journal of Applied Behavioural Science,* 18(3), 257–273.

Smith, B. R., Barr, T. F., Barbosa, S. & Kickul, J. R. (2008). Social Entrepreneurship: A Grounded Learning Approach to Social Value Creation. *Journal of Enterprising Culture,* 16(4), 339–362.

Snow, R. E., Corno, L. & Jackson III, D. (1996). Individual Differences in Affective and Conative Functions. In D. C. Berliner & R. C. Calfee (Eds.), *Handbook of Education Psychology.* New York: Simon and Schuster McMillan.

Steyaert, C. (2007). Entrepreneuring as a Conceptual Attractor? A Review of Process Theories in 20 years of Entrepreneurship Studies. *Entrepreneurship & Regional Development,* 19(6), 453–477.

Van de Ven, A. (2007). *Engaged Scholarship: A Guide for Organizational and Social Research.* Oxford: Oxford University Press.

Vesper, K. & Gartner, W. B. (1997). Measuring Progress in Entrepreneurship Education. *Journal of Business Venturing,* 12, 403–421.

Weick, K. E. (1969/1979). *The Social Psychology of Organizing.* Reading, MA: Addison-Wesley.

Weick, K. E. (1995). *Sensemaking in Organizations.* Thousand Oaks, CA: Sage Publications.

Wenger, E. (1998). *Communities of Practice: Learning, Meaning and Identity.* Cambridge: Cambridge University Press.

Ylinenpää, H. (2012). Entrepreneurship and Innovation Systems: Towards a Development of the ERIS/IRIS Concept. In B. Johannisson & Å. Lindholm Dahlstrand (Eds.), *Enacting Regional Dynamics and Entrepreneurship: Bridging the Territorial and Functional Rationales.* Abingdon: Routledge.

7 Employees as Social Intrapreneurs

Active Employee Participation in Social Innovation

Catharina Juul Kristensen

Employees form an important but less explored and utilized resource in social innovation in social welfare organizations in the third and public sectors. The employees have important knowledge of the everyday challenges of the organizations, the wishes and needs of their users and customers and of the local communities that can inspire and refine innovations. They are active, albeit not always consciously so, and potential social intrapreneurs. Although wider international research exists, the Nordic research seems to dominate the field. The aim of this chapter is to contribute to the existing research on employees as social intrapreneurs (the fields of employee-driven innovation and social intrapreneurship) by conceptualising active employee participation in social innovation and elucidating the potential and multiplicity of the phenomenon. The chapter is theoretically explorative.

Employees: A Resource in Social Innovation

Ordinary employees, such as social administrators, social workers and technicians, constitute an important but less acknowledged resource in the development of modern, sustainable social welfare organizations. Many employees possess valuable knowledge and experience of the everyday practice, procedures and problems at their workplace, and of its users, customers and collaborators that can spur or improve innovative initiatives and create value (Kristensen, 2011; Høyrup, Bonnafous-Boucher, Hasse, Lotz & Møller, 2012). They are active or potential social intrapreneurs.

The implementation of a professionally run, street-level night shelter for women in the Danish capital of Copenhagen is just one example of such social intrapreneurship. In Copenhagen, an academic municipal administrator played an important role in the enhancement of the knowledge and awareness of socially vulnerable and excluded women among administrators, practitioners and politicians during the late 1990s and early 2000s. Through collegial collaboration and persistent networking and negotiation, her work laid the ground of the creation of the night shelter. The work was later taken over by others. The night shelter constitutes an innovative supplement to the (few) existing women's shelters in the city by offering anonymous help, advice and, of course, shelter for women in crisis. It is run by a non-profit organization in collaboration with the municipality (Kristensen, 2012).

The aim of this chapter is to conceptualise employee participation in innovations in social welfare organizations, that is, social intrapreneurship by employees, and to present a theoretical framework for an analysis of the phenomenon. Social intrapreneurship by employees holds, is the underlying thesis argued for here, great importance for the development of welfare services and products in challenged welfare states such as the Nordic welfare states. The chapter is theoretically explorative. The empirical examples included are chosen to illustrate some of the theoretical points made. They are all research based.

The exploration focuses on *active* participation by employees in social innovation processes. The employees not only produce, implement, provide or sell innovations: they influence the innovation processes and the services and products produced. The employees furthermore generate social, economic and other forms of value on behalf of their workplace.

Active employee participation in social innovation constitutes a somewhat neglected but developing field of study. Although wider international research exists, the Nordic research seems to predominate.[1] These countries have a relatively long history of active employee participation in formal and informal organizational change and decision-making processes. Furthermore, the employees experience a relatively high degree of work autonomy (Åmo, 2006; Jacobsen, 2010). This may also encourage active participation in innovation processes and research interest in these.

The chapter first encircles and defines the form of innovation found in social welfare organizations: social innovation. Along with the subsequent account of the central concept of intrapreneurship and its private sector heritage, the section forms the theoretical setting for the exploration of social intrapreneurship and social intrapreneurs. The scene is then almost set for the conceptualisation of the phenomenon of employees as social intrapreneurs. An additional concept, which focuses explicitly on innovative employees, is presented, namely the Danish-coined concept of employee-driven innovation. After defining the concept of innovative employees, two general forms of innovation involving employee initiative and action are introduced: bottom-linked and bottom-based innovation. Whereas bottom-linked innovation includes active collaboration and negotiations between managers and employees, the small, tacit innovations at the 'bottom' of the organization are often unacknowledged by management. In the final section, the key concepts are recapitulated and discussed.

Social Innovation

Social innovation concerns innovation, creativity and change-oriented action with the wide goal of creating social value. Whereas it was possible to identify two general approaches to social innovation within Western European research only five or six years ago—a more pragmatic, praxis-oriented approach represented by, among others, Mulgan (2006), and the explicitly critical, empowerment and change-oriented approach represented by Moulaert and colleagues (see e.g. Moulaert, Martinelli, Swyngedouw & González, 2005; MacCallum, Moulaert, Hillier & Haddock, 2009)—the picture is more blurred today (Kristensen, 2015). This chapter draws on both these traditions.

In his definition, Mulgan emphasises the aim and the organizational anchorage of social innovation. The aim is to meet new or known social needs in organizations whose primary aim is to create social value. Social innovation thus "refers to innovative activities and services that are motivated by the goal of meeting a social need and that are predominantly diffused through organizations whose primary purpose are social" (Mulgan, 2006, p. 146). This type of innovation can in principle be carried out by organizations in the public, third and private sectors, or in collaboration between these. In this chapter, the focus is delimited to social innovations in non-profit organizations, i.e., social welfare organizations in the third and public sectors.

The term social value is an inclusive term, covering a wide range of activities at different societal levels. Social value here includes a variety of non-for-profit initiatives that benefit different groups of users and citizens, the organization and/or the local community. Social value can be generated by improving services, expanding social services to embrace previously neglected groups of citizens and by improving the living conditions in a local community through inclusive, empowering change processes. Social value creation is often combined with the generation of economic value. But the former is again the primary purpose. If an economic surplus is generated, it is used to benefit the organization and its users, not private investors or owners. Value creation can further include the creation of democratic, cultural and aesthetic values (Thompson, 2002; Mair & Martí, 2006; Moulaert, 2009).

Like other types of innovations, social innovations vary in scale and effect. Whereas some innovations involve the development of something radically new within a specific area (radical innovations), others are small, delimited or incremental. In practice, innovations take different forms. They may thus start out as small and almost unnoticeable innovations and develop into larger and more radical innovations over time. Often, these developments can only be identified retrospectively (Sundbo, 1997; Kristensen, 2012).

Newness constitutes an important factor in the conceptual distinction between change and innovation. In contrast to change, innovations thus have to represent something new. But what constitutes this 'something new'? Whereas some researchers define innovations as a discontinuity, a break with former practice (Osborne, 1998; Osborne & Brown, 2005), others weigh the power and scale of the initiatives (Light, 1998). In line with

Swedberg (2000), two general forms of innovations are included in this current delimitation of the phenomenon: innovations can represent something radically new or be based on combinations of known and new knowledge used in new ways or in new contexts. Innovations are furthermore seen to form a break with former practice, but this break can equally be created through single initiatives and incremental change.

Finally, the innovative ideas must be put into practice and create value. This value can be created at all stages of the innovation process—not only in the final stage of the service provision or sale. The involved employees and managers may have gained new useful knowledge during the process, new professional networks may have been formed and users and citizens may have enjoyed improved living conditions or health during the initial implementation and refinement. Social innovation can lastly generate critically founded social change, as well as social improvements within the existing societal, social and organizational structures (Moulaert et al., 2005; Kristensen, 2015).

In order to capture the multiplicity of active employee participation in social innovation and to accentuate the importance of the organization as the setting of the employees' innovative activities, this theoretical inquiry takes its outset in research on intrapreneurship and corporate entrepreneurship.

Social Intrapreneurship and the Invisibility of Employees

The vast majority of research on intrapreneurship and the related concepts of corporate entrepreneurship engage with private sector organizations. Although diverse, two main conceptions of intrapreneurship can be identified: intrapreneurship as the creation of new ventures within corporations/organizations (organizational proliferation), and intrapreneurship as entrepreneurship and innovation within existing organizations (Antoncic & Hisrich, 2003; Sharma & Chrisman, 2007; Kristensen, 2011). As Antoncic and Hisrich elaborate:

> Intrapreneurship refers not only to the creation of new business ventures, but also to other innovative activities and orientations such as development of new products, services, technologies, administrative techniques, strategies and competitive postures.
>
> (Antoncic & Hisrich, 2003, p. 9)

A number of different innovative and entrepreneurial activities are thus possible.

The private sector research within this field has a pronounced management perspective and/or focus on what is articulated as the necessity of management strategies and organizational change processes to facilitate intra-organizational innovation to increase the organizations' competitiveness and sustainability (see, e.g., Kanter, 1985; Chisholm, 1987; Seshadri &

Tripathy, 2006). When mentioned, the intrapreneurs are often identified as middle managers or as more diffuse groups of managers and employees (Kanter, 1982, 1985; Hisrich, 1990; Sundbo, 1996; Brunåker & Kurvinen, 2006). This is now changing. Employees are slowly but increasingly seen as important actors and, in all its ambiguity, unexploited sources of innovation (Kristensen & Voxted, 2009; Kesting & Ulhøi, 2010). Their innovative work can be utilized in more or less management-led processes in order to maintain or improve the performance of organizations.

The research on *social* intrapreneurship builds on, and is in some instances perhaps best described as, a proliferation of the private sector research. Most of this research includes organizations from all three societal sectors. Yusuf's work is a case in point. In her definition, social intrapreneurship "encompasses entrepreneurial activity that generates social value undertaken within the confines of an organization, either in the private, public or non-profit sectors" (Yusuf, 2005, p. 121). Social value creation is present, but is not necessarily the primary purpose of the organizations. She adds, however, that government and non-profit organizations are the heart of social intrapreneurship, as they have "discovered and put into practice opportunities to create value by fulfilling unmet societal needs or finding better ways to deliver products or services" (Yusuf, 2005, p. 121). In this chapter, private sector organizations are excluded, as their primary aim is to create an economic surplus for private owners.

As is the case within intrapreneurship research in general, *active* employee participation is less explored within social intrapreneurship. When focusing on innovation in the Nordic countries, however, more research is found. This present inquiry into employees as social intrapreneurs is informed by the insights of the research on employee-driven innovation. The term employee-driven innovation was coined in Denmark in the mid-2000s. The first reports on the matter were published (LO, 2007, 2008), and the concept was used in different national political strategy papers on innovation (Regeringen, 2006; Forsknings- og Innovationsstyrelsen, 2008). Around the same time, the first research-based conceptualisations were published (Klitmøller, Lauring & Christensen, 2007; Kristensen & Voxted, 2009; Høyrup, 2010). Today, the concept is gaining ground in the Nordic and in other European countries (see, e.g., Høyrup et al., 2012; Wihlman, Hoppe, Wihlman & Sandmark, 2014).

Employee-Driven Innovation: Employees as Social Intrapreneurs

The notion employee-driven innovation is based on the thesis that given the right circumstances, all groups of employees can contribute to innovation processes at their workplace. The employees in question are thus employees who are not formally employed to initiate or facilitate innovation. They can hold different formal positions within the organization and carry out different work tasks. They are ordinary employees (Kristensen & Voxted, 2009). Existing studies suggest that innovative employees are encouraged and provoked by factors such as the awareness of unmet social problems and needs, demands of change and innovation, and professional ambition. The employees tacitly carry out the innovative work as a part of their everyday work activities or visibly and persistently negotiate the necessary support and resources to implement their ideas (Hubbard & Ottoson, 1997; Kristensen, 2012; Voxted, Kristensen & Hagedorn-Rasmussen, 2015).

Employee-driven innovation implies active participation by the employees. They thus partake in and influence the innovation processes and products. In their work, Kristensen and Voxted propose the following definition:

> Employee-driven innovation is innovation processes where employees' ideas, knowledge, time and creativity are put into play. The innovation processes involve the generation, acceptance and implementation of new ideas, processes, products and services in all types of organizations.
> (Kristensen & Voxted, 2009, author's translation)

Employee-driven innovation can be part of management strategies and initiatives, be initiated by employees or emerge from collaboration between managers, employees and other stakeholders. Beyond initiating innovations, the employees may be actively involved in or lead such processes.

Although emphasising the dynamic and hence changeable nature of innovation processes, the work of Kristensen and Voxted (2009) and others (e.g. Van de Ven, Polley, Garud & Venkataraman, 2008) delimits idea creation and development to specific, identifiable phases. In other studies, however, the idea creation has shown to be a long and complex process, including the identification of new and unmet social needs, gathering knowledge and creation of entrepreneurial opportunities to meet these, and requiring persistence (Piihl, 2011; Kristensen, 2012; Mulgan, 2012).

In their inspiring work, Mair and Martí define social entrepreneurship as "a process involving the innovative use and combination of resources to pursue opportunities to catalyse social change and/or address social needs" (Mair & Martí, 2006, p. 37). Employees, managers and other stakeholders can consequently be seen as actors who more or less deliberately observe and utilize opportunities of innovation. As Piihl (2011) argues, the opportunities of entrepreneurship and innovation can also be created by the actors. Innovators thus not only observe and utilize opportunities, they can also create them.

Based on these insights, *innovative employees* are defined as employees who create, observe and utilize opportunities of social innovation on behalf of their workplace. These employees can either take initiative to innovate themselves or be invited to participate actively in such processes by managers or other stakeholders. The innovative employees contribute their ideas, knowledge, creativity, persistence and time. The employees finally make up a central group of *social intrapreneurs*. The other groups are managers and perhaps also volunteers. The social intrapreneurs all engage in social intrapreneurship. They undertake entrepreneurial activity that generates value in or on behalf of their workplace.

In the below section, the concepts of bottom-linked and bottom-based innovation are presented. The concepts elucidate and facilitate the analysis of two important forms of social intrapreneurship involving active employee participation: collaborative innovation between employees and managers, and tacit everyday innovations amongst employees.

Bottom-Linked and Bottom-Based Innovation

Employee participation in innovation processes is often associated with bottom-up processes or described as such, and contrasted to top-down innovations, i.e., innovations initiated and led by top management or politicians (Osborne & Brown, 2005; Bason, 2007; Høyrup, 2010). Although the role of middle managers in such processes is also stressed, the conceptual dichotomy of bottom-up and top-down innovation easily disguises the collaboration between managers and employees in innovation processes on the one hand, and the tacit, small-scale innovations implemented by employees as part of their everyday work activity on the other. Recent empirical studies show that such innovations are indeed taking place (Andersen, 2008; Sundbo, 2008; Kristensen & Voxted, 2009; Voxted et al., 2015). The concepts of bottom-linked and bottom-based innovation offer a conceptualisation of these.

Bottom-linked innovation refers to innovations created in more or less planned collaboration between managers and employees (Kristensen, 2011). The concept thus bridges the conceptual dichotomy of bottom-up and top-down innovation within organizations. Bottom-linked innovations can be based on ideas posed and developed by managers and employees or in collaboration between the two groups and implemented and consolidated in the same way. The managers involved may be managers at different levels, i.e., middle managers and top managers. In his work, Sundbo argues that innovation processes involving the bottom level of organizations (i.e., employees and middle managers) and top managers appear naturally in all organizations and may form part of a formal innovation strategy (Sundbo, 2008). Such collaboration is also possible between middle managers and employees (Kristensen & Voxted, 2009). Here, the middle managers are seen as central actors in social intrapreneurship, as they may facilitate and negotiate resources and support of innovations (Kanter, 1982; Cummings, Phillips, Tilbrook & Lowe, 2005; Sundbo, 2008). They constitute the formal link to other middle managers and to the top management.

Finally, the ability to create supportive formal and informal networks or different forms of social capital seems pertinent in all types of social innovation processes (Sundin & Tillmar, 2008; Westlund & Gawell, 2012). These are likely to be created by employees as well as by managers.

In a case study in a Danish public sector institution, the manager was found to use bottom-linked innovation as an active tool in the development of a new employment programme for the long-term unemployed, thus encouraging and demanding active and inventive participation by her employees. The employees contributed with professional, knowledge-based ideas of in-house activities and external practice training, social work methods and of possible external collaborators (experts, companies and external colleagues). The ideas were discussed, dismissed or developed by the employees and the manager at staff meetings and workshops, and the most viable ones were then selected by the manager, implemented and adjusted. The process resulted in a successful innovative programme for the unemployed (Kristensen & Voxted, 2009).

The concept of *bottom-based innovation* concerns the many inconspicuous and informal innovations that are believed to take place in organizations without the knowledge or attention of management (Andersen, 2008; Voxted, 2011). Studies show that the innovative employees behind such innovations do not always see their initiatives as innovative. They are just doing their job or finding better ways to meet management goals (Voxted, 2011; Voxted et al., 2015).

Bottom-based innovation is innovations coined and implemented by employees without the participation or attention of management. They unfold at the bottom level of the organization. They are practice-based innovations, drawing on everyday creativity and workplace learning (Ellström, 2010) to solve everyday tasks and challenges in better or more effective ways. In order for such innovations to move from the spheres of the innovative employees, they must be observed, critically evaluated and perhaps also developed. Managers must, in other words, observe and strategically utilize the most viable bottom-based innovations. Bottom-based innovations can thus become bottom linked or perhaps taken over by management and diffused to other parts of the organization.

Bottom-based innovations may seem unimportant or even inferior at first sight. The creation of an indoor meeting place for social workers and homeless women studied by Juul Kristensen in 2011 is a case in point. In their quest to get in contact with and help the homeless women they met on the streets, two Danish social workers decided to negotiate the allocation of an indoor site where they could meet with the women. The street workers in the municipal Homelessness Unit had not previously had such a site. The room was allocated by the municipality on the condition that no costs were involved. On the streets, the homeless women often mixed with other people, and it was thus difficult to have conversations about personal and sensitive issues. The social drop-in facilities and commercial cafes were not suitable either. The room solved the social workers' problem and improved the quality of their work. The indoor meetings constituted an important means to help the women and to meet the formal politico-administrative goals. No meeting place—no viable contact—no help.

No help—no reduction of social needs. Small-scale, bottom-based innovations like this is not captured by an analysis of formal innovation strategies or bottom-linked initiatives. As they are inconspicuous and tacit in nature, they require an analytical employee-based perspective.

Conclusion

The aim of this chapter has been to conceptualise intrapreneurship by employees in social welfare organizations, and thus to present a theoretical outset for empirical analyses of this important phenomenon. As a first step in this quest, social innovation was defined as innovation processes that are undertaken by organizations whose primary purpose is social. Such non-profit organizations generally aim to create social value for the organization, its users or a wider community, but other forms of value can also be created. Their activities can thus aim to change exiting socio-political structures and practices, and improve or supplement existing services and products. In concurrence with this definition, social intrapreneurship was defined as innovative and entrepreneurial activities in social welfare organizations.

The concept of social intrapreneurs not only includes employees, but also managers who innovate on behalf of their workplace. The emphasis has naturally been on the employees. These innovative employees are defined as employees who create, observe and utilize opportunities of social innovation on behalf of their workplace or are invited to participate actively in such activities. The innovative employees contribute with their ideas, knowledge, creativity, persistence and time. They are, among other things, motivated, provoked and pressured by demands of change and increased efficiency, and by the observation of unmet social needs and neglected social problems.

The employees often create and implement social innovations in collaboration with colleagues and managers, but some are implemented in tacit and more solitary ways. The innovations can be part of formal innovation strategies, be less formalized or non-conscious, i.e., not articulated or perceived of as innovations. Two such general types of innovations were termed and defined: bottom-linked and bottom-based innovations. Whereas bottom-linked innovations are created in more or less planned interaction between managers and employees, bottom-based innovations are created and implemented by employees without the participation or attention of management. They unfold at the bottom level of organizations.

In order to meet the current demands of up-to-date, high-quality services and inter-organizational competition and create sustainable social welfare organizations on the one hand, and meet the current challenges of the welfare states on the other, the employees' innovative and entrepreneurial activities call for equally innovative and entrepreneurial managers and politicians. These central actors must consciously observe, encourage, acknowledge and support social intrapreneurship by employees, and thus conscientiously and strategically utilize its potential.

The chapter has so far focused on the positive contributions of employees. But employees can, of course, also oppose and obstruct innovation. The resistance to innovation can be caused by groups of employees (or managers) who fear that their status and formal position within the organization will be threatened, or that power relations will change in unfavourable ways. Some may dislike or feel stressed by change. Others may not be convinced by the necessity or prospects of the proposed or enforced innovations—and perhaps rightfully so (Shane, 1995; Kanter, 2000; Janssen, Van de Vliert & West, 2004; Seshadri & Tripathy, 2006; Jacobsen, 2010; Kristensen, 2011). Critique and resistance can also be productive. These matters are important to include in empirical analyses of social intrapreneurship by employees.

It is furthermore important to recognise the different statuses of hierarchies and struggles of interest and power within organizations, not only between managers and employees, but also between employees. Collaboration can be a productive but also a highly politicised and competitive venture. In this chapter, the employees are treated as a unified and homogenous group. In practice, the group is likely to be heterogeneous. The employees are not only employed by the same organization, they hold different formal positions, have different educational backgrounds and work experience and are thus likely to be ascribed different statuses and power within the organizations. This can both spur and obstruct collaboration and innovation.

While this chapter contributes to the exploration of one important but neglected group of social intrapreneurs, it leaves another, the volunteers, almost invisible. Future empirical studies of social intrapreneurship in social welfare organizations should also focus on the role of the volunteers in innovations and their possible collaboration with employees and managers. Seen in a Nordic perspective, volunteers are primarily found in third-sector organizations, but local authorities in Sweden, Norway and Denmark have recently opened up to the possibility of using volunteers. It may thus become a more widespread phenomenon.

Note

1. This is based on a literature search on employee participation in innovation in the public and third sector carried out by the Roskilde University Library and on literature studies by the author. Note also Crepaldi et al. (2012).

References

Åmo, B. W. (2006). Employee Innovation Behaviour in Health Care: The Influence from Management and Colleagues. *International Nursing Review*, 53, 231–237.
Andersen, O. J. (2008). A Bottom-Up Perspective on Innovations: Mobilizing Knowledge and Social Capital Through Innovative Processes of Bricolage. *Administration & Society*, 40(1), 54–78.

Antoncic, B. & Hisrich, R. D. (2003). Clarifying the Intrapreneurship Concept. *Journal of Small Business and Enterprise Development*, 10(1), 7–24.

Bason, Chr. (2007). *Velfærdsinnovation: Ledelse af nytænkning i den offentlige sektor København*. Børsens: Forlag.

Brunåker, S. & Kurvinen, J. (2006). Intrapreneurship, Local Initiatives in Organizational Change Processes. *Leadership & Organization Development Journal*, 27(2), 118–132.

Chisholm, T. A. (1987). Intrapreneurship and Bureaucracy. *S.A.M. Advanced Management Journal*, 52(3), 36–40.

Crepaldi, C., De Rosa, E. & Pesce, F. (2012). *Literature Review on Innovation in Social Services in Europe (Sectors of Health, Education and Welfare Services)* Report. Work Package 1. Milano: Istituto per la Ricerca Sociale/The European Commission

Cummings, R., Phillips, R., Tilbrook, R. & Lowe, K. (2005). Middle-Out Approaches to Reform of University Teaching and Learning: Champions Striding Between the "Top-down" and "Bottom-Up" Approaches. *International Review of Research in Open and Distance Learning*, 6(1), 1–18.

Ellström, P. E. (2010). Practice-Based Innovation: A Learning Perspective. *Journal of Workplace Learning*, 22(1/2), 27–40.

Forsknings- og Innovationsstyrelsen. (2008). *Strategi for styrket innovation i den offentlige sektor*. København: Forsknings- og Innovationsstyrelsen/Rådet for Teknologi og Udvikling.

Hisrich, R. D. (1990). Entrepreneurship/Intrapreneurship. *American Psychologist*, 45(2), 209–222.

Hubbard, L. A. & Ottoson, J. M. (1997). When Bottom-Up Innovation Meets Itself as a Top-down Policy: The AVID Untracking Program. *Science Communication*, 19(1), 41–55.

Høyrup, S. (2010). Employee-Driven Innovation and Workplace Learning: Basic Concepts, Approaches and Themes. *European Trade Union Institute, etui, Transfer*, 16(2), 143–154.

Høyrup, S., Bonnafous-Boucher, M., Hasse, C., Lotz, M. & Møller, K. (2012). *Employee-Driven Innovation: A New Approach*. Houndsmill: Palgrave Macmillan.

Jacobsen, D. I. (2010). Deltakelse som virkemiddel i organisatoriske erindrings processer—et tveegget sverd? In H. Kundsen, J. Falkenberg, K. Grønhaug & Å. Garnes (Eds.), *Mysterion, strategike og kainotomia*. Oslo: Novus Forlag.

Janssen, O., Van de Vliert, E. & West, M. (2004). The Bright and Dark Sides of Individual and Group Innovation: A Special Issue Introduction. *Journal of Organizational Behaviour*, 25, 129–145.

Kanter, R. M. (1982). The Middle Manager as Innovator. *Harvard Business Review*, 60(4), 95–105.

Kanter, R. M. (1985). *The Change Masters: Corporate Entrepreneurs at Work*. London: Unwin Paperbacks.

Kanter, R. M. (2000, first published in 1991). When a Thousand Flowers Bloom: Structural, Collective and Social Conditions for Innovation in Organizations. In R. Swedberg (Ed.), *Entrepreneurship: The Social Science View*. Oxford: Oxford University Press.

Kesting, P. & Ulhøi, J. P. (2010). Employee-Driven Innovation: Extending the License to Foster Innovation. *Management Decision*, 48(1), 65–84.

Klitmøller, A., Lauring, J. & Christensen, P. R. (2007). Medarbejderdreven innovation i den offentlige sektor. *Ledelse & Erhvervsøkonomi*, 4, 207–216.

Kristensen, C. J. (2011). Medarbejderdrevet innovation. In C. J. Kristensen & S. Voxted (Eds.), *Innovation og entreprenørskab*. København: Hans Reitzels Forlag.

Kristensen, C. J. (2012). Social innovation i indsatsen for hjemløse kvinder— tilblivelsen af en natcafé. *Dansk Sociologi*, 23(4), 55–73.

Kristensen, C. J. (2015). Social innovation og socialt entreprenørskab. In B. Greve (Ed.), *Socialvidenskabelig grundbog: Fem perspektiver*. Frederiksberg: Nyt fra Samfundsvidenskaberne.

Kristensen, C. J. & Voxted, S. (2009). *Innovation: Medarbejder og bruger*. København: Hans Reitzels Forlag.

Light, P. (1998). *Sustaining Innovation: Creating Nonprofit and Government Orientations That Innovate Naturally*. San Francisco: Jossey-Bass Publishers.

LO. (2007). *Employee-Driven Innovation—A Trade Union Priority for Growth and Job Creation in a Globalised Economy*. Copenhagen: LO, the Danish Confederation of Trade Unions.

LO. (2008). *Employee-Driven Innovation: Improving Economic Performance and Job Satisfaction*. Copenhagen: LO, the Danish Confederation of Trade Unions.

MacCallum, D., Moulaert, F., Hillier, J. & Haddock, S. V. (2009). Introduction. In D. MacCallum, F. Moulaert, J. Hillier & S. V. Haddock (Eds.), *Social Innovation and Territorial Development*. Aldershot: Ashgate.

Mair, J. & Martí, I. (2006). Social Entrepreneurship Research: A Source of Explanation, Prediction, and Delight. *Journal of World Business*, 41, 36–44.

Moulaert, F. (2009). Social Innovation: Institutionally Embedded, Territorially (Re) Produced. In D. MacCallum, F. Moulaert, J. Hillier & S. V. Haddock (Eds.), *Social Innovation and Territorial Development*. Aldershot: Ashgate.

Moulaert, F., Martinelli, F., Swyngedouw, E. & González, S. (2005). Towards Alternative Model(s) of Local Innovation. *Urban Studies*, 42(11), 1969–1990.

Mulgan, G. (2006). The Process of Social innovation. *Innovations*, 1(2), 145–162.

Mulgan, G. (2012). The Theoretical Foundations of Social Innovation. In A. Nicholls & A. Murdock (Eds.), *Social Innovation: Blurring Boundaries to Reconfigure Markets*. Basingstoke: Palgrave Macmillan.

Osborne, S. P. (1998). Naming the Beast: Defining and Classifying Service Innovations in Social Policy. *Human Relations*, 51(9), 1133–1154.

Osborne, S. P. & Brown, K. (2005). *Managing Change and Innovation in Public Service Organizations*. London: Routledge.

Piihl, J. (2011). Entreprenørielle muligheder—diffusion eller translation? In C. J. Kristensen & S. Voxted (Eds.), *Innovation og entreprenørskab*. København: Hans Reitzels Forlag.

Regeringen (2006). *Fremgang, fornyelse og tryghed: Strategi for Danmark i den globale økonomi*. København: Statsministeriet.

Seshadri, D. V. R. & Tripathy, A. (2006). Innovation Through Intrapreneurship: The Road Less Travelled. *Vikalpa*, 31(1), 17–29.

Shane, S. (1995). Uncertainty Avoidance and the Preference for Innovation Championing Roles. *Journal of International Business Studies*, 26(1), 47–68.

Sharma, P. &. Chrisman, S. J. J. (2007, first published in 1999). Toward a Reconciliation of the Definitional Issues in the Field of Corporate Entrepreneurship. In Á. Cuervo, D. Ribeiro & R. Salvador (Eds.), *Entrepreneurship: Concepts, Theory and Perspective*. Berlin & New York: Springer Verlag.

Sundbo, J. (1996). The Balancing of Empowerment: A Strategic Resource Based Model of Organizing Innovation Activities in Service and Low-tech Firms. *Technovation*, 16(8), 397–409.

Sundbo, J. (1997). Management of Innovation in Services. *The Service Industries Journal*, 17(3), 432–455.

Sundbo, J. (2008). Innovation and Involvement in Services. In L. Fuglsang (Ed.), *Innovation and the Creative Process*. Cheltenham: Edward Elgar.

Sundin, E. & Tillmar, M. (2008). A Nurse and a Civil Servant Changing Institutions: Entrepreneurial Processes in Different Public Sector Organizations. *Scandinavian Journal of Management*, 24(2), 113–124.

Swedberg, R. (2000). The Social Science View of Entrepreneurship: Introduction and Practical Applications. In R. Swedberg (Ed.), *Entrepreneurship: The Social Science View*. Oxford: Oxford University Press.

Thompson, J. L. (2002). The World of the Social Entrepreneur. *The International Journal of Public Sector Management*, 15(5), 412–431.

Van de Ven, A. H., Polley, D. E., Garud, R. & Venkataraman, S. (2008, first published in 1999). *The Innovation Journey*. New York: Oxford University Press.

Voxted, S. (2011). Upåagtet innovation. In C. J. Kristensen & S. Voxted (Eds.), *Innovation og entreprenørskab*. København: Hans Reitzels Forlag.

Voxted, S., Kristensen, C. J. & Hagedorn-Rasmussen, P. (2015). *Lederens rolle i den innovative praksis*. København: Væksthus for Ledelse.

Westlund, H. & Gawell, M. (2012). Building Social Capital for Social Entrepreneurship. *Annals of Public and Cooperative Economics*, 83(1), 101–116.

Wihlman, T., Hoppe, M., Wihlman, U. & Sandmark, H. (2014). Employee-Driven Innovation in Welfare Services. *Nordic Journal of Working Life Studies*, 2(2), 159–180.

Yusuf, J. E. (2005). Putting Entrepreneurship in Its Rightful Place: A Typology for Defining Entrepreneurship Across Private, Public and Nonprofit Sectors. *Academy of Entrepreneurship Journal*, 11(2), 113–127.

8 The Added Value of Social Entrepreneurship in Contemporary Social Design in Norway

Brita Fladvad Nielsen and Jonas Asheim

Social designers and social entrepreneurs share the common goal of improving life quality through products and services. These two approaches are, however, to a large extent separated. This chapter explores differences and similarities with the aim to discuss meeting points of the two in the contemporary and geographically focused context of Norway. Insights on the 'social designer' extracted from six open-ended interviews are compared with the image of the 'social entrepreneur' found in a selection of social entrepreneurship literature. A central finding is that social designers are trained to emphasise empathy and environmentally sustainable solutions, whereas social entrepreneurs strengthen the economic sustainability of design solutions as well as providing the necessary leadership and risk-taking role that designers often feel they lack. Increased partnerships between social entrepreneurs and social designers could lead to empathic, user-centred and environmentally sustainable business models that can meet the increasing demands form the Norwegian public sector and potentially also in other geographical areas.

The Convergence of Perspectives

Public sector actors in the Nordic countries are increasingly looking to include the private sector in solving emerging social challenges. One illustration of this tendency is that the Norwegian State from 2005 until 2013 increased its spending on private welfare services for the Norwegian population for more than 30 per cent in order to complement what the public service system could offer (Aarøy, 2013). Social entrepreneurship is generally seen as an ethically defendable alternative to for-profit privatization by social democratic governments. In order to support the creation of social enterprises within Norway, research communities and political institutions put emphasis on clearly defining social entrepreneurship (Galera & Borzaga, 2009; Järvenpää, 2012)

Simultaneously, designers are experiencing a growing demand from public sector and non-profit organizations that recruit designers for the purpose of solving social challenges through design. Designers apply 'designerly'

(Cross, 2001, 2006) analytic approaches centred around ways of understanding the end user and create solutions based on this insight; approaches frequently referred to as 'design thinking' (Rowe, 1991; Brown, 2008; Wylant, 2008; Stickdorn & Schneider, 2010).

Within design literature, social design is often defined as a design or a design process that contributes to improving human well-being and livelihood. Defining the social designer and her or his characteristics is secondary in literature. Social designers are inspired by ideas of what the mission of the designer should be, such as Papanek and Fuller (1972), who argue that designers have a responsibility to create positive change through design (Papanek & Fuller, 1972). Design literature includes many thoughts on what are the designer's approach should be, whereas less is known about the designer's individual characteristics and skills needed in order to apply tools and meet these responsibilities as 'world changers'. Social entrepreneurship literature, on the other hand, includes many descriptions of the 'social entrepreneur' (Leadbeater, 1997; Dees, 1998; Barendsen & Gardner, 2004). These are characteristics perceived as necessary to run a social enterprise, an enterprise based on the human as the main capital rather than profit.

Designers are left wondering what the role of social design should be in relation to social entrepreneurship due to the increased focus within politics and research on this area. In order to discuss what this role should be, an understanding of the current situation should be created as a starting point for a debate. This study therefore seeks to explore the convergences and divergences between social entrepreneurs and social designers. This contribution will be useful both to policy makers and researchers in both the design and social entrepreneur fields. For designers, it will highlight areas for improvement and partnership, while the study and analysis will add to a 'definition' of the social entrepreneur in Norway by seeking to draw a boundary between social entrepreneurship and the related field of social design.

Research Question and Literature Selection

The question this chapter answers is: how can the added value of social entrepreneurs in contemporary socially responsible design in Norway be understood?

The research question was based on the notion that social entrepreneurship is a growing field, whereas social design has similar values yet seems to not get similar attention by the research community at the time of writing. We selected the literature based on that they included descriptive studies and ideas of what social entrepreneurship is. In other words, the more normative, value-oriented perspectives were selected. These were identified in a few early influencers from European and USA traditions (Leadbeater, 1997; Dees, 1998; Barendsen & Gardner, 2004; Kidwell, 2015) that are devoted to defining which *characteristics* are required to be a successful 'social entrepreneur'. Within social entrepreneurship research, there is an increasing amount of emerging efforts in Northern Europe that are describing social entrepreneurship in the Nordic countries, for example, through the Social Entrepreneurship Research Network for the Nordic Countries initiative. These types of research networks have resulted in an increase in country- and sector-specific insights on the potential of social innovation and enterprise in Nordic countries (Järvenpää, 2012). There has been no equivalent initiative in the same geographic region to define the role of the social designer in public-private partnerships. Therefore, a descriptive comparison of 'the social designer' and the 'social entrepreneur' in the Norwegian context will be presented in this chapter.

Due to the lack of geographically based studies focused on the characteristics of the social designers, the authors decided to conduct interviews with the purpose of extracting the data necessary for making such an analysis. The method choice is therefore based on the assumption that the description of a social designer is, as the social entrepreneur, highly context driven.

First, prominent characteristics of 'the social entrepreneur' and 'the social designer' were extracted through a literature review. Next, the perspectives from six semi-structured interviews with social designers were analysed. By comparing the interview data to a sample of influential academic descriptions of the social entrepreneur, a model is presented showing the overlaps and differences between social designers and social entrepreneurs. The model exemplifies the potential added value of including designers and design thinking in social enterprise. The chapter is summed up by a discussion of the findings and a list of questions for further investigation.

The participants were chosen based on the criteria that they are Norwegian industrial designers with a master's degree in industrial design engineering. They have to be familiar with and currently working to solve social issues and not only profit. Some of them are presented in the section "Introducing the Social Designer" in order to illustrate to the reader who is unfamiliar with design what their projects may look like. Included are both examples of designers working with local challenges in Norway and also designers working on a global scale. The interviews were recorded, transcribed and coded into categories describing characteristics of the individual, and the researchers discussed until consensus which were the patterns comparable to the social entrepreneurship vocabulary. The authors discussed categories until consensus. The repeated 'labels' describing the 'social entrepreneur' were put in a diagram together with the descriptions of a social entrepreneur drawn from literature. This allowed the researchers to extract the difference between social entrepreneurship and socially responsible design based on the perspectives from the participants.

Highlighted Characteristics of the Social Designer

Social design or socially responsible design (at times referred to as SRD) originates within the social innovation movement and resulted in a generation of designers whose aim is to achieve an impact on people's well-being. Dean Nieusma (2004) describes 'alternative design scholars' as scholars who seek to "understand how unequal power relations are embodied in, and result from, mainstream design practice and products". Within these alternative design scholars, Nieusma lists socially responsible designers, but also universal design, participatory design, ecological design and feminist design. All of the above provide inspiration for designers who seek to improve society rather than simply creating products for a market. Further, Woodhouse and Nieusma (2001) refer to expertise as a capital through a definition that is highly comparable to the use of 'social capital' in social entrepreneurship.

The difference between social model design and market model design is, according to Margolin and Margolin (2002), the priorities of the designer rather than the method of design, production or distribution. A few indicators to describe the design thinker have been introduced, for example, by Tim Brown (2008), who argues that a design thinker's characteristics 'should' include empathy, integrative thinking, optimism, experimentalism and collaboration skills (Brown, 2008). Empathy is a central theme within social design literature. Designers are, according to social design and design researchers in general, not trying to generate new knowledge, test a theory or validate a scientific hypothesis. Instead, the mission of design thinking may rather be to "move from observations and interaction into understandings of end-users and from there seek solutions through appropriate and creative methods in form of products and services that will improve lives [. . .] designers have learned that it is possible to apply the principle of empathy not just to individuals, but also to groups and the interactions among them" (Brown & Katz, 2011, p. 2).

As Nieusma (2004) highlights, there is a need to find new alliances around socially relevant projects, emphasising that the designer can take the role as an advocate in important alliances to work with designers who want to achieve a real social impact, to balance the political side of public institutions and make sure marginalized groups really are heard.

In a short article, "What Social Entrepreneurship Can Teach Social Design" (Ford, 2010), Ford emphasises how the criteria for successful social design projects require "management, fundraising, design and engineering". Ford believes designers should "recognize their own limitations and network with others to fill project needs", seeking both to establish closer partnerships with other fields such as social entrepreneurs and investigate the potential of educating designers broadly within other fields, to better be able to manage the main goal of all social projects making a 'positive' social impact.

Introducing the Social Designer

In order to introduce social design for readers unfamiliar with design and design research, three of the interview participants will be presented below.

One of the participants of the interviews, Kristine Holbø, is an industrial design researcher based in Trondheim, Norway. The main goal of her project is to develop GPS solutions with sensors and support systems to track people with dementia so that they still can go for walks or hikes if they are capable of doing so. The growing proportion of the elderly presents many challenges for Nordic welfare systems. Supporting the needs of people with dementia is only one of these issues that technology design and services can alleviate.

Industrial designer Kristin Wigum Støren runs the project "Joy of life for elderly" in Trondheim, Norway, where she has been searching for ways to improve lives of elderly people living in public nursing homes. Funding and other contributions have allowed to do this "through a more holistic and needs driven view of the user experience". She sought to identify what changes the elderly people's moods and health through a year of user-centred observation in order to figure out what can make them feel more like home and less as if they were in an institution. One of the emerged solutions was 'bringing the seasons inside', as the Kristin puts it; in other words, to introduce summer, autumn, winter and spring visually to the nursing home. One of the measurable results is that the elderly are now requiring less medication than before the changes were implemented.

A third participant was Tor Inge Garvik, a designer working for Laerdal Global Health. Laerdal Global Health is a not-for-profit company (a company with no goal to earn profits for its owners) based in Stavanger, Norway. Laerdal Global Health was created with the aim to help developing countries significantly reduce infant, child and maternal mortality. One of their successful products is MamaNatalie, an affordable and realistic birth simulator for medical personnel, which according to UNICEF could save 800 of the 1 000 deaths that occur every day.

All participants share that they chose to devote their careers to improve people's well-being and primary needs instead of focusing primarily on business profits.

Reflections From the Social Designers

Through the interviews, several patterns of agreement were identified. The participants' descriptions of future and present challenges and strategies regarding social welfare issues and strengths of the designer for solving these overlapped. All citations in this section originate from these interviewees.

Loneliness was singled out as a priority among all the participants when asked what they perceived was the biggest challenge for the Nordic societies in the future. Answers concerning global challenges diverge, but one finding is that questions regarding global challenges generated more answers involving product innovation and object focus rather than immaterial solutions and systems-oriented design. When seeking to solve challenges within Norway, the designers observe and participate in an increase in systems and service-oriented design:

> How we view our future as a design company? We are not only focusing on service design now because it is so much fun in itself. If we had hired three new staff on service design we would have a greater market in Norway immediately. Secondly, there will be more and more service oriented companies; they will become larger than the product producing companies in the future I believe. First off, all production is outsourced to Asia.

Five out of six participants mention that their motivation differs from product or business strategic-oriented designers. The sixth explains that he thinks the shift from product to system and service is a response to demand rather than motivation. The five participants explain that they find more motivation in solving a problem or a need through design or redesign of an existing service than in developing a new product. Service design is one of the emerging areas among Norwegian designers and the socially responsible designers, according to the participants. The socially responsible designers emphasise that working with service design for the public sector makes regional counties common employers or partners for design enterprises. Working with the public health sector or education equals small budgets, changes the focus of the designer's effort and moves this focus away from products and onto solving social needs through services rather than products. These participants believe that there is much potential for changes that can have positive impacts on people's lives. Changing attitudes and work patterns are one of the challenges they mention. For example, introducing new technologies that require extra tasks by public personnel, or labor-intensive solutions, can be difficult, whereas redesigning *how* systems are designed and how people work together is efficient and effective and according to them, a good task for 'design thinking'.

All participants mentioned 'empathy' as an important characteristic of designers that led them to seek increasingly challenging and fulfilling work. *"I believe that we need the freedom to work thoroughly with one problem and enough time to meet the people who are going to use our products"*.

The participants express that they find themselves working frequently as facilitators, intuitively seeking to include and 'empower' the social group in focus through their entire work process. All designers in this review also focused on user-centred design as a core component of a social designer's work strategy. They tend to spend much time at the beginning of projects trying to extract something referred to as the 'real need' of the end user. When asked what they meant by 'real need', we find that it is characterized by its solution, that the solution should really be the *best* solution to a real problem, not creating a need for a business to fill. *"It is important to design for the whole system, if not your solution for the one little problem will create five new problems that you need to solve".*

Another of the informants expressed "the importance of realizing that we who reside in the 'Western world' represent ideals for the unfortunate rest" and that "we (designers) have to carry this responsibility". Another notes the large-scale challenges such as the elderly wave or loneliness. Every fourth Norwegian feels that his life situation is affected by loneliness, according to Statistics Norway (2012). One of the participants who emphasised loneliness as a contemporary future challenge for designers to solve in Norway, and who is working on a large-scale research innovation project concerning the elderly, expressed that "new products may not be the right solutions". As she puts it, sometimes we even 'design ourselves' into more loneliness and less problem-solving attitudes. Technology and other products can make us less creative and less capable of solving our own problems, something that she believes that social designers should try to prevent. This leads to another commonly repeated finding within this research sample: 'immaterial solutions' to social needs.

> *We do not only need food and clothes but we also have our fundamental needs such as identity, experiences and togetherness. Many of our needs are non-material, right, and this has to come in somehow.*

Half of the participants expressed the belief that there is a current trend and will among designers and their employers to explore how to improve people's lives *without* necessarily introducing new technologies and sometimes without introducing a product at all. Sometimes what is needed is to think 'new' and innovative with what already exists. *"[I] feel that because we haven't learnt enough about communication in our study, we could have had much more ethics and that kind of stuff. I have thought a lot about what I have perceived as the right. I have actually torn down many of my earlier principles about what I thought was right . . . and rather taken an open approach where I take in what others perceive as the right thing, to . . . to find the right solution!"*

Ethics and accountability was also seen an important part of the analytical process for all but one of the participants. One participant expressed a newfound awareness working within a global context for the motives behind designing a product leading to a newfound integrity being reflected on the design process at home, seeing his integrity closely connected to the ethics of his decision. Participants propose that an increased focus on ethics in education can increase the designers' capabilities of facing future societal challenges. *"Our solutions have a highly social meaning in the sense that it makes people able to perform better in their job and help others with what they do".*

The participants often get feedback from their management that they think more holistically and analyse a situation better than others, which prevents them from making the wrong decisions on behalf of the end users.

This also goes hand-in-hand with the next key description of the social designer: design for real needs, not for markets. The participants mention shortcomings when related to budget administration, business model design and management when faced with questions when discussing whether they believe that designers are ready to step into the role as social entrepreneurs. They have one solution for this:

> *I think that we need to make partnerships with other; this will strengthen your project. Get more people in, more perspectives, at the same time as increasing quality. We cannot read all the subjects that are needed. Budgeting and marketing. We are a little bit like the architects: we think we know everything; we don't.*

Highlighted Characteristics of the Social Entrepreneur

The focus of the literature review was to use a sample of literature to extract characteristics of the 'social entrepreneur' rather than 'social entrepreneurship', which again has limited our literature selection to descriptive literature within social entrepreneurship. Categories and nuances in terminology can be identified from chosen literature, and these are illustrated in Table 8.1. The characteristics are referred to as 'agents' by Dees (1998), 'aims' by Peredo and McLean (2006) and 'criteria' by Defourny and Nyssens (2010), whereas McMahon and Bhamra (2012) divide them into 'capacities' and 'skills' (Table 8.1). The reviewed literature highlights the need for the social entrepreneur to be a 'risk taker' (Peredo & McLean, 2006; Defourny & Nyssens, 2010), someone who 'acts boldly' (Dees, 1998) and in general is the catalyst of innovation or business progress within a social enterprise. Dees makes an early attempt to define a set of proposed requirements as a means to define the social entrepreneur. There is a clear factor of moral or ethics in Dees's view of the social entrepreneur. Dees considers the social entrepreneur as 'one species in the genus entrepreneur', where the difference between a business and a social entrepreneur lies in the entrepreneur's mission and how he/she acts in relation to the market. Where the social entrepreneur has the social mission explicit and central as a component to how the entrepreneurship will act and be evaluated in the market, the business entrepreneur will be more confined to the framework and the constraints of economic value creation.

The work of Dees (1998) is influential in most social enterprise research with his descriptions of the social entrepreneur. Dees regards social entrepreneurs as the solution to a problem. "Many governmental and philanthropic efforts have fallen far short of our expectations. Major social sector institutions are often viewed as inefficient, ineffective, and unresponsive. Social entrepreneurs are needed to develop new models for a new century"(Dees, 1998). Still others have joined the discussion of how to conceptualise and distinguish the social entrepreneur from any other entrepreneur. Dees (1998) also puts large responsibility on the social entrepreneur by requesting her or him to "exhibit a heightened sense of accountability to the constituencies served and for the outcomes created" (Dees, 1998).

These requirements, although perhaps more finely elaborated, are recognised by Pedrero and McLean (2006) as the "aim to create social value, either exclusively or at least in some prominent way" as the main criterion for distinguishing social entrepreneurship from other entrepreneurial enterprises (Peredo & McLean, 2006). By looking at Table 8.1, the reader will see that the social entrepreneur is frequently described as a single individual, acting as a driving force and a key factor for the success of the enterprise. The social entrepreneur is responsible and a risk taker at the same time.

Table 8.1 Characteristics of the Social Entrepreneur Based on a Review of Chosen Literature

Dees, 'Agents'	*Peredo et.al 'Aim'*	*Defourny et.al, 'Criteria'*	*McMahon, 'Capacities'*	*McMahon 'Skills'*
Adopting a mission to create and sustain social value	Aim exclusively or in some prominent way to create social value of some kind	An explicit aim to benefit the community	Empathy	Social cohesion
Recognising and relentlessly pursuing new opportunities to serve that mission	Recognising and exploiting opportunities to create this value		Openness Engagement Diversity	
Engaging in a process of continuous innovation, adaptation and learning	Employing innovation	A continuous activity of producing goods and/ or selling services	Understanding	
Acting boldly without being limited by resources currently in hand	Tolerating risk Declining to accept limitations in available resources	A significant level of economic risk, a minimum amount of paid work	Investment	
Exhibiting a heightened sense of accountability to the constituencies served and for the outcomes created			Openness Reflection Questioning Comparison	
		A high degree of autonomy		Decision-making

Dees, 'Agents'	Peredo et.al 'Aim'	Defourny et.al, 'Criteria'	McMahon, 'Capacities'	McMahon 'Skills'
		An initiative launched by a group of citizens		Teamwork
		A participatory nature, which involves various parties affected by the activity	Communication Participation Dialogue Sharing	Social interaction
		A limited profit distribution		

McMahon & Bhamra (2010) ties social entrepreneurship to design thinking in emphasising 'understanding' and 'empathy' (McMahon & Bhamra, 2012), which by the other researchers are expressed as 'opportunity' or 'learning' (Dees, 1998; Peredo & McLean, 2006) rather than being directly linked to seeking a deep understanding of the needs of the end user. McMahon also mentions collaboration and teamwork skills more strongly than other social enterprise scholars, who use more individualistic characteristics such as 'openness' and 'accountability' (Leadbeater, 1997; Dees, 1998; Peredo & McLean, 2006; Defourny & Nyssens, 2010;)

The cultural and geographic context of the discussion is also a central issue of social enterprise research (Defourny & Nyssens, 2010; Muñoz, 2010), as social entrepreneurship is understood through how a society is constructed, for example, through its political and welfare systems. For this study, we have therefore limited our context for literature selection and interview focus to their relevance in the context of the Norwegian welfare state. This will also benefit the appropriateness of the study as an example for comparisons with other socio-cultural contexts at a later stage.

Meeting Points, Differences and Discussion

The analysis of the reviewed literature as compared to the findings from the interviews allowed the researchers to draft a figure that illustrates how social entrepreneurs and socially responsible designers differ and complement each other in attention, approach and responsibilities (see Figure 8.1).

A major difference between the two fields is that the entrepreneur focuses on the managing opportunities and risks in relation to economy. Designers emphasise empathy and ways of finding the needs of the user. Perhaps more interestingly, the design discourse focus seems to be more process oriented,

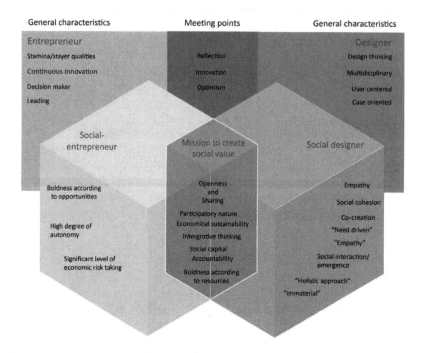

Figure 8.1 Map of General Characteristics and Meeting Points

whereas the entrepreneurial discourse emphasises the personal characteristics of the social entrepreneur.

'Empathy' is the term most frequently repeated by the social designers in this study (Black, 1998; Brown & Katz, 2011). Empathy, or user insight and understanding of the end user's real needs, may be equivalent with what the entrepreneurial vocabulary expresses as 'opportunity'. Design thinking stands for design-specific cognitive activities that designers apply during the process of designing and is described as a designer's approach of using empathy to understand, creativity to generate ideas and analytical methods to finally solve problems (Rowe, 1991; Brown, 2008). In other words, the end user insight is the core of the business idea, whereas for the designer, it may be the core of the solution (which may not even entail a business possibility). This illustrates how the social entrepreneur, according to the chosen literature, focuses on the possibility of making a business model based on a 'consumer need', whereas the designer sees it as more important to solve this need and to define what the 'real' need is, rather than directly regarding it as a business opportunity. Empathy may indeed be the strongest meeting point and the area designers can assist social entrepreneurs to strengthen (Leonard & Rayport, 1997) and spark innovation. Dees argues that it is the social entrepreneur's responsibility to innovate and continuously adapt to change. The social entrepreneur may have a broader concept of what these changes involve, whereas for the designer, the sensitivity to the end user's needs and experiences and the best solution seen from their perspective is more important.

The designer moves towards a role as social innovator or entrepreneur due to demand and strengths of empathic approaches within the demand change. In order to increase the impact of social design, however, the participants express that they could gain from learning from social entrepreneurship in several areas. The participants thought that this could be solved through increased collaborative and multi-disciplinary efforts, seeing design as an added value in social entrepreneurial enterprise.

Another reoccurring topic amongst the responding social designers was the emphasis on the issues of sustainability and immaterialism. While these issues where not elaborated on in the chosen literature on social entrepreneurs, the respondents highlighted that design thinking can be used to create a better product or solution with the elements already at hand. The respondents had different motivations for doing so, some more business strategic and others seeming to lie closer to the designer's personal convictions.

In either case, including social designers on the team would, according to the findings, increase the possibility of finding solutions that really fill the existing need without creating new ones and often without requiring more material resources.

Other important differences are found in the collaboration characteristics: a social entrepreneur is described as be willing to act more independently, whereas a social designer seems more comfortable with the role as a team player or a project leader within a social project.

Regarding shortcomings, the design participants argued the need for capacity building to increase their capabilities as primary decision-makers and for more economic understanding.

The move towards service and systems-oriented design as opposed to object-oriented design (Booch, 1982) that the participants describe has been part of design research (Woodson, Tillman, & Tillman, 1992; Sevaldson, 2009; Sevaldson, 2010;). Service design is defined as a way to improve existing or to create new services to make them more useful and usable for clients and efficient and effective for its organizations (Moritz, 2005). In contrast to tangible product design and services, systems design requires a more multi-disciplinary approach (Stickdorn & Schneider, 2010). According to Sevaldsson, "The main mission of Systems Oriented Design is to build the designers own interpretation and implementation of systems thinking so that systems thinking can fully benefit from design thinking and practice and so that design thinking and practice can fully benefit from systems thinking". System thinking is the process of understanding how things regarded as systems influence one another within a whole (Emery, 1969; Checkland, 1999). In order for the designer to develop the best-fitted and most sustainable solution, Sevaldson and other design researchers following the systems design approach highlight that in a complex and fast-changing globalised world, designers need to take system's thinking into their toolbox to be able to understand the holistic system relevant to the product or service that they are designing. That designers increasingly work on the systems level may lead to designers having even more in common with the entrepreneurs since they are less and less defined by products and production processes and more by understanding larger systems, including business and service solutions.

A Joint Venture or Merging Roles?

If mental models somewhat resonate with reality, the findings in this study argue that by combining the characteristics and skills of social entrepreneurs with those of designers, a balance between economic, social and environmental sustainability, referred to as the *triple bottom line*, and more empathic solutions can be offered to the Norwegian public sector and other similar contexts. 'Design thinking' would in partnership with social entrepreneurs achieve less resource-dependent social enterprises and products, while the skills of the social entrepreneur would increase the chances of economic viability. An alternative to partnerships is, according to the participants, that the designer tries to become a social entrepreneur by improving his/her business skills and leadership skills through an increased educational focus.

Another perspective well known to design researchers is, of course, that all design is, per definition, aimed at achieving social improvement (Plattner, Meinel & Leifer, 2010).

Upon reflection, one could ask if these suggested approaches are representing a new approach, or if the basic idea, although not conceptualised, could be found within former development processes in Norway. An example is how establishing the 'Nordic model' combined free market capitalism with the creation of a comprehensive welfare state. One could argue that social design was utilized in that social change process even if the concept 'social design' was not used. Still, as a profession, the authors are not aware of designers being used actively within projects aiming at social impact in Norway until recent years. Consequently, there might a potential for a new and innovative phase in which social designers, combined with social entrepreneurs, can contribute to a social and economically sustainable renewed model.

References

Aarøy, T. (2013). *Vi behandler 1,6 millioner flere enn vi gjorde i 2005*. Available at http://www.bt.no/nyheter/innenriks/faktasjekk/Vi-behandler-1_6-millioner-flere-enn-vi-gjorde-i-2005–2950020.html#.Uh3Dxj-NCrM, accessed 15 October 2015.

Barendsen, L. & Gardner, H. (2004). Is the Social Entrepreneur a New Type of Leader? *Leader to Leader*, 34, 43–50.

Black, A. (1998). Empathic Design: User Focused Strategies for Innovation. In *Proceedings of the New Product Development*, IBC Conferences, London, UK.

Booch, G. (1982). Object-Oriented Design. *ACM SIGAda Ada Letters*, 1(3), 64–76.

Brown, T. (2008). Design Thinking. *Harvard Business Review*, 86(6), 84.

Brown, T. & Katz, B. (2011). Change by Design. *Journal of Product Innovation Management*, 28(3), 381–383.

Checkland, P. (1999). *Systems Thinking, Systems Practice: Includes a 30-year Retrospective*. Chichester: John Wiley & Sons.

Cross, N. (2001). Designerly Ways of Knowing: Design Discipline Versus Design Science. *Design Issues*, 17(3), 49–55.

Cross, N. (2006). *Designerly Ways of Knowing*. London: Springer.

Dees, J. G. (1998). *The Meaning of Social Entrepreneurship*. Comments and suggestions contributed from the Social Entrepreneurship Funders Working Group.

Defourny, J. & Nyssens, M. (2010). Conceptions of Social Enterprise and Social Entrepreneurship in Europe and the United States: Convergences and Divergences. *Journal of Social Entrepreneurship*, 1(1), 32–53.

Emery, F. E. (1969). *Systems Thinking*. Harmondsworth: Penguin Books.

Ford, R. (2010). What Social Entrepreneurship can Teach Social Design. Available at http://designobserver.com/feature/what-social-entrepreneurship-can-teach-social-design/15148/, accessed 14 October 2015.

Galera, G. & Borzaga, C. (2009). Social Enterprise: An International Overview of Its Conceptual Evolution and Legal Implementation. *Social Enterprise Journal*, 5(3), 210–228.

Järvenpää, E. (2012). *Towards More Strategic Corporate Social Responsibility— Partnerships with Social Enterprises*. Aalto: Aalto University.

Kidwell, R. E. (2015). *The Social Entrepreneur: Moral Courage in Organizations: Doing the Right Thing at Work*, 88. New York: Routledge.

Leadbeater, C. (1997). *The Rise of the Social Entrepreneur*. London: Demos.

Leonard, D. & Rayport, J. F. (1997). Spark Innovation Through Empathic Design. *Harvard Business Review*, 75, 102–115.

Margolin, V. & Margolin, S. (2002). A 'Social Model' of Design: Issues of Practice and Research. *Design issues*, 18(4), 24–30.

McMahon, M. & Bhamra, T. (2012). Design Beyond Borders. International Collaborative Projects as a Mechanism to Integrate Social Sustainability into Student Design Practice. *Journal of Cleaner Production*, 23(1), 86–95.

Moritz, S. (2005). *Service Design: Practical Access to an Evolving Field*. Cologne: Köln International School of Design.

Muñoz, S. A. (2010). Towards a Geographical Research Agenda for Social Enterprise. *Area*, 42(3), 302–312.

Nieusma, D. (2004). Alternative Design Scholarship: Working Toward Appropriate Design. *Design Issues*, 20(3), 13–24.

Papanek, V. & Fuller, R. B. (1972). *Design for the Real World*. London: Thames & Hudson.

Peredo, A. M. & McLean, M. (2006). Social Entrepreneurship: A Critical Review of the Concept. *Journal of world business*, 41(1), 56–65.

Plattner, H., Meinel, C. & Leifer, L. (2010). *Design Thinking: Understand–Improve– Apply*. Berlin: Springer Science & Business Media.

Rowe, P. G. (1991). *Design Thinking*. Cambridge, MA: MIT press.

Sevaldson, B. (2009). *Systems Oriented Design: The Emergence and Development of a Designerly Approach to Address Complexity*. Paper presented at the 2nd International Conference for Design Education Researchers, Oslo, Norway.

Sevaldson, B. (2010). *Discussions & Movements in Design Research: FORMakademisk, Vol. 3 2010, 8–35 Statistics Norway (2012) Levekårsundersøkelsen*. Available at http://www.ssb.no/sosiale-forhold-og-kriminalitet/statistikker/soskon/hvert-3-aar/2013–10–01, accessed 14 October 2015.

Stickdorn, M. & Schneider, J. (2010). *This Is Service Design Thinking: Basics—Tools—Cases*. Amsterdam: BIS Publishers.

Woodhouse, E. J. & Nieusma, D. A. (2001). *Democratic Expertise: Integrating Knowledge, Power, and Participation: Knowledge, Power, and Participation in Environmental Policy Analysis*. New Brunswick: Transaction Publishers.

Woodson, W. E., Tillman, B. & Tillman, P. (1992). *Human Factors Design Handbook: Information and Guidelines for the Design of Systems, Facilities, Equipment, and Products for Human Use*. New York: McGraw-Hill.

Wylant, B. (2008). Design Thinking and the Experience of Innovation. *Design Issues*, 24(2), 3–14.

9   Social Entrepreneurship

Between Odysseus's Scar and Abraham's Sacrifice

Daniel Ericsson

In the City of Malmö, social entrepreneurship initiatives are being proposed to reduce health inequalities among citizens. How do these initiatives acquire legitimacy? Taking a narrative turn, I suggest that social entrepreneurship in theory and practice is shaped by the narrative styles of Homer and the Old Testament and that building the legitimacy of social entrepreneurship apparently entails not only aligning biased interests with neoliberal and managerial discourses, but also narrating the reality of social entrepreneurship by means of enchanting digressions and tacit truth claims. However, such acquired legitimacy comes at a cost, giving rise to specific consequences for social entrepreneurship in general and for the City of Malmö specifically.

Shaping the Reality of Social Entrepreneurship in Malmö

In the last few decades, areas such as economic geography, cultural planning and urban studies have come under the influence of a managerial discourse on creativity, suggesting not only the desirability but also the possibility of developing cities into creative centres (see, for instance, Florida, 2002). Criticism of this creativity discourse has been harsh, however. For instance, Peck (2005) has argued that the focus on talented, creative individuals and the strategies for creating cities in which creative talent thrives are parts of a neoliberal agenda leading to gentrification and interurban competition. In a study of Copenhagen, a city largely governed by this managerial discourse on creativity (Bayliss, 2007), Lund Hansen, Andersen and Clark (2001) state that the creative city "on closer inspection [becomes] a dubious ideological smokescreen to cover up the social costs associated with compulsive adaption to the 'requirements' of the 'new' flexible globalized economy" (Lund Hansen et al., 2001, p. 866).

As Bayliss (2007) emphasises, however, there are alternatives to the managerial discourse on creativity when it comes to urban development. One of these is a strategy that places bottom-up participatory initiatives originating in local neighbourhoods (instead of top-down initiatives originating in municipal authorities) at the centre of attention, stressing aspects such as social cohesion, improved life skills and a democratic citizenry. Instead of creativity, one could say that it is *social entrepreneurship* that is placed at the top of the agenda.

This chapter addresses a city that, at least partly, seems to be applying such a social entrepreneurship strategy, namely, Malmö, Copenhagen's twin city across the Öresund, long troubled by the aftermath of the 1970s crisis and socio-economic problems such as poverty, unemployment and alienation. To come to grips with increasing health inequalities among citizens, in 2012, the City of Malmö formed the Commission for a Socially Sustainable Malmö. The commission's 2013 report emphasised two 'overall recommendations' to the City of Malmö: 1) Establish a policy for social investments directed towards reducing differences in citizens' living conditions and 2) Make existing municipal managerial processes more cooperative and democratic. The commission introduced the concept of 'knowledge alliances' defined as "co-operation on equal terms between researchers and stakeholders from, for example, the public sector, the voluntary sector and the business community" (Stigendal & Östergren, 2013, p. 6) and stressed the importance of the voluntary sector due to its capacity for social entrepreneurship (Stigendal & Östergren, 2013, p. 48). The voluntary sector should be involved in political decision processes and be used by the municipality "as a resource in the development of health-promoting and cohesive actions" (Stigendal & Östergren, 2013, p. 48). "What is needed", the commission stated, "is an infrastructure within the municipality which can take advantage of the voluntary sector's innovative capacity and knowledge" (Stigendal & Östergren, 2013, p. 48).

The commission's report was well received by the public, media and politicians and the nearly 70 official responses to the report (Malmö Stad, 2014, p. 10). Contrary to what one might expect, there were few divergent political opinions about the meaning and importance of the report, and the turn towards social entrepreneurship seemed to encounter few legitimacy problems. This experience is not only at odds with the lack of legitimacy usually experienced by actors interested in social entrepreneurship, especially those wanting to promote and develop it (see, for instance, Nicholls, 2010), but is also at odds with the problematic aspects of the social entrepreneurship field that Nicholls (2010) has identified. According to Nicholls (2010, p. 624), different paradigm-building actors draw on different legitimating discourses to shape the field in accordance with their 'own internal logics', and this is something that may "undermine and perhaps even destroy the normative and cognitive legitimacy of social entrepreneurship to a wider audience" (Nicholls, 2010, p. 625): for instance, government officials who seek to deliver public goods in an efficient manner legitimize their actions discursively in terms of 'business models', fellowship organizations that seek to build social capital by maximizing leverage gain legitimacy by referring to the discourse of 'the hero entrepreneur', and pure network organizations that try to initiate communitarian action are in alignment with the discourse of 'social justice' (Nicholls, 2010, p. 624).

In Nicholls's (2010) framework for tackling these problems, however, no particular attention is paid to *how* the paradigm builders actually strive for legitimacy: Nicholls does not question how they present their arguments, and he displays little interest in how they describe the reality of social entrepreneurship. Could blind spots such as these also be part of the problem to which Nicholls draws attention? Could such blind spots explain why the initiatives proposed by Malmö's commission seem to be facing a kind of surplus legitimacy?

To address these questions, I consider the social entrepreneurship discourse through the lens of narrative analysis. Such a turn is largely embedded within a grander theoretical discourse on entrepreneurship comprising a Foucaldian discourse analysis of the discourse's unexamined assumptions, challenging the discourse's hegemony (see, for instance, Ogbor, 2000; Bruni, Gherardi, & Poggio, 2004; Jones & Spicer, 2005), as well as narrative and rhetorical analyses highlighting the social aspects of entrepreneurship (see, for instance, Steyaert & Bouwen, 1997; Hjorth & Steyaert, 2004). The narrative interest of the present chapter, however, is not primarily directed towards *what* is being narrated within the theoretical discourse on social entrepreneurship, but towards *how* social entrepreneurship is narrated. From this perspective, the present chapter is aligned with the literatures on reality representations (Potter, 1996) and written representations (van Maanen, 1988), focusing specifically on the concept of *narrative styles* as introduced by Auerbach (1953/1968). He identified two narrative styles, the Homeric as expressed in *The Odyssey* and the Old Testament style, specifically as expressed in the story of Abraham's sacrifice, and argued that these two styles have exerted a determining influence on the Western literary representation of reality (Auerbach, 1953/1968, p. 23). The question here is to what extent these two narrative styles also shape the reality of social entrepreneurship.

The overarching purpose of this chapter is to advance understanding of how paradigm-building actors, by their actions, shape the reality of social entrepreneurship by using different narrative styles, and to tentatively outline the consequences of such reality shaping in terms of the legitimacy of social entrepreneurship in general and for the City of Malmö specifically.

To achieve this purpose, the chapter is organized in three parts. The first section presents Auerbach's two narrative styles, while these styles, as theories of interpretation, are employed in the second section in critically examining how social entrepreneurship is represented in the relevant theoretical discourse. The empirical material consists of two recently published books taken to be representative of the social entrepreneurship discourse: *The Search for Social Entrepreneurship* (Light, 2008) and *Social Entrepreneurship: What Everyone Needs to Know* (Bornstein & Davis, 2010). The main argument presented here is that the social entrepreneurship discourse indeed seems to recall the narrative styles of Homer and the Old Testament: the paradigm-building actors are captured between Odysseus's scar and Abraham's sacrifice, depicting the reality of social entrepreneurship in terms of either entertaining digressions or tacit truth claims, both of which might hamper the paradigm-building actors' pursuit of legitimacy.

In the third and final section, the initiatives following in the wake of the Commission for a Socially Sustainable Malmö come in focus as being shaped between Odysseus's scar and Abraham's sacrifice.

Section One: Odysseus's Scar and Abraham's Sacrifice

In "Odysseus's Scar", Auerbach (1953/1968) draws attention to the scene in *The Odyssey* in which the protagonist has finally arrived home, but for political reasons has not yet revealed his true identity. Odysseus passes himself off as a stranger to his wife Penelope and all the people of the court. As a sign of hospitality, the old housekeeper Euryclea, once Odysseus's nanny, is ordered to wash the stranger's feet. As she goes about this, however, Odysseus remembers an old scar on his thigh that he got as a child, and he begins to fear that Euryclea will recognise him by the scar and reveal his identity. What follows is an analepsis more than seventy verses long in which the reader is taken back to Odysseus's childhood and given a very detailed description of how he actually got the scar on his thigh. At the moment of crisis, when Odysseus's identity is about to be revealed, Homer seamlessly interrupts the progress of the narrative, transcending time and place in the very same sentence. After the digression, Homer just as seamlessly takes the reader back to the scene in which Euryclea detects the scar:

> His father and his honoured mother rejoiced at his return, and asked him all the story, how he got his wound; and he told them all the truth, how, while he was hunting, a boar had struck him with his white tusk when he had gone to Parnassus with the sons of Autolycus.
>
> This scar the old dame, when she had taken the limb in the flat of her hands, knew by the touch, and she let fall the foot. Into the basin the leg fell, and the brazen vessel rang. Over it tilted, and the water was spilled upon the ground. Then upon her soul came joy and grief in one moment, and both her eyes were filled with tears and the flow of her voice was checked.
>
> (Homer, 1942, Book 19)

According to Auerbach (1953/1968), the narrative style of these scenes is characteristic of Homer. His writings are replete with gracefully narrated digressions full of concrete details, adjectives and actions, as if it did not matter that there was a grand narrative to return to. The environments in these digressions are thoroughly described, the people are carefully portrayed and their actions, thoughts and gestures are illuminated to the extent that it seems as if everything is spelt out and presented in the foreground, in 'full light'. In this sense, Homer "knows no background"; Auerbach concludes,

"What he narrates is for the time being the only present, and fills both the stage and the reader's mind completely" (Auerbach, 1953/1968, pp. 4–5).

Adding to this characteristic Homeric narrative style is the absence of lacunae. Everything that is thus foregrounded is also contextualized so that the reader is always informed of the when and where of the narrative, of how the actors and their actions are interrelated. In this regard, Auerbach argues, there are no secret meanings, hidden motives or hidden actions in Homer's works. *The Odyssey* is completely transparent to the reader, who consequently does not need to engage in interpretation: there is simply no need for it, as there is nothing to decipher.

This shifting in time and place, interrupting the narrative flow, yet always written in the present tense to create an absolute 'here and now', could be seen as a modernist device to create suspense. Auerbach's reading, however, presents a contrarian interpretation. The seventy-verse-long interlude between Euryclea's recognition of the scar and her reaction to it is not intended to keep the reader in suspense, but rather to dispel the reader's tension. Homeric poems, Auerbach writes, do not simply strive for narrative closure by means of suspense; they are written to delight, entertain and enchant the reader by their sheer narrative joy and power. In this sense, they are based on legend making, a combination of make-believe and legenda (Latin for 'things to be read'), rather than on any historical and accurate reality.

To further inculcate the Homeric narrative style, Auerbach turns to the Bible and the text in the Old Testament in which Abraham is told to sacrifice his son Isaac. Quoting the opening of the story in Genesis (22:1)—"And it come to pass after these things, that God did tempt Abraham, and said to him, Abraham! And he said, Behold, here I am"—Auerbach (1953/1968, p. 8) pinpoints how underdeveloped the biblical narrative is in both detail and context compared with Homer's works. The reader is essentially told nothing about the actors, about where they come from or about why God is tempting Abraham. It is as if they have no history, no present circumstance and no motives.

Abraham's sacrifice stands out as a lacuna, a tacit narrative without any detailed and contextualizing digressions. The fact that so much remains unspoken not only creates a suggestive atmosphere of incompleteness and ambiguity, but also keeps the reader in suspense, building psychological tension. This atmosphere becomes even more suspenseful as readers are only apprised of seemingly disconnected episodes and can only guess how the protagonists interpret and understand the situations that they face. The story "unrolls with no episodes in a few independent sentences whose syntactical connection is of the most rudimentary sort" (Auerbach, 1953/1968, p. 9).

This narrative style leaves no room for adjectives, epithets or descriptions of actors and landscapes: they would even be 'unthinkable', Auerbach (1953/1968, p. 8) concludes, given the atmosphere created. The only gesture mentioned, Abraham's lifting of his eyes, in "its uniqueness . . . heightens the impression that the journey took place through a vacuum . . . the journey is like a silent progress through the indeterminate and the contingent, a holding of the breath" (Auerbach, 1953/1968, pp. 9–10).

Compared with the Homeric narratives, those of the Old Testament are 'fraught with background' (Auerbach, 1953/1968, p. 12), and as such, they call for interpretation in order to reveal their hidden secret meanings, although this call is not a particularly overt one. Old Testament texts seek to make history, claiming to convey the truth about the history of the world, and as such they *must* be interpreted to be understood. With Homer's narratives, the opposite is the case, argues Auerbach: they cannot be interpreted. They are nothing but fairy tales, pure entertainment without any need for interpretation or understanding, whereas the biblical texts are written to educate and subject the reader. Homer's text resists the type of exegesis that a reading of biblical texts demands, and if one were to attempt such an interpretation of *The Odyssey*, it would be 'forced and foreign' (Auerbach, 1953/1968, p. 13).

Section Two: Entertaining Digressions and Tacit Truth Claims

In the preface to *The Search for Social Entrepreneurship* (2008), Paul C. Light states that the book is based on his own research journey. That journey began in 2005 "with a reasonably deep reading of the literature on social entrepreneurship" (Light, 2008, p. xi) and deepened in 2006 and 2007, theoretically as well as empirically, with a survey of 131 organizations in the entrepreneurship field. Light concludes that his book can best be seen as a 'travel guide' reflecting his field observations. Almost as if apologizing for the subjectivity of his research endeavour, throughout the book, Light warns the reader that his study "contains both biases and caveats" (Light, 2008, p. 196), and he rounds off the preface with a kind of disclaimer: "I have no doubt missed many important vistas in my journey, but I have enjoyed the trip more than I ever imagined I would" (Light, 2008, p. xii).

Light's disclaimer sets the tone of the book, but it also alerts the reader to the possibility of intertextual allusions to Homer's *Odyssey* in terms of both content and narrative style. In terms of content, the protagonist, trained in political science and a professor of public service at New York University, is getting himself into deep waters. Just as Odysseus is adrift on unknown waters searching for Ithaca, his home, Light is carrying out research in a new theoretical field, seeking a theoretical home where the true assumptions about social entrepreneurship have been sorted out from the false ones (see, for instance, Light, 2008, Chapter One). Just as Odysseus had to confront the dangers of Scylla and Charybdis in the strait of Messina, Light is facing the dilemma of choosing between inclusive and exclusive definitions of social entrepreneurship (Light, 2008, p. 20), and just as the protagonist of *The Odyssey* is characterized by his wisdom and cunning, *mētis*, the protagonist of *The Search for Social Entrepreneurship* is characterized by a knowledgeable (dis)position. Both books are also characterized by happy endings.

Regarding the narrative style of *The Search for Social Entrepreneurship*, it is striking that both Light's research journey and the book's narrative more or less start in 2005. There are very few attempts, besides references to Drayton (2002) and Dees (1998), to present the history of social entrepreneurship as it has been externalized in theory and practice, and there are no major attempts to place social entrepreneurship in the wider context of, for example, 'entrepreneurship', 'innovation', or 'civil society'. Social entrepreneurship is not given any prior history or background: it is as if the field were non-existent before Light's entry into it. Light writes in the present tense and unfolds his research journey accordingly, *in media res*, with himself as both narrator and protagonist, just as Homer narrates the adventures of Odysseus.

This lack of history and context does not mean that Light does not intend to make a theoretical contribution to the field of social entrepreneurship. On the contrary, the book is full of theoretical digressions and in-depth discussions. For instance, Light thoroughly scrutinizes the forty basic assumptions of the field's 'state-of-the-art' research in order to 'chisel out' a definition that clearly makes it possible to distinguish social entrepreneurship from other forms of action, and carefully compares the extensive literatures on business and social entrepreneurship in order to winnow true assumptions from false ones as regards the natures of entrepreneurs and of their ideas, opportunities and organizations. In carrying out this theoretical work, Light analyses all possible ideas and thoughts, iteratively structuring his explication, returning to previously presented theoretical arguments, either testing them against empirical data or confronting them with theoretical counterarguments.

Light's Homeric meticulousness in putting seemingly all theoretical details in the foreground could be seen as a consequence of his research ethos. Light (2008, p. 88) writes, "Researchers can only be a force for good if they let the evidence take them where it will. They must confront the field with hard questions about its assumptions, tough analysis of the facts, and a readiness to speak truth to power". From this ethical stance, it follows that there must not be any theoretical lacunae: every gap must be spotted and closed by means of empirical research.

Also following from this ethical stance is a specific epistemological orientation implying deductive reasoning and the possibility, not to say the desirability, of creating objective knowledge. In contrast to the hermeneutic traditions, such an orientation excludes the very idea of interpretation as well as any notions of hidden or secret meanings in a text. It produces a combination of the realist telling of tales that are filled with details (see, for instance, van Maanen, 1988) and a narrative that renders interpretation superfluous. From the reader's point of view, Light's book evokes a corresponding reading strategy: 'telling it as it is' simply demands that the reader 'read it as it is' and not indulge in exegesis.

Light's epistemological orientation leaves little room for 'interpreting' or 'understanding' his book in the hermeneutic sense. Instead, it seems as though Light wants the book to be acted on: on the one hand, he urges his reader to engage in empirical field studies to validate the conceptual knowledge presented in the book; on the other hand, he wants researchers and practitioners to join together to overcome the high failure rates, the "sunk costs, missed opportunities, or needless sacrifice" (Light, 2008, p. 215) of social entrepreneurs, and ultimately to achieve sustainable change. "The question facing the field is not whether a new generation of social entrepreneurs will accept the call to action—that much is clear from the remarkable increase in student interest in coursework on the topic . . . Rather, the question is how researchers can work together to increase the odds of success" (Light, 2008, p. 215).

This call for action might seem to stand in stark contrast to the delight of the Homeric narrative style, and it might be somewhat farfetched to interpret Light's book as pleasing and/or enchanting. However, two considerations speak in favour of such an interpretation. First, it seems as though the theoretical discourse on social entrepreneurship, of which the book is part, is an enchanting one: researchers are drawn into the research field because they find it a "source of explanation, prediction and delight" (Mair & Marti, 2006). In this regard, it comes as no surprise that Light found his research trip enjoyable, and a reader who shares Light's ethical (dis)position could plausibly find the book at least as enjoyable and 'epic' in the Homeric sense. The praise on the back cover of the book leads in that direction, as it says the book is "a must-read for leaders who will engage in the future sculpting of our world".

Second, the subject matter and the narrative style seem to reinforce each other, making the book a heroic and legend-making endeavour. The social entrepreneur is celebrated throughout the book as a legendary figure, i.e., someone who possesses extraordinary powers and whose social and historical significance are perceived to be paramount. This legendary figure is made the protagonist of a narrative legend, that is, Light places the social entrepreneur outside of history, yet within the realm of the possible.

Legends, however, are not recognised only by their verisimilitude, according to Auerbach (1953/1968), but also by their tendency to run 'far too smoothly' (Auerbach, 1953/1968, p. 19). In legendary tales such as *The Odyssey*, real-life experiences are reduced and simplified: "cross-currents, all friction, all that is causal, secondary to the main events and themes, everything unresolved, truncated, and uncertain, which confuses the clear progress of the action and the simple orientation of the actors, has disappeared" (Auerbach, 1953/1968, p. 19). In Light's (2008) book, this reduction and simplification of real-life experience is mainly achieved by means of the quantitative methods adopted in the 2006 survey of 131 social benefit organizations. Designed to offer an opportunity to explore differences in the material, Light nevertheless concludes that, in the material, the organizations and the social entrepreneurs working for them were generally more similar than different.

In both legendary senses, the narrative style of *The Search for Social Entrepreneurship* could well be understood as a sort of legend making to please and enchant the reader.

Comparing *The Search for Social Entrepreneurship* with Bornstein and Davies' *Social Entrepreneurship: What Everyone Needs to Know* (2010), it could be argued that the books are written for different audiences and different purposes. Whereas Light is a university professor and presumably writes for an audience mainly comprising researchers in an endeavour to advance the theoretical conversation, Bornstein, a best-selling author, and Davis, a practitioner in the field, envision an innovative society and presumably write for an audience larger in scope—that is the 'everyone' named in the book's title. Regarding the content of the books, though, there are great similarities between the two in that they both include lengthy discussions of how to define the concept of social entrepreneurship and they both focus intently on delivering normative recommendations to the reader.

One of the major differences between the books' narrative styles is found in how Bornstein and Davis embrace the history and context of social entrepreneurship. While starting from the same references cited by Light (for example Dees, 1998 and Drayton, 2002), instead of ending up in Light's myopic narrative position, they unfold what could be conceptualised as an 'eternal' narrative of social entrepreneurship. "Social entrepreneurs have always existed", they write, "but in the past they were called visionaries, humanitarians, philanthropists, reformers, saints, or simply great leaders" (Bornstein & Davis, 2010, p. 2). From this broad historical perspective, it makes perfect sense for Bornstein and Davis to include classic economists such as Jean-Baptise Say, Joseph A. Schumpeter and Adam Smith as theoretical interlocutors, and to position social entrepreneurship amidst organizations such as the Salvation Army, Rotary International and the Boy and Girl Scouts (Bornstein & Davis, 2010, p. 6).

Bornstein and Davis's historical awareness is offset by their somewhat shallow narrative style in which important historical actors and arenas are indeed inscribed in the narrative, but only to be mentioned in passing. The authors do not digress into the areas they open up for discussion and they do not immerse themselves in detail. For instance, the history of ideas from the Middle Ages to the post-industrial era is rushed through in a few pages (Bornstein & Davis, 2010, pp. 3–7), and throughout the book, both empirical and theoretical references are used eclectically to illustrate lines of thought rather than to strengthen the authors' arguments.

Bornstein and Davis bring a lot of empirical and theoretical material to the foreground, but make very little effort to present a coherent and meaningful context to facilitate the reader's in-depth understanding of the treated phenomenon. In this regard, their book is 'fraught with background'—to use Auerbach's expression—and as such is written in a narrative style like that of the Old Testament: there is an absence of concrete details, the reader is vaguely informed of how actors and things are interrelated and the text is full of gaps waiting in vain to be filled. The book calls for interpretation, just as the Old Testament does.

A 'blurb' on the cover of the book from the *New York Times* alludes to the book's biblical point of reference: "A bible in the field". This allusion, however, has at least two meanings: on one hand, it conveys a truth imperative; on the other, it brings power issues to the fore.

The Old Testament's truth imperative is wide ranging and pervasive: the reader is told the 'true' story about how heaven and earth were created, how humans came to exist and inherited the earth generation by generation and how humans should live life righteously. As such, the Old Testament is written to educate the reader, in terms of both genealogy and ethics, and the knowledge that resides on the biblical pages is simply 'what everyone needs to know' to be part of the religious community. Compared with this biblical truth imperative, the truth claims made by Bornstein and Davis's book are indeed weaker. The subtitle "*What Everyone Needs to Know*" does not have the universal aspirations that the scriptures have, and is not supported by the same kind of strong convictions about the consequences of ignorance that biblical readers might have.

Bornstein and Davis's narrative style, however, has distinct features in common with the scriptures, that is genealogical history-making as well as a rigorous sense of morality inscribed in the narrative. This morality is spelt out in the descriptions of the social entrepreneur's personality or 'temperamental qualities' (Bornstein & Davis, 2010, p. 26). Disguised as empirical evidence of the psychological traits and constitution of social entrepreneurs, the *portraits parlés* offered (Bornstein & Davis, 2010, p. 26 ff) convey a moral message to the reader in which the importance of being 'comfortable with uncertainty' as well as having 'a high need for autonomy', 'a bias towards action' and an 'inner locus of control' (Bornstein & Davis, 2010, pp. 26–27) is stressed. The description of the social entrepreneur thus entails a prescription: what 'is' simultaneously means what 'ought to be'.

Bornstein and Davis's message of truth and morality is further emphasised in the appendix entitled "Thoughts for Changemakers" (Bornstein & Davis, 2010, p. 129 ff). Just as God handed down the Ten Commandments to Moses at Mount Sinai, Bornstein and Davis here provide the reader with proverbial 'laws' of social entrepreneurship, telling acolytes how to think and act to foster and mould the desired (dis)position. Among these 'laws' the reader finds advice such as, "Do what you do best", "Apprentice yourself with masters (Work without pay if necessary)", and "Take a finance course". The meanings of these 'laws', however, are not elaborated on, but are taken for granted or hidden between the lines, forcing readers to engage in acts of interpretation—or at least to question why on earth they should take a finance course or work without pay.

As the bringer of truth and morality, *Social Entrepreneurship: What Everyone Needs to Know* does not attempt to please or enchant the reader in the same manner as Light's book does. Instead, it seeks to subject the reader, to make the reader want to be part of the universal history being outlined and to live life in accordance with its righteous laws. If the reader refuses to be subjected, then the reader is a rebel (Auerbach, 1953/1968, p. 15 ff)—or worse yet, a renegade. In this sense, Bornstein and Davis's book is not only educational in character and style; it is also a political project. The book represents an absolute authority, not by the arguments or narratives it presents, and not by its missionary purpose of teaching people "how to make a positive difference in the world" (as suggested on the book's cover), but by its very narrative style. The text, fraught with background, hails the readers, and disciplines them by tying them to never-ending acts of interpretation.

Section Three: Malmö: Between Odysseus's Scar and Abraham's Sacrifice

The literature on social entrepreneurship seems either to invite the reader to approach social entrepreneurship 'as it is' in a joyful manner or to subject the reader to the never-ending study of the alluring but evasive phenomenon of 'social entrepreneurship'. The reader either is enchanted by the legend making or wants to become part of a mysterious history-making process. What about the consequences of the narrative styles for the paradigm-building actors in the City of Malmö?

In Malmö, many of the strivings for municipal-level social entrepreneurship are currently aligned with and promoted and legitimized by the Commission for a Socially Sustainable Malmö. In particular, the idea of knowledge alliances seems to have struck a chord among municipal politicians and officials, who are now eagerly trying to meet the commission's objective 3.1.3, which stipulates that Malmö should "create new forms of collaboration between the private and public sectors as well as the voluntary sector" (Stigendal & Östergren, 2013, p. 134). The main action proposed by the commission for meeting this objective is to "further develop an infrastructure for social innovation and urban integration" (Stigendal & Östergren, 2013, p. 134), the idea being to utilize existing platforms for collaboration between the City of Malmö and Malmö University and to attach new 'nodes' to them, particularly voluntary-sector organizations that have successfully created social value and capital. These organizations—such as the 'Yallatrappan' women's cooperative, the 'Drömmarnas hus' youth centre, and the 'Glokala folkhögskolan' folk high school—are seen as 'important sources of inspiration' for social entrepreneurs. They illustrate how social innovation can occur, and the commissioners foresee that a social entrepreneurship infrastructure, with nodes such as these organizations and ties between them, could contribute to increased knowledge "through regular conferences and a continuous exchange of knowledge" (Stigendal & Östergren, 2013, p. 134).

The Malmö City Council decided to adopt the commission's report and proposals for action on 5 March 2014, and a strategy to implement the decision was soon formulated. In the hands of city council officials, the commission's objective 3.1.3 was deemed of the utmost importance to the leadership and organization area. "It encompasses", the Declaration of Intent states, "activities that focus on increased cooperation, development of methods, and the creation of joint platforms and meeting places" (Malmö Stad, 2014, p. 21, author's translation). However, instead of developing the infrastructure as proposed by the commission and continuing to work on municipal initiatives for social entrepreneurship, such as the 'Områdesprogrammen' (an 'area project' to foster bottom-up initiatives in areas where well-being is lowest), a decision was made to consider joining the Forum for Social Innovation Sweden (FSIS) (Malmö Stad, 2014, p. 21) and to calculate the costs of joining.

According to its own history-making at www.socialinnovation.se, FSIS emerged from the Knowledge Foundation, which since 1994 has been a governmental initiative to strengthen Sweden's competitiveness and create growth. The Knowledge Foundation funds research at new universities in Sweden and a prerequisite for funding is that the research be conducted in cooperation with Swedish companies. In 2008, SEK 120 million were earmarked to initiate a programme to promote social entrepreneurship co-production by various stakeholders, and in 2009, after slightly changing the target of the funding, the foundation announced a call for 'meeting places', i.e., neutral platforms for knowledge exchange between actors in the field, and Malmö University together with Mid Sweden University were funded to run the Forum for Social Innovation and Social Entrepreneurship. As the Knowledge Foundation funding ended in 2012, the two universities went their separate ways, and Malmö University decided to continue operating the forum on a permanent basis jointly with the Region Skåne authority under the current name, FSIS. In December og the same year, the Swedish government formally designated FSIS a "national platform for knowledge of social innovation and social entrepreneurship" with SEK 6 million of funding for the years 2013 and 2014.

Since 2012, FSIS has acted in line with its Programme Declaration (2012), which says that FSIS is a 'knowledge platform' based on practical and theoretical knowledge of leadership and organization, design processes, finance, social investment and corporate social responsibility. The declaration states that FSIS aims to "develop, coordinate and diffuse knowledge" of social innovation and entrepreneurship, and that this is to be done digitally through Facebook, Twitter and www.socialinnovation.se, where information about research, publications, events, conferences and 'best practices' is gathered. Set up primarily as an environmental scanning organization and an arena for knowledge sharing, FSIS in practice also provides a network by arranging seminars and conferences as well as publishing short publications such as "ABCs of Social Innovation".

The possibility of Malmö municipality's joining FSIS was investigated by the city council's Working Committee for Healthcare and Welfare. The committee's recommendation to the city council was to join FSIS at an annual cost of SEK 2 million, and the official letter accompanying the recommendation specifies the reasons for doing so (STK, 2014–238). First, by joining FSIS, the City of Malmö can gain access to 'important information' about social innovation and social entrepreneurship. Second, the committee believes that the City of Malmö together with FSIS can build suitable infrastructure in line with the idea of knowledge alliances, as proposed by the Malmö Commission. "If the knowledge alliances consist of people from FSIS, the county council, civil society, trade and industry, universities, and governmental agencies, the City Council thinks that FSIS can play an important role by providing access to knowledge and a large national and international network" (STK, 2014–238, p. 7, author's translation). FSIS can arguably contribute knowledge of social innovation and entrepreneurship that, it is hoped, will inspire the creation of more social enterprises, leading to more new jobs.

As a third reason, the Working Committee identifies FSIS as a way to continue the area project's work on innovation methods and culture. Joining FSIS, the argument goes, "could be a way forward for the area project, instead of its termination" (STK, 2014–238, p. 8, author's translation), and as such would be aligned with the city council's decision to profile Malmö as a city that takes social challenges seriously. To influence FSIS's work in this direction, however, the recommendation to join FSIS is made conditional: besides being entitled to conduct annual follow-ups, the City of Malmö is to be given a place on FSIS's steering committee, Region Skåne and Malmö University must support FSIS with the same amount of money as Malmö contributes and Malmö's logo should be featured whenever FSIS undertakes any marketing activities.

The image value that the City of Malmö will acquire by joining FSIS is also highlighted in the written material from FSIS that accompanies the official letter (STK, 2014–238, Appendix, author's translation): "Via FSIS the city will gain access to . . . a strong network built around issues of social innovation and a knowledge bank concerning how cities can address social sustainability, which might have a value for the city . . . In terms of image, we believe that it is important that Malmö be associated with social innovation and social entrepreneurship".

Based on the official letter and the recommendation of the city council's Working Committee for Healthcare and Welfare, the city council resolved to join FSIS and support its operations with SEK 2 million per year with no specified time horizon. A short press release was published on the city's website on 28 November 28 2014 in which the Director of Welfare is quoted as saying, "With our financial support, we will develop FSIS and give the organization greater legitimacy. We can see that this is needed, because from this approach come solutions we would otherwise never see".

* * *

What the future will bring the City of Malmö in terms of social entrepreneurship remains to be seen. However, there seems to be a fairly loose connection between the commission's notion of knowledge alliances and actions taken by city council officials. The commission's objective 3.1.3, which stipulated that the City of Malmö should "create new forms of collaboration between the private and public sectors as well as the voluntary sector" has been 'lost in translation', translated first by the city council's Working Committee for Healthcare and Welfare into the joining of FSIS, and then by the Director of Welfare into the pursuit of legitimacy. In the process, the objective of creating an infrastructure that facilitates participatory bottom-up initiatives for the sake of urban integration has been replaced by buying into a 'knowledge bank' and network for the sake of job creation and acquiring a positive image for the city. That is, social entrepreneurship seems to have been hijacked by the very same neoliberal, managerial discourse that has made creativity into an essential feature of urban planning.

However, behind the neoliberal, managerial discourse and its focus on knowledge and inspiration, the narrative styles of Homer and the Old Testament are lurking.

Regarding the type of knowledge that the city council officials envision, it is not relational knowledge, as in the commission's idea of knowledge alliances. Instead of being appreciated as more or less unconditionally created in and by alliances of stakeholders, knowledge is treated in line with an objectivist epistemology. The making and meaning of social entrepreneurship is therefore predefined either in lexical terms (as in 'ABCs of . . .') or in terms of 'best practices'; FSIS is accordingly approached and narrated by the city council as the bringer of the truth, just as Bornstein and Davies (2010) position their book. However, the truth about social entrepreneurship, or about FSIS for that matter, is apparently neither particularly transparent nor detailed. Social entrepreneurship and FSIS are indeed defined, but the definitions are multiple and divergent. Being fraught with background in this manner, one could argue that the narrative of FSIS and social entrepreneurship hails the city council officials and subjects them not only to eternal funding, but also to eternal acts of interpreting the value and meaning of social entrepreneurship.

As regards the inspiration that the city council officials hope for, it will probably be conveyed via the same kinds of activities embraced by the commission: social entrepreneurs who have been particularly successful in creating social value and capital are envisioned as narrating their experiences, presumably at seminars, fora and conferences. Not much is said about these activities in the official letter from the city council, but one can assume that these narratives are intended to be promotional in character—realistic and full of detailed descriptions of hardships, but of course with happy endings. As such they could, in line with Homer's narrative style, be conceptualised as a kind of heroic legend-making intended to please and enchant the audience, just as FSIS's own history-making can be conceptualised as a narrative constructed to delight city council officials.

Either way, these particular constructions of knowledge and inspiration—and the narrative styles and their accompanying constructions of reality—might hamper the actors' pursuit of legitimacy in that both subjection and enchantment could be considered illegitimate narrative strategies for both researchers and practitioners. Enchantment might encourage an ethos that induces researchers and practitioners to seek new adventures as soon as their journeys into social entrepreneurship are no longer enjoyable, whereas subjection might lead to blind faith and messianism, with or without a Messiah (Dey & Steyaert, 2010). In the former case, the legitimizing activities are offset by an ephemeral attitude; in the latter case, the striving for legitimacy is compromised by biased self-interest, although in the guise of a greater cause. In the case of Malmö, this gives rise to a paradox: on one hand, social entrepreneurship and the enrolment of FSIS as a partner of the City of Malmö are characterized by blind faith and self-interest, while on the other hand, the partnership is conditioned by annual evaluations to be conducted in relation to the budget process. It seems as though the city council has faith in social entrepreneurship and FSIS only as long as it pays off, presumably in jobs and goodwill.

Enchantment and subjection might also have devastating effects on the ability to relate to the social entrepreneurship field in a nuanced and reflective manner. One who stands enchanted or subjected before a phenomenon is unlikely to level criticism or question its value or raison d'être, and is more likely, not to say inclined, to (re)produce a reality in which the phenomenon is treated as intrinsically and indisputably good, as an objective fact. In this sense, it is no wonder that Light (2008) and Bornstein and Davis (2010) are united in an effort to define social entrepreneurship: it is simply the strategy of those who favour a reality they know to be enchanting or mysterious. As such, their writings on social entrepreneurship could be also conceptualised as showcases for ontological gerrymandering (Woolgar & Pawluch, 1985; Potter, 1996). In and by their use of narrative styles, the complex, multiple facets of social entrepreneurship are demarcated and delimited so that certain aspects of the desired reality are emphasised and assembled into a representation of 'Reality'—the One and Only, whereas other aspects are downplayed and disregarded. Such ontological gerrymandering may very well lead to a coherent paradigm; however, it may at the same time be undermined by those who have been disregarded—or those with a different ethos.

In the City of Malmö, the reality of social entrepreneurship could have been shaped into a matter of governance and could have been legitimized in terms of knowledge alliances. Instead, social entrepreneurship has predominantly been interpreted as a government issue and as such been assumed to concern job creation and image management. For social entrepreneurship, however, legitimacy seems not only to be about aligning biased interests with neoliberal and managerial discourses, but also about narrating the reality of social entrepreneurship by means of enchanting digressions and tacit truth claims.

In this sense, the City of Malmö seems to be caught between Odysseus's scar and Abraham's sacrifice.

References

Auerbach, E. (1953/1968). *Mimesis: The Representation of Reality in Western Literature*. Princeton: Princeton University Press.

Bayliss, D. (2007). The Rise of the Creative City: Culture and Creativity in Copenhagen. *European Planning Studies*, 7, 879–903.

Bornstein, D. & Davis, S. (2010). *Social Entrepreneurship—What Everyone Needs to Know*. Oxford: Oxford University Press.

Bruni, A., Gherardi, S. & Poggio, B. (2004). Entrepreneur-Mentality, Gender and the Study of Women Entrepreneurs. *Journal of Organizational Change Management*, 17(3), 256–268.

Dees, J. G. (1998). Enterprising Nonprofits. *Harvard Business Review*, 76, 55–67.

Dey, P. & Steyaert, C. (2010). The Politics of Narrating Social Entrepreneurship. *Journal of Enterprising Communities: People and Places in the Global Economy*, 4(1), 85–108.

Drayton, W. (2002). The Citizen Sector: Becoming Entrepreneurial and Competitive as Business. *California Management Review*, 44, 120–132.

Florida, R. (2002). *The Rise of the Creative Class: And How It's Transforming Work, Leisure and Everyday Life*. New York: Basic Books.

Hjorth, D. & Steyaert, C. (Eds.). (2004). *Narrative and Discursive Approaches in Entrepreneurship: A Second Movements in Entrepreneurship Book*. Cheltenham: Edward Elgar.

Homer. (1942). *The Odyssey*. Vol. 2. Cambridge, MA: Heinemann.

Jones, C. & Spicer, A. (2005). The Sublime Object of Entrepreneurship. *Organization*, 12(2), 223–246.

Light, P. C. (2008). *The Search for Social Entrepreneurship*. Washington: Brookings Institution Press.

Lund Hansen, A., Andersen, H. T. & Clark, E. (2001). Creative Copenhagen: Globalisation, Urban Governance and Social Change. *European Planning Studies*, 9, 851–869.

van Maanen, J. C. (1988). *Tales of the Field—On Writing Ethnography*. Chicago & London: The University of Chicago Press.

Mair, J. & Marti, I. (2006). Social Entrepreneurship Research: A Source of Explanation, Prediction, and Delight. *Journal of World Business*, 41, 36–44.

Malmö Stad. (2014). *Det fortsatta arbetet för ett social hållbart Malmö*. Malmö: Exakta.

Nicholls, A. (2010). The Legitimacy of Social Entrepreneurship: Reflexive Isomorphism in a Pre-Paradigmatic Field. *Entrepreneurship, Theory and Practice*, 34(4), 611–633.

Ogbor, J. O. (2000). Mythicizing and Reification in Entrepreneurial Discourse: Ideology-Critique of Entrepreneurial Studies. *Journal of Management Studies*, 37(5), 605–635.

Peck, J. (2005). Struggling with the Creative Class. *International Journal of Urban and Regional Research*, 29, 740–770.

Potter, J. (1996). *Representing Reality: Discourse, Rhetoric and Social Construction.* London: Sage Publications.

Programme Declaration. (2012). *Mötesplatsen Social Innovation: Programförklaring.* Malmö: Mötesplatsen för Social Innovation. Available at http://social innovation.se/wp-content/uploads/2013/08/Programf%C3%B6rklaring-M%C3%B6tesplats-Social-Innovation-ars-2013.pdf.

Steyaert, C. & Bouwen, R. (1997). Telling Stories of Entrepreneurship—Towards a Narrative-Contextual Epistemology for Entrepreneurial Studies. In R. Donckels & A. Miettinen (Eds.), *Entrepreneurship & SME Research: On Its Way to the Next Millenium.* Aldershot: Ashgate.

Stigendal, M. & Östergren, P. O. (2013). *Malmö's Path Towards a Sustainable Future: Health, Welfare and Justice. Commission for a Socially Sustainable Malmö.* Malmö: Malmö Stad.

STK 2014-238. (2014). *Fråga om Malmö stads anslutning till Mötesplats social innovation.* August, 19. Malmö: Malmö Stad.

Woolgar, S. & Pawluch, D. (1985). Ontological Gerrymandering: The Anatomy of Social Problems Explanation. *Social Problems*, 32, 214–227.

10 Social Entrepreneurship as Collaborative Processes in Rural Sweden

Yvonne von Friedrichs and Anders Lundström

Since the mid-1990s, Sweden has had one of the fastest urbanization processes of any of the countries in the European Union. However, such a fast urbanization process causes severe problems, especially in regions with sparsely populated communities. In this chapter, entrepreneurship is discussed as a collaborative force for local communities to retain and develop prosperity and well-being for local residents. Five examples of how sparsely populated communities have developed various collaborative models of social entrepreneurship to meet the structural changes in society are presented. The results of the cases presented show that there are no quick fixes; that community-based entrepreneurship implies long-term oriented activities, which have to be integrated in each local context. Decisions to make the work successful must to a large extent be taken in each local community, since the knowledge and understanding of possibilities and limitations can only be found in the community in question.

Entrepreneurship as a Collaborative Force

The definition of an entrepreneur has for a long time focused on the individual aspect: who the entrepreneur is and what s/he does, and frequently in a private sector context. But since entrepreneurship "is concerned with the discovery and exploitation of profitable opportunities" (Shane & Venkataraman, 2000), the concept could also embrace non-solitary individuals, i.e., collectives of individuals from various contexts. As the notion of entrepreneurship is strongly connected to innovation and opportunism (Bjerke, 2013), cultural and institutionalized patterns are constantly challenged by innovative solutions and new models for how to create wealth for people around the world. Such innovative movements will occur at different levels in society, such as on the individual level, that is the entrepreneur her/himself, but also on a common level, as the community or regional level.

Recent research shows that the concept of entrepreneurship is intertwined with societal responsibility, e.g., social and community-based entrepreneurship, which means that social benefits could be the major organizational outcome of entrepreneurship processes (Johannisson & Nilsson, 1989;

Dees, 1998; Austin, 2000; Gawell, Johannisson, & Lundqvist, 2009). Such perspectives have challenged institutionalized norms and values related to entrepreneurship research. A wider perspective on entrepreneurship as a conceptual notion that incorporates not only economic but also human and social values can be found in various contexts and sectors in society (Lundström, Zhou, von Friedrichs & Sundin, 2014). Cooperation and partnerships between regional public, private and civic actors have become strategies to meet the increasing global competition between regions regarding residents and local business activity, especially in regions where local welfare and well-being are threatened as a result of economic depletion due to closures and poor tax assessment. Recent research has shown that strategic collaboration and partnerships between stakeholders from the public, private and civic sectors, and sometimes academia as well, may explain structural development in economies, e.g., the Triple Helix (Etzkovitz & Leydesdorff, 1995; Leydesdorff, 2012) and public-private partnership (Jacobson & Choi, 2008; UNDP, 2015).

In the wake of the current rapid structural changes in society, social and community-based entrepreneurship is becoming more important as a way to encourage businesses and public policy practitioners to focus on the significance of people working together to facilitate regional development (see, Kapelus, 2002). "Many empirical studies have been carried out, but the majority of them have been oriented to summarising experiences and opinions related to this area [*social entrepreneurship*] or addressing conceptual issues in order to establish some core ideas in this particular field of academic research. It is clear that more solid, qualitative empirical work is needed" (Pierre, von Friedrichs, Wincent, 2013, p 19).

The aim of this chapter is to elaborate on social entrepreneurship, and, more specifically, what in Sweden is called societal or community-based entrepreneurship[1] as a collaborative counterforce to rural local societies' decrease in a welfare context. In particular, we will focus on how such collaborative initiatives are initiated, how they are organized and their development strategies and resource allocation. We will look at five cases from the two Swedish counties of Jämtland and Västernorrland, both peripheral and sparsely populated regions located in the middle of Sweden affected by structural changes in local society. The chapter will provide examples of regional stakeholder collaboration and partnership initiatives aimed to meet the challenges of rural communities in Sweden. Five local initiatives from the two counties are emphasised to illustrate the different modes of this type of social entrepreneurship. The initiatives are examples of communities where the inhabitants have managed to create long-term change and development through involvement of entrepreneurship with social purposes. In the chapter, the analysis of the five initiatives is presented as an example of how collaborative entrepreneurship in a welfare nation such as Sweden could be managed. The impact on local society and the outcome of the initiatives will be discussed, as well as examples of different organizing solutions and resource allocation challenges. Finally, the challenges of public-private partnership in rural communities will also be mentioned.

The chapter proceeds as follows. In the first section, there is a discussion about the field of entrepreneurship as a collaborative process, organizational challenges and development in the context of small, rural localities. In the second section, a number of models in use are presented based on the cases of Jämtland and Västernorrland, where five initiatives were initiated to develop prosperity and wealth in local communities. The third section includes an analysis of the role of collaborative entrepreneurship in attempting to reach prosperity and wealth in small communities located in sparsely populated regions. Finally, conclusions are drawn based on the five cases, and several implications are proposed for policy and practice as an outcome when applying collaborative entrepreneurship in regional development.

Embedded Community Entrepreneurship

The European Union " has placed the social economy and social innovation at the heart of its concerns, in terms of both territorial cohesion and the search for new solutions to societal problems, in particular the fight against poverty and exclusion, under the Europe 2020 strategy" (European Commission, 2011). The OECD (2011) shows that collaborative work between the public and private sectors has helped local economies to transform into entrepreneurial and innovative communities with the ability to create more and better jobs, to avoid economic crisis and to achieve sustainable development. It is argued that structural changes in society will open up for the employment of a regional entrepreneurial mindset (von Friedrichs & Boter, 2009), as it provides opportunities for different actors to challenge established norms and values in society. The more globalized the world becomes and the more impact it has on people, the more opportunities are given for alternative thinking on how to support regional dynamics. People and businesses worldwide "think globally but act locally", which means that problems can often be found very close to the local residents in a community.

Social entrepreneurs have been proposed to make significant and diverse contributions to communities and societies, adopting business models in their work to find innovative solutions to complex and pressing social problems (Zahra, Gedajlovic, & Schulman, 2009; Nicholls, 2010;). If entrepreneurship is approached in a wider sense than business and profit and also embraces the social good, it may provide opportunities for different actors to question cultural and institutionalized patterns and solutions on how to solve problems and how to create wealth in different contexts, e.g. rural communities.

Social entrepreneurship has, like most commercial entrepreneurs, its primary focus on the creation of social value, while the type of generated value differs between the entrepreneurs. Whereas economic value creation is central for most of the commercial entrepreneurs, the primary focus for the social entrepreneur is social value creation (Smith & Stevens, 2010). The scope and impact of social entrepreneurship depend on the closeness and relevance of the problem. Drawing on a typology proposed by Zahra et al. (2009), Smith and Stevens (2010) add the two dimensions of geography and embeddedness to the three suggested types of social entrepreneurs: the social engineer, the social constructionist and the bricoleur (Zahra et al., 2009). Smith and Stevens (2010) point to the importance of embeddedness for the development of variants of social entrepreneurship and its mobilizing of resources. A high degree of embeddedness in a society facilitates the 'bricoleur' function (Baker & Nelson, 2005) when social entrepreneurship is based upon a pragmatic mobilization of resources (Di Domenico, Haugh, & Tracey, 2010). The embeddedness can take the form of organizational affiliation (Zahra et al., 2009). Such affiliation provides the social and community-based entrepreneur with a net of contacts, which facilitates the gathering of necessary resources for their initiatives, since it implies a context in which resources can be found and mobilized. The organization itself can belong to the non-profit sector or the commercial sector, and it can be a public organization (Austin, Stevenson & Wei-Skillern, 2006; Mair & Martí, 2006).

Sweden is the country in the European Union with the fastest urbanization, which has been the case ever since the mid-1990s, and this poses severe challenges for many regions in Sweden. Rural regions and communities who are situated far from the three most urbanized areas in the country are those who are most concerned with how to reconstruct local service support systems in order to keep regional and local prosperity and welfare development. A major problem for several rural areas is that young people move to urban areas looking for work and education, leaving aging people (+50 years) behind. The distorted age structure in rural areas makes new solutions and models on how to adapt to the structural changes in Swedish regions urgent. There are people and organizations in a number of small Swedish communities and villages that have realised that if they want to have a good quality of life for themselves and their families, they will have to arrange it themselves.

Entrepreneurship as Collaborative Processes

Entrepreneurship and entrepreneurial behaviour are most often discussed from a profit-making perspective. The mainstream definition of entrepreneurship is linked to private companies, but there are also broader perspectives linked to the creation of new organizations (Gartner, 1985) and various types of entrepreneurial activities associated with, and often within, larger companies and organizations, e.g. corporate entrepreneurship and intrapreneurship (Zahra, Jennings & Kuratko, 1999). Entrepreneurship in this market-oriented tradition most often aims at economic return and firm creation (see, e.g., Shane & Venkataraman, 2000). However, Holcombe (2002), among others, has found that entrepreneurship also exists in the public sector, e.g. political entrepreneurship. During the last decade, there has been a growing interest in entrepreneurship and local/regional development, which brings in a focus on social issues as in the concept of social entrepreneurship. Social entrepreneurship is a powerful means to stimulate innovative and creative actions aiming to develop and organize functions that are beneficial for society (Hartigan & Elkington, 2008). Nicholls (2006, p 23) has tried to define social entrepreneurship as: "innovative and effective activities that focus strategically on resolving social market failures and creating opportunities to add social value systematically by using a range of organizational formats to maximize social impact and bring about change".

Gawell et al. (2009) claim that in Sweden, there is a problem with this definition of social entrepreneurship, as it mainly focuses on the individual social entrepreneur experimenting with new venture forms and how to transform social good to private transactional offerings. Instead, Gawell et al. (2009) offer a complementarity contrast to this view in the notion of a more balanced view on the role of individuals, which has engaged Swedish scholars and policy makers. In the wake of this, the concept of societal entrepreneurship has been developed as an attempt to capture a multifaceted phenomenon depending on focus and context. Gawell et al. (2009, p. 15) argue that, "Swedish societal entrepreneurship has been strongly related to local mobilization, to employment, to the will and opportunity to remain in and reclaim a local context, and to mobilize around new business opportunities". Societal entrepreneurship unites research perspectives with different focuses depending on the purpose and actors involved. Further, it is argued that the concept has been developed to draw attention to the Swedish tradition of solidarity and non-transactional collective actions in local proximity. The concept of societal entrepreneurship is, therefore, most often related to actors, individuals and groups, foremost in local proximity where community-based problems play an important role (Bjerke, 2013; Pierre, von Friedrichs & Wincent, 2013).

Much of the value of research on social entrepreneurship lies in the non-restricted and innovative manner in which the societal entrepreneurs pursue their goals, i.e., considering several pressing issues in society without getting 'locked in' a certain institutional setting. The people involved make a difference to societal entrepreneurship, as they are responsive, have strong emotional bonds to the community and are able to build networks and interact with other societal actors (Johannisson, 2005). The social and societal entrepreneur, in other words, acts innovatively towards relevant structures while attempting to reach a predefined social goal (see Zahra et al., 2009; Smith & Stevens, 2010). These goals can vary greatly even if they have a common denominator, i.e. 'social'. The goals of societal as well as social entrepreneurship are, however, always collective and related to a greater social need (Nicholls, 2010; Bjerke, 2013).

Local Development Through Entrepreneurship

When meeting changes in a specific regional or local context, it becomes necessary to mobilize a wide range of actors in order to meet the challenges linked to the new situation (Arbuthnott & von Friedrichs, 2012). A wide set of actors within the business community and the civic sector will, together with various public organizations, come forward in order to adapt to changes and find solutions to their own and common problems (Elkington & Fennel, 1998). Partnership models such as the Triple Helix (Etzkowitz & Leydesdorff, 1995; Leydesdorff, 2012), private-public partnerships (Osborne, 2000; UNDP, 2015) and cross-sector social partnerships (Selsky & Parker, 2010) have been used as approaches for various actors to collaboratively and innovatively tackle societal transformation processes. In contemporary perspectives on entrepreneurship, it is shown that innovative and opportunistic behaviour not only exists in the private sector, but also in other sectors in society (Bjerke, 2013). For example, the corporate entrepreneurship perspective is in many ways well adapted to non-profit activities. Scholars such as Morris and Jones (1999) found many similarities between corporate entrepreneurship and the public context, for example, a strong cultural environment and the importance of effective and well-developed routines for administrative control. Johannisson and Nilsson (1989) indicate that public sector organizations not only work with concrete entrepreneurial activities, but that their core assignments as public authorities and public service providers can be conducted in an entrepreneurial way and in close cooperation with companies.

The public sector becomes more and more influenced by globalization and finds itself in a more complex environment that calls for a different public organizational behaviour. While the public sector becomes more businesslike, businesses are encouraged to take on a social responsibility perspective, although the public sector often has less flexibility than actors in the business sector when it comes to acting depending on external and internal environments (Kearney, Hisrich & Roche, 2009). Previous research by Kearney et al. (2009) found that there are similarities between private and public sector entrepreneurship, but also that there are important differences related to some of what they pinpoint as established key dimensions defining entrepreneurial orientation, namely: innovativeness, risk taking and proactiveness. However, Bjerke (2013) argues that the notion of risk taking is outdated in contemporary entrepreneurship research and that it is innovation and opportunism that are the main features of entrepreneurship. Following this view, entrepreneurship can be found in various contextual settings where systems and individuals meet, incorporating actors and perspectives in borderless organizations and at different levels in society. It could be claimed that there are few empirical studies on the organization and outcome of social and community-based entrepreneurship. In particular, there is a knowledge gap on what kinds of measures small communities and villages take to meet current structural changes in society, especially from a social welfare perspective, like in the Nordic countries.

The Swedish Context: A Strong Welfare Structure

Sweden is in the top 20, at number 15, of the wealthiest nations in the world, and it is a welfare country (Global Finance, 2013). In Sweden, as in many other nations, there are regional differences in gross regional product within the country (SCB, 2012), but Sweden has an extensive tradition of solidarity and equal opportunities, meaning that all Swedes should have equal access to publicly funded local services, regardless of where in the country they live. This is a challenge for the Swedish society and its 1,838 small municipalities (defined as 200 to 10,000 inhabitants, (Growth Analysis, 2011), who are facing the challenge of erosion of the Swedish welfare model and demands of the same level of access to local social services as urban areas.

For quite a long time, Sweden has experienced major reductions in employment opportunities due to public and private sector closures, which have lead to unemployment (von Friedrichs, 2009). Several municipalities have been adversely affected by this development, with the result that young people move to find education and work elsewhere, leaving aging people in need of local social services behind, which in turn creates problematic local economic performance (see, e.g., von Friedrichs & Boter, 2009; Arbuthnott & von Friedrichs, 2012). Sweden is known for having a predominantly tax-financed public sector, and most municipalities are dependent on a well-functioning public sector financing social services, e.g., schools, health and elder care and road maintenance etc. The two counties of Jämtland and Västernorrland are both regions that have been extensively affected by urbanization. Especially the small rural communities have experienced a negative trend where people and businesses are leaving the two counties, which in turn leads reduced tax revenues to finance social functions in the local community, and this in turn makes it difficult for people to stay. Outside the urban areas in Sweden, this development is a contemporary problem for Swedish rural municipalities, resulting in depleted regions.

In times of such major structural changes, traditional structures, norms and values have been challenged in Swedish society. During the last decades, several municipalities, like the counties of Jämtland and Västernorrland, have had a reduction in the total number of inhabitants, and the people still living in these municipalities are forced to find new solutions on how to secure wealth and prosperity for themselves and for the enterprises in the local society. Cross-border collaborations between actors from private, public and civic sectors have been developed in various ways, and through these initiatives, the communities try to solve how to organize several functions that have previously been taken care of by the public sector and financed by taxes (see Swedish Agency for Economic and Regional Growth, 2014). There is still little research on how and why such initiatives are established, how they are organized and resources mobilized and what strategies and actions are used to deal with local community concerns in a welfare context.

Evidence From Rural Sweden

This section provides five examples of how small Swedish communities develop various models of soci(et)al entrepreneurship in order to meet problems in the wake of structural changes in local society. The five local communities are: Trångsviken, Näsbygden, Kallbygden, Oviken and Docksta. An explorative study was conducted in August 2009 and in November 2011 in the five small communities in the two remote and sparsely populated counties of Jämtland and Västernorrland in the middle of Sweden (see Figure 10.1).

All five communities are located between 20–44 kilometres from a municipality centre. The five informants in the study were local residents or engaged locally on a regular basis. They all had powerful and influential positions in the local society and had been involved in the development of the community for many years. Four of the interviews took place in 2009 and one in 2011, and all took place on the community premises, lasting two hours each. The data from the informants was also supplemented by Internet-based information, e.g. characteristics about the communities.

Figure 10.1 Locations of Jämtland and Västernorrland

Table 10.1 Summarizing Five Local Cases of Community-Based Entrepreneurship

Characteristics	Trångsviken	Näsbygden	Kallbygden	Oviken	Docksta
Population 2013	700	900	550	1750	900
Distance from municipality centre	44 km	20 km	23 km	33 km	32 km
Number of businesses	80 SEs	50 SEs	10 MEs + 60–70 SEs	400 SMEs	70 SMEs
Initiation of mobilization	2000	1984	1991	1997	1963
Organization	Ltd company	Ltd company	Interest association + Ltd company	Limited Company	Interest association + Ltd company
Community entrepreneur	Trångsviken Limited Company	Näsbygdens Development Company	Kallbygden Interest Association	Oviken Local Business Association	Docksta Table Tennis club
Strategy	Encouraging entrepreneurship Mentorship Venture capital	Local service Housing Windmill power	Local service Housing Windmill power	Doing business Housing Encouraging entrepreneurship	Sports activities Doing business Housing School Elderl care Lobbying
Activities	Networking activities New ventures	Networking activities Projects Study circles	Networking activities Projects Immigration	Networking activities Projects	Networking activities Sports activities New ventures Investments
Major achievement	Increase of households 20% the last 10 years	Mobilized local residents to solve residential problems	Increase of Dutch families	Mobilization of residential interest for common problems	Local mobilization of human, financial social capital
Collaborators	Locals Business	Locals Business	Locals Business Public	Locals Business	Locals Business Non-profit organization

SE = SMALL ENTERPRISE ME = MEDIUM SIZED ENTERPRISE
SME = SMALL AND MEDIUM ENTERPRISE

Trångsviken

Characteristics: Trångsviken is a small community in the county of Jämtland, with about 400 residents and 80 smaller businesses. The community is located 44 km from the municipality centre. The geographical location is relatively favourable, close to both the mountains and the regional centre, to the European Route 45 and only half an hour by car from the regional airport. The community is a unique place with respect to its entrepreneurial culture and positive business climate.

The start: social entrepreneurs mostly work on a local basis in the case of Trångsviken. Through a dialogue with the people concerned, local needs were identified, which resulted in the construction of a new community centre building in the mid-1990s, financed jointly by the residents. This became a platform for the involvement of local people and functioned as a supportive structure for the subsequent initiatives for business development.

Organization: with a non-profit association as the organizational basis, the local residents managed to support new business ventures as well as existing local businesses development. Trångsviken has inspired and supported several other communities in various parts of the county and is often considered a role model for social and community-based entrepreneurship in the country. Local companies and the local community have evolved side by side, which resulted in the non-profit business association being converted into Trångsviken Limited Company in 2000. The business idea was to offer a platform for individuals with the same idea of contributing to keep and develop the local welfare and for the platform to have good financial strength to support ideas. 65 individuals, 24 companies and two associations invested around 3.6 million Swedish crowns in the company. The conversion of the previous non-profit business association into a limited company mainly aimed at broadening the ownership.

Strategy: the preservation of basic social services vital for local prosperity and welfare has meant that initiatives have been taken to save local service facilities, such as the local grocery store, the local school, the library and the local bank office. From the start, the objective of the company was to pursue development projects to improve the living conditions and invest in infrastructure, such as broadband and facilities for new industries. The company's main operation was renting out premises and to function as support for businesses in the area.

Resourcing: the residents of Trångsviken have always felt a strong commitment to the place and have used their personal networks as assets to achieve common goals, i.e., to create an attractive place for people to live in and for businesses to invest in. The residents used a collaborative approach to entrepreneurship, having, e.g., the local sports club, bank capital and politics join forces to reverse negative development, which many municipalities in the Swedish countryside, especially in inland Norrland, are experiencing.

Major achievement: about twenty new businesses have launched since the end of the 1990s. During the same period, the number of households has increased by 20 per cent. "Entrepreneurship for all ages" is the motto the villages live by, and therefore the company Trångsviksbolaget Ltd committed itself from the very beginning to the development of an entrepreneurial school, an entrepreneurial youth camp and a company developed to care for people with business ideas, among other things.

Näsbygden

Characteristics: this example is also a small community with about 850 residents and about 50 small businesses. The community is located 20 km from the municipality centre.

The start: in 1984, a couple of residents realised that they were experiencing a negative community development, so they decided to do something about it. A small group of residents, six active local politicians, decided to contact someone from another small community who they had been told was an expert in local development issues. This expert recommended the group that all activities aimed to develop the community should be done in a limited company and not as a voluntary association. The reason for this was that the commercial banks had little knowledge about voluntary businesses and were likely to hesitate to lend out money to such an association.

Organization: the six local politicians decided to leave politics when they started the limited company 'Näsbygdens Development Company' (NDC). The group of six became the company's board and main owners. In addition to this, other residents in the community were invited to buy B-shares in the NDC. At the time of the study, there were 40 shareholders in the company. The main objective of the development company was to work towards making it possible for people of all ages to be able to live and work in the local community.

Strategy: all earnings of the company were reinvested in to the community. The main strategy of the NDC was to engage people in workshops, which meant that they organized a new study circle for each new project. When the NDC had no projects of their own, they lent a hand to other activities in the community, which meant that when residents encountered a problem or something had to be fixed in the community, the NDC was expected to help out.

Resourcing: at times, the NDC also organized large meetings, inviting people from all over the community. At these meetings, they discussed common interests related to the future of the community, such as school issues, wind power, new housing and uranium exploration. After each such meeting, volunteers were appointed to workgroups specifically dealing with different prioritized issues. In each project, the chairman of the NDC mixed people with different backgrounds, ages, previous experience, networking skills etc. that were likely to affect whether or not the project would succeed.

Major achievement: the driving force of the community and the NDC was that each individual resident had to take responsibility for the community to survive. Each one of them had to work hard to keep the important local service providers, such as the local grocery store, the post services and catering to the elderly. The collective power of the NDC seemed to be obvious. One example of this was that residents identified the lack of housing as a problem for people who wanted to move to the area. The NDC succeeded in convincing the municipality to build new apartments in the area. At the time of the study, the wind power development, uranium exploration and new housing for the elderly had become prioritized areas of NDC.

Kallbygden

Characteristics: Kallbygden is a district that consists of six communities with about 550 residents and about 10 medium-sized companies and 60–70 very small businesses. The district area is as big as the country of Monaco and is located 23 km from the municipality centre.

The start: for several years, Kallbygden consisted of a number of small villages, and the cooperative work was fairly unstructured and turbulent. Every year, the district received compensation from the state for the regulation of the lakes, which meant that they received 2–2.5 million Swedish crowns ($\approx$ € 200,000–250,000) each year from the local government. The amount was placed in a community trust be shared out among the villages. Who was entitled to receive the money caused a conflict each year. In 1991, the Kallbygden Interest Association (KIA) was established, and all six villages were included. KIA became a strong negotiator in relation to the municipality government. The association included two people from each village, a treasurer, a secretary, two vice presidents and a chairperson.

Organization: the collaboration between the local government and the villages started when the six villages participated in an experimental project run by the central municipality concerning models for local democracy. An experimental group was formed to function as a district board responsible for the municipal budget for the Kallbygden district. The experiment that started as a project is now a permanent solution for the governance of Kallbygden. At the time for the study (2009), it was the only of its kind in Sweden, and the district board managed a budget of 10 million Swedish crowns (> € 1,000,000) annually. The money was used to manage schools and elder care, among other things. The board consisted of six people, three directly elected from the district and three politicians who were elected by the municipality. Prior to each year, people from the district could nominate people to represent the directly elected.

Strategy: residents were encouraged to come up with ideas for new project proposals and submit these directly to the association. But it was the association that decided and prioritized the projects according to what was most beneficial for the district. The main aim of KIA was to retain local services for the villages and to attract more settlers. KIA submitted all the project proposals to the municipality government. This has meant that the money nowadays is more likely to go to large projects that are expected to benefit the whole district, that is, projects supporting something that they all want and can use. So far, KIA has built a new local grocery store, a retirement home, a wind power plant, a service building close to the campsite and a swimming pool etc. A small amount of the money was used to maintain the roads and other types of refurbishments. The strategy has been "urgent response, rapid solutions to urgent problems". KIA also invested money into the water supply in the six villages.

Resourcing: in Sweden, living far from the municipality centre constitutes a major problem when it comes to lending money from banks for investments. The problem is related to the fact that the valuation of properties located on the Swedish periphery is very different from city centres. To solve this problem, KIA established a limited company, Kalls Fastighetsförvaltning (Kall's Property Management, KPM) as a way to finance current expenses. As KIA managed the various projects, KPM could benefit from various forms of public assistance and in turn, KIA purchases services from KPM.

Major achievement: KIA collaborated with a Norwegian company that brokered contacts with Dutch families interested in moving to Kallbygden, and so far, 17 people have moved to the area from Holland. At the time of the study, KIA was trying to resolve the funding of new housing and broadband. The informant from Kallbygden explained that in order for local development to proceed in the long term, a degree of commercialism is necessary in community-based social entrepreneurship.

Oviken

Characteristics: in the Oviken district, there are approximately 1,750 residents and 400 businesses. The district is located 33 km from the municipality centre. Most businesses, 236 to be exact, are companies working with agriculture and forestry. Oviken is well known for its culture, music, strong community life and a voluntary commitment from its residents.

The start: in the Oviken district, the Oviken Business Association (OBA) was committed to the district's development. The board of the business association consisted of seven people, women and men of a relatively low average age; more people got involved in the work when needed.

Organization: the informant at Oviken believed that OBA would have to reorganize to improve for the future to be able to succeed with the development needed in the area, and also that they needed to hire permanent staff. A role model for OBA was Trångsviken, which is why they decided to start a limited company in 2009. They are of the opinion that it is important to have some form of commercial activity for local development efforts to be sustainable and therefore, they had to start a company.

Strategy: a very important issue for the future was to encourage more people to move to the community and to attract more companies with new jobs. But OBA was also involved in the development of the school and the health centre and the maintenance and expansion of the roads etc.

Resourcing and major achievement: OBA was committed to showcasing the district and to developing the trade. To this end, they started a yearly Christmas market for local residents and visitors, but also a spring market fair for associations and companies. OBA discussed local problems in meetings with banks, insurance companies and the municipality government; the problems discussed were major as well as minor issues in the municipality.

Docksta

Characteristics: Docksta is a small community in the county of Västernorrland in the middle of Sweden. In 2010, there was a population of 900 people and about 70 companies. The community is located 32 km from the municipality centre. The development of the society at large is more negative than the development of the population, with enterprises struggling with financial problems and a school and housing for elders that are both threatened with being closed down for economic reasons.

The start: Docksta Table Tennis Club (DBTK) started as a sports club association in 1963 and currently has about 500 members. There was a great reliance on the industry as a driver of societal development in the 1970s. The Swedish government and administration discussed the possibility to support local economies through investments in industry facilities. In Docksta, there were also discussions about the municipality investing in an industry facility to support the local economic development, but nothing came of it. The club's 'core members' brought this up for discussion as a problem for the local society. The club members knew there was an entrepreneur who was willing to rent facilities for his business, so they decided to do something about it. This was the main event that marked the development of the club into a social entrepreneur committed to the economic development of the local society. The objective was to maintain the local community so that it remained a vibrant and attractive countryside.

Organization: the board of DBTK consists of eight members, three substitutes and one representative and one substitute from each sports section. DBTK started a joint stock company, Docksta BTK Ltd, which was responsible for the operation and maintenance of the association's real estate as well as the tourist cable car owned by the company.

Strategy: DBTK has focused on the community's unique local conditions and developed these conditions in a pragmatic way, rather than focusing on a specific type of social problem. This approach has brought with it a great variety of activities, including the development of tourism activities (holiday cottages), sports activities (tennis, climbing and downhill) and a music festival, as well as industrial activities and local social services. These activities were the result of local needs.

Resourcing: essential for DBTK's success as a social entrepreneur was their ability to attract various forms of capital, and not just financial capital, but also human and social capital. The human capital primarily comprised of the skills that were found among the members of the board of the club. The cash flow resulting from their properties and other activities, like the music festival, has been the economic backbone of the club's involvement in the development of the community. They have also received project money and bank loans as well as money from the municipality, e.g., to run the school and the home for elderly. Social capital is the network of relationships that DBTK has been included in. Crucial to this network has been the trust that the club has received through the activities they pursued. The driving force of the club's development has been that they have been able to mobilize club members for volunteer work.

Major achievement: to counteract the negative development, the volunteer non-profit organization DBTK has developed into a social entrepreneur to save local jobs and mitigate the consequences of the negative development at large. They function as the local bricoleur.

Lesson Learned From Rural Sweden

The counties of Jämtland and Västernorrland in the northern parts of Sweden are from different perspectives perceived, geographically as well as mentally, as sparsely populated and peripherally located in relation to larger markets. Furthermore, as a region with a less developed infrastructure, these sparsely populated counties are by all means representative of many rural regions in Sweden that are facing the challenge of an emigrating population. Regions like Jämtland and Västernorrland are in many ways affected by the current transformation of society, and that is why local actors are becoming more and more interested in and motivated to focus on community-based and social entrepreneurship, as collaboration means making it possible to retain structures and functions that today's public sector no longer are or have not been able to maintain.

The county of Jämtland is known for a positive spirit of collaboration between authorities, organizations and the civil society, and also as a county with long-standing traditions of entrepreneurship and social networking. The county is one of the most sparsely populated in all of Europe, and various collaborative networks have substituted the social service that the public sector was not always able to provide and that have not been profitable enough for the market. The county of Västernorrland is different from Jämtland, with a tradition of larger industrial investments, primarily in the pulp industry. Västernorrland has more of a patriarchal structure and a less developed entrepreneurial tradition in the local society. The social and economic development of the disadvantaged communities in both counties is, however, based on teamwork between private, public and non-profit actions. Collaborative solutions for child and elder care, schools and pre-schools, as well as many other functions, have been established to meet the lack of public-funded community services.

The strong tradition in Jämtland of co-operation and collaborative solutions to solve shared functions and problems is often based on the contribution of volunteers and enthusiasts. The problem with these kinds of efforts is that it seems that after a period of intense involvement, these enthusiasts lose interest and the general development work ceases. To combine volunteer engagement with more commercial elements in work of this type seems to increase the persistency and innovative capacity of a small community.

When summarizing all five cases, it appears that the initiative to engage in community-based entrepreneurship comes from people who live close to each other and local business owners. In all cases, the main reason for local residents to organize themselves seems to be the urge to solve local issues perceived as problems related to the residents' daily lives. As a first step, when establishing a local collaboration, in most cases they decided to pursue their goals within the frame of a non-for-profit organization. When the organization grew and matured, more capital was needed, e.g., to invest locally or to maintain property, and as a solution, the non-profit or volunteer organizations transformed into limited companies. The reasons for this transformation were both to get bank loans for investments and to invite the local residents to ownership in the company. So far, there is only in one case, Kallbygden, where a partnership has been formalized between the private, public and civic sectors in order to invest in and govern local services.

These cases can tell us something about the development of sparsely populated areas. It is primarily about the initiation process, which is of course important, but our main conclusion is that to mobilize community developments takes a lot of time. For our five cases, the process has been going on between 15 to 50 years, and in some cases, it is still difficult to present concrete results from these activities. It is impossible to know what would have happened if these processes had not been initiated. The number of new businesses and small businesses differs in the different communities, between five to 23 per cent of the number of local inhabitants. It should also be noted that in all cases, the private community has played a very important role, even if the role differs between each community. What can be learned from this is that there is no one solution as to how to develop local successful processes. Since the forces reducing, e.g., the number of inhabitants, changing the age structure or diminishing the service in the community are so strong, the main purpose of the actions taken is to create anti-forces to such development or at least to reduce the effects. In all communities, we can find processes that will not end, but must continuously be developed from local experience and knowledge. It is also interesting that these processes have been mostly unknown outside the local communities, perhaps with some exception.

Collaborative Entrepreneurship Means Enabling Local Development

Different places and regions have different opportunities and obstacles in terms of development; therefore, it could be assumed that models of social and community-based entrepreneurship could also vary depending on circumstances and context. Even if the concept has not been described until recently, community-based entrepreneurship has been a reality for many years in different organizational forms. These long processes have provided knowledge of what seems to be/not be productive in different communities. In the initiation phase, there have obviously been different approaches, depending on the local context. The initiative could have come from individuals in the public and/or private sector, but it has to be developed by individuals in the local community in question. What can be learned from the process is that it is of vital importance to realise that these processes must be regarded as a never-ending story. It may take years before we can measure any real effects of all the efforts.

The individuals involved in the processes could all be regarded as soci(et)al entrepreneurs, since the main focus is to create forces that can create an alternative development based on different local contexts. Furthermore, it cannot be done without all partners involved using a 'thinking outside the box' perspective. Much of the work has to be carried out by non-profit forces that are able to see the importance of keeping a vital local context to make it worthwhile to develop further.

These collaborative movements in different local communities are more common than many of the actors on the national level know. Therefore, there is a political concentration on development in urban areas, since similar processes in these areas probably are much shorter in time and there is no need to be as creative as in sparsely located contexts. In local contexts, there are also factors that can be developed to prevent the rate of negative development. So far, we have not seen any politicians participating and supporting these developments on the regional and national levels. We believe that in the future, there are lessons to be learned when it comes to how to develop local communities in different contextual settings. There are no quick fixes: these are long-term activities that have to be worked on in each local context, and decisions on how to make the work successful must be taken locally. Knowledge of possibilities and limitations can only be found in each community.

In Sweden's sparsely populated and geographically peripheral and rural villages and communities, volunteer and non-profit organizations take over previous fiscal activities. In this chapter, we have shown that successful soci(et)al entrepreneurship is local and community-based, with networking activities involving actors from private, public and civil sectors in collaborative models. A Nordic model for soci(et)al entrepreneurship is community-based entrepreneurship enabling people living in sparsely populated regions in welfare societies like the Nordic countries to engage in and organize to innovatively meet the erosion of the Swedish welfare model—they become powerful geographically embedded bricoleurs.

Note

1. The differences and relation between these concepts will be elaborated on later in the text.

References

Arbuthnott, A. & von Friedrichs, Y. (2012). Entrepreneurial Renewal in a Peripheral Region: The Case of a Winter Automotive-Testing Cluster in Sweden. *Entrepreneurship and Regional Development*, 5(5–6), 371–403.

Austin, J. (2000). Strategic Collaboration Between Nonprofits and Business. *Non-Profit and Voluntary Sector Quarterly*, 29(1), 69–97.

Austin, J., Stevenson, H. & Wei-Skillern, J. (2006). Social and Commercial Entrepreneurship: Same, Different, or Both? *Entrepreneurship Theory & Practice*, 30(1), 1–22.

Baker, T. & Nelson, R. (2005). Creating Something from Nothing: Resource Construction through Entrepreneurial Bricolage. *Administrative Science Quarterly*, 50, 329–266.

Bjerke,B. (2013). *En bok om entreprenörskap*. Lund: Studentlitteratur.

Dees, J. G. (1998). *The Meaning of 'Social Entrepreneurship'*. Stanford University, Draft Report for the Kauffman Center for Entrepreneurial Leadership, 6.

Di Domenico, M., Haugh, H. & Tracey, P. (2010). Social Bricolage: Theorizing Social Value Creation in Social Enterprises. *Entrepreneurship: Theory & Practice*, 34, 681–703.

Elkington, J. & Fennel, S. (1998). Partners for Sustainability. *Geographic Focus Global*, 24, 49–60.

Etzkowitz, H. & Leydesdorff, L. (1995). The Triple Helix—University, Industry, Government Relations: A Laboratory for Knowledge-Based Economic Development. *EASST Review*, 14, 14–19.

European Commission. (2011). *Social Business Initiative: Creating a Favourable Climate for Social Enterprises, Key Stakeholders in the Social Economy and Innovation*. Communication from the commission to the European parliament, the council, the European economic and social committee and the committee of the regions. Available at http://eurlex.europa.eu/LexUriServ/LexUriServ.do?uri=COM:2011:0682:FIN:EN:PDF, accessed 12 October 2015.

von Friedrichs, Y. (2009). *Omvandling, omställning och omstrukturering i närsamhället—en studie hur försvarsnedläggningen i Sverige under 2000-talet påverkar lokal näringslivsutveckling*. (Social Science Reports from Mid Sweden University, 2009:1). Östersund: Mittuniversitetet.

von Friedrichs, Y. & Boter, H. (2009). Meeting Radical Change and Regional Transition: Regional Closedowns and the Role of Entrepreneurship. *Managing Global Transitions*, 7(2), 99–122.

Gartner, W. (1985). A Conceptual Framework for Describing the Phenomenon of New Venture Creation. *Academy of Management Review*, 10(4), 696–706.

Gawell, M., Johannisson, B. & Lundqvist, M. (2009). *Entrepreneurship in the Name of Society*. Stockholm: KK-stiftelsen.

Global Finance. (2013). *The World's Richest and Poorest Countries*. Available at http://www.gfmag.com, accessed 12 October 2015.

Growth analysis. (2011). *Orter med befolkningsökning—exempel på "attraktiva orter" perioden 2000–2010* (Report 2011:11). Östersund: Tillväxtanalys. Available at www.tillvaxtanalys.se.

Hartigan, P. & Elkington, J. (2008). *The Power of Unreasonable People: How Entrepreneurs Create Markets That Change to World*. Cambridge, MA: Harvard Business Press.

Holcombe, R. (2002). Political Entrepreneurship and the Democratic Allocation of Economic Resources. *The Review of Austrian Economics*, 15(2–3), 143–159.

Jacobson, C. & Choi, S. (2008). Success Factors: Public Works and Public-Private Partnerships. *International Journal of Public Sector Management*, 21(6), 637–657.

Johannisson, B. (2005). *Entreprenörskapets väsen*. Lund: Studentlitteratur.

Johannisson, B. & Nilsson, A. (1989). Community Entrepreneurs: Networking for Local Development. *Entrepreneurship & Regional Development*, 1, 3–19.Kapelus, P. (2002). Mining, Corporate Social Responsibility and the "Community": The Case of Rio Tinto, Richards Bay Minerals and the Mbonambi. *Journal of Business Ethics*, 39(3), 275–296.

Kearney, C., Hisrich, R. D. & Roche, F. (2009). Public and Private Sector Entrepreneurship: Similarities, Differences or a Combination. *Journal of Small Business and Enterprise Development*, 16(1), 26–46.

Leydesdorff, L. (2012). The Triple Helix, Quadruple Helix, and an N-Tuple of Helices: Explanatory Models for Analyzing the Knowledge-Based Economy? *Journal Knowledge Economy*, 3, 25–35.

Lundström, A., Zhoue, C., von Friedrichs, Y. & Sundin, E. (2014). *Social Entrepreneurship—Leveraging Economic, Political, and Cultural Dimension*. International Studies in Entrepreneurship. Springer International Publishing.

Mair, J. & Marti, I. (2006). Social Entrepreneurship Research: A Source of Explanation, Prediction, and Delight. *Journal of World Business*, 41(1), 36–44.

Morris, M. H. & Jones, F. F. (1999). Entrepreneurship in Established Organisations: The Case of the Public Sector. *Entrepreneurship Theory and Practice*, 24(1), 71–91.

Nicholls, A. (2006). *Social Entrepreneurship: New Models of Sustainable Social Change*. Oxford: Oxford University Press.

Nicholls, A. (2010). The Legitimacy of Social Entrepreneurship: Reflexive Isomorphism in a Pre-Paradigmatic Field. *Entrepreneurship Theory & Practice*, 34(4), 611–633.

Osborne, S. P. (2000). *Public-Private Partnerships: Theory and Practice in International Perspective*. London: Routledge.

Pierre, A., von Friedrichs, Y. & Wincent, J. (2013). A Review and Definition of Community-Based Entrepreneurship Research. In A. Lundström, C. Zhou, Y. von Friedrichs & E. Sundin (Eds.), *Social Entrepreneurship—Leveraging Economic, Political, and Cultural Dimensions*. New York & Heidelberg: Springer.

SCB. (2012). *Svag Bruttoregionprodukt (BRP) följdes av stark*. Press release from SCB 2012-12-12 09:30 Nr 2012:948. Available at http://www.scb.se/Pages/PressRelease___345460.aspx, accessed 12 October 2015.

Selsky, J. W. & Parker, B. (2010). Platforms for Cross-Sector Social Partnerships: Prospective Sensemaking Devices for Social Benefit. *Journal of Business Ethics*, 94(1), 21–37.

Shane, S. & Venkataraman, S. (2000). The Promise of Entrepreneurship as a Field of Research. *Academy of Management Review*, 25(1), 217–226.

Smith, B. R. & Stevens, C. E. (2010). Different Types of Social Entrepreneurship: The Role of Geography and Embeddeddness on the Measurement and Scaling of Social Value. *Entrepreneurship & Regional Development*, 22, 575–598.

Swedish Agency for Economic and Regional Growth. (2014). *Lokala servicelösningar* (Report N2009/465/RT, Dnr 012–2009–905934). Stockholm: Tillväxtverket. Available at www.tillvaxtverket/publikationer.

UNDP. (2015). *United Nations Development Programme*. Available at http://www.undp.org/.

Zahra, S. A., Gedajlovic, D. & Schulman, J. (2009). A Typology of Social Entrepreneurs: Motives, Search Processes and Ethical Challenges. *Journal of Business Venturing*, 24, 519–532.

Zahra, S. A., Jennings, D. F. & Kuratko, D. F. (1999). The Antecedents and Consequences of Firm-level Entrepreneurship: The State of the Field. *Entrepreneurship: Theory & Practice*, 24(2), 47–67.

11 Microfinance as a Case Study of Social Entrepreneurship in Norway

Unni Beate Sekkesæter

In this chapter, microfinance in Norway and in the Nordic countries are analysed as a case study of social entrepreneurship, as a social capital building process and as an arena for learning and exchange of experience among self-employed and small business owners in Norway. The chapter draws on data from fieldwork in Norway, Hordaland County and the author's involvement in building a microfinance organization in Norway as well as being part of organizing a Nordic Microfinance Network. The challenge of transferring from welfare to self-employment is briefly discussed. The benefit for those who managed to start their own enterprise and for society overall may be huge as seen in Hordaland, where the total financial turnover of members of the 21 network groups was NOK 65,200,701($\approx$ € 7,130 550) in 2013. Consequently, the women can continue to live and work in rural areas.

Microfinance as Network Credit Methodology in the Nordics

The first European microfinance institutions (MFIs) were idealistic organizations: they were founded by people who had personally seen the success of microfinance in developing countries and who sought to import it to their home countries. These pioneers were followed by a host of small and large organizations, and the years after 2000 saw rapid growth in the number of MFIs in Europe. This period also saw ordinary banks entering the field of microfinance through collaborations with MFIs, with MFIs taking responsibility for client relations and business development services, and banks taking responsibility for providing capital and loan handling. In 1996, Unni B. Sekkesæter (the author of this chapter) founded a project (based in Norwegian People's Aid) that brought micro lending to refugees and immigrants in Norway. In 2003, the project was turned into Network Credit Norway, the predecessor of Microfinance Norway, and in collaboration with Hordaland County Council and Cultura Bank, Network Credit Norway also created the Microinvest Foundation, a fund dedicated to financing microcredit initiatives. The Hordaland County Council supported some administrative costs related to lending from 2000 to 2003, and other supporters of the project, such as the Norwegian Directorate for Immigration, Innovation Norway and some municipalities, provided financing for the loan fund. Cultura acted as the financial intermediary and managed the operational activities of the fund, whereas Network Credit Norway coordinated lending activities and provided business training and support (Wiggen, 2005, p. 71–75). The initiative was backed by a guarantee from the European Investment Fund under the EU Multiannual Programme for Enterprise, and subsequently the EU Competitiveness and Innovation Framework Programme 2006 (Hektoen, 2011, p. 176).

In 2014, a new independent loan fund, Mikrofinans Norge AS, was founded. Since 2015, it provides microloans to financially excluded start-up and small enterprises who cannot get access to finance in other ways (Mikrofinans Norge AS, 2015). The potential gains from the exchange of knowledge about microfinance and adult education in relation to microfinance and micro enterprise development are huge in the Nordic countries. Most practitioners of microfinance in the Nordic context consider themselves to be social business entrepreneurs. The three partners, Norway (Mikrofinans Norge), Sweden (Mikrofinans Instituttet and Nätverk för Entreprenörer från Etniska Minoriteter, or NEEM) and Denmark (Dansk Forum for Mikrofinans), have been developing a Nordic microfinance network funded by the Nordic Council of Ministers from 2010–2013. Microfinance works as a tool to enable more inclusion of those who fall outside the target of mainstream financial institutions. It is also about building opportunities for those who need a bit more educational/mentoring support in order to succeed, since training and finance need to walk hand in hand in the complex business context of the Nordics. In other words, we are talking about social entrepreneurship in practice where the microfinance institution or program operates as a social enterprise.

This chapter focuses on a case from Hordaland, Norway, where the building of social capital has been substantial since 1998. The case study is part of a PhD student longitudinal research project covering the period from 2002–2015 that has followed the same group of entrepreneurs in Hordaland County, Norway, starting with interviews, a survey and focus groups in 2002, followed by in-depth interviews and a follow-up survey in 2013. In general, very little information and research exist related to microfinance organizations based in the Nordic region—primarily reports and evaluations (Sekkesæter, 2002; Lotherington & Ellingsen, 2002) and master theses (Width, 2010; Aase, 2014). The theoretical focus includes building social capital as an outcome from the close collaboration in the network groups, as well as stakeholder theory. Freeman (1984, p. 46) defines a stakeholder as "any group or individual who can affect or is affected by the achievement of the organization's objective". Adding to this, Gibson (2000, p. 245, quoting Carroll, 1993) is included because he also has important insights on an organization's stakeholders, pointing to "Those groups or individuals with whom the organisation interacts or has interdependencies and any individual or group who can affect or is affected by the actions, decisions, policies, practices, or goals of the organization".

Nordic Microfinance Institutions in a Welfare State Context

The Nordic microfinance institutions have different structures in their organizations. Whereas Denmark tried to start its association in 2013 (still not registered), Norway and Sweden have similar small NGOs where they provide mentoring and loans for their customers, mainly immigrants, but also women in the rural areas of Norway (as the case from Hordaland will show). In Norway, the microfinance approach has a strong focus on their customers forming loan groups where the group members evaluate each other's business plans, give advice and exchange experiences and also function as lenders (Hordaland). In Sweden, the loans were given individually with mentoring and advice for the customers. The form of education and mentoring differs, but the focus on the importance of education/training/ mentoring is similar. In Sweden, the MFI approach was to work on developing the structure of the organization to be as self-sufficient as possible. This was meant to happen primarily through lending directly to its customers instead of working in partnership with a bank. This would give the organization income from interest accrued. In 2012, Mikrofinansinstitutet i Sverige AB in Sweden got their first investment and started lending to their customers. As of November 2013, nine loans had been granted.

Mikrofinansinstitutet i Sverige AB was created in Katrineholm, Sweden, in August 2009 as a joint-stock company, with the mission "to increase access to finance for individuals who are socially and financially excluded, in particular migrants and women who have difficulties entering the Swedish labour market and who would like to start micro enterprises in order to sustain themselves". By early 2011, the company increased its effort to have a loan portfolio of its own, rather than via partnerships. As of June 2013, MFI AB had provided only six loans for a gross loan portfolio of SEK 1,2 million (≈ € 128,000). The typical loan size was SEK 50–250,000 (≈ € 5,300–26,700). The MFI AB was bought by Plantagon International AB in February 2014 for SEK 1 (≈ € 0,1). The reason for this was that the company was poorly managed and was at risk to go into bankruptcy. A decision was made to integrate MFI AB into Plantagon International AB after the summer of 2015. The outstanding seven loans amounting to SEK 286,865 (≈ € 30,500) were transferred to Plantagon (Pattersson & Platagon, 2015).

However, there are other microfinance actors in Sweden that have given far more loans to women and immigrants, such as ALMI, which originated from an entrepreneurship association covering the whole of Sweden. Through their partnership with IFS Counselling, an organization supporting entrepreneurs with foreign backgrounds in Sweden, ALMI/IFS has provided a steadily growing number of loans. Since 2014, it also accessed the

European Investment Fund guarantee facility under the Progress Microfinance Initiative (EIF, 2015). Figures from ALMI show that out of the SEK 206 million (≈ € 22 million) lent out through the microfinance initiative in 2013, SEK 76 million (≈ € 8 million) were given to women. Similarly, SEK 88 million (≈ € 9 million) were given to immigrants (ALMI, 2013). This level of lending has been consistent over the last few years and shows that women and especially immigrants are in fact overrepresented relative to the wider population of entrepreneurs. It is therefore clear that ALMI has managed to expand coverage while maintaining its outreach towards women and immigrants as prioritized groups. ALMI was not part of the attempt to set up the Nordic Microfinance Network, and is therefore not the focus of this chapter. Time will show if future Nordic initiatives will bring more success than these first attempts.

In Norway, two microfinance organizations participated in the last Nordic network meeting: Microfinance Norway and Nettverk Vest (Network West) based in Hordaland County on the west coast of Norway. Microfinance Norway has been operating microfinance activity under several names since 1996 and has been giving microloans independently through the Microinvest Foundation and lately in partnership with a bank, Cultura Savings Bank, during the period from 2008 to 2013. However, now the situation is similar to that of Sweden, and Foreningen Mikrofinans Norge, which is a membership association, wishes to deliver all loans by itself from 2016 on. Microfinance Norway is still working on getting investors for its new loan fund, Mikrofinans Norge AS, a social business loan fund which is, according to the definition of Muhammad Yunus, "A non-loss, non-dividend company, dedicated entirely to achieving a social goal" (Yunus & Weber, 2010, p. xvii). This fund is owned by the membership association Mikrofinans Norge. This more independent operation of the organizations generates several positive opportunities of becoming more self-sufficient, but also challenges: logistic issues regarding efficient lending (with IT platform), reporting and evaluation systems, getting investors and regulatory issues, which is a particular challenge since it will lend as a non-banking actor. As of January 2016, the financial regulatory authorities in Norway (Finanstilsynet) have recommended to give the new loan fund the permission to lend, but have only passed this recommendation to the Finance Ministry for the final decision so far (Finanstilsynet, 2015).

Although the Nordic countries have similar welfare systems, we see differences: a stronger decentralisation in the Danish system, with more possibilities for municipalities to independently make microloans, for example through a project in Århus, started by SUS (Danish Forum for Microfinance, 2013). In Denmark, they have achieved greater acceptance and cooperation with the municipalities compared to other Nordic countries. All the organizations experience challenges helping to ensure their customers' rights to continued social benefits when they start as self-employed and/or get microloans. In cases where they fail in business, they also often lose their right to unemployment benefit, as this is based only on income from salary employment. This effectively removes much of the 'safety net' for a person who takes the risk of creating self-employment and even jobs for others. If the income of the business disappears or declines, or illness occurs, there are very few rights to gain support from the welfare states in Norway and Denmark; however, the situation has improved in Sweden. In Norway, for instance, a self-employed person has no right to unemployment benefits, and the minimum social welfare support is only given if all personal or business assets are sold first. It is also risky to get sick unless a special insurance has been taken out—and this is based on what the self-employed person pays him/herself from the business surplus over a three-year period. In many cases, a small business owner takes out very little income for personal use, but uses most of the income for developing the business further, and thus they have no rights to welfare support unless they have insurance or there is a delay of 17 days, at least in the case of Norway (Breivik, 2015). All these rules put many potential entrepreneurs off, even if they have a great business idea, and a lot of potential businesses and new jobs are not created.

Still, there are very good results: a recent study carried out by the EU initiative 'Progress Microfinance' found that 61 per cent of all assisted businesses in the EU during the last period of support (2010–2014) were new enterprises started by unemployed persons (EIF, 2015), so there is clear potential. In a long-term perspective, the potential for job and enterprise creation from entrepreneurship and innovation may be lost due to the stringent rules of the Nordic welfare state that are not well enough adapted to the realities of the entrepreneurs. There are good examples to learn from in Ireland and Germany, where similar issues have been dealt with in different ways, such as through the Back to Work Enterprise Allowance scheme in Ireland. Within the Nordic countries, there are different degrees of experience with microfinance, combined with entrepreneurial and financial adult education as a strategy; there is a need for a closer exchange of experience in this relatively new field. And since the summer of 2009, the three Nordic countries Norway, Sweden and Denmark decided to launch a Nordic Microfinance Network with the purpose of sharing knowledge about using microfinance linked with adult education as a tool in the Nordic welfare system.

Inclusion efforts for migrants and others who are financially and socially excluded from the labour market have focused on conventional employment as tool. However, analyses and experience indicates that support to self-employment and entrepreneurship might be a new and powerful tool as a supplement to the existing approaches to integration and inclusion. The Nordic microfinance concept was meant to be the coordinated provision of coaching, training and mentor support, combined with a possibility of getting small loans, and hopefully it will continue, but after March 2014, no coordinated effort across the Nordic countries exists to continue the work of the Nordic Microfinance Network. The future of this Nordic cooperation effort is very uncertain due to the lack of finance and coordination across the Nordic countries (Nordic Microfinance Network, 2014).

The Norwegian Network Credit Methodology

Network Credit is the commonly used name of microfinance/microcredit in the Norwegian context, but it is also known as the 'Women's Bank' in some places. As an adapted version of the Grameen Bank model from Bangladesh, Network Credit was first implemented in the Lofoten and Vesterålen islands in 1992. Mohammad Yunus, the founder of Grameen Bank, has had a close connection with the initiators in Norway and described the growth of this Grameen-type project in Norway in his book *Banker to the Poor* (Yunus, 1998). This first microcredit institution was incorporated in Lofoten and Vesterålen, northern Norway. It was established as a pilot project to help women start their own businesses. As in other countries, many women in Norway had problems obtaining small loans from lending institutions, including from the government's lending schemes for entrepreneurs. Six other factors were also identified as creating barriers for women (Yunus, 1998):

1. The economy in this particular region was seasonal (fishing); thus, additional jobs were needed in periods with low economic activity.
2. Lending institutions were often not interested in giving credit to these women because banks were not interested in the kinds of businesses women wanted to establish.
3. Women were disadvantaged in seeking credit from banks because of difficulties assessing risk, high interest rates, bureaucracy and a certain unfamiliarity as to how the financing system works.
4. Women have little or no capital to invest.
5. Women want co-operation and networks.
6. Women are less interested in 'quick fixes'.

The 'saving linked credit group/solidarity group' model is most widely applied, and it functions so that five women together stand liable for group repayments. However, this form of joint liability is not implemented in Hordaland or elsewhere in Norway as group members did not accept this rule, and the group lending might not have worked, according to interviews in 2002 with several project leaders and members in Hordaland.

What was formerly called Hordaland Network Credit had by 2013 changed its name to the Association Nettverk Vest, Hordaland and Sogn & Fjordane, and had 26 network groups with an average of five members each. The turnovers of those businesses were about NOK 65 million (≈ € 7 million) in 2013. The outstanding amount of loans in 2013 was NOK 1,7 million (≈ € 185,000) (Hvidsten, 2015), but the number of loans is not known. In the whole country, the last available number from 2008 estimated that 265 network groups with more than 1 320 members and a total loan capital of NOK 53 million (≈ € 5,7 million) existed in Norway (Width, 2010; Width, 2011). These groups are modelled on the 'Grameen Bank' model introduced by Prof. Muhammad Yunus and brought to Norway first by Bodil Maal in 1992 to the Lofoten islands and Vesterålen, but soon the whole country was covered by such network groups. Then in 1996, a slightly different model, the Self-Help Project: Network Credit to Refugees and Immigrants (now called Microfinance Norway), also based on the same Grameen Bank model was introduced by Unni Beate Sekkesæter. The difference was that its main focus was on immigrants in some of the big cities: Oslo and Bergen, and later, Trondheim. However, the rural and city models are very similar and have existed side by side throughout the years. Around 70 network groups have been formed through the program now called Mikrofinans Norge (named Network Credit Norway 2003–2010 and the Self-Help Project: Network Credit to Refugees and Immigrants from 1996).

According to the principles laid out in this network credit model, groups of four to seven individuals are responsible for making decisions regarding enterprise loans to each other in a small network group (also referred to as peer group or loan group). The group liability has been modified in the Norwegian model, so the group is only in charge of assessing the loan applications. Otherwise, the group gives mutual support and shares experiences of starting and running small enterprises, but there is no joint liability for group debt. This method of microfinance enables individuals with relatively low capital requirements to access the credit needed to create or expand micro enterprises in their local community. Apart from the accessibility to loans, these groups create a very strong network for support and learning and building social capital, and this is an *integral* part of the Grameen model. In Norway, microcredit/microfinance (also referred to as 'Network Credit') has been utilized almost exclusively by women, particularly in rural areas where communities are dependent on traditional forms of livelihood, such as agriculture, handicrafts and fishing. The failure rate has been relatively low, although neither the repayment rate nor the delinquency rate are monitored. This form of micro lending has proved an effective vehicle for creating micro-enterprises in Norway, as hundreds of new micro-enterprises have been started since the start of Network Credit in Norway 1992. Microfinance of this type was introduced in Hordaland County in 1997. Hordaland, and Norway in general, has a major problem sustaining rural communities because of the increasing migration of women and youth to urban areas. There are more jobs for men in these communities related to fishing/farming, etc., but for women, it is more difficult to find jobs.

For some years, these islands, situated in a rather desolate spot off the Northern coast of Norway, had been experiencing a serious depopulation problem. Though young men often returned to the islands after university, the young girls did not. There was little incentive. While the women waited for their fishermen husbands or fathers to return from sea, there was almost no social or commercial activity to occupy them. They suffered from loneliness . . . Thanks to the ceaseless efforts of Bodil Maal, the government of Norway decided to initiate a Grameen project through the Fisheries Ministry. This project offered women commercial credit for income generating activities to help keep them on the islands and make their lives less lonely and more meaningful . . . Now for the first time, the women of the arctic circle had access to credit. And thanks to the program, they had access to community support groups and financial opportunities . . . More important, however, the Norwegian project promotes micro-credit as a tool for social integration and an effective way to add new meaning to people's lives.

(Yunus, 1998)

The Hordaland Case Study

Hordaland County on the west coast of Norway comprises 33 municipalities and has a population of 511,357. The county is the second most populated in Norway, and more than half the population live in Bergen, the centre of Hordaland and Western Norway. The Hordaland County Council was part of the Equal Credit Project of the EU in the early phase of Network Credit, and this influenced the way the model developed in this part of Norway, partly due to international networking, and partly because of a different approach to public-private partnership than in some of the other counties.

Through the Equal Credit project (1998–2002), the Hordaland County Council has sought to target women (and some men), and refugees and immigrants in selected areas (through its partnership with the Self-Help Project, Norwegian People's Aid until 2003). Funding through the EU RECITE II program and the Strategic Development Plan (SNP) as well as the Norwegian Industrial and Regional Development Fund (later called Innovation Norway) was used to create 24 network groups as of 2014 (although not all were under Equal Credit).

Some of the objectives of the Equal Credit Project included:

1. To stimulate job creation using microcredit schemes and thereby to improve job opportunities in deprived urban and rural communities.
2. To develop and test models of microcredit to widen the EU experience and demonstrate what can be achieved by Structural Fund support in co-operation with the private sector.
3. To increase wealth created in deprived areas for deprived groups.

The Norwegian experience is also documented in a few reports, mainly evaluations (Kassah, 1993; Abrahamsen, 1995; Esbensen, 1998; Thomassen, 1998, 1999; Kvinnebanken Norgesnett, 1998; Pettersen, Alsos, Anvik, Gjertsen, Ljunggren,1999; Dupont, 2001; Lotherington & Ellingsen, 2002)).

A national evaluation carried out by the NORUT Research Institute in Tromsø (Lotherington & Ellingsen, 2002) and a master thesis (Width, 2010) have given a deeper understanding of Network Credit as an instrument for micro-entrepreneurs in Norway.

Case Methodology

The data for this chapter combines a qualitative and quantitative methodology through survey data, semi-structured qualitative interviews and a focus group. The informants are various stakeholders of the Hordaland micro-enterprise development program. Project leaders were interviewed in a focus group discussion. A survey, "Hordaland Network Credit Survey 2001", was filled out by a random sample of 50 per cent of the 60 members of Hordaland Network Credit. Twenty-nine respondents participated in the questionnaire survey, and 24 of them also participated in focus group discussions. The informants included in the analysis were all members of peer groups of four to six people who were planning their start-up (15 per cent) or were in business (77 per cent) or had been in business (eight per cent) as of 2001.

The survey was designed to explore the characteristics of Hordaland Network Credit's members, their level of participation in the program, characteristics and evolution of their businesses, the changes in the sources of business credit they used, members' assessment of the quality and usefulness of Hordaland Network Credit's services, level of joint marketing and joint venturing among members, changes in self-confidence, quality of life, community involvement and family relations resulting from the group process. The questionnaire was filled out at the end of the focus group discussions to ensure a substantial response rate (100 per cent). The dataset was based on responses from 29 informants and has been analysed by using the statistical software package SPSS. The analysis has been carried out at the following levels: the institutional level, the peer group level and the level of the individual micro-entrepreneur. From a methodical point of view, it was difficult to obtain a completely representative sample. In this study, the systematic random sampling technique was used, with every first, third and fifth member of each peer group being selected for the focus group discussions. In August 2013, a round of follow-up in-depth interviews and update of the responses given in the survey from 2001 was carried out (using the same survey forms for each person as in 2001 and comparing the data). Also, a focus group discussion and interview with the coordinator, Elin Hvidsten from Nettverk Vest (the new name of Hordaland Network Credit), was carried out.

Micro Enterprise Development in Hordaland

The history of the Hordaland program goes back to a visit from a representative of the Women's Bank, or Network Credit, from Lofoten. This visit to Hordaland in the autumn of 1996 led to a visit by representatives of Hordaland County Council to the Lofoten Islands in 1997, and this visit then led to the start of the first three network groups in 1997–98 as part of the SNP. The project was a pilot project, and each group was assigned an external project leader for support and advice. A savings and credit scheme was part of the model. Business development services were given to a limited degree, and the main learning took place in the network groups through peer support and the sharing of experiences, advice, customer referrals, joint marketing and joint venturing. Through its peer-lending program, Hordaland Network Credit extends credit to self-selected groups of five to seven members that review and approve each other's loans. Each group manages a loan capital of NOK 200,000 (≈ € 29,000). Up to 80 per cent of this amount may be loaned to the group's members at any time.

The model is still used in Hordaland, and a high rate of loan repayment by all the members is required to access new loans, which may be up to a maximum of NOK 80,000 (≈ € 8,700). There is no 'stepped lending', meaning a gradual increase in loan amounts (such as in Microfinance Norway), and the network group may decide the loan amount, including for the first loan. Each network group has its own group fund consisting of the group's saving and NOK 200,000 (≈ € 21,700) as their loan fund. Each member has to save at least NOK 150 (≈ € 20) per month, and the savings may be used by the group in the way they decide is best. However, no member may withdraw their savings before leaving the group. The group fund functions as a form of collective collateral for the loans given by the group. Groups are virtually self-managed after an initial period of coaching by a program employee called the 'project leader'. The project leaders were in the past employed by *regional development agencies* in Hordaland and work for Network Credit as a small part of their normal job; however, during the last period until 2013, Innovation Norway paid for a part-time position. The project leaders used to have a contract with the county council, and invoice the county council on an hourly basis for the work carried out in relation to work with the groups (recruitment, monitoring and reporting). This model enabled a high degree of local knowledge among the project leaders, and it was very flexible in terms of the costs involved. Average annual administrative costs per group are very low. This is an important finding: the model is cost effective because the staff of the program participates in group meetings only one or two times per year. This form of organization in Hordaland County is unique in the Norwegian context and has proved to function well, but funding for project leaders stopped in 2014.

Important local adaptations of the national Network Credit model (the Lofoten model) have been made. Self-employment provides at least some income for a growing percentage of the active labour force in Norway, with geographic variations. Many of these enterprises are concentrated in rural communities and provide an alternative way of earning income in places where few or no suitable employment options exist. The self-employed thereby contribute to a diversification of the local labour market. Most of the business owners in this study were in some form of employment (full or part time) when they started their own business, but these jobs were often not suited well to their competence. This means that their former jobs now (in many cases) are available to somebody else. Only a couple of informants in this study of Hordaland started their new business as a way out of unemployment (as opposed to, for instance, immigrants in the cities). However, when women in Norway start their business, they often start very small businesses, which they grow over time. In many cases, they do this without walking away from other sources of employment income. In most cases, the 'big step' is taken after long periods of 'patching' income and making sure the rest of the family would not be too much affected by the woman taking the full step into self-employment. Because of this fact, the group (or network) within the network credit system is important for motivating and encouraging the micro-business owner so she doesn't have to rely on her family to understand her 'sudden new idea/dream' or to provide finance for the business or collateral for loans. The study points out the fact that very often, the family is less understanding/supportive when it comes to putting new ideas/dreams into practice. The Network Credit model is a welcome solution to some of these problems as a new arena for sharing business issues with somebody who understands and supports, as well as being a source of business finance.

Detailed Findings From the Hordaland Case Study

Only one of the informants was dependent on income from social welfare and unemployment benefits now. A few others talked about their experience with unemployment and depending on social welfare in the past and saw the option of being self-employed as a way out of unemployment. Many saw it

Table 11.1 Importance of Network Credit Services

Importance of These Hordaland Network Credit Services for Your Business	Very Important	Important	Little/Not Important At All
The advisers that NC provides me	29.2%	50%	20.8%
What I learn from participating in network group meetings	61.5%	26.9%	11.5%
The advice and help from project leader/the enterprise agent	36%	44%	20%
The NC business training sessions.	30.4%	47.8%	21.7%
The Hordaland Network Credit loan	50%	21.4%	4.4%
The friendship and support from other members	76%	20%	4%
The business advice from other members	44%	40%	16%
The chance to make my own decisions	60%	36%	4%
Increasing my self-confidence	64%	32%	4%

as a way to enable them to use their skills and work with something more suitable/desirable for them than an ordinary job. Since all the respondents are members of the peer groups (loan groups), there are several qualities of these group/networks that contribute to the building of social capital. When asked to rate the importance of the various services offered by Hordaland Network Credit (now Nettverk Vest), the members rated the different services in the following way.

Social Capital: The Product or By-Product of Micro-Enterprise Development?

Hordaland Network Credit is designed around the idea that membership in a group strengthens the links between business owners and makes them responsible for virtually all decisions, including loan approval, and it encourages business growth. This part of the survey explored if and how the respondents were interacting with other members of their groups.

> They [group members] get the whole thing [the responsibility for running the group and loan administration] in their hands without forming the strategy. We as project leaders make the decisions, often without consulting the groups. Many of the ideas for changes come from the groups, and we give the ideas to Hordaland County Council, who send the suggestions to Innovation Norway . . . regional office, which sends it to Innovation Norway nationally. But we often forget to go down with the proposition to the group. (Interview, project leader)

The least-explored outcome of microcredit is the production of social capital arising from group-based microfinance programmes (van Bastelaer, 1999). "The social capital of a society includes the institutions, the relationships, the attitudes and values that govern interactions among people and contribute to economic and social development. Social capital, however, is not simply the sum of the institutions that underpin society, it is also the glue that holds them together. It includes the shared values and rules for social conduct expressed in personal relationships, trust, and a common sense of 'civic' responsibility that makes society more than a collection of individuals" (The World Bank, 1998, p. 1).

Interest in social capital's role in economic growth has been growing since the work of Coleman (1990) and Putnam et al. (1994). It is fairly well understood how microfinance programmes use the existing networks of horizontal associations to lower some information and other transaction costs (Stiglitz, 1990; Besley, 1995; Conning, 1999; Morduch, 1999). In the Western context, this can have outcomes like the creation of 'business arenas' like networks, groups, hubs etc. Some microfinance programmes also do advocacy on behalf of their members as well as providing linkages to networks of importance to micro-entrepreneurs. This includes, for example, linkages with banks that give loans to clients who 'graduate' from the program (with or without partial guarantees from the Microfinance Institution).

Less understood is how MFIs create new social capital. Microfinance programmes in the south often use existing social capital, particularly in their peer group lending techniques, but it can also be argued that MFIs create social capital through their meetings and other services. Microfinance has the potential to enable collective action by bringing together the community and supporting more sustainable community-based organizations such as the network groups. Finding ways that may contribute to the strengthening of a community's social capital may aid in solving even more complex problems related to local and regional development. The Network Credit model is used mostly in scarcely populated rural areas and therefore, the building of social capital may make a considerable difference for people who are looking for ways of enhancing their lives in rural communities instead of moving to a city.

The findings from Hordaland provide many examples showing the value added by Network Credit as a strategy that can contribute to making people's quality of life better. The field study in Hordaland shows clear indications of the importance of the network and resources provided by the peer group. In a questionnaire survey among 50 per cent of the participants, 75 per cent of the informants state that the friendship and support from other members in their peer group is 'very important' to them, whereas 20,8 per cent find it 'important'. However, the effect on the community was less clear in the Hordaland findings: a majority of 52,2 per cent said their participation in the micro-enterprise program had little or no importance at all for increasing their involvement in their local community. It should be noted, however, that the enhancement of social capital is generally a salutary by-product of microfinance, not its primary objective. Therefore, there may be more efficient ways to enhance social capital in any given setting (Anderson, Locker & Nugent, 2002). Schreiner (2001) and Stiglitz (1990) argue that groups can reduce social costs if they tap into existing social capital and use it to shift screening, monitoring and contract enforcement from the lender to the group. Total costs may decrease if the social capital has already been established.

Peer Group Lending Challenges

Group loans may increase social benefits if their financial intermediation relaxes financial constraints or if their social intermediation relaxes non-financial constraints (Schreiner, 2001). Groups in developing countries typically build on trust and social capital that already exists, since group members often live and work in the same community, and have various types of social ties that may strengthen a lending situation. The general situation of many peer group lending programmes in the north is quite different. Schreiner (2001) gives four main reasons why peer group lending have struggled in many cases: 1) Social capital among people is weak and it evaporates when people move (mobility can be high); 2) The target groups of programmes in the north are more diverse; thus, it becomes difficult to form homogenous groups of like-minded people; 3) Even where joint liability is the rule (not in the Hordaland program), it is not always enforced, and lack of enforcement from the organization may unleash an avalanche of arrears because peers no longer have selfish reasons to select trustworthy peers; and 4) Groups break down because even poor people in the north—if they have a clean credit record—can get individual loans through credit cards; thus, most borrowers would prefer to avoid groups and the high transaction costs of maintaining friendship and contact.

One of the premises of a group-based approach is that, with sufficient training and experience, group members can become effective owners and managers. Projects can be designed to prepare customers to advance along the continuum of increased responsibility by including significant investment in building up local institutions and training clients in accounting and other skills they need to manage their own institutions (Bennet, 1998).

A study focused on combining social and financial intermediation to reach the poor (Bennet, 1998) provides a useful framework for an analysis of participation:

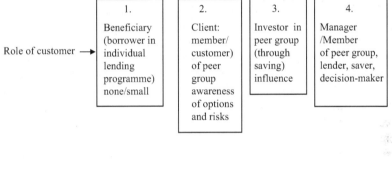

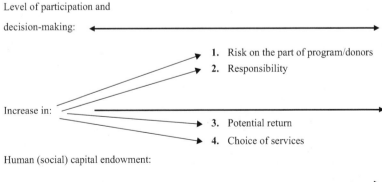

Figure 11.1 Roles, Level of Participation and Decision-Making

Adapted from (Bennet, 1998) (p. 101)

The high degree of self-management in the groups of Hordaland Network Credit supports Bennet's argument. In the Norwegian model of Network Credit, there has been an effective shift of screening, monitoring and contract enforcement from the lender (Hordaland County Council/Innovation Norway) to the group. Most of the group meetings are held without program staff being present. Most groups meet with the project coordinator only once or twice per year. This is different for new groups, but already after an initial period of five to six months, most groups are almost totally self-managed.

The degree of self-management of these groups would easily fit with the roles identified in box four of Bennet's adapted model above. The groups even manage their own loan fund and saving scheme. In the questionnaire survey, 84% of the respondents rated the 'chance to make our own decisions' as an important quality of the Network Credit programme. The implications of this 'self-managed model' are highly interesting, as costs related to managing the scheme are low and the level of importance to the members involved is still very high. Measurements of the importance of group processes and the self-managed loan process are mainly based on qualitative findings (2002 and 2013), but they are backed up by the survey data and in-depth interviews from 2013. All participants rated the group-lending model as very valuable for their business and personal growth. Only two of the focus group participants would prefer to make a shift from the group-based model to a purely individual lending model. Exchanges about business matters within the network peer group have positively influenced their family lives as well. Evidence about women in the sample shows that even when bank loans might be available, they might only be so if collateral is provided, such as a home equity loan, thereby involving the family economy in their business. In Hordaland, even those who could get loans from other sources preferred the group loans and highly valued the social intermediation perspective of the program that strengthened social capital among the group members and their wider community by creating much-needed jobs in the area around Bergen.

Stakeholders as Participants in the Formation of Program Strategy

The influence of the different stakeholders on the strategic decision-making process is highly important for the realisation of the organization's strategy. To a large extent, the different categories of the organization's policy may be adaptable over time, and it would be desirable to have all stakeholders being active rather than passive in influencing such change. Actors have the power to be both 'strategy context setters' as well as players who may support or sabotage the strategy the organization is seeking to play out (Eden, 1998). The members of the program have roles as managers and stakeholders through their self-managed network groups.

However, this may give rise to risks for the donors/program management. The money the group manages is, after all, public money, given as an interest-free loan from Innovation Norway or other donors and which can be managed by the group as long as it is functioning. However, if the money is lost because of bankruptcy, it may be possible to negotiate an exemption from this rule of repayment. For Innovation Norway, giving funding for micro-entrepreneurs as a grant through their 'etablererstipend' (a grant scheme for start-up businesses) is something they normally do. Network Credit transforms a portion of this grant money into interest-free loans for the groups. In this way, the grant money is reused time after time as new loans and thus may assist many more entrepreneurs than if it was given as a normal grant to one person. The money is constantly revolving in the group fund, as the same money is lent time after time, allowing for many micro-businesses to benefit from the loan scheme. Microfinance Norway has NOK 1,6 million (≈ € 173,400) loan capital (from Innovation Norway and others), which resulted in 155 loans of a total value of NOK 5,5 million (≈ € 596,000). The nature of this public funding (grants) is important for judging the level of risk involved in having the self-managed group model. Of course, the individual businesses have the same level of risk, but we are here talking about the loan model as such and the benefit of using limited public funds in such an efficient manner that leads to such a high degree of value creation AND the saving of public funds for welfare support. In Norway, the microfinance model is substantially different from other industrialized countries and has proved to be an effective way of ensuring a more effective use of grant money as well as the building of social capital through networking, exchange of experience and support.

The issue of individual versus group loans was discussed in both focus groups and individual interviews in 2002 and 2013. All the informants saw the group aspect of the program as important, and since the element of group guarantee is not part of the Network Credit model, they did not see the group aspect as a burden compared with individual loans. The process of building social capital was found to be strong within the program, and the people participating in the focus groups indicated that they appreciated the process. A new round of interviews in 2013 with almost 50 per cent of the participants from the study in 2002 proved this point very clearly: the building of social capital was very important for all informants. They also reflected around how close/distant these relations should be, and most pointed to the importance of the right mix of friendship and business relationship in the network groups. None of them wanted the group members to be 'their very best friend', and they all felt that having family members in the same group would be wrong. This point is in line with findings about most customers joining because of the promise of getting a loan, but staying in because of the network and support from their peers. Without the peer lending aspect, the networking process would have been substantially weakened.

In other countries like the United Kingdom and the USA, either the loans are given as individual loans or the group lending is taking place as part of a more stringent organizational policy where the staff are much more involved in the running of the groups and program (Pearson, 1997). The loans are given through the organization from their loan fund, although the group often makes the loan decision. The most similar model to the 'Network Credit model' internationally is the village bank model where groups re-lend each other's saving, but this often happens without investment in a loan fund from any outside institution (Burkey, 1993; Ashe, 2014). The Norwegian model of Network Credit is therefore quite unique.

The Network Credit model grew out of grassroots initiatives and has different cultural specificities than the rest of the Innovation Norway programmes. For this reason, it has to be treated differently from the other programmes of Innovation Norway, as it is a collective lending system. The model is a participative development tool built around the idea that group members through their collective action can strengthen each other as micro-business owners both socially and financially. For a public agency subject to bureaucratic and regulatory procedures, it may be difficult to manage a scheme like Network Credit, and this may have been a factor in Innovation Norway stopping its central coordination of the network groups in 2009, as it no longer wanted to prioritize the program. Instead, something called gründer groups were started (entrepreneurship groups). In their 2009 annual report (Innovasjon Norge, 2009), it was mentioned in a footnote (p. 40) that the program was changed and is now called Gründer Groups. No explanation was given. At the same time, self-managed groups continued to exist all over Norway. About 50 per cent of the original nation-wide funding of NOK 53 million (€ 5,743,400) might still be circulating in the network groups in 2015, but the most recent numbers available are from 2009, as estimated by Width (2010). For the groups in Hordaland, this change meant that they had to continue without any central coordination. Their own county association 'Nettverk Vest' (Network West, 2015) continues to be a coordinating network for the groups, but more resources are needed. All funding from the local Innovation Norway office ended in 2013 (Hvidsten, 2013).

Conclusion

The strategies used by the peer lending micro-enterprise program 'Nettverk Vest' presented in this study demonstrate an effective means for growing micro-businesses in rural and semi-rural areas in Hordaland, Norway. Substantial increases were documented in networking amongst members and the impact that the groups have had on member self-confidence, their involvement in the community and thus on building social capital.

The level of the social capital of the members has clearly been increasing through their active participation in the program. The program is highly participative, and it is fairly easy for members to voice their opinions and be heard. Finally, the survey results show that participating in a loan group not only increases mutual assistance among business owners and helps businesses grow; it also has important psychological and social consequences. A clear majority of participants (75 per cent) said their participation in Hordaland Network Credit was 'very important' for increasing their self-confidence. The program was seen as important or very important by a majority, and there were also indications that relations with family and community had improved.

In more general terms in Norway, the picture is still complex, with constant attention to the problems related to welfare, to enterprise transfer and the lack of welfare security. The government's lack of interest in the EU-wide programmes like the EU Programme for Employment and Social Innovation (2015–2020), even though they could strengthen the microfinance sector, is also a challenge. Innovation Norway is restructuring itself currently under new leadership, and it remains to be seen how this will affect the situation for social entrepreneurship and microfinance in Norway. The story of Microfinance Norway documented by Aase (2014) illustrates how political support towards microfinance in Norway was shaped by a lack of official interest and a constant struggle of attracting funds. Aase argues that the approach to welfare provision advocated by Microfinance Norway competed with that of the government, where the former has promoted self-employment and microfinance, whereas the latter has preferred either labour or welfare provisions. Over the last few years, however, we have been seeing signs of change. With the emergence of social entrepreneurship as a concept and the new Solberg government (2013), there is a reconceptualisation of welfare state sustainability, more focus on innovation and entrepreneurship and more focus on social entrepreneurship as a strategy.

References

Aase, M. G. (2014). *Who Will Finance the Financiers? A Comparative Study of Microfinance Initiatives in Norway, Sweden and the United Kingdom*. Oslo: University of Oslo.

Abrahamsen, K. S. (1995). *Felles skjebne—felles løft: Om sosiale nettverk, selvhjelp og livskvalitet*. Oslo: Universitetsforlaget.

ALMI. (2013). *Almi Årsredovisning 2013*. Stockholm: ALMI Företagspartner.

Anderson, C. L., Locker, L. & Nugent, R. (2002). Microcredit, Social Capital, and Common Pool Resources. *World Development*, 30, 95–105.

Ashe, J. and Neilan, K. J. (2014). *In Their Own Hands: How Saving Groups Are Revolutionizing Development*. San Fransisco: Berret-Koehler.

Bennet, L. (1998). Combining Social and Financial Intermediation to Reach the Poor: The Necessity and Dangers. In M. S. Kimenyi, R. C. Wieland & J. D. von Pischke (Eds.), *Strategic Issues in Microfinance*. Aldershot: Ashgate Publishing Ltd.

Besley, T. & Coate, S. (1995). Group Lending, Repayment Incentives and Social Collateral. *Journal of Development Economics*, 46, 1–18.

Breivik, T. (2015). *Stakkars Jan Arild Snoen! Aftenposten Debatt*. Oslo: Aftenposten.

Burkey, S. (1993). *People First: A Guide to Self-Reliant, Participatory Rural Development*. London: Zed Books.

Carroll, A. (1993). *Business and Society: Ethics and Stakeholder Management*. Cincinnati: South-Western Publishing.

Coleman, J. (1990). *Foundations of Social Theory*. Cambridge: Harvard University Press.

Conning, J. (1999). Outreach, Sustainability and Leverage in Monitored and Peer-Monitored Lending. *Journal of Development Economics*, 60, 51–77.

Danish Forum for Microfinance. (2013). Referat af møde i Nordisk Mikrofinansnetværk København.

Dupont, M. (2001). Evaluation of Network Credit, Norwegian People's Aid. In M. Dupont & J. A. Lian (Eds.), *Evaluering av Norsk Folkehjelps Nettverkskredittprosjekt*. Oslo: Fafo.

Eden, C. & Ackermann, F. (1998). *Making Strategy: The Journey of Strategic Management*. London: SAGE Publications.

EIF, The European Investment Fund. (2015). *EaSI Microfinance and Social Entrepreneurship*. Paper presented at EMN Conference, Dublin. Available at www.emnconference.org/images/Dublin/EaSI_-_Microfinance_and_Social_Entrepreneurship_EIF.pdf, accessed 27 August 2015.

Esbensen, A. M. V. (1998). *Evaluering av nettverkskreditt i Norge*, unpublished report.

European Investment Fund. (2014). First Progress Microfinance Agreement in Sweden for Micro Enterprises. Available at: http://www.eif.org/what_we_do/microfinance/news/2014/almi.htm, accessed 10 January 2016.

Finanstilsynet. (2015). *Letter with Recommendation to the Finance Ministry Regarding Application for Permit to Establish Mikrofinans Norge AS*. Date: 15.12.2015 ref. 14/12240.

Freeman, R. E. (1984). *Strategic Management: A Stakeholder Approach*. Boston, MA: Pitman.

Gibson, K. (2000). The Moral Basis of Stakeholder Theory. *Journal of Business Ethics*, 26, 245–257.

Hektoen, L. (2011). Micro Finance in Norway. Cultura Bank and Access to the European Investment Fund's Loan Guarantee. In E. P. Delia (Ed.), *Microcredit as a Tool of Ethical Financing for Sustainable Development*. Malta: APS Bank.

Hvidsten, E. (2013). Interview with U. B. Sekkesæter.

Innovasjon Norge. (2009). *Årsrapport 2009: Hovedrapport til departementene 2 utgave*. Oslo: Innovasjon Norge.

Kassah, B. L. (1993). *Erfaringshåndbok fra prosjektet Nettverkskreditt*. Oslo: Fiskerinæringens kvinneutvalg.

Lotherington, A. -T. & Ellingsen, M.-B. (2002). *Små Penger og Store Forventninger: Nettverkskreditt i Norge 1992–2002*. Tromsø: Norut Samfunnsforskning AS.

Mikrofinans Norge AS. (2015). *Årsberetning Mikrofinans Norge AS 2014*. Kolbotn: Mikrofinans Norge AS.

Morduch, J. (1999). The Microfinance Promise. *Journal of Economic Literature*, 37, 1569–1614.

Network West. (2015). Available at www.nettverkvest.no/hjem, accessed 7 October 2015.

Nordic Microfinance Network. (2014). *Nordic Microfinance Network: Final Report and Minutes from Meetings Related to Nordplus Adultproject ID: AD-2012–1a-30720.* Oslo, Norway: Foreningen Mikrofinans Norge.

Kvinnebanken Norgesnett. (1998). *ABC i Nettverkskreditt.* Lofoten: Kvinnebanken Norgesnett.

Pearson, R. & Watson, E. (1997). Giving Women the Credit, Gender and Development: Poverty in the North. *Oxfam Journal, 5*(3), 52–57.

Pettersen, L. T., Alsos, G. A., Anvik, C. H., Gjersten, A. & Ljunggren, E. (1999). *Blir det arbeidsplasser av dette da, jenter? Evaluering av kvinnesatsingen i distriktspolitikken.* Bodø: Nordlandsforskning.

Pettersson, O. (Plantagon) (2015). *RE: E-mail message: Re: Haster! Input til artikkel— oppdatert statistikk!* E-mail dated 09 October 2015 to U. B. Sekkesæter.

Putnam, R. D., Leonardi, R. & Nanetti, R. Y. (1994). *Making Democracy Work: Civic Traditions in Modern Italy.* Princeton, NJ: Princeton University Press.

Schreiner, M. (2001). *Microenterprise in the First and Third Worlds.* Center for Social Development Working Paper 00–2. St. Louis: Washington University.

Sekkesæter, U. B. (2002). *Evaluation of Hordaland Network Credit.* Bergen: Hordaland Fylkeskommune (Hordaldn Couty Council).

Stiglitz, J. E. (1990). Peer Monitoring and Credit Markets. *World Bank Economic Review,* 4, 351–366.

Thomassen, B. (1998). *Nettverkskreditt: Positive og Negative Sider.* Tromsø: NORUT Samfunnsforskning.

Thomassen, B. (1999). *Nettverkskreditt i Norge: Erfaringer og utfordringer.* Oslo: KRD—Ministry of Local Government and Regional Development and Fiskerinæringas Kvinneutvalg.

Van Bastelaer, T. (1999). *Imperfect Information, Social Capital and the Poor's Access to Credit. A Review of the Literature.* Center for Institutional Reform and the Informal Sector IRIS. College Park: University of Maryland.

Width, E. (2010). *Nettverkskreditt som tilgang til kompetanse, nettverk og kapital: En sammenliknende case studie.* Tromsø: Universitetet i Tromsø.

Width, E. (2011). *Norske mikrofinans grupper/föreninger.* Bardufoss.

Wiggen, M. (2005). *Fra almisser til verdighet? Mikrokreditt – bank for fattiga.* Oslo: CIVITA Senter for næringsliv og samfunn.

The World Bank. (1998). *The Initiative on Defining, Monitoring and Measuring Social Capital: Overview and Program Description.* Washington, DC: The World Bank.

Yunus, M. (1998). *Banker to the Poor: The Autobiography of Mohammed Yunus Founder of the Grameen Bank.* London: Aurum Press.

Yunus, M. & Weber, K. (2010). *Building Social Business: The New Kind of Capitalism That Serves Humanity's Most Pressing Needs.* New York: Public affairs.

12 Social Change Through Temporary, Short-Term Interventions

The Role of Legitimacy in Organizing Social Innovations

Anders Edvik and Fredrik Björk

The literature on social innovation is growing quickly, covering many aspects of the phenomenon. However, in this chapter, we argue that organizational aspects of social innovation is a topic that deserves more attention. Using institutional theory, more specifically, the concept of legitimacy, the aim is to look at why project grants have become an important way of organizing social innovation processes, especially those that are structured around cross-sector collaboration. The argument is illustrated by five examples of initiatives working with social innovation and social entrepreneurship in the Region of Skåne in southern Sweden.

Projects and Social Innovation

Social innovation and social entrepreneurship are often discussed in terms of definitions (Moulaert, Martinelli, Swyngedouw & Gonzalez, 2005; Mulgan, Tucker, Ali & Sanders, 2007; Phills, Deiglmeier, & Miller, 2008) or in terms of narratives of interventions addressing societal challenges. These discussions include normative assumptions related to either classical economic theory, such as Schumpeter's view on entrepreneurship, or citizen participation (Hjort & Bjerke, 2006; Hulgård & Lundgaard Andersen, 2012; Rasmussen, 2013). In these discussions, there are also frequent claims that society is undergoing a dramatic change that requires new ways of cross-sector collaboration (Leadbeater, 1997; Moe, 2009; Bornstein & Davis, 2010; Murray, Caulier-Grice & Mulgan, 2010; Scharmer & Kaufer, 2013). These claims, however, rarely include organizational aspects or consideration of national institutional contexts related to the conditions under which social entrepreneurs and associations are operating. In fact, we argue that there is a need for organizational perspectives on how social innovation becomes operative within a Scandinavian, social democratic, welfare regime.

In the editorial chapter of this book, it is argued that there is a need to explore in order to broaden the understanding of social entrepreneurship and social innovation in relation to the role and extent of the welfare state. This chapter focuses on conditions and institutional factors that have a structuring impact on the way social innovations are being materialized into welfare services in Sweden. The theoretical point of departure comes from institutional theory, which enables us to broaden our understanding of a practical issue: why social innovation initiatives tend to be organized as temporary and often short-term interventions although the innovations are addressing complex and long-term social challenges.

The examples that provide the empirical foundation for this text are by no means unique or extreme. Rather, *project-driven operations* have become the standard procedure for many social entrepreneurship organizations working on issues with the overall purpose of contributing to socially sustainable development. At the same time, these organizations are actors within a predominantly tax-funded regional innovation system. In 2013, tax-based funding for the regional innovation system in Skåne Region reached 90 million euros, to a considerable extent in the form of project grants (Kalin, 2013, December 14th). The 120 initiatives in the regional innovation system are related not only to actors in academia, business and public administration, but also to organizations rooted in the third sector. Not infrequently, these initiatives focus on societal challenges, such as integration, unemployment, health and environmental issues: in other words, complex societal long-term challenges that temporary funding is intended to generate solutions for. Political discourse argues for collaboration across sectorial boundaries where academia, public and private sectors and sometimes the third sector, are supposed to join forces in order to achieve outcomes which they are not able to do on their own (Danermark & Kullberg, 1999; Anell & Mattisson, 2009). Frequently, it is also claimed that this will lead to greater efficiency in delivering welfare services, especially to vulnerable groups (Anheier, 2004; Wijkström, 2012). Such claims have a fundamental impact on the field of social entrepreneurship, and third-sector organizations as well as public administration have to respond to this in a legitimate way.

As mentioned above, temporary conditions seem to be well known to most third-sector organizations. We argue that *projects*, which have become more or less a standard organizational format, are of particular interest. Projects, as the discourse is claiming (Sahlin, 1996), enable opportunities for experiments, learning and cross-boundary collaboration, but for social entrepreneurs, the project format also represents uncertainty and short-term conditions. The Swedish Government and the European Union, as well as other major project funders, enable financial support through project grants that public administration, local or regional, are able to apply for in collaboration, often manifested through co-financing with businesses and/or third-sector organizations. This means that the innovation process is not only about the challenge of coming up with solutions or services to meet citizen needs, but it is also about developing sustainable organizational forms in line with the diverging interests of a heterogeneous constellation of stakeholders.

The purpose of this chapter is to highlight institutional structures that are conditioning the way social entrepreneurs are organizing their operations.

Our point of departure is five empirical examples that will help to identify challenges and opportunities associated with project-based operations in the field of social innovation. As we will present in the next sections, legitimacy is a mechanism that structures both the actions of social entrepreneurs and the organization of how project grants are distributed and used.

The Tempting Idea of Collaboration

One of the institutional factors that has a structural impact on the organization of operations is the tempting idea of collaborations between public administrations and third-sector organizations. This idea is associated with normative beliefs stating that collaboration is contributive and innovative in providing complementary services to the welfare sector (Goldsmith, Georges & Burke, 2010; Rønning, Knutagård, Heule & Swärd, 2013). However, cross-sector collaboration is not a new phenomenon. There are numerous examples of the close relationship between the government and the third sector, such as in sports, culture, and voluntary adult education and health care (Salamon, Sokolowski & List, 2003; Jegermalm, Svedberg & von Essen, 2010). However, currently collaboration or co-production (Pestoff, 2011) is often associated with prototypes aiming to develop new knowledge, methods of treatment and forms of cooperation (Danermark & Kullberg, 1999). These claims are evident in concepts such as *penta helix* (Ahonen & Hämäläinen, 2012; Calzada, 2013). The penta helix concept is developed from the quattro helix (Danilda, Lindberg & Torstensson, 2009), a critique of the triple helix, arguing for the addition of third-sector actors to join forces in innovation processes in addition to academia, business and public administration. The penta helix, in the understanding of the CPE example below, additionally involves the category of *public entrepreneurs*. This dynamic can be related to the 'bees and trees' concept (Mulgan et al., 2007), where entrepreneurial agents "operate across the boundaries [. . .] Innovation thrives best when there are effective alliances between small organizations and entrepreneurs (the 'bees' who are mobile, fast, and cross-pollinate) and big organizations (the 'trees' with roots, resilience and size) which can grow ideas to scale" (p. 5).

By involving external actors in the renewal processes of public services, often in the name of social innovation, it is from the government perspective cognitively legitimate (in Suchman's, 1995 terminology) to *fail* as long as some prototypes are successful. In terms of governance (Hedlund & Montin, 2012; Pierre & Sundström, 2009; Löfström, 2010) or management bureaucracy (Hall, 2012), this way of addressing social challenges is a shift from Max Weber's bureaucratic focus on public organization that ensured efficient administration, civic equality and generic and large-scale solutions. Today's emphasis on the need for a *new* post-bureaucratic network-oriented public administration (Quirk, 2011) is an expression of a transition from general solutions based on bureaucratic principles towards smaller and more localized solutions in which the local community is supposed to have an important role. From this perspective, the boundary between the different sectors is no longer distinct (Swan, Scarbrough & Robertson, 2002; Murray et al., 2012).

Thus, new post-bureaucratic ideas not only enable collaboration within the welfare sector, but they also present a strong pressure on both public administration and social entrepreneurs to collaborate. This pressure becomes apparent when government encourages municipalities and third-sector organizations to collaborate by providing temporary project funding. Thus, collaboration and cross-sector partnership represent tempting ideas in an innovation system in which both third-sector organizations and public administration operate.

Temporary Funding and Project Organizing

A second institutional mechanism that has a structural impact on the way social innovations materialize into operations lies within temporary short-term funding. One reason for this is the dominance of public providers within the welfare sector along with an almost non-existing market for social services. Third-sector organizations are largely dependent on grants or economic support from government—local, regional or national. Many of these organizations have just a small number of employees or voluntary workers, and the services provided are aimed at citizens with little or no ability to pay for the services themselves. In these cases, membership fees do not enable a permanent economic base to build an operation because of the small number of members. These conditions have made social innovators in the third sector dependent on external funding, something that makes their position vulnerable from a long-term perspective. Moreover, in Sweden, philanthropic contributions to third-sector welfare service providers have been on a lower level than in many other countries for decades, leading to a situation where government funds are the major option.

A common approach is that government addresses social challenges by turning them into overall objectives for a funding program. In this aspect, temporary grants can be seen in terms of institutional pressure on organizations to produce social values in addition to their regular operations. An example could be a sports association that participates in a social integration program—a tempting opportunity for an organization with scarce economic resources. 'Extra' resources enable activities that are not usually part of the daily operations (Edvik & Björk, 2012), but receiving project grants often requires administrative skills and increased efforts, which can become a burden for small organizations. It is not uncommon for smaller organizations that receive project grants to find out that they are in need of professional assistance to cope with administrative tasks, which in turn may force them to apply for new project grants. Project funding thus tends to transform the direction of third-sector organizations into becoming instruments for policy objectives addressing the social challenges that are at the top of the current political agenda.

Even if the temporary funding system consists of different public funders, there is a Weberian history within public administration through which the distribution of funding is organized. This bureaucratic tradition defines not only regulative (DiMaggio & Powell, 1991; Scott, 1995) criteria or how public tax money should be applied, but also involves norms and values constituting the use of such. From a bureaucratic perspective, both distribution criteria and the use must be in accordance with the democratically legitimate management regime (Berg & Jonsson, 1991). It is required that grants are used efficiently, that public authorities have insight into how applicants are using the money and that funds are properly used for the intended purpose. These institutional norms and regulations are well in line with the goal-oriented rationality of the project format (Sahlin, 1996; Forssell, Fred & Hall, 2013; Löfgren & Poulsen, 2013). The focus on a clear objective to be achieved within a predetermined time frame and with designated resources gives the impression that projects are an efficient form of control (Sahlin, 1996) and a format that can be made distinct from other operations in an organization (Söderlund, 2005).

The project format thus enables opportunities for funders to control both application and evaluation criteria (Sahlin-Andersson, 1996). This opportunity for double control represents a pressure on the organizations receiving funding to respond in a legitimate way in line with bureaucratic, rationalistic principles. In practice, this means that funded projects have to be valued in relation to defined objectives within the project application. However, this governmental way of controlling is not per definition in line with the understanding of innovation processes, which are often associated with high degree of uncertainty, risk taking and failure. Thus, the application process enables insight into what the project intends to implement, and through monitoring and reporting systems, funders are given an opportunity to ensure the intended objectives are achieved.

Temporary grants are often associated with regulative institutional requirements, such as co-financing, which require a permanent organization as a partner. This can be either with resources in kind or in the form of financial contribution. Thus, one needs to collaborate with a partner association, and by co-operating with others, each participant's legitimacy is strengthened (Suchman, 1995). On the other hand, organizations that do not have the ability to co-finance a project will jeopardize future opportunities to be part of collaborative networks.

To insist that the *project*, as a temporary organization, dominates the contemporary perception of organizational efficiency may go a little too far (Sydow, Lindkvist & Defillippi, 2004). However, projects are currently seen as a relevant response to a growing need for development, innovation, creativity and unique and customized solutions, which is a result of globalisation and a perceived rapid pace of change. Today, the traditional principles of the efficient organization, founded in the principles of bureaucracy, seem to have been replaced by more flexible forms, such as projects and networks (Midler, 1995; Sahlin, 1996; see also the concept of projectification: Lundin & Söderholm, 1998; Hodgson & Cicmil, 2006; Packendorff & Lindgren, 2014). The *rational project discourse* (Sahlin, 1996) claims that a project should be understood in terms of a given objective that will be achieved within a certain time, with a defined amount of resources, based on an activity plan (Blomberg, 1998, 2003). The temporary nature of the project format allows a conception that projects are easier to end in comparison with regular operations, where resources are often tied up in long-term commitments. Projects provide a funding flexibility in that grants can, after an audit, be withdrawn, which may be seen as a reduction of risk (Meeuwisse, 1996). Nevertheless, understanding projects based on the assumption that deviations from the plan mean failure is contrary to claims stating that projects must adapt to changes during execution in order to succeed in achieving the desired effects. Isolating projects from history and context may lead to a failure in terms of not fulfilling needs (Sahlin, 1996; Svensson & von Otter, 2001; Blomberg, 2003; Engwall, 2003).

The Role of Legitimacy

Thus, collaboration beyond sectorial boundaries is politically viewed as desirable, and through project grants, the government is able to stimulate such initiatives in accordance with bureaucratic norms. However, the way social innovations are materialized into operations is also structured (thirdly) by the need of being legitimate in relation to project stakeholders. To establish a productive and innovative relation between partners, time is essential in order to prove trustworthiness among participants (Maurer, 2010). Positive experiences from previous collaborations makes the process work more smoothly, but when it comes to forming new constellations without historical references, *legitimacy* is a key factor in enabling constructive partnerships (Suchman, 1995). The challenge is, however, to form a strong project organization in accordance with funding criteria and thereby respond in a legitimate way while at the same time acting in accordance with institutionalized norms and values within the organizational field where the social innovation is developed. Even if cross-sector collaboration is articulated as something good, different institutional logics make it difficult in practice. It is therefore common that in practice, cross-sector means a separated form of collaboration between public and third-sector organizations (Johansson, Löfström & Ohlsson, 2007).

As mentioned above, cross-sector collaboration in the field of social innovation in Sweden is often based on partnerships between public administration and third-sector organizations. The reason for this can be found both in legislation linked to institutional contract rules (procurement rules), and internal opportunities for public administrations to

Table 12.1 Summary of Empirical Examples

Institutional factors Empirical examples	Organization and financial support	Obtained legitimacy
CPE	Permanent association based on short-term grants	'Trustworthy' partners
WinWin	Temporary operation based on short-term grants	Weak institutional network
Maggan	Temporary operation based on short-term grants	'Trustworthy' partners
FIFH	Permanent association supplemented with project-based business and short-term grants	A strong record
Brightful	Permanent association based on voluntary work combined with short-term grants	Voluntary efforts and a strong record

expand operations without affecting the maintenance budget. Temporal short-term funding enables public administration to find informal ways, less bureaucratic, routinized and hierarchical, to develop new services or to engage in a project without political insight (Forssell et al., 2013), and since it may be less administratively burdensome and more legitimate to collaborate with a third-sector organization, these have become natural project partners.

Before presenting the five empirical examples, a summary is presented in Table 12.1. Each example is illustrated from the institutional factors of legitimacy and organization.

Developing the Regional Ecosystem for Social Innovation: The Centre for Public Entrepreneurship

To illustrate the point we are making in this chapter, we have chosen five empirical examples of initiatives in the field of social innovation from the Skåne Region.[1] The examples have been chosen in order to illustrate a range of different institutional aspects of projects in order to facilitate temporary short-term interventions.

The Centre for Public Entrepreneurship is clearly within the category of capacity building organizations, while the other four examples (WinWin, Mötesplats Maggan, FIFH and Brightful) represent a range from service delivery to political advocacy. All the latter four represent initiatives that have received support from the Centre for Public Entrepreneurship and, except for Brightful, their resources are to a large extent provided through project funding from public authorities.

Even though several of the initiatives and organizations in the regional innovation system are supporting the development of innovations targeting societal challenges, the orientation has predominantly been towards market-based solutions, and less on aspects such as community resilience (Moore, Westley, Tjornbo & Holroyd, 2012) or the involvement of third-sector organizations (Nicholls & Murdock, 2012). This led several actors in the regional social innovation ecosystem (Cameron, 2012; Björk, Hansson, Lundborg & Olofsson, 2014) to argue for the need to develop a function that could provide capacity building for organizations in the region that were developing social innovations. In 2009, Folkuniversitetet took the initiative together with Glokala Folkhögskolan, both third-sector civic education organizations, to apply for a project grant from the European Regional Development Fund to initiate the Centre for Public Entrepreneurship (CPE). Co-financing was provided from, among others, Skåne Regional Council, the Swedish Knowledge Foundation, Malmö University and the City of Malmö. Today, CPE is in the process of turning the project into a permanent organization, which is also strengthening CPE's autonomy. The overall objectives have been to support projects and initiatives that encourage citizen participation in both local as well as regional development and to help build cross-sector networks that can increase collaborative governance through supporting *public entrepreneurship* (Bjerke & Hjort, 2006). Since 2009, CPE has supported the development of more than 220 initiatives.

> We support social entrepreneurial initiatives in the whole Skåne Region by offering mentoring and advice on financing, organization, project management, communication, and access to our multidisciplinary network. (CPE, 2015. Translation from Swedish by the authors)

A common feature of CPE's services is the provision of knowledge and experience for those who are starting up initiatives. This is often done by bringing a broad range of local partners together to build coalitions. CPE also works to support networks that aim to strengthen third-sector organizations in relation to the public sector. To facilitate this, collaborations with academia and developing international connections are also important activities, as well as facilitating knowledge sharing and development through workshops, conferences and seminars.

WinWin: Trading Resources Between Sectors

"The Immanuel Church receives furniture for our transitional accommodation for homeless people in return for letting the company 4Cycle use our excellent conference facilities. This creates a win-win situation and marks the start of a good cooperative effort", argues pastor Johan Pernryd, who participated in Sweden's first WinWin event at Malmö City Hall in April 2012.

The WinWin project, based on a German model, is an event where third-sector organizations and businesses meet and connect. But the meeting should not just end with the exchange of business cards. The basic concept of WinWin is that it should lead to actual deals: agreements that are signed by both parties. This is a way of getting private businesses and third-sector organizations to meet and create shared value.

Agreements could be about anything: the important thing is that money is not involved, either in sponsorship or in selling. Instead, other resources are to be used. Several departments from the City of Malmö and local enterprise and local third-sector organizations were partners in the WinWin project. Funding was provided from the European Regional Development fund, with co-financing from the city of Malmö. The aim was that WinWin would become an annually recurring event and that the concept would spread to other parts in Skåne. However, when the project ended in May 2013, it was not possible to find a model for organizing and financing future WinWin events. One important reason for this was that several of the stakeholders from the City of Malmö questioned whether the public sector should engage in this kind of initiative at all (Ullman, 2013).

Meeting Place Maggan: Cross-Sector Collaboration to Promote Community Development

"Being an active participant within your local residential area is taking a step into society. Our hope is that Meeting Place Maggan will provide our tenants with increased understanding on how society functions and how to participate more actively in its development", says Sonja Lastre at LKF, Lunds Kommuns Fastighets AB. Meeting Place Maggan opened in March 2012 with singing, dancing and music. It is a meeting place by and for the people living in Norra Fäladen, developed in collaboration between local third-sector organizations, real estate companies and local enterprise organizations. The project receives project grants from the European Regional Development fund and is co-financed by the City of Lund and the Swedish Public Employment Service.

Welfare dependency, unemployment and segregation are part of daily life in Norra Fäladen. Maggan's objective is to change this and its operations are, therefore, especially focused on work integration. You can receive help in applying for work, writing your CV and attending job interviews, but also get advice on how to start your own business. "We need to be patient now in the start-up phase. It takes time to spread the word", says Marzieh Momenian, project assistant at Maggan with a special responsibility for English training, homework help and the women's group. Together with communicator Andreas Ragnarsson, she walked from door to door, posted information notices and visited SFI (Swedish for Immigrants) classes in order to spread the word about the initiative. "Many people in Norra Fäladen come from countries with different lifestyles and cultures and are unemployed or have no knowledge on how to start their own business. It is vital to disseminate information and see the growth potential in the area", says Andreas. The goal was for Maggan to be run by the local residents after the project period ended in December 2014, but unfortunately, this could not be accomplished. The plan is now to develop new project applications during 2015 in order to acquire resources.

FIFH: Focus on Abilities Instead of Disabilities

FIFH is Sweden's largest association for sportsmen and women with disabilities, but it increasingly focus also on the inclusion of disabled people in the labour force. One objective is to create a social business with disabled consultants who, among other things, can provide advice on accessibility. The part of FIFH that involves sports will continue as a voluntary association, with a small amount of regular financial support from the City of Malmö. Peter Nilsson is one of the driving forces in developing FIFH's new direction. "We must highlight people as being resources. When disabled people live off welfare instead of being tax payers, this unnecessarily leads to illness and poor health", he says. He speaks from his own experience. After graduating with a degree in economics from university, he applied for over two hundred jobs without luck. But in 2005, he became the project manager for one of FIFH's EU financed projects. Now he wants to provide better opportunities for others. At FIFH, young people meet role models who are self-sufficient and have jobs. This is important as inspiration and motivation. "I welcome tougher requirements. People with disabilities must solve their own problems instead of waiting for non-disabled people to solve them for us", Peter says. FIFH works continuously to develop projects. One example is Hotel Funktionell, a project financed by VINNOVA, Sweden's innovation agency, aiming to develop a hotel concept where people with disabilities are the 'normal' guests, also providing job opportunities for disabled people (FIFH, 2015).

Brightful: Only When You Receive Acknowledgement Do You Dare to Dream

At Värner Rydénskolan in Rosengård on a sunny Friday afternoon in May, a small classroom is still packed with pupils from the 7th and 8th grades. Everyone is there because they want to be, and they talk about their visions of the future. A former pupil, Fatime Nedzipovska, and her friend, Elnaz Barjandi, have succeeded where many have previously failed: getting young people in disadvantaged neighborhoods to engage in their own future, to set their own personal goals and then encourage them to see that these goals are actually attainable. The organization they have created is called Brightful. To facilitate this, the Brightful program engage in individual coaching and joint workshops, giving young people access to various stakeholders in the community, such as schools, local organizations and businesses, as well as role models. Today, Brightful has dedicated mentors (about 40) who are involved with coaching and engaging young people on their goals, dreams and aspirations. The ambition is that Brightful should not become yet another short-lived project that leaves pupils stranded, but instead exist as a community. It started entirely without funds in 2012, but has since then been able to acquire a number of minor awards and grants, both from government and philanthropic providers, in addition to a small amount of regular financial support from the City of Malmö.

> The important thing is that young people continuously dare to dream real dreams, not dreams according to what other people say they should become, but dreams of what they themselves want to become, deep down inside. It is then that you become Brightful. I went to the same school myself and can show them that you can reach far, even though you come from an neighborhood with a bad reputation. (Fatime)

Analysis

The empirical examples above illustrate how institutional factors, to a different extent, have an impact on the way social innovation becomes operations within a regional innovation system. The three analytic factors this chapter proposes, the tempting idea of collaboration, temporary funding and need for legitimacy, help us to understand how social entrepreneurs and associations materialize social innovation initiatives into operations. The CPE example shows not only the provision of welfare services, but also how the infrastructure of the innovation system has become dependent on project funding. In this example, the idea about cross-sector collaboration, based on the penta helix model, is at the very heart of the operational setup. CPE have achieved legitimacy not only from their operations, but also largely from the fact that they are funded mostly by Region Skåne while having a third-sector organization as project owner. The fact that they managed to secure project funding for two consecutive project cycles (the second was called CPE 2.0) also increased their legitimacy. The transformation of CPE from project format to permanent organization is an indication that key actors in the organization see it as counter-intuitive to continue with a capacity building organization in project format and that a more permanent organizational setup would be purposeful. However, this has proven difficult, as there are only a limited number of examples of cross-sector organizational management in Sweden. Even as a permanent organization, it is probably through project funding that the organization will acquire resources for the foreseeable future. Cooperation between CPE and other actors that support social innovation processes regionally is also made possible by the co-location with related organizations such as Third Sector

Network Skåne and Coompanion (an organization that supports cooperative business development), who both, incidentally, also get a large part of their funding from Skåne Regional Council.

In addition to the CPE example, the tempting idea of collaboration was even more significant in the example of WinWin. Here, a successful idea from one context was adapted to Swedish conditions, which seemed to be the main challenge for WinWin when the project was being planned. However, the format seemed to appeal to participants from different sectors, and the event turned out quite well despite the fact that collaboration was not smooth and there was no clear candidate for future project ownership. The role of key partners, such as the City of Malmö, was decidedly vague, and the relation to societal challenges was at best indirect, which led to a loss of legitimacy and eventually to the discontinuation of the initiative.

In the third example, temporary funding illustrates both the opportunities that project grants enables in a short-term perspective, but also the challenges with providing long-term operation. For the people behind Mötesplats Maggan, project funding provided an opportunity to create something that would not have taken place otherwise. The organizational set up of the project brings together a truly cross-sectorial range of organizations, which also provided the project with considerable legitimacy. Nevertheless, while the actors involved voiced their satisfaction with the project outcomes, the interest in making this project permanent was not enough, and it is now on hold until new project funding opportunities occur.

The FIFH-example illustrates how institutional pressure, in terms of temporary funding, transforms an association into a provider of projects within the field of social entrepreneurship. The example also illustrates the need for legitimacy when an operation within the third sector becomes a project provider of social services. FIFH has a long organizational history as a sports club, but the recent development of projects, especially with the purpose of providing new and better opportunities for people with disabilities to get jobs, has changed the organization profoundly. FIFH receives legitimacy for its projects because it has a unique relationship to a vulnerable group of beneficiaries, a successful track record and only to a lesser extent, because it builds on collaborative projects.

The fifth and last example illustrates the need for legitimacy when a third-sector association provides social services, but also a critique against project funding. While Brightful was initiated without financial resources, eventually the need to acquire some financial resources to keep a stable operation management has become evident. Funding has been received from various sources, but the organization has decided to keep external funding at a minimum to avoid building an internal bureaucracy that will use an disproportionate amount of resources. Similar to FIFH, Brightful receives legitimacy mainly through their unique relationship to its beneficiaries and their successful track record.

Conclusions

The purpose of this text is to highlight and to discuss the impact of three institutional factors that we claim have significance on the way social entrepreneurs set up an operation. This is, we argue, highly relevant as third-sector organizations will continue to struggle with project applications, reporting, monitoring, evaluation efforts and seeking new cross-sector partnerships, as there are few other options to finance operations under the current system.

In particular, the focus has been on the idea of collaboration, temporary, short-term funding and the need for legitimacy. Five examples illustrate how these factors affect the organizing of initiatives in the regional context of Skåne. Our findings contribute to this overall discussion by focusing on the role of legitimacy and the challenges that third-sector organizations are facing in a project-oriented distribution system. Based on the five examples, three conclusions can be drawn.

First, the distribution of resources is built on the legitimacy of taxpayers. It is taken for granted that tax money should be used in an efficient and proper way, and it would appear odd if public funders were organizing the distribution of grants based on criteria not in line with this. This also means that the concrete project activities as well as the values of the organizations receiving project funding must be in line with public policy goals.

Second, the project format is legitimate since the form provides funders both with control opportunities and minimum risk. This makes sense in a public sector environment, as government is not supposed to take unnecessary risks with taxpayers money. There is no need to motivate the discontinuation of support for initiatives once the project phase is over, and the responsibility for finding new resources or developing permanent funding models often ends up with the project group, rather than with the formal project owners or funders.

Third, by collaborating with others, or participating in a partnership, each single actor strengthens their legitimacy, which increases possibilities for grant acceptance. Cross-sector collaboration in itself has a strong normative legitimacy in providing new solutions to shortcomings in the provision of welfare services. On the other hand, developing permanent cross-sector organizational setups has been proven to be difficult, and thus the solution tends to become to search for new project funding once a collaborative project is finished.

These three conclusions also point towards questions that need to be discussed. Most importantly, the question is to what extent these institutional factors are leading to consequences that are desirable for different stakeholders. If the consequences, especially the difficulties in turning social initiatives into more permanent operations, are not desirable, then how may conditions be changed in order to enable such a climate? At the same time, it is also important to acknowledge that the Scandinavian welfare regimes are part of a historical legacy with strong contemporary political importance, which also means that they are loaded with ideology.

Some of these systems were, in their day, social innovations that changed societal relations fundamentally in Sweden. It is thus equally important to ask if, and if so, to what extent, some of the institutional qualities of these systems need to be transformed in order to respond to the change in social relationships that can be observed today and to enable socially innovative initiatives to become more sustainable.

Note

1. The examples are from a booklet published by the Centre for Public Entrepreneurship: "The art of inviting participation" (Dagerbo & Ohm, 2012), used and edited with permission.

References

Ahonen, L. & Hämäläinen, T. (2012). CLIQ: A Practical Approach to the Quadruple Helix and More Open Innovation. In S. P. Macgregor & T. Carleton (Eds.), *Sustaining Innovation: Collaboration Models in a Complex World*. New York: Springer Science & Business Media.

Anell, A. & Mattisson, O. (2009). *Samverkan i kommuner och landsting—En kunskapsöversikt*. Lund: Studentlitteratur.

Anheier, H. (2004). *Civil Society: Measurement, Evaluation, Policy*. London: Earthscan Publications.

Berg, P. O. & Jonsson, C. (1991). *Strategisk ledning på politiska marknader—Opinionsbildning och intern förankring i förvaltningar och folkrörelseorganisationer*. Lund: Studentlitteratur.

Bjerke, B. & Hjorth, D. (2006). Public Entrepreneurship: Moving from Social Consumer to Public Citizen. In C. Steyaert & D. Hjort (Eds.), *Entrepreneurship as Social Change*. Cheltenham: Edward Elgar.

Björk, F., Hansson, J., Lundborg, D. & Olofsson, L. (2014). *An Ecosystem for Social Innovation in Sweden—A Strategic Research and Innovation Agenda*. Lund: Lund University.Blomberg, J. (1998). *Myter om projekt*. Stockholm: Nerenius & Santérus.

Blomberg, J. (2003). *Projektorganisationen—kritiska analyser av projektprat och praktik*. Malmö: Liber ekonomi.

Bornstein, D. & Davis, S. (2010). *Social Entrepreneurship: What Everyone Needs to Know*. New York: Oxford University Press.

Calzada, I. (2013). Critical Social Innovation in the Smart City Era for a City-Regional European Horizon 2020. *P3T. Journal of Public Policies & Territories, Social Innovation and Territory*, 6, 1–20.

Cameron, H. (2012). Social Entrepreneurs in the Social Innovation Ecosystem. In A. Nicholls & A. Murdock (Eds.), *Social Innovation: Blurring Boundaries to Reconfigure Markets*. Basingstoke: Palgrave Macmillan.

CPE. (2015). Center for Public Entrepreneurship, www.publiktentreprenorskap.se/om-oss/vad-vi-gor/, accessed 15 April 2015.

212   *Anders Edvik and Fredrik Björk*

Dagerbo, E. and Ohm, H. (2012). *The Art of Inviting Participation*. Malmö: Denter for Public Entrepreneurship. Available at www.publiktentreprenorskap.se/wp-content/uploads/2012/12/CPE-Booklet-English.pdf, accessed 15 April 2015.

Danermark, B. & Kullberg, C. (1999). *Samverkan: Välfärdsstatens nya arbetsform*. Lund: Studentlitteratur.

Danilda, I., Lindberg, M., & Torstensson, B-M. (2009). Women Resource Centres: A Quattro Helix Innovation System on the European Agenda. Paper presented at Triple Helix VII, Glasgow, United Kingdom.

Dimaggio, P. J. & Powell, W. W. (1991). *The New Institutionalism in Organizational Analysis*. Chicago: University of Chicago Press.

Edvik, A. & Björk, F. (2012). *Den projektkompetenta idrottsföreningen: En studie av idrottsföreningarnas förmågor att genomföra projekt*. Malmö: Malmö högskola.

Engwall, M. (2003). No Project Is an Island: Linking Projects to History and Context. *Research Policy*, 32(5), 789–808.

FIFH. (2015). *All Inclusive Movement: En samhällskatalysator som breddar normalitetsbegreppet*. Malmö: FIFH.

Forssell, R., Fred, M. & Hall, P. (2013). Projekt som det politiska samverkanskravets uppsamlingsplatser: En studie av Malmö stads projektverksamheter. *Scandinavian Journal of Public Administration (SJPA)*, 17(2), 37–59.

Goldsmith, S., Georges, G. & Burke, T. G. (2010). *The Power of Social Innovation: How Civic Entrepreneurs Ignite Community Networks for Good*. San Francisco: Jossey-Bass.

Hall, P. (2012). *Managementbyråkrati: Organisationspolitisk makt i svensk offentlig förvaltning*. Malmö: Liber.

Hedlund, G. & Montin, S. (2012). *Governance på svenska*. Stockholm: Santérus Academic Press Sweden.

Hodgson, D. & Cicmil, S. (2006). *Making Projects Critical*. New York: Palgrave Macmillan.

Hulgård, L., & Andersen, L. L. (2012). Socialt entreprenørskab-velfærdsafvikling eller arenaer for solidaritet?. *Dansk sociologi*, 23(4), 11.

Jegermalm, M., Svedberg, L. & von Essen, J. (2010). *Svenskarnas engagemang är större än någonsin*. Stockholm: Ersta Sköndal högskola.

Johansson, S., Löfström, M. & Ohlsson, Ö. (2007). Separation or Integration? A Dilemma When Organizing Development Projects. *International Journal of Project Management*, 25(5), 457–464.

Kalin, K.-S. (2013, December 14). *Rörigt system möter skånska innovatörer: Sydsvenskan*. Available at http://8till5.se/2013/12/14/rorigt-system-moter-skanska-innovatorer/, accessed 15 April 2015.

Leadbeater, C. (1997). *The Rise of the Social Entrepreneur*. London: Demos.

Löfgren, K. & Poulsen, B. (2013). Project Management in the Danish Central Government. *Scandinavian Journal of Public Administration*, 17(2), 61–78.

Löfström, M. (2010). *Samverkan och gränser: Studier av samverkansprojekt i offentlig sektor*. Borås: Skrifter från Högskolan i Borås, 25.

Lundin, R. A. & Söderholm, A. (1998). Conceptualizing a Projectified Society Discussion of an Eco-Institutional Approach to a Theory on Temporary Organizations. In R. A. Lundin & C. Midler (Eds.), *Projects as Arenas for Renewal and Learning Processes*. Boston, MA: Kluwer Academic.

Maurer, I. (2010). How to Build Trust in Inter-organizational Projects: The Impact of Project Staffing and Project Rewards on the Formation of Trust, Knowledge

Acquisition and Product Innovation. *International Journal of Project Management*, 28(7), 629–637.

Meeuwisse, A. (1996). Projektens dolda funktioner. In Sahlin, I. (Ed.), *Projektets paradoxer*. Lund: Studentlitteratur.

Midler, C. (1995). 'Projectification' of the Firm: The Renault Case. *Scandinavian Journal of Management*, 11(4), 363–375.

Moe, E. (2009). Vi behöver fler samhällentreprenörer. In M. Gawell, B. Johannisson & M. Lundqvist (Eds.), *Samhällets entreprenörer: En forskarantologi om samhällsentreprenörskap*. Stockholm: KK-stiftelsen.

Moore, M., Westley, F., Tjornbo, O. & Holroyd, C. (2012). The Loop, the Lens, and the Lesson: Using Resilience Theory to Examine Public Policy and Social Innovation. In A. Nicholls & A. Murdock (Eds.), *Social Innovation: Blurring Boundaries to Reconfigure Markets*. Basingstoke: Palgrave Macmillan.

Moulaert, F., Martinelli, F., Swyngedouw, E. & Gonzalez, S. (2005). Towards Alternative Model(s) of Local Innovation. *Urban Studies*, 42(11), 1969–1990.

Mulgan, G., Tucker, S., Ali, R. & Sanders, B. (2007). *Social Innovation: What It Is, Why It Matters and How It Can Be Accelerated*. London: The Young Foundation.

Murray, R., Caulier-Grice, J. & Mulgan, G. (2010). *The Open Book of Social Innovation*. London: NESTA & The Young Foundation.

Nicholls, A. & Murdock, A. (2012). The Nature of Social Innovation. In A. Nicholls & A. Murdock (Eds.), *Social Innovation: Blurring Boundaries to Reconfigure Markets*. Basingstoke: Palgrave Macmillan.

Packendorff, J. & Lindgren, M. (2014). Projectification and Its Consequences: Narrow and Broad Conceptualisations. *South African Journal of Economic and Management Sciences*, 17(1), 7–21.

Pestoff, V. (2011). Co-production, New Public Governance and Third Sector Social Services in Europe. *Ciências Sociais Unisinos*, 47(1), 15–24.

Phills, J. A., Deiglmeier, K. & Miller, D. T. (2008). Rediscovering Social Innovation. *Stanford Social Innovation Review*, Fall 2008, 34–43.

Pierre, J. & Sundström, G. (2009). Politikens roll i samhällsstyrningen. In J. Pierre & G. Sundström (Eds.), *Samhällsstyrning i förändring*. Malmö: Liber.

Quirk, B. (2011). *Re-Imagining Government: Public Leadership and Management in Challenging Times*. Basingstoke: Palgrave Macmillan.

Rasmussen, P. (2013). Uddannelse og Social Innovation. *Dansk Sociologi*, 23(4), 75–90.

Rønning, R., Knutagård, M., Heule, C. & Swärd, H. (2013). *Innovationer i välfärden—möjligheter och begränsningar*. Stockholm: Liber.

Sahlin, I. (1996). Vad är ett projekt. In I. Sahlin (Ed.), *Projektets paradoxer*. Lund: Studentlitteratur.

Sahlin-Andersson, K. (1996). I styrbarhetens utmarker. In I. Sahlin (Ed.), *Projektets paradoxer*. Lund: Studentlitteratur.

Salamon, L. M., Sokolowski, S. W. & List, R. (2004). Global Civil Society: An Overview. In L. M. Salamon (Ed.), *Global Civil Society: Vol. 2: Dimensions of the Nonprofit Sector*. Bloomfield, CT: Kumarian.

Scharmer, O. & Kaufer, K. (2013). *Leading from the Emerging Future: From Ego-System to Eco-System Economies*. San Francisco: Berrett-Koehler Publishers.

Scott, W. R. (1995). *Institutions and Organizations*. Thousand Oaks, CA: Sage.

Söderlund, J. (2005). *Projektledning och projektkompetens: Perspektiv på konkurrenskraft*. Malmö: Liber.

Suchman, M. C. (1995). Managing Legitimacy: Strategic and Institutional Approaches. *Academy of Management Review*, 20(3), 571–610.

Svensson, L. & von Otter, C. (2001). *Projektarbete: Teori och praktik: Med sagan om diamanten som sprängdes*. Stockholm: Santérus.

Swan, J., Scarbrough, H. & Robertson, M. (2002). The Construction of Communities of Practice in the Management of Innovation. *Management Learning*, 33(4), 477–496.

Sydow, J., Lindkvist, L. & Defillippi, R. (2004). Project-Based Organizations, Embeddedness and Repositories of Knowledge: Editorial. *Organization Studies*, 25(9), 1475–1489.

Ullman, M., (2013). Bygga Gemensamt. Processutvärdering av WinWin Malmö. (http://mip.sverigesforeningar.se/wp-content/uploads/2013/04/bygga-gemensamt. pdf), accessed 4 December 2015.

Wijkström, F. (2012). *Civilsamhället i samhällskontraktet: En antologi om vad som står på spel*. Stockholm: European Civil Society Press.

13 Entrepreneurship Invited Into the (Social) Welfare Arena

Malin Gawell, Elisabeth Sundin and Malin Tillmar

Social services such as childcare, elder care, health care and education have primarily been provided by the public sector in the welfare society that emerged during the twentieth century in Sweden. Non-profit organizations had a limited role in delivering social services. Businesses had almost none. This absence of the civil society and non-profit organizations from social services does not imply a weak civil society, but rather that the engagement takes other forms of expression.

The public sector in Sweden has undergone a major transformation during the last decades. Deregulation, procurement and client choice models have been used to invite private entrepreneurs into the social welfare arena in which public and private actors are expected to contribute to diversity and efficiency in the provision of social services in a society where social welfare services have been provided predominantly by the public sector. In this chapter, we explore and discuss how entrepreneurship is invited into the social welfare arena, how this invitation is handled by different actors and what the conditions are for entrepreneurship. We will do this by means of a variety of empirical cases from the private, public and non-profit sectors that illustrate expressions of social entrepreneurship in the current welfare society. Neither social considerations nor entrepreneurship are new phenomena in any sector, so what is described and discussed is current changes and new expressions—not something entirely new.

Social Entrepreneurship in a Transformed Welfare Society

Entrepreneurship, in the basic understanding of *entre prendre*, or in other words, *entering into* and *grasping something* (Hjorth, Johannisson & Steyaert, 2003), is increasingly being recognised in social spheres even if what is referred to as *social* varies (Steyaert & Katz, 2004; Gawell, 2006; Mair, Robinsson, & Hockerts, 2006; Nicholls, 2006). On the one hand, social relates primarily to general social interaction between people and the construct of practices (Steyaert & Katz, 2004; Steyaert & Hjorth, 2006). On the other hand, it is related to the start-up and running of ventures providing social services or addressing social problems (Leadbeater, 1997; Dees, 1998). It is not only in the field of social entrepreneurship that the understanding of *social* varies. Different types of ventures and different branches of activities are referred to as social—frequently with variation between countries. In Sweden, the public sector deals with many of the issues and services that we would generally call social. In the Swedish context, the concept of societal has been used to emphasise a way of thinking and arguing developed in historical traditions that is illustrated in both this chapter and in others.

Sweden, a mature welfare state, provides data for illustrative examples of how the definition of 'social' varies over time and space as well as the perception, or rather, the common understanding, of who is responsible. Acknowledgement is necessary to transform needs into demands and actions. Society is never static. Even today, in a mature welfare state, changes that challenge the common solutions are taking place—some of the changes are substantial, some concern ideas and perceptions. Demographic changes, a growing number of elderly people, many of them in need of care, and a growing number of immigrants are examples of the former. An example of the latter is how the needs and rights of people with learning disabilities are improved. The current examples lead to discussions as to which needs are social here and now and which community is best suited to meet these needs.

During the first half of the twentieth century, a relatively extensive public sector was developed and organized in a way that has been labelled the Scandinavian welfare model (Esping-Andersen, 1990). It was based on the idea of equal access to health care, childcare, elder care, education, housing etc. and that these services were best governed and run collectively. Distribution of these social services was to be based on needs and funding based on payment capacity and channelled through the public tax system. The starting point was low, in an international perspective, but dramatically changed the position of the country. The creation of the welfare state that took place after the Second World War has been presented as an entrepreneurial project (Kovalainen & Sundin, 2012). The development of the public welfare system was an expression of a collective approach to social problems as well as to more general structural issues in society, even if other reasons for the development of the public sector also existed. The labour movement, and more specifically, the Social Democratic Party, had a strong influence, as did streams within farmers' associations and social liberals. But it has been also argued that collective solutions were seen as an opportunity for individual freedom, not least for women, who traditionally cared for the children, the sick and the elderly within family structures (Berggren & Trägårdh, 2006). The collective solutions released women from some family obligations and also provided work opportunities and thereby financial independence—or at least decreased dependence on husbands and family (Berggren & Trägårdh, 2006). This paradoxical relation can also be observed in the World Value Study in which Sweden and the other Nordic countries score very highly on measurements related to valuing collective solutions, and the same countries also score highly on valuing individualism (World Value Study, 2015).

The position of women in a Scandinavian welfare state has been recognised in both politics and research. The Norwegian political scientist Helga Hernes (1987) coined the phrase the *women-friendly welfare state*, which has also explained why women have a more positive attitude than men towards the public sector. Despite that, we should remember that Sweden is not a society where equality between men and women is a fact (Statistics Sweden, 2014). The differences show a pattern that has resulted in another expression—the *gender system* (Hirdman, 1988).

The public sector was and is governed by elected politicians and therefore is under democratic control. In the early 1990s, the public sector accounted financially for more than 60 per cent of the GDP, but this has since decreased to slightly more than 50 per cent. Since year 2000, the decrease is explained by a combination of changes—the Swedish Church is no longer a public unit, some producing units have been transformed from agencies to companies and, as will be discussed in more detail below, Swedish applications of international trends have been influenced by New Public Management (NPM). Approximately one-third of the labour force currently works in the public sector or publicly owned ventures (Statistics Sweden, 2014). Social security, including financial transactions in relation to sick leave, unemployment, public pensions children and families and people with disabilities, accounts for approximately 40 per cent of public spending. Health care accounts for approximately 15 per cent and education approximately 12 per cent (Statistics Sweden, 2014).

The extensive public sector also meant that civil society organizations were given a complementary role, providing few social services of a conventional kind (Lundström & Wijkström, 1997). Instead, they have developed their advocacy and deliberative role (Wijkström & Lundström, 2002). It seems as if organizations whose main tasks are far away from what is considered to be social themselves interpret activities as having social dimensions. One example is an appeal from a Swedish municipality to all organizations that undertake social duties, which was responded to by a number of sport clubs and the like (Hallström, 2015). This perception is shared by public opinion.

Entrepreneurship Invited Into (social) Welfare Branches

The Swedish welfare model was increasingly debated during the 1980s and the following decades. There were arguments that it was ineffective and that high public costs hindered economic growth. Arguments favouring market-based solutions and restrained public intervention grew stronger in Sweden, as in many other countries around the world. The changes have been described and interpreted from different perspectives, often influenced by political convictions. Here, we will mainly refer to 'from government to governance' and NPM. Both are international but have national and, in the case of Sweden, also local interpretations. Government is associated with hierarchy and centralisation, and governance with networks and decentralisation. In many ways, decentralisation is a Swedish tradition, as local self-government is an integrated part of the Swedish democratic system. The changes that have taken place during the last decades, however, mean something completely new, which will be illustrated in connection with the presentation of our cases below.

The current state is highly influenced by an NPM approach that has permeated the governance of the public sector since the 1980s. NPM is characterized by a quest for efficiency and a belief in business-like transactions as a tool to match resources efficiently (Jacobsson, Pierre & Sundström, 2015). NPM has become a norm within the public sector, and through the policy shifts in which private actors are invited as sub-contractors, it has now spread into the private sector, both profit and non-profit organizations—at least as an approach to relate to in the welfare arena, which will be illustrated below (see also Wikjström & Zimmer, 2011).

The welfare arena is far from simplistic. National policy-making processes are interrelated with regional and local processes. In Sweden, almost 300 municipalities have a large responsibility for social care, education etc. and some twenty counties have primary responsibility for health care as well as public transport (Association for Local Authorities and Regions, 2015). These municipalities and counties are, to a large extent, independent and governed by autonomous, democratically elected bodies. They are, however, obliged to follow national law.

The 1990s saw the deregulation of the financial, telecommunication and transport sectors (Munkhammar, 2009). Furthermore, an educational reform in 1992 allowed private schools to become recipients of public school funding (Parding, 2011). Prior to the reform, only a very small percentage of schools were privately owned. In 2014, 27 per cent of pre-schools, 17 per cent of compulsory schools (grades 1–9) and 33 per cent of upper secondary schools were privately owned (Skolverket, 2014). In some municipalities, primarily in larger cities, 40 to 60 per cent of the students in compulsory and upper secondary education attend privately owned schools (Friskolornas Riksförbund, 2014). Since then, other social sectors such as health care, childcare and elder care, psychiatric care and also labour market initiatives have followed similar transformations through public procurement and different types of client choice models. It is difficult to fully disclose this development statistically, since these ventures are classified under different codes. Apart from the figures related to schools above, we can here also mention a 60 per cent increase in the number of private actors in the field of health care from 2001 to 2014 (Statistics Sweden, 2014). There has, however, only been an increase of 10 per cent in the number of people working in these ventures, which means an increase primarily in relatively small ventures.

On the one hand, this has meant a privatization of social services. On the other hand, these services are still publicly funded, which means that there has been a partial privatization with strong public governance structures due to conditions of payment (see also Christensen & Laegreid, 2005, 2006). In terms of policy, this discussion has been strangely avoided for a long time. Instead, politicians have highlighted 'competitive neutrality', that is to say, they have not explicitly targeted or limited procurement to one type of venture or the other. An analysis of the outcome of procurement and also client choice model practices indicates certain biases, which will be elaborated on below.

Different Interpretations of and/or Different Types of Entrepreneurship

During the last decades, the interest in entrepreneurship has also grown and attitudes have shifted from being rather sceptical to overwhelmingly cherishing—first as a key force for economic growth and then, gradually, as a panacea for all types of aspects of development. The business approach to entrepreneurship was accompanied by references to societal entrepreneurship and social entrepreneurship. A rather confused discussion emerged in which aims, forms and sector of activities were at times alternately mixed. For example, there are assumptions that business in general and, related to the topic of this anthology, more specifically in the social fields, is commonly ascribed a profit maximization aim, even though studies indicate that this is not necessarily the case (Sundin, 2010, 2011). It is also assumed that social engagement is generally related to altruistic non-profit ventures. The complexity of connections between profit/non-profit, self-interest/benefit to others and different organizational forms is at times underestimated, as representatives for different approaches argue, which will be illustrated in the cases presented below.

It is not easy to pinpoint the concept of entrepreneurship that is cherished nowadays, which can also be seen in the debate on and practices of entrepreneurship in relation to welfare services. There are several underlying references to entrepreneurship as a dynamic innovative force and thereby to a Schumpeterian view of entrepreneurship. There are also references to entrepreneurship as swift and flexible organizers detecting 'demands' in society and thereby a Kirzner-influenced approach. Demand is here in citation marks due to an imprecise use of terms, which creates confusion when applied interchangeably in economic and social discussions. Needs, demands and wishes in social terms do not automatically correspond with demands in economic terms. The latter consist of a willingness, combined with an ability, to pay (Gawell, 2013). But there are also several references to entrepreneurship as the creation of, and operations run by, private enterprises, depending on who makes this type of statement. Enterprise can mean exclusively for-profit enterprises or include different types of enterprises, of which some are large/medium-size/small and some are profit-maximising, whereas others aim for decent economic output to be distributed to owners or ventures that re-invest potential profit or simply view funding as a means to operate without profit aims.

With a basic understanding of social entrepreneurship as social engagement combined with some kind of entrepreneurial action (Gawell, 2008), initiatives can take different forms depending on decisions and other factors that influence the process. A for-profit business, a co-operative or a non-profit organization can emerge during the entrepreneurial process. In practice, the principles of these different types are not always clear. There are for-profit enterprises, not least small ventures, that prioritize aspects other than maximising profit, such as care for a community or working opportunities for employees, as presented below. There are also non-profit organizations that at times seem to prioritize economic efficiency over needs in society. This leads us to argue that it is not analytically possible, or at least not meaningful, to initially differentiate various forms. The different ventures engaging in welfare services that aim for social security and activities in the social sectors such as different types of care can thereby all be viewed as forms of social entrepreneurship—despite their different legal forms.

To clarify the discussion above, the following illustration shows the different versions of social entrepreneurship and the emergence of different types of ventures and the rather elastic relation to concepts such as business/industry, social economy and civil society (Gawell, 2014). The organizational form is not clear when the entrepreneurial initiative emerges. The form—related to legal structures as well as norms and practices in the different categories—is taken on as the entrepreneurial initiative proceeds. The concepts of *entrepreneurship* and also, more specifically, *social entrepreneurship* are used in all the different sub-categories. Also, references to *social enterprises* as a label for social ventures are being made in the business, co-operative and non-profit spheres. In the business sphere, this is in line with the so-called Anglo-American business school approach. In the co-operative and, to some extent, the non-profit sphere, this is in line with the co-operative influenced EMES approach. In the non-profit sphere, entrepreneurship is connected and at times intertwined with general non-profit discussions (Gawell, 2014). In this chapter, we also elaborate on entrepreneurship as a driver for development of public ventures. We recognise and stress that the 'logics' of the different spheres, and thereby the different versions of social entrepreneurship, are not easily separated, even though different practices appear. In the transformation of the Swedish welfare society, all these versions of social entrepreneurship are highly relevant—albeit not explicitly referred to due to references to 'competitive neutral' policies, that is, to not relate to different legal forms in procurements, etc. Further, conceptual complexity, as well as difficulties to relate the elusive aspects of social entrepreneurship, for example, related to legal structures or statistics, contributes to a rather vague social entrepreneurship debate.

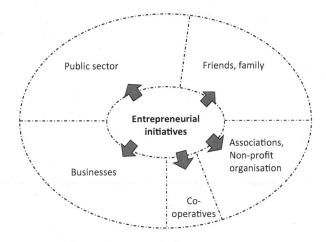

Figure 13.1 Different Versions of Social Entrepreneurship
Source: Gawell (2014), printed with permission from Springer.

Illustrations

In this section, we will take a closer look into policy measures as well as adjustments of established actors and new actors responding to the invitation to act within the welfare arena. We will start with the social sector, and in particular an organization called Criminals Return Into Society (CRIS) that was established long before the changes in the public sector in the social arena belonging to the non-profit sector. CRIS had to adapt to the new situation. The subsequent section is also taken from the social sector and illustrates entrepreneurship as a construction of organizations, since the meta-organization Famna was established as a positive response by non-profit organizations operating in the field of health care to the invitations to enter the social welfare arena. In the third part, we meet organizations in the private business sector with obvious social aims. We start with an example to show that social considerations have always been an incentive for entrepreneurs. This is followed by two examples connected to political decisions inspired by NPM. Different types of entrepreneurship are manifested to put the services at hand on the market.

Fellow Human Beings Become Customers and Factors of Production

Social entrepreneurship relates as much to individuals engaging in entrepreneurial activities and beneficiaries as to how ventures, and even society at large, are organized. Based on three different studies,[1] let us look more

222 *Malin Gawell, Elisabeth Sundin and Malin Tillmar*

closely into some aspects of the social entrepreneurship discourse. The organization CRIS is an illustrative example. Their primary aim is to help each other to stay free from drugs and establish honest lifestyles in spite of former drug abuse and/or criminality (CRIS, 2015). The organization was started and is run by people sharing 'the background' and is essentially a fellowship association in which fellow human beings support each other and together construct a functional everyday life—even when temptations and distress are difficult to bear. Based on this fundament, members of CRIS meet inmates who so wish as they are released from prison, celebrate in a drug-free community and try to help with housing, jobs etc. Thus far, relationships are based on fellow solidarity and the fostering of mutual trust.

With the ambition to help each other and to reach out to more beneficiaries, efforts to mobilize resources call for the 'packaging' of activities according to the donor's logic. In the case of Sweden this has been, and to a large extent still is, governed by public authorities and/private funds providing grants for social activities. The Swedish Prison and Probation Services (Kriminalvården), municipalities, the European Social Fund and the Swedish Inheritance Fund (Arvsfonden) are examples of influential donors. Suddenly, terms such as *target groups, objectives, activity plan, measurable results* become part not only of applications for funds, but also of the organization, as a response to new principles and demands of the public sector. This might seem like semantics. But the people involved hesitate to label themselves and fellow human beings *target groups* since it creates stereotype images that are inconsistent with the friendship and the aim of empowerment (Gawell, 2013).

The discourse on social entrepreneurship, at least as expressed by actors promoting (economic) market-influenced ideals, takes the discussion on relations yet another step further. Target groups are relabelled *customers*. But even if beneficiaries are the clients/users of services, funding bodies dictate the terms. The understanding of the concept of customer is thus split into the relation to beneficiaries on the one hand, and the relation to donors and their conditions on the other hand. Again, the people involved hesitate, this time since, as beneficiaries, they are called customers—but without having the control of purchasing power.

Organizations like CRIS develop so-called work-integrating social enterprises as a means to provide job training and work opportunities for their members, as well as running halfway houses or other services that support people who want to change their lives for the better. Other organizations, frequently with influences from the co-operative movement, do the same. They commonly target people who have been unemployed for a long time without specification of the reasons for unemployment. The policy interest in these work-integrating social enterprises has led to opportunities for ventures in which beneficiaries and the funding eligible to support them on the labour market become factors of production in the social venture.

The reaction from people involved, first and foremost as beneficiaries, is divided. Some argue that this mobilization of resources benefits them in a positive way. They argue that the social enterprise is also a catalyst for the empowerment process. Others, however, argue that they are being used as factors of production or even exploited without favourable reciprocity (Gawell, 2013). And it seems, but is not fully proven, to have something to do with the position in the social enterprise. Of the 320 social enterprises identified by the Swedish Agency for Economic and Regional Growth (Tillväxtverket), only a third of the approximately 6,000 people who participated in training programmes and/or ordinary activities participated on the basis of employment (www.sofisam.se). Most of the others had more temporary agreements.

Established Non-Profit Organizations Mobilize and Adjust

The Swedish Association for Non-Profit Health and Social Service Providers (Famna) is an umbrella organization that lobbies the government as well as national, regional and local parliaments for the role of non-profit alternatives. The importance of increasing the diversity of service providers is one of the organization's key messages. Famna was founded in 2004 and acts in various ways on the national level to strengthen the role of non-profit organizations in public markets for care and health services (Famna, 2015). The organization has acted as an intermediary between service providers (their members) and policy makers, for example, in the field of quality improvements (Neubeck, Elg & Schneider, 2014). Famna also facilitates competence development among its organizations by providing seminars, leadership training and advice. After a lobbying process from the civil society organizations, a national-level compact between the civil society and the public sector was signed simultaneously (Johansson, 2011). Local-level compacts are currently being negotiated in a number of municipalities (see Hallström, forthcoming).

The leaders of the national organization Famna found that the interest of health-related non-profit organizations in providing services was lower than they had expected. In 2010, they therefore requested a study on how idea-driven organizations perceive opportunities and obstacles to provide welfare services.

The study that was conducted clearly illustrated the different logics in national umbrella organizations and within their locally situated member organizations (Skåmedal & Tillmar, 2010). Five umbrella organizations took part in the study (in addition to Famna; these were HSO, the Swedish Disability Federation; SIOS, the Co-operation Group for Ethnic Associations in Sweden; PRO, the Swedish National Pensioners' Organization; and SPF, the Swedish Pensioners' Association). The leaders of these organizations were at the time reluctant to advise member organizations to become service providers. One main reason was the conflict between voice and service (see Wijkström & Lundström, 2002). That is to say, the organizations view themselves as lobby organizations defending the rights of the individual (the members of their member organizations, for example). At times, they defend the individual's rights against service providers and public organizations such as municipalities or county councils. The leaders of the umbrella organizations interviewed argued that if their member organizations also became service providers, the role of the organizations as a 'voice' would be eroded. Furthermore, they perceived themselves to be lacking financial as well as human capital; i.e. the idea that they or their members were entrepreneurs or business operators was alien to them.

Having experienced the pros and cons of public quasi-markets, Famna pointed to the price competition and the large units being put out for tender as posing obstacles to their member organizations, which are often smaller (see Tillmar, 2004). However, when it came to the overall issue of non-profit providers of care, Famna itself was the most positive of the umbrella organizations, highlighting opportunities such as procurement procedures that increasingly focus on quality issues and less on prices, and the broad political agreement on the advantage of non-profit organizations in welfare services.

On the local level, all the umbrella organizations had, in fact, members that were already providing welfare services. Among these, perceptions of non-profit service production were much more positive. While in practice, they saw tough competition and economies of scale as benefiting large for-profit companies, they interpreted the increased interest in non-profits on behalf of the government as very promising for them. In sum, whereas many of the umbrella organizations for the established non-profits at the national level were reluctant on ideological grounds to enter into the market as providers of services, local-level organizations were more pragmatic and optimistic.

Social Dimensions in Private Sector Organizations: Possibilities and Problems

Social dimensions are often an integrated part of the incentives for individuals starting an enterprise and for individuals working as owner-managers (Sundin & Holmquist, 1989; Holmquist & Sundin, 2002). For some, the social aspect is a large, not to say dominating element of the decision to establish an organization. We will here give three examples from our own research: the midwife who started an enterprise to provide advice and support on sexuality for young people with learning disabilities, the parents who established a school and the cleaners who established a company that would do a good job and give workmates a job and an income. The first example is from the pre-NPM era and shows one of the many entrepreneurs and enterprises with social considerations as one of their incentives. The second, the parents who established schools, was possible thanks to the liberalization of schools and the construction of a schools market. The third is a direct consequence of NPM principles and a political will to reduce the public sector in the municipality.

The first example is of a midwife who, during her work for the county council, met young people with learning difficulties who had problems with their sexuality, as well as others who had problems with their sexuality. Parents and other adults were anxious that the young people with learning difficulties should not be abused and used by others. There was a need, the midwife said, for people with learning difficulties to receive help to 'say no' but also to 'say yes' to having a positive relationship. Their families needed help and support as well. The midwife talked to her employer, the county council, about this and proposed a time and resources to work with the issue. Her superiors, that is, medical doctors as well as the decision-makers, the politicians, understood the problem but did not support her proposal that these issues should be put into organizational practice. As she was so convinced of the need, she found that she had to start a firm of her own. Her customers were groups of parents and stakeholder associations. To earn a living, she also worked part time as a midwife for the county council. She found that that was beneficial, as she met new colleagues. She acted as an entrepreneur both inside the big organization and through her own enterprise.

The second example relates to the response of parents to changes in school policies. In 1992, various changes were introduced into the Swedish school system. Schools could be established by anyone who met some rather modest criteria, and children and their parents had to choose which school they wanted to attend. Schools had been the responsibility of the municipalities since 1991. As the economic conditions were hard and the demands for efficiency were growing with NPM, many municipal managers and politicians centralised schools and closed down small units in villages outside the centre of the municipality. This was resisted in many villages and, with the help of the new regulations, parents established themselves as owner-managers of schools—sometimes they chose a co-operative model, sometimes a private company. The reasons for the start-ups were not just their own children, but the survival of the village and its inhabitants. The school was an important organization in protecting a lifestyle, both symbolically and as a hard economic fact (Sundin & Tillmar, 2010).

The third example relates to cleaners who had to adapt to new conditions. When the municipality started their customer choice practices, the cleaning services for their own facilities and for the elderly who had been granted cleaning assistance were no longer to be provided by the municipality. The cleaning unit within the municipality was closed down and almost 500 cleaners, most of them women, lost their jobs. The politicians responsible did not expect unemployment to follow, as they hoped that many of the cleaners would establish themselves as entrepreneurs in the cleaning market and provide the services that the municipality requested. What followed was far from these hopes (Sundin & Rapp, 2006). Here, however, we will concentrate on around 100 cleaners who decided to establish a company together. The initiative was taken by some entrepreneurial cleaners for a number of reasons. One was that their professional pride was insulted by the decision to close the unit. They thought that they were doing an excellent job not only as cleaners, but also in taking care of colleagues with problems, since the municipality had established a practice of asking the cleaning unit to take care of individuals in need of replacement. This meant that they did not simply produce cleaning services but also care services, and that a number of the employees were not effective cleaners.

Business advisers told the entrepreneurs to exclude the individuals with health problems when they started their venture. But they refused to make a selection, even though it was not only the health issues that were a problem, but sometimes also the attitude towards being an owner-manager. "But what could we do?" says one of those interviewed. "With my health problems, I would not hire myself."

Concluding Analysis and Discussion

By means of a number of different cases, we have illustrated that entrepreneurship, which through the social focus of activities can be referred to as social entrepreneurship, is a vivid phenomenon in contemporary society, as well as throughout history. Entrepreneurship for social purposes has also previously existed in private businesses, co-operatives, non-profit organizations and public organizations. Sometimes it is and was individual, and sometimes it is and was collective. Sometimes the focus is on the social dimensions, and the economic purposes are a minor part. Sometimes it is the other way around. And due to the intertwined complexity, it is very difficult to specify in categorical or quantitative terms.

Specifically, we have set out to explore and discuss: 1) How entrepreneurship is invited into the social welfare arena, 2) How this invitation is handled by different actors, and 3) What the conditions for entrepreneurship have become.

The Invitation

Much of the Swedish welfare state is decentralised and the municipalities are largely autonomous—which is of importance in more way than one in the cases referred to in this chapter. Care for children and the elderly is the responsibility of municipalities and thus it is organized in a way decided upon by local politicians. This implies that despite clear intentions from the national government to increase what they called diversity and freedom of choice through competition in public markets, organizations in the societal sectors have been invited to different extents and in different ways in different municipalities. A recent quantitative overview shows differences in market development, in particular between larger metropolitan areas on the one hand, and smaller towns and rural contexts on the other. For example, in metropolitan areas, there was a greater increase in the number of small and medium-sized enterprises in welfare industries (Sköld, 2015). In short, the trend is the same across the country—but the extent and the organizational models vary between municipalities. The explanations are many—the size of the municipality influences the size of the market. Ideology also has relevance for this phenomenon.

Over time, the dominating organizational models for public markets have changed as reactions to unintended practice and as actions to create markets. During the first wave of privatization, the Public Procurement Act (SFS, 2007:1091) regulated municipal decisions regarding service suppliers. Since 2009, the use of The Act on the System of Choice in the Public Sector (SFS, 2008:962) has been advocated. The former was directed towards the suppliers—private companies, non-profit organizations and public sector organizations. The latter aimed to involve the clients and give them freedom of choice.

How the Invitation Was Handled by Different Actors

As we have illustrated, private, public and non-profit organizations were all affected by the introduction of entrepreneurialism in the welfare arena. First, as far back as the 1980s, the municipalities' own production was divided into units, presenting bids to win contracts and managed as private companies with time-limited contracts. Overall, principles of care were exchanged for economic principles. When other suppliers were invited to join 'their market', it meant a great change. The main issue was to handle austerity policies and not to solve an expanding demand, as it had been for a long time.

The big companies gained a new market with an increasing demand (in economic terms) and a reliable payer—the public sector. All they had to do was to respond to formulations in calls for tender that were listed by regional counties within health care and municipalities within child and elder care as well as other social services in their responsibilities. Some of these large, at times multinational enterprises were successful and have been able to make a significant profit. However, this is a politically sensitive issue, which makes it hard to make relevant comparisons between different owners.

The small, local companies also gained a new market with fierce competition, which they, as a rule, found too tough. So even if there has been an increase in the number of smaller enterprises in particular, this does not necessary mean lucrative ventures or an increasing share of the market. The same conclusion was reached by the third-sector/non-profit organizations. Some of them had been suppliers of social services in the municipalities with support from the public sector. They were forced to make changes, as illustrated in some of the cases. The internal difficulties with contradictory logics and identities posed major challenges to these organizations. It is still an open empirical question whether we are witnessing a genuinely increased role of non-profit organizations in society, or if we are witnessing a 'sister process' to the NPM system—a *New Non-Profit Management*. Within service provision, the pressure is hard. But some organizations still combine service provision with advocacy—and many organizations focus on advocacy rather than service.

The Conditions for Social Entrepreneurship

In both public procurement processes and client choice systems, our studies indicate that larger private corporations have a competitive advantage at the expense of small and medium-sized enterprises and non-profit organizations (Tillmar, 2004; Sundin & Tillmar, 2010; Sköld, 2015; Högberg, 2015) and public sector organizations. A case study of a particular municipality showed that both the municipality's production unit and the non-profit organizations that had been contracted for special services for many years lost the most in the transformation. The third-sector organizations could not, and at times would not, adapt to the new NPM principles and regulations. The conflict with the ideologies governing the organizations and/ or the interest of their individual as well as organizational members had become too big. This comes as no surprise, as the purpose of NPM is to make all organizations adapt to the principles of a market. However, some of the consequences were not wanted by many decision-makers, and there are currently some indications of changes.

The use of NPM within the public sector and in an extension into the market, like conditions on the welfare arena, aims to increase efficiency and therefore reduce slack in 'the system'. And even if social entrepreneurship and social innovations in which civil society organizations are ascribed a vital role are praised by politicians, for example, in the innovation strategy (Ministry of Enterprise, 2012), the NPM approach decreases the space for creativity and trying out new ideas and thereby a fundamental base for entrepreneurship, intrapreneurship and innovation.

It is difficult to draw a clear line between ventures run as for-profit, non-profit or public organizations. We have seen different examples in this chapter. There are, however, differences in how ventures prioritize social and economic aims. Some act only if there are lucrative financial conditions. Others, especially small enterprises and non-profit organizations, act if there are means to cover costs. And some non-profit organizations mobilize many other types of resources in order to be able to act—even if there are no obvious funds accessible. Activities are then dependent on individual engagement and capacity to act upon what they perceive as necessary, over time.

As mentioned earlier in this chapter, the former welfare structures were formed by a perceived *women-friendly state* (Hernes, 1987), since the state both ensured social care and legal rights that emancipated women from traditional non-paid duties and roles and provided a labour market in which women could earn their own income—albeit generally with lower salaries than equivalent male-dominated sectors. Women were dominating some parts of the public sector on all levels, although they were under-represented as managers.

During the transformation addressed in this chapter, the established position of women in the public sector organizations is challenged, as it is "to a large extent a management and managerial project" (Kovalainen & Sundin, 2012, p. 277; Sejestad, 2002) However, advocacy groups and politicians raised arguments that the transformation addressed would improve women's opportunities to start businesses and thereby improve both working conditions and income. The fact is that more women have started businesses in the social fields in which many women have previously worked as employees (Gawell & Sundin, 2014). However, these fields have also been subject to strong financial pressure due to public procurements and other payment measurements, which means that the women-dominated parts of the public sector have a weaker position. There are also studies revealing gender structures in which men are over-represented in more lucrative ventures, whereas women are (still) over-represented in ventures addressing less lucrative, everyday social challenges (Gawell & Sundin, 2014; Sköld, 2015). The consequences from a gender perspective are equivocal and far from offering satisfactory closure.

Note

1. Seven projects funded by the European Social Fund in Sweden, Criminals Return Into Society, sixty-seven projects funded by the Swedish Inheritance Fund (Arvsfonden) (Gawell, 2011a, 2011b, 2012, 2013).

References

Berggren, H. & Trägårdh, L. (2006). *Är svensken människa?* Stockholm: Norstedts.
Christensen, T. & Laegreid, P. (2005). *Organisationsteori för offentlig sektor.* Malmö: Liber.
Christensen, T. & Laegreid, P. (2006). *New Public Management: The Transformation of Ideas and Practice.* Farnham: Achgate.
CRIS. (2015). Available at www.kris.a.se, accessed 12 May 2015.
Dees, G. (1998). *The Meaning of "Social Entrepreneurship".* Available at www.redf.org/from-the-community/publications/262, accessed 8 April 2013.
Esping-Andersen, G. (1990). *The Three Worlds of Welfare Capitalism.* Cambridge: Polity Press.
Famna. (2015). Available at www.famna.se, accessed 12 May 2015.
Friskolornas Riksförbund. (2014). *Fakta om friskolor.* Available at www.friskola.se, accessed 9 August 2015.
Gawell, M. (2006). *Activist Entrepreneurship: Attac'ing Norms and Articulating Disclosive Stories.* Stockholm: Stockholm University.

Gawell, M. (2008). Socialt entreprenörskap—en kombination av socialt engagemang och entreprenöriellt handlande. In *Ungt entreprenörskap*. Luleå: Luleå University.

Gawell, M. (2011a). *Entreprenörskap och företagande i projekt finansierade av Europeiska socialfonden. Rapport från en kartläggning av projekt som beviljats medel 2008-2009*. Stockholm: Tillväxtverket, report 89.

Gawell, M. (2011b). *Inte vilket entreprenörskap och företagande som helst. En fältstudie av 7 projekt med finansiering från den Europeiska socialfonden*. Stockholm: Tillväxtverket rapport 90.

Gawell, M. (2012). *Kreativa Hederliga Företagare - det krävs både mod och tålamod*. Analys av ett KRIS-projekt finansierat av Europeiska socialfonden. Stockholm: Criminals Return Into Society.

Gawell, M. (2013). Social Entrepreneurship as Innovative Challengers or Adjustable Followers? *Social Enterprise Journal*, 9(2), 203–220.

Gawell, M. (2014). Soci(et)al Entrepreneurship and Different Forms of Social Enterprises. In A. Lundström, A. C. Zhou, Y. von Friedrichs & E. Sundin (Eds.), *Social Entrepreneurship: Leveraging Economic, Political, and Cultural Dimensions*. Heidelberg, New York, & London: Springer.

Gawell, M. & Sundin, E. (2014). Social Entrepreneurship—Gendered Entrepreneurship? In A. Lundström, A. C. Zhou, Y. von Friedrichs & E. Sundin (Eds.), *Social Entrepreneurship: Leveraging Economic, Political, and Cultural Dimensions*. Heidelberg, New York, & London: Springer.

Hallström, V. (2015). *Samhällsentreprenörskap över gränser mellan ideell- och offentlig sektor: Exemplet Norrköping*. Helix: Linköping University.

Hernes, H. (1987). *Welfare State and Women Power: Essays in State Feminism*. Oslo: Norwegian University Press.

Hirdman, Y. (1988). Genussystemet: Teoretiska reflektioner kring kvinnors sociala underordning. *Kvinnovetenskaplig Tidksrift*, 9(3), 49–63.

Hjorth, D., Johannisson, B. & Steyaert, C. (2003). Entrepreneurship as Discourse and Lifestyle. In B. Czarniawska & G. Sevón (Eds.), *The Northern Lights: Organization Theory in Scandinavia*. Malmö: Liber.

Holmquist, C. & Sundin, E. (2002). *Företagerskan: Om kvinnor och entreprenörskap*. Stockholm: SNS förlag.

Högberg, L. (2015). *Eget val: En uppföljning med focus på etniskt företagande*. Helix Vinn Excellence Centre: Linköping University.

Jacobsson, B., Pierre, J. & Sundström, G. (2015). *Governing the Embedded State: The Organizational Dimension of Governance*. Oxford: Oxford University Press.

Johansson, M. (2011). *I dialogens namn,—idén om en överenskommelse mellan regeringen och ideella organisationer*. Växjö: Linnaeus University Press.

Kovalainen, A. & Sundin, E. (2012). Entrepreneurship in Public Organizations. In D. Hjort (Ed.), *Handbook on Organizational Entrepreneurship*. Cheltenham: Edward Elgar.

Leadbeater, C. (1997). *The Rise of the Social Entrepreneur*. London: Demos.

Lundström, T. & Wijkström, F. (1997). *The Nonprofit Sector in Sweden*. Manchester: Manchester University Press.

Mair, J., Robinsson, J. & Hockerts, K. (2006). *Social Entrepreneurship*. Hampshire: Palgrave.

Ministry of Enterprise. (2012). *Den nationella innovationsstrategin*. Stockholm: Ministry of Enterprise.

Munkhammar, J. (2009). *Försäljning av statliga bolag under tre decennier*. Stockholm: Timbro.

Neubeck, T., Elg, M. & Schneider, T. (2014). Managing the Gap Between Policy and Practice Through Intermediaries for Quality Improvement. *Scandinavian Journal of Public Administration*, 18(4), 73–90.

Nicholls, A. (2006). *Social Entrepreneurship: New Models of Sustainable Social Change.* New York: Oxford University Press.

Parding, K. (2011). Forskning om den svenska friskolereformens effekter. *Didaktisk Tidskrift*, 20(4), 231–247.

Sehestad, K. (2002). How New Public Management Reforms Challenge the Roles of Professionals. *International Journal of Public Administration*, 25(12), 1513–1537.

SFS 2007:1091. *Public Procurement Act: Swedish Law Based on EU Directive 2004/18/EG, Which Replaced Former Law on Public Procurements 1992:1528).* Stockholm: Swedish Government.

SFS 2008:962. *The Act on System of Choice in the Public Sector.* Stockholm: Swedish Government.Skåmedal, J. & Tillmar, M. (2010). *Idéburna organisationers förutsättningar att utveckla vård och omsorg: Famna.* Stockholm: Tillväxtverket.

Sköld, B. (2015). *Vad hände? Kvinnors företagande och de strukturella villkoren—en studie i spåren av den offentliga sektorns omvandling.* Linköping: Linköping University.

Skolverket (2014). *Statistik och utvärdering.* Available at www.skolverket.se, accessed 9 August 2015.

Statistics Sweden. (2014). *På tal om kvinnor och män.* Örebro: Statistics Sweden.

Steyaert, C. & Hjorth, D. (2006). *Entrepreneurship as Social Change.* Cheltenham: Edward Elgar.

Steyaert, C. & Katz, J. (2004). Reclaiming the Space of Entrepreneurship in Society: Geographical, Discursive and Social Dimensions. *Entrepreneurship & Regional Development*, 16(3), 179–196.

Sundin, E. (2010). Masculinisation of the Public Sector: Local Level Studies of Public Sector Outsourcing in Elder Care. *International Journal of Gender and Entrepreneurship*, 2(1), 49–67.

Sundin, E. (2011). Entrepreneurship and the Reorganization of the Public Sector: A Gendered Story. *Economic and Industrial Democracy*, 32(4), 631–654.

Sundin, E. & Holmquist, C. (1989). *Kvinnor som företagare: Osynlighet, mångfald, anpassning.* Malmö: Liber.

Sundin, E. & Rapp, G. (2006). Städerskorna som försvann. *Arbetsliv i omvandling*, 2.

Sundin, E. & Tillmar, M. (2010). The Intertwining of Social, Commercial and Public Entrepreneurship. In A. Fayolle & H. Matlay (Eds.), *Handbook of Research on Social Entrepreneurship.* Cheltenham: Edward Elgar.

Swedish Association for Local Authorities and Regions. (2015). Available at http://skl.se/tjanster/englishpages.411.html, accessed 18 October 2015.

Tillmar, M. (2004). *Är det möjligt? Om villkor för småföretagande inom vård-och omsorgssektorn.* Stockholm: Nutek.

Wijkström, F. & Lundström, T. (2002). *Den ideella sektorn: Organisationerna i det civila samhället.* Stockholm: Sober Förlag.

Wijkström, F. & Zimmer, A. (2011). *Nordic Civil Society at a Cross-Roads.* Baden-Baden: Nomos.

World Value Study (2015). Available at www.worldvaluessurvey.org/WVSContents.jsp, accessed 28 May 2015.

14 Narratives of Social Enterprises

Their Construction, Contradictions and Implications in the Swedish Debate

Ulrika Levander

Work-integration social enterprises today stand out as an important remedy for social challenges, such as mass unemployment and social marginalization. As the political legitimacy of these enterprises to a great extent is founded in their role as unique and effective 'labour market policy tools', what does this imply for their capabilities of simultaneously embracing ideals of democratic grassroots participation, where the perspectives of marginalized groups are taken into consideration? In this chapter, the construction of work-integration social enterprises and their internal contradictions and implications is explored in a Swedish context—both regarding these innovating organizations and the associated discourse framed at a policy level.

Social Entrepreneurship as a Panacea Of 'Social Ills'

'A growing industry of social goods.' 'Welfare recipients becoming business leaders.' And 'a highway to the labour market.' A lot of claims are—and have been—made about social enterprises in the socio-political debate in Sweden. Frequently, the enterprises are portrayed as an innovative and growing part of the third sector, and as such, they are often framed as groundbreaking and flexible actors, more suitable to effectively take on current welfare challenges than 'ordinary', 'unwieldy' and 'bureaucratic' public organizations. The fact that the enterprises combine non-governmental and market-based approaches to address social issues helps position them as less dependent on the public sphere than other third-sector organizations. By having limitations on profit distribution, they simultaneously stand out as something quite different from regular, private, for-profit businesses. In this sense, social enterprises appear not only as new and innovative, but also as very unique performers in the Swedish welfare landscape (Levander, 2011).

The increased interest in social enterprises and social entrepreneurship as a solution of today's 'social ills' is not a trend purely isolated to Sweden. Rather, the concept of social entrepreneurship has gained a strong recognition globally in recent years, often being framed as a new policy paradigm whereby welfare delivery transcends the traditional boundaries between market, state and family (Nyssens, 2006; Defourny & Nyssens,

2008; Nicholls, 2010; Santos, 2012). Although the understanding of the concept varies between different cultural and national contexts, it is frequently conceptualised as social innovation processes undertaken by social entrepreneurs, which could refer to a broad range of activities from voluntary activism to corporate social responsibility in the for-profit sector (Kerlin, 2006; Defourny & Nyssens, 2008; Nichols, 2010). The concept of social entrepreneurship is often used in a broad sense as an umbrella term that also incorporates social enterprises. In the European discussion, the understanding of such concepts is generally linked to initiatives taking place in the third sector. In this understanding, social entrepreneurship has gained strong political support, both as a contribution to the production of welfare services and as a way of increasing the role of 'active citizenship' and political participation in society (Gawell, Johannisson & Lundqvist, 2009; Hulgard, 2010; Gawell, 2014).

In discussing the potential role of the third sector as a facilitator of re-democratization and new forms of citizen participation in European welfare states, Pestoff (2012) argues that this is only possible when social services are co-produced by citizen groups that have direct democratic control over the provision of publicly financed services. As participation by key stakeholders and democratic decision-making are two core criteria in the definition of social enterprise developed by the European EMES Research network, Pestoff contends that this definition endorses such valuable forms of co-production. However, the willingness of European governments to recognise the importance of citizen participation in policy making is according to him crucial for taking up future opportunities to implement 'real'—or as he refers to it, 'heavy'—forms of co-production in welfare provision. In analysing the relationship between social entrepreneurship and public sector governance in Sweden, Gawell (2014) finds indications of close ties between what policy makers promote and what social entrepreneurs choose to target, and this raises questions regarding the power relationships between involved public and civil society actors.

As discourses of social entrepreneurship both hold ideas of remedying social ills and creating participation and active citizenship amongst socially vulnerable groups, the overall discourse of the phenomenon tends to be constructed in positive terms, with normative claims for its definite—and 'good'—outcomes (Dey & Steyaert, 2012; Gawell, 2014). In this sense, social entrepreneurship appears as a sort of panacea for the grand 'social ills' of the post-industrial world. However, Dey and Steyaert (2012) refer to the contemporary discourse of social entrepreneurship, in both political and scientific fields, as 'myth-making'—a process of which they are critical (Dey & Steyaert, 2012, p. 91):

> Constructing social entrepreneurship as necessary, even indispensable, for tackling today's most serious ills, and framing the matter in the language of morality and rationality, forms part of a myth-making process,

which chiefly suggests that anyone who considers him- or herself reasonable cannot but embrace social entrepreneurship. On the face of it, the conditions of today's scholarship leave little if any space for substantial critique of social entrepreneurship—simple because others suggest that the solution already exist.

In a study to map the contours of social enterprise activities that the EU Member States initiated in 2013, Sweden is portrayed as one of the European countries where a broad variety of support schemes specifically designed for social enterprises have been initiated (European Commission, 2014). However, the Swedish state support initiatives are identified as narrowly focused on work-integrating social enterprises (WISEs), whereas those in several other countries are recognised as aiming at the much broader 'social economy'. Thus, the Swedish the concept of social enterprise focusing on WISE, although supported by national regulations, appears as narrower in scope than in most other European countries. Across Europe, WISEs today stand out as the most dominant type of social enterprise (Defourny & Nyssens, 2008). This implies a specific concern for labour market inclusion, which reflects today's political need to address and find solutions to high levels of long-term and structural unemployment numbers within the European Union.

Apart from combating social exclusion and long-term unemployment, WISEs in Sweden are currently politically framed as effective instruments to foster participation and empowerment among excluded groups (Ministry of Enterprise, 2010). Considering that the idea of social enterprise, in mixing principles of the market, the voluntary sector and the public sphere, is blending traditionally conflicting understandings of institutional logics and organizational fields (DiMaggio & Powell, 1983), the implications of legitimating certain aspects of the discourse of WISEs are not self-evident or obvious. For example, whereas ideals of participation and empowerment increasingly are articulated as important issues to address in prevailing socio-political discourses, new forms of regulatory techniques are implemented in current practices with marginalized individuals, whereby enhanced control and disciplining mechanisms are exercised (Rose, 1999; Levitas, 2004). This is apparent, for example, in the increased focus of activation and performance requirements implemented in Swedish labour market policies over the last couple of decades (Johansson, 2010), which in many aspects influenced the discretion of Swedish WISEs. As the political legitimacy of these enterprises to a great extent is founded on the identity of them being unique and effective 'labour market policy tools', what does this imply for their possibilities to simultaneously embrace ideals of democratic grassroots participation, where the perspectives, discretion and ideas of marginalized groups are taken into consideration in the everyday dealings of the companies?

Departing from a critical sociological perspective, which leads to an analysis of power effects in shaping and controlling dominant discourse, the aim of this chapter is to explore the construction of WISEs, the democratic gains ascribed to them and their internal contradictions and implications in a Swedish context. In the contemporary Swedish debate, expressions like 'entrepreneurship of the civil society', 'value-based enterprising', 'societal entrepreneurship' and 'social economy' are often used synonymously with the concept of social entrepreneurship (Prop, 2009/10:55). As social entrepreneurship appears as quite a vague concept in Sweden, lacking a clear and hegemonic understanding, this chapter specifically focuses on the discourse of WISEs conducted both in public policies and among social enterprise actors from the early 2000s up until 2011. In analysing the constructions and contradictions of the narratives conducted, the implications of participation, co-governance and advocacy opportunities of marginalized groups in social enterprise are specifically discussed and highlighted.

Examining Social Entrepreneurship From a Critical Perspective

In exploring what consequences the understanding of WISEs imply, both for the innovating organizations concerned and for the political discourse framed, Foucault's concept of 'governmentality' is employed, as it adopts a social constructivist perspective on power and control (Foucault, 1991/1978; Rose, 1999; Miller & Rose, 2008). Foucault (1980) refers to governmentality as a specific form of mentality that has developed as fundamental in the political thought of the modern and post-modern worlds, in which the overall construction of knowledge is closely linked to power and the ability to control commonly accepted 'truths'. Using this analytic platform helps develop an understanding of how power stipulates certain frames of truth that provide amenable forms of self-control to individuals and organizations in the contemporary world.

Miller and Rose (2008) refer to the prevailing governmentality of the post-industrialized world as 'advanced liberal', a rationality which according to them is characterized by an increased localization of power to individual citizens and civil society-driven initiatives. Rose (1999) identifies the third sector, or *the third sphere*, as he refers to it, as a moral space with the capacity to connect people in durable relations. He stresses that the discourse of the third sector initially came forward as a form of social criticism that over time has come to be suffused with professional claims. In the more expert-oriented emerging discourse of civil society, this sector increasingly tends to be represented as a field of activities that are carried out and controlled by professional actors. This implies a state-colonisation of a space that previously has been fairly free from controlling practices. Now, this space is constructed as a new sector of regulation (Rose, 1999).

In analysing how entrepreneurial improvements in the third sector are legitimated and normatively framed as needed and 'good', Rose's (1999) identification of a shift in the predominant discourse of the third sphere is of interest. This shift is fundamentally allied to today's socio-political linking of the third sector as a way of problematizing contemporary social challenges. For example, as the form of control executed within the advanced liberal rationality is increasingly focused on the need to include marginalized people in society through active labour market measures, an ethical reconstruction of socially excluded people can be identified (Rose, 1999). Here, activation measures provided by various forms of experts—preferably located in the civil society—are to be used and directed towards people subject to 'exclusion'. This implies a weakened focus of the potential of civil society's *deliberative* democratizing processes in favour of the control and regulations carried out through the advanced liberal form of governmentality. Thus, a characteristic of the discourse of the third sphere is how it tends to construct itself as the solution to the social problems it portrays. According to Rose, the prevailing discourse of the third sphere is hence constructed as a solution to the problems it identifies. This makes critiques of the 'positive' discourse of the third sector, and the normative claims linked to it, difficult to address.

In this chapter, concepts from neo-institutional analysis, such as *institutional rationality*, and *cognitive* and *normative legitimacy* (Powell, 1991; Scott, 1995; Suchman, 1995) are also used to examine the implications of various institutional framings of social enterprises and their possible contradictions. Empirically, the chapter draws on the discourse and narrative analysis (Fairclough, 1992, 2000, 2005; Edley, 2001; Wagner & Wodac, 2006) of the documents produced by state authorities involved in the reporting about of WISEs in Sweden, and qualitative interviews with participants, workers and staff in three different Swedish WISEs trying to achieve the inclusion and participation of marginalized people through social entrepreneurship. Depending on the kind of institutional rationality operating in the specific accounts, different narratives of WISEs can be identified. The different use of discourse and narratives emerging in the material is analysed, compared and discussed in the light of the theoretical frameworks used.

From Deliberation to Inclusion

In recent years, there has been a tendency to conceptualise disadvantaged positions in society in terms of 'social exclusion' in political as well as theoretical discourse; this is of fundamental importance for the construction of work-integrating social enterprises as an effective and desirable solution to today's social ills. A shift in the understanding of the concept 'social exclusion' has been identified by various scholars, entailing a redirection of attention in the European understanding of the concept from excluding processes and social structural factors causing marginalization towards deficiencies of the excluded ones (Jessop, 1999; Young, 1999; Esping-Andersen, 2002; Gilbert, 2002; Steinert, 2003; Levitas, 2004; Martin, 2004). The use of 'social exclusion' in today's political discourse suggests that an ideological shift has taken place, where welfare solutions to an increasing extent are accommodated to neoliberal and conservative ideals. Similar changes in the understanding of the concept of social exclusion can be discerned in the Swedish political debate, which implies that the overall view of the traditional 'universal' Swedish welfare model is undergoing transformation (Davidsson, 2009). This discursive shift, focusing on proactive labour market integration as the 'overall' solution to problems of marginalization and social exclusion, is for instance evident when the predeceasing agency to the Swedish Agency for Economic and Regional Growth in 2005 described labour market exclusion in the following terms:

> Today, about one million people are excluded from the Swedish labour market, and are being supported by passive subsidies. Many can and want to work but the road to the labour market is closed.
>
> (Nutek, 2005, p. 3)

The statistics behind the figures presented reveal that about 65 per cent of the people being categorized as 'excluded from the labour market' are either on long-term sick leave or have retired early due to physical or mental disabilities; this latter group was not included in earlier official unemployment numbers in Sweden and hence was not considered as 'excluded' from the labour market. In categorizing people with early retirements and long-term sick leaves as being excluded from the labour market, social exclusion is here framed as a serious and large-scale social problem. Further, in characterizing subsidies as 'passive', the quote clearly positions social exclusion, here understood as not being self-sufficient, as a 'bad' and unwanted situation in society. So, what does this framing of 'social exclusion' as an immediate and undesirable problem imply in the political construction of WISEs as a desired vehicle to improve the situation of socially marginalized groups?

A Shifting Discourse

In the macro discourse on social enterprises framed at a policy level in Sweden, a discursive shift can be identified between early articulations of the phenomenon found in the late 1990s and early 2000s and later political accounts. The main concern in the early official discussions about Swedish social enterprises—then mainly referred to as 'social work-cooperatives'—primarily focuses on processes of collective action and democratic governance as a means to reinforce the influence and power of marginalized groups in society:

> the uniqueness of social work-cooperatives is that they are owned and operated by people working in them; and these people have a need for work on their own terms.
>
> (Swedish State Authority of Work-Related Issues, 2002, author's translation)

> The whole idea with the social enterprise is that the power of running the company is held by the people working in it. If you let go of that critical function the employees lose their power, and in the end their engagement in the company. A social enterprise has been disarmed.
>
> (The National Board of Health and Welfare, 2001, author's translation)

The localization of power to the social entrepreneurs running the companies is here positioned as central. Further, this is framed as a vital possibility for marginalized groups to be empowered and enhance their position, not only in society but also in relation to public authorities:

> Successful social enterprises have great capacities to improve the living conditions—create a good or better life—for marginalized groups. Thereby, people would be given the chance to regain the power and control over their lives through liberating or reducing their dependency on welfare, health and correctional authorities, and on the psychiatric services.
>
> (The National Board of Health and Welfare, 2001, *author's translation*)

> In creating cooperatively run businesses a change of identity among people who have been subjected to various welfare-state measures can take place. In the social work-cooperatives they actively take the power in their own hands [. . .] This creates empowerment and an identity as a co-operator, employee and social entrepreneur.
>
> (Swedish State Authority of Work-Related Issues, 2002, p. 6 *author's translation*)

Implicitly, public authorities and their dealings with marginalized groups are here positioned as paternalistic. In documents dealing with WISEs in the early 2000s, structural and institutional factors are repetitively highlighted as causes of exclusion. Also worth noting is that the buzzword 'marginalization' at this juncture is used to refer to underprivileged groups, rather than people in 'social exclusion'. What is at stake in the early discourse on WISEs is clearly the need to implement more participative modes in welfare creation in order to generate good living conditions for marginalized groups. In this regard, the early discourse on WISEs implies a critique of the traditional welfare ideology in Sweden where welfare officers, 'experts' and public authorities traditionally have had a dominant position in 'calling the shots' and coming up with suitable solutions for welfare needs. Consequently, this discourse is allied with the initial discourse of the third sector described by Rose (1999), where civil society organizations are framed mainly as a critical force in the societal construction of political power.

However, a discourse on social exclusion[1] addressing a need for a more proactive attitude to labour market integration emerged in later years. Rather than framing the legitimacy of WISEs in terms of finding new ways of challenging excluding structures in society by making marginalized groups more participative in welfare provision, labour market inclusion is positioned as the central issue. This is also reflected in official discussions on social enterprises appearing in political documents:

> Social enterprises have created hundred of thousands new job-openings in Europe. Also in Sweden the number of jobs created in social enterprises has grown. These are jobs established for and by people who for various reasons are excluded from the labour market and risk permanent social exclusion.
>
> (Nutek, 2005, p. 2)

In the text quoted, being excluded from the labour market is linked to risks of permanent social exclusion. In this way, social exclusion is put forward as a severe welfare challenge. Here, the concept of 'social exclusion' emerges as a central buzzword in the political discourse and is also equated with being positioned outside the labour market. Further, the social enterprise is framed not only as a possible but a highly relevant and effective solution to the problem. In Europe, hundred of thousands new job openings have been established by social enterprises.

As the WISE is increasingly portrayed as an effective solution to problems of social exclusion, the perspectives on the individuals operating the companies are reframed. For example, in the white paper "From Subsidies to Paid Employment" (SOU, 2007:2), people living on subsidies are recurrently talked of as people with a 'subsidy-dependence'. In portraying people who are excluded from the labour market as having a 'dependency', exclusion is here principally framed as a problem due to individual deficiencies rather than institutional or societal excluding structures. Whereas social work cooperatives in the Swedish government paper "Wage Subsidies Investigation" (SOU, 2003:95, p. 241) from 2003 are described as a model for people to 'create work and solidarity on their own terms', the commission paper "From Subsidies to Paid Employment" (SOU, 2007:2) published five years later talks of 'people who need societal support'. Accordingly, in the latter paper, a target group in need of support is constructed, rather than a group of people being framed as able to create solutions on their own. Rather than being positioned as acting subjects able to take action on their own, the participants of social enterprises are here framed as passive objects of change (Fairclough, 1992; Wagner & Wodak, 2006). In summary, in the latter discursive formulation, the WISE is mainly framed as an active labour market policy tool aiming to amplify excluded people's work abilities in order to enhance their possibilities to be included in society. Here, the excluded individuals' capacities to change in order to be included in society are in focus.

Consequently, a discursive shift in the official discussion of social enterprises emerges in Sweden. From being comprehended as a way of increasing the participation of marginalized groups in society, the WISE is reframed as an effective labour market policy tool. This does not only imply a shift in the view of social solutions similar to the one identified in the socio-political understanding of 'social exclusion'. In being framed as an effective labour market policy tool, the latter discourse on WISE is also suffused with political objectives, which implies a weakened focus of the potential of civil society's *deliberative* democratizing processes in favour of the control and regulations carried out through the advanced liberal form of governmentality (Rose, 1999).

Contradicting Narratives of Social Enterprises

In the ideological gaps appearing in the political reframing on social enterprises at a national level, various narratives appear in the discussions conducted and documents produced by the WISEs examined in the study. An institutionally constructed narrative of fundamental significance in the framing of social enterprises emerging in several WISEs is *the success story of the social enterprise*. In this story, the social enterprise is presented as a social innovation possessing the unique ability to turn welfare recipients into entrepreneurs and business managers. Below, an example of how the success story is articulated in an information sheet from Basta, one of the biggest social enterprises in Sweden, is illustrated:

> Within few companies, if any, is the possibility to make a career faster than at Basta—as one of the co-owners expressed the matter: 'four years ago I was in prison with a drug-problem that had lasted longer than twenty years. Today I am an enterprise executive'.
> (*Basta—Ett nykooperativt företag*, 2005 p. 2–3, author's translation)

In the above story, a problem identity—the long-time drug user—is transformed into a success identity—the enterprise executive. The fact that the transformation process is portrayed as fast and effective is both implicitly and explicitly put in the quote; explicitly, it is a fast career that is offered at Basta, and implicitly, the person being quoted says that in less the four years he has moved on from being a drug addict to becoming an executive. On the one hand, the WISE is here constructed in a similar way as in the later discourse on WISE framed in policies, i.e. as an efficient labour market policy tool. On the other hand, the story does not only claim that the WISE is able to bring people into the labour market. It also claims that it can make entrepreneurs and executives out of them. In short, a 'success story' is told where quite pretentious claims are made about the social enterprise; claims that no other organizations in society can compete with. The enterprises effectively turn welfare recipients into business managers. In this respect, the success story shapes an image of the social enterprise as a highly valuable initiative in the societal battle against social exclusion and unemployment. Hereby, the narrative constructed helps the WISE to gain a strong cognitive legitimacy (Scott, 1995; Suchman, 1995) as an efficient and unique labour market policy tool.

However, similar to the earlier discourse on social enterprises framed in policies, the success story constructs the jobs created in these enterprises as having the capacity to empower marginalized groups. This is explained by the democratic governing structures and the non-discriminating views built into the companies, which allows for the enterprises to recognise the skills of marginalized people—people that are usually not regarded as skilful. In an application for project grants launched by The National Board of Health and Welfare in Sweden, the organization Vägen ut, which is running a handful of social enterprises, writes:

> People with a history of drug-abuse or criminality are not used to their capacities and skills being well regarded in society. Rather, their problems are constantly in focus. But, to survive as a drug-addict for many years is actually a sign of great creativity and energy, a strength and creativity which it is possible to turn into something constructive.
>
> (Vägen ut, 2003)

In this narrative, the abilities and capacities of former addicts and criminals are in focus. This articulation challenges traditional categorizations of people with addictions, as it is these people's problems and problem identities that typically are in focus in 'ordinary' casework assessments by welfare institutions (Järvinen & Mik-Meyer, 2003). Thus, what implicitly is said is 'as others view problems, social enterprises identify resources'. In this sense, the WISE is framed as an actor who can utilize human resources that other societal actors are missing out on. Consequently, the social enterprise is framed as an actor that does not adopt discriminating structures and attitudes typical of 'ordinary' companies, workplaces and societal institutions. By pointing out discriminating norms as causing social exclusion, the success story here implies a structural critique and advocates solutions that imply reduced scope for institutional actors to exclude vulnerable groups from participation in society. In this way, the story helps to create a normative legitimacy (Scott, 1995; Suchman, 1995) of the social enterprise as 'human-centred' and morally good, where the voices and resources of marginalized groups are constructed as central. In this regard, a moral legitimacy is constructed for the WISE (Meyer & Rowan, 1991; Suchman, 1995). Further, the societal critique identified by Rose (1999) as emerging in the initial discourse of the third sector is also interwoven in the success story. Accordingly, the success story blends accounts and perspectives from both the early and the later discourses on social enterprises, discourses with various ideological roots and implications.

In some ways, this ideologically contradictory way of constructing an understanding of the social enterprise can, of course, be viewed as paradoxical. At the same time, the hybrid and conflicting ideas that are interlaced in the story allows for new and defiant connections to be made in the comprehension of marginalized individuals and their capacities. In articulating the possibility for excluded people not only to get a job and become self-sufficient but also to become business managers and entrepreneurs, the success story challenges commonly accepted notions of marginalized groups. In the earlier discourse on social enterprises framed in policies, it is emphasised that the people operating social enterprises usually are, or have been, in excluded positions themselves. By emphasising the great creativity needed to survive in socially exposed positions, for example, as a drug addict or as a former prisoner, and by stressing the capability to use these traits as resources—as a social entrepreneur—the identities of people ordinarily perceived as problematic are reframed and discursively charged with positive and resourceful connotations.

In starting and operating social businesses and thereby creating job openings for themselves, marginalized people are also located as active subjects able to create their own solutions, rather than passive objects of official labour market policies (Fairclough, 1992, 2000). Hence, rather than passive and problematic, the success story reconstructs marginalized individuals as able and potentially successful. Thus, in mixing discourses with various ideological implications, the success story challenges discriminating and oppressing ideas of socially exposed groups in the post-industrialized society. In this sense, the success story offers a form of resistance to dominant discourses and norms that challenge the rationality of today's neoliberal political accounts.

Yet Another Narrative With Contradictory Constructions

But the success story is not the only narrative appearing in the discussions of social enterprises exercised by the WISEs examined. Depending on what kind of institutional rationality (Powell, 1991) is operating in specific accounts of the social enterprise, various narratives were found in the study conducted. For example, a narrative that is quite contradictory but still very similar to the success story emerges when the ability of the WISE to act as a human service organization offering rehabilitation, job training and work-fare measures is articulated. The need to give adequate support to people facing exclusion, rather than to use their unique experiences and abilities, is highlighted within this story, here referred to as *the rehabilitation story*. The following quote from an interview with an employee in a social enterprise exemplifies how this narrative is framed:

INTERVIEWER: And what would you say that (this social enterprise) is doing with and for people?

EMPLOYEE: Well, it is about coming back to an ordinary everyday routine. With structures, with good and regular habits, that it can lead to employment, work [. . .] What we do is to offer routes to people in exclusion to get back into the labour market. (Interview with an employee in a Swedish social enterprise)

Here, the human-service oriented content of the social enterprise's dealing is emphasised. The enterprise is said to offer training to individuals in exclusion on how to gain sound everyday structures and routines. The focus on the human-service orientation is also evident in the following interview excerpt with another social entrepreneur:

EMPLOYEE: You own your own problems, and you are the one who can do something about it for yourself. I can be there for you to offer support, structures and be there for you when it's needed [. . .] You know, I can make a person feel important, get that person to feel he or she is growing [. . .] But, the change within you, that is to take place—which will make you become a more whole and healthier individual—you have to do that yourself. (Interview with an employee in a Swedish social enterprise)

The identities of the people in this story are not constructed as capable and potentially successful social entrepreneurs. Rather, they are framed as lacking important capabilities and skills. The social enterprise, on the other hand, is portrayed as the actor able to give the support needed, due to its human-centred ability to 'see' and 'believe in' people and who, according to the rehabilitation story, help excluded people to grow and reach personal development. In addition, in this rehabilitation story, personal growth is constructed as a precondition for excluded people to eventually fit into society—and into the labour market. Just as in the success story, labour market integration is outlined as the goal of the social enterprise's efforts. Further, the ability to 'recognise' and 'see' people is highlighted. But rather than recognising people's skills and resources, the ability to meet people's needs is stressed here. Moreover, in contradiction with the success story, the goal of the labour market integration is not articulated in terms of being an employed social entrepreneur in a social enterprise. Instead, the integration is located in 'the ordinary' labour market 'outside' the social enterprise. Rather than turning welfare recipients into business leaders and social entrepreneurs, the rehabilitation story constructs the aim of the social enterprise to prepare excluded people for a job in the 'ordinary' labour market. Consequently, the implications for the concerned individuals differ between the stories. Rather than being framed as active subjects with resources and abilities, marginalized people are now constructed as objects of change (Fairclough, 1992).

Primarily, the rehabilitation story is articulated when the legitimacy of the social enterprise as a human service organization is at stake. The success story, on the other hand, is expressed when the social enterprise is portrayed as a unique and innovative business form creating economic growth and new job openings in the societal battle against social exclusion. Hence, the various stories hold different rhetorical resources that provide possibilities to address various assets of the enterprise depending on the legitimacy issues at stake in the institutional context. The different constructions of the social enterprise in the success story and the rehabilitation story also entail different understandings of the kinds of work positions offered in social enterprises. In the success story, the entrepreneur, executive and employee is put forward. In the rehabilitation story, it is rather the people in training that are portrayed, i.e., 'clients', as undergoing workfare measures.

One Concept, Several Understandings

In the definition of work-integrative social enterprises provided by the Swedish state authority in charge of the growth and development of social enterprises, the Swedish Agency for Economic and Regional Growth (Tillväxtverket, formerly Nutek), three forms of WISEs are described. These are social enterprises focusing on: 1) Work with wage employment, 2) Job training as a preparation for taking a job in the ordinary labour market and 3) A sense of fellowship and meaningful pursuit (Nutek, 2008, p. 23). In this regard, the WISE does not come forward as one uniform phenomenon. More accurately, it appears as a concept with several possible understandings, aims and goals. In offering activation measures to excluded people rather than paid employment, the second form of social enterprise comes across as a form of welfare service, contracted out from the public authorities responsible for labour marker integration. The understanding of social enterprises as organizations being fairly independent of the public sector and creating new job openings for excluded people in the battle of exclusion are partly challenged here.

As previously discussed, the hybridization of resources (e.g., contracts and subsidies) and combination of various institutional logics within the social enterprises enables different and partly contradictory framings. As a business, the social enterprise can be institutionally located within business and industry policy. As initiatives that create new job openings and integrate people into the labour market, the enterprises appear as actors involved in labour market policy. Creating other welfare solutions, such as various forms of rehabilitation or occupational therapies for marginalized and disabled people, the enterprises can also institutionally be located to the socio-political sphere. Depending on what kind of WISE is in focus and what kinds of positions the people within the company can hold, it is possible to outline a variety of routes offered by social enterprises. As a matter of fact, Swedish social enterprises today are predominantly related to welfare services, such as job training and rehabilitation to address long-term unemployment. As these services are contracted by public authorities through public procurement (quasi-) markets, the border is often blurred between the 'business part' of the companies and the part involving welfare service. In conducting welfare service, the social enterprise both creates new job openings for their employed staff and acts as a human service organizations, conducting 'casework' and workfare measures with marginalized groups. However, in the dominating political discourse on social enterprises in Sweden, these contradictions between business and welfare provision and their implications for the people they concern are rarely discussed. Instead, the WISE is principally—and somewhat uncritically—constructed as an effective and innovative solution to social exclusion and unemployment. In this way, contradictions between the companies' ability to perform empowering participation for marginalized groups as civil society organizations and carrying out controlling practices in the realm of active labour market policies are made somewhat invisible.

Conclusions and Reflections

In the Swedish political debate, it is evident that the work-integrating social enterprise—often referred to as the social enterprise in public discourse—has been framed successfully as an efficient solution to problems of social exclusion, a problem that in the political debate generally is considered as 'standing outside the labour market'. Here, as in many other European countries (Nyssens, 2006), the WISE is pretty much framed as a custom-made solution to address one of today's most comprehensive societal challenges. In this sense, the framing made in the Swedish socio-political language very much reflects a myth-making process of social enterprises as a taken-for-granted, morally good phenomenon similar to the one discussed by Day and Steyart (2012) concerning the general discussions of social entrepreneurship in an international context.

The discursive shift identified in the Swedish policy discussions of social enterprises further reflects a contemporary alteration in Swedish labour market policies, where the later discourse of WISE is consistent with today's political accounts. Hence, in referring to the social enterprise as an effective labour market policy tool, it can be legitimized as a rational and coveted solution to problems on the political agenda. As a means to reach social inclusion, the later discourse on social enterprise concentrates on the need to change excluded people, rather than to create solutions that can decrease the level of structural, institutional or cultural marginalization. Hence, the change identified in the Swedish policy discourse of WISE is consistent with what Nicolas Rose (1999) points out as typical for the discourse of the third sector in the post-industrialized world: once initiated as a societal critique, it has over time become more aligned with the overall political objectives. In Rose's interpretation, the third sector in this way risks losing ground in the contribution to 'real' social innovation and change.

Political Objectives, Narrative Negotiations and Participatory Implications

As a contribution to the research field on Nordic social entrepreneurship, this chapter visualises the importance of ongoing critical studies to be conducted in the field, not least regarding the implications of participatory aspects of social entrepreneurship. Gawell (2014) concludes that "the question of representation and social entrepreneurship as a channel for people's own representation [. . .] needs further analyses". The analysis conducted in this chapter further illustrated this need. The idea of social enterprise as an activity involving multiple goals, multiple institutional logics and multiple resources opens up for a wide range of competing discourses in the discussions of the phenomenon. The different understandings of social enterprises described by the Swedish state authority in charge of the development and growth of WISEs has a similar effect. Consequently, in the discourses and narratives of the social enterprise examined in this study, the lines are repeatedly blurred between what is to be understood as a business with paid employees and what is to be understood as a human service organization conducting welfare services and offering workfare measures for marginalized groups. The various institutional logics at play in the organizational fields surrounding the WISE provide possibilities for the enterprises to creatively use and negotiate various narratives in the struggle for legitimacy. Hence, from a neo-institutional point of view, the discursive negotiations illustrated in this chapter can be interpreted as a way for the WISEs to gain legitimacy, both cognitively and normatively, in different institutional domains (Powell, 1991). In the process of institutionalization that the social enterprises are subject to in Sweden today, this kind of creative negotiation is also needed in order for institutional entrepreneurs, such as social enterprises, to gain access to resources available in different institutional domains, and hence to survive as organizations.

Gawell and Westlund (2014) note how the understanding of social entrepreneurship differs between Swedish ministries and in various government bills and that participatory and democratic approaches are not always recognised, for example, in the innovation strategy of the Ministry of Enterprises. Although this is not the case in policies surrounding WISEs, the ideological blending of logics and ideas identified in the narratives used by the social enterprises both suggest possibilities to address social change and to make the form of power exercised over marginalized individuals appear less visible. In framing labour market integration as the overall—and common—goal for the work conducted by WISEs, initiatives enabling people to become fully employed business managers with discretion over the operation of the company are frequently discussed in similar ways as initiatives for people subject to workfare measures. Primarily, this happens when the social enterprise is being portrayed according to the success story, but also conducts tasks similar to the rehabilitation story. Here, the kind of power exercised over marginalized people that are subject to workfare measures is not made visible, and this is especially problematic as the labour market policies carried out in Sweden today include an increased focus on activation and performance requirements.

This implies a contradictory position for the people it concerns, especially as they are being talked of as people being empowered (Foucault, 1980; Rose, 1999; Järvinen & Mik-Meyer, 2003; Börjesson & Palmblad, 2008). In this regard, the concept of 'heavy co-production' discussed by Pestoff (2012) in analysing the potential role of the third sector as a facilitator of re-democratization in European welfare states does not seem to cover all possible aspects of participation, democratic decision-making and empowerment in social enterprise activities, particularly for more marginalized people.

As the various forms of subject positions and power relations available as discursive resources in the discussions on WISEs are not recognised and problematized in the Swedish political debate, the institutional conditions of the human-service activities carried out by the enterprises are frequently unclear. Who is subject to workfare measures, what participation means and how it formally relates to the different status positions that may occur in various types of social enterprises are therefore frequently difficult to comprehend. In this respect, the actions carried out by WISEs can be viewed as an example of how the power and control exercised over individuals in welfare interventions, such as rehabilitation and activation measures, may become less visible—especially when the activities conducted are carried out by actors independent from the state and who are renowned as participatory and democratically run third-sector organizations, rather than public authorities exercising official authority.

At the same time, the findings show that the discursive negotiations taking place in the discussions of WISEs have the capacity to recharge the identities of marginalized and discriminated groups with resourceful properties, which over time has the capacity to challenge the overall understanding of low-status and marginalized positions in society and thereby to empower vulnerable groups (Foucault, 1980; Cohen & Arato, 1994; Butler, 1999;

Lilja & Vinthagen, 2009). As the Nordic welfare countries historically stand out as role models for universal and inclusive welfare solutions and the overall discourse of social enterprise tends to be constructed in positive terms, it could be particularly important to extend the kind of problematizing analysis conducted here to other kinds of social innovations and progressive change in such contexts.

Note

1. A frequent terminology used in the Swedish political debate from 2006 and onwards is 'utanförskap' ('outsidership'), referring to people in social exclusion. In this chapter, the concept of 'utanförskap' is hence translated to 'social exclusion' (see Davidsson, 2009).

References

Basta—Ett nykooperativt företag. (2005). *Information Booklet Produced 2005 by Basta.* Available at http://www.basta.se/bilder/original/NykooperativtFöretagande.pdf, accessed 14 March 2008.Börjesson, M. & Palmblad, E. (2008). *Strultjejer, arbetssökande och samarbetsvilliga: Kategoriseringar och samhällsmoral i socialt arbete.* Malmö: Liber.
Butler, J. (1999). *Gender Trouble: Feminism and the Subversion of Identity.* New York: Routledge.
Cohen, J. L. & Arato, A. (1994). *Civil Society and Political Theory.* Cambridge, MA: MIT Press.
Davidsson, T. (2009). *Utanförskapet—en diskursanalys av begreppet utanförskap.* Masteruppsats. Göteborgs universitet, Institutionen för socialt arbete.
Dey, P. & Steyaert, C. (2012). Social Entrepreneurship: Critique and the Radical Enactment of the Social. *Social Enterprise Journal,* 8(2), 90–107.
Defourny, J. & Nyssens, M. (2008). Social Enterprise in Europe: Recent Trends and Developments. *Social Enterprise Journal,* 4(3), 202–228.
DiMaggio, P. D. & Powell, W. W. (1983). The Iron Cage Revisited: Institutional Isomorphism and Collective Rationality in Organizational Fields. *American Sociological Review,* 48, 147–160.
Edley, N. (2001). Analyzing Masculinity: Interpretative Repertoires, Ideological Dilemmas and Subject Positions. In M. Wetherell, S. Taylor & S. Yates (Eds.), *Discourse as Data: A Guide for Analysis.* London: Sage.
Esping-Andersen, G. (2002). Towards the Good Society, Once Again. In G. Esping-Anderen (Eds.), *Why We Need a New Welfare State.* Oxford: Oxford University Press.
Fairclough, N. (2000). *New Labour, New Language?* London: Routledge.
Fairclough, N. (2005). Peripheral Vison: Discourse Analysis in Organizational Studies: The Case for Critical Realism. *Organizational Studies,* 26(6), 915–939.
Foucault, M. (1980). *Power/Knowledge: Selected Interviews and Other Writings 1972–1977.* Edited by C. Gordon. Translated by C. Gordon, L. Marshall, J. Mepham & K. Sober. New York: Pantheon.
Foucault, M. (1991/1978). Governmentality. In B. Graham, G. Colin & P. Miller (Eds.), *The Foucault Effect: Studies on Governmentality.* Chicago: University Chicago Press.Gawell, M. (2014). Social Entrepreneurship and the Negotiation

of Emerging Social Enterprise Markets. *International Journal of Public Sector Management*, 27(3), 251–266.

Gawell, M., Johannisson, B. & Lundqvist, M. (2009). Utgångspunkter, tankelinjer och textramar. In M. Gawell, B. Johannisson & M. Lundqvist (Eds.), *Samhällets entreprenörer*. Stockholm: KK-stiftelsen.

Gawell, M. & Westlund, H. (2014). Social Entrepreneurship as a Construct of Liberal Welfare Regime? In H. Douglas & S. Grant (Eds.), *Social Entrepreneurship and Enterprise: Concepts in Context*. Prahran: Tilde University Press.

Gilbert, N. (2002). *Transformation of the Welfare State: The Silent Surrender of Public Responsibility*. Oxford: Oxford University Press.

Hulgard, L. (2010). *Discourses of Social Entrepreneurship—Variations of the Same Theme?* EMES Working Paper 10/01.

Järvinen, M. & Mik Meyer, N. (2003). Institutionelle paradokser. In M. Järvinen & N. Mik Meyer (Eds.), *At skabe en klient. Institutionelle identiteter i socialt arbejde*. København: Hans Reitzels Forlag.

Johansson, H. (2010). Den europeiska unionens politik mot fattigdom. *Socionomens forskningssupplement*, 4, 22–30.

Jessop, B. (1999). The Changing Governance of Welfare: Recent Trends in Its Primacy Functions, Scale, and Modes of Coordination. *Social Policy and Administration*, 33(4), 348–359.

Kerlin, J. (2006). Social Enterprises in the Unites States and Europe: Understanding and Learning from Differences. *VOLUNTAS: International Journal of Voluntary and Nonprofit Organizations*, 17(3), 247–263.

Levander, U. (2011). *Utanförskap på entreprenad: Diskurser om sociala företag i Sverige*. Göteborg: Daidalos.

Levitas, R. (2004). Let's Hear It for Humpty: Social Exclusion, the Third Way and Cultural Capital. *Cultural Trends*, 13(2), 41–56.

Lilja, M. & Vinthagen, S. (2009). Motståndsteorier. In M. Lilja & S. Vinthagen (Eds.), *Motstånd*. Malmö: Liber.

Martin, S. (2004). Reconceptualising Social Exclusion: A Critical Response to the Neoliberal Welfare Reform Agenda and the Underclass Thesis. *Australian Journal of Social Issues*, 39(1), 79–94.

Meyer, J. & Rowan, B. (1991). Institutionalized Organization: Formal Structure as Myth and Ceremony. In W. Powell & P. DiMaggio (Eds.), *The New Institutionalism in Organizational Analysis*. Chicago, IL: University of Chicago.

Miller, P. & Rose, N. (2008). *Governing the Present, Administrating Economic, Social and Personal Life*. Cambridge: Polity Press.

Ministry of Enterprise. (2010). *Handlingsplan för arbetsintegrerade sociala företag*. Swedish Government: N2010/1894/ENT.

The National Board of Health and Welfare. (2001). *Socialt företagande. Om den sociala ekonomins dynamik. Exemplet Basta arbetskooperativ*. Stockholm: Socialstyrelsen.

Nicholls, A. (2010). The Legitimacy of Social Entrepreneurship: Reflexive Isomorphism in a Pre-paradigmatic Field. *Entrepreneurship Theory & Practice*, 34(4), 611–633.

NUTEK. (2005). *Socialt företagande—en väg till arbetsmarknaden*. Stockholm: Swedish Agency for Economic and Regional Growth.

NUTEK. (2008). *Programförslag för fler och växande sociala företag*. Stockholm: NUTEK.

Nyssens, M. (2006). *Social Enterprise—at the Crossroads of Market, Public Policies and Civil Society*. London: Routledge.

Pestoff, V. (2012). Co-production and Third Sector Social Services in Europe: Some Concepts and Evidence. *VOLUNTAS: International Journal of Voluntary and Nonprofit Organizations*, 23(4), 1102–1118.

Powell, W. (1991). Expanding the Scope of Institutional Analysis. In W. Powell & P. DiMaggio (Eds.), *The New Institutionalism of Organizational Analysis*. Chichago, IL: University of Chicago Press.

Prop. (2009/10:55). *En politik för det civila samhället*. Stockholm: Ministry of Gender Equality and Integration.

Rose, N. (1999). *Powers of Freedom: Reframing Political Thought*. Cambridge: Cambridge University Press.

Santos, F. (2012). A Positive Theory of Social Entrepreneurship. *Journal of Business Ethics*, 111(3), 335–351.

Scott, W. R. (1995). *Institutions and Organization*. Thousand Oaks, CA: Sage.

SOU 2003:95. *ArbetsKraft: Betänkande från Lönebidragsutredningen*. Stockholm: Fritzes.

SOU 2007:2. *Från socialbidrag till arbete*. Stockholm: Fritzes.

Steinert, H. (2003). Participation and Social Exclusion: A Conceptual Framework. In H. Steinert & A. Pilgram (Eds.), *Welfare Policy from Below*. Aldershot: Ashgate.

Suchman, M. C. (1995). Managing Legitimacy: Strategies and Institutional Approaches. *Academy of Management Review*, 20(3), 571–610.

Swedish State Authority of Work-Related Issues. (2002). *Sociala arbetskooperativ. Funktionshindrades möjligheter till arbete genom sociala arbetskooperativ. Strukturella förutsättningar i Sverige, Storbritannien och Italien*. Stockholm: Arbetslivsinstitutet).

Vägen ut. (2003): Project Description of the Halfway House 'Villa Karin'. Attached to an application for project grants from the organisation 'Vägen ut' directed to The National Board of Health and Welfare in Sweden.

Wagner, I. & Wodac, R. (2006). Performing Success: Identifying Strategies of Self-Presentation in Women's Biographical Narratives. *Discourse & Society*, 17(3), 385–411.

Wilkinson, C., et al. (2014). A Map of Social Enterprises and Their Eco-systems in Europe. Executive Summary. ICF Consulting Services, European Commission: 1–16.

Young, J. (1999). *The Exclusive Society*. London: Sage Publications.

15 Democratic Innovations

Exploring Synergies Between Three Key Post-New Public Management Concepts in Public Sector Reforms

Victor Pestoff

The concepts of democratic innovations share much with those of social enterprise, social innovation and co-production. They all refer to highly complex phenomena involving multiple dimensions that require a multi-disciplinary approach. Yet, the academic debate normally oversimplifies them, often from the perspective of a single discipline. This chapter notes their complex nature and explores links between them in relation to the delivery of public services. Evidence of greater client and staff influence stems from social enterprises providing childcare in Sweden. It concludes that governments need to develop more flexible, service-specific and organizational-specific approaches for renewing public services that promote social enterprise, social innovation and co-production, rather than looking for simple 'one size fits all' solutions to the challenges facing public service delivery. Similarly, our understanding of democratic governance should build on multi-dimensional and multi-disciplinary approaches and not look for simple solutions.

A Field With Different Dimensions

The academic debate on social enterprise, particularly in Europe, emphasises the importance of several different aspects or dimensions. According to the EMES approach (presented in the first chapter in this volume), social enterprises are not merely private firms that indirectly promote social values, provide social services or practice corporate social responsibility. Rather, they are organizations or firms that successfully combine several economic, social and governance functions. Similarly, the academic discourse on public sector innovations has moved beyond the traditional perspective employed by industry and manufacture, since it does not fit well with the provision of public services. This debate recognises that public sector innovations take various forms and promote a variety of goals. In addition to efficiency and effectiveness, they include both social and/or governance goals. Also, the debate on co-production recognises the existence of different kinds of citizen participation in the provision of public services: economic, social and political (Pestoff, 2006, 2009). If the concept of democratic governance is to become a more robust tool for understanding and analysing public sector reforms, it too must become truly multi-dimensional and multi-disciplinary.

The concept of co-production is probably older (Parks, Baker, Kiser, Oakerson, Ostrom, Ostrom, Perry, Vandivort & Whitaker, 1981, 1999; Ostrom, 1996, 1999) than the other two, but it disappeared from the academic and political debate in the early 1980s in the wake of New Public Management (NPM). In the post-NPM era, its two cousins, social enterprise and social innovation, became key elements of alternatives to purely market solutions for the challenges facing the public sector and public services. So, co-production may appear to some as the 'new kid on the block', but in fact, it has a lot in common with its cousins, social enterprise and social innovation. The aim of this chapter is to make their common elements clear and discuss the implications of this for the study of democratic innovations.

Can social enterprise, social innovations and co-production eventually lead to a more democratic regime of governance? Hirst argues that the concept of 'governance' points to the need to rethink democracy and find new methods of control and regulation of the big public and private organizations that dominate the public and private sectors. He defines governance as "a means by which an activity or ensemble of activities is controlled or directed, such that it delivers an acceptable range of outcomes according to some established social standards" (2000:24). In the space below, we intend to explore how these three post-NPM concepts might contribute to a more democratic regime of governance.

The UNDP (2015) considers co-production a major social innovation in the provision of public services, one that can provide greater user control and influence over public services. Osborne, Radnor and Nasi (2013) argue that co-production is an essential part of a broader framework to provide a new theory for public service management—a service-dominant approach, in contrast to the manufacturing dominant approach of NPM, that is based on a 'fatal flaw' in public management theory that views public services as manufacturing rather than as service processes. However, services demonstrate three major differences from goods: 1) They are intangible, 2) They are subject to different production logics, and, most important here, 3) The role of the user is qualitatively different in manufacturing and services. The latter are often co-produced by the professional providers and consumer of the services (Osborne et al., 2013). Thus, public service needs to be understood from a broader framework called New Public Governance (Osborne, 2010). Co-production can, therefore, make an important contribution to the debate on public management, since it is a key concept that goes to the core of both effective public services delivery and the role of public services in achieving societal ends, such as social inclusion and citizen participation (Osborne et al., 2013, p. 145).

This chapter considers the main three dimensions of each of these key concepts. We will start by discussing the economic, political and social aspects of social enterprise, then turn to social innovation and co-production.

Recognising their separate dimensions as well as understanding the similarity between them facilitates forging links between them and also emphasises the mutuality or synergy of the goals they promote. Greater space is given to co-production, as the lesser-known or newer concept, including some comparative evidence from social enterprises providing childcare in Sweden. Co-production facilitates greater client and staff participation and influence than either public or for-profit services.

Social Enterprise

We will begin with the public debate on social enterprise and then turn our attention to the academic discourse.

The Public Debate

The public debate about social enterprise and social entrepreneurship suffers from a mix of the vagaries of two contrary tendencies. The first tendency is so broad that the rule seems to be 'anything goes', where almost any and every business firm, including those with only an indirect or vague social value and those practicing some form of corporate social reporting or corporate philanthropy can qualify as a 'social enterprise', although this is clearly part of a strategy to achieve greater sales, turnover and profit. The second tendency reflects the opposite rule, here 'almost nothing qualifies, and very few organizations are able to meet the strict criteria necessary to gain public recognition as a social enterprise in some European countries. These two tendencies help illustrate the risk of market or bureaucratic capture of central academic concepts.

In the first case, some definitions of social enterprise are so vague or loose that a big international fast food chain might qualify as a social enterprise, since it offers many young people their first job and helps them get a foot into the labour market. In addition, it may also support or provide some important social services for a small group. However, while such activities may represent important social values, they don't comprise the main focus of such a big international food chain's business activities. Rather, they are related to its business strategy of employing cheap, unskilled labour in order to keep its costs down and/or promoting its public image. So, they are a means to an end, rather than an end in themselves. Similarly, a mammoth retailer may provide jobs in many communities across the nation, which is very laudable in times of high unemployment, but it is also notorious for its low wages and poor working conditions. Would it also qualify as a social enterprise under such vague criteria? Perhaps it might. Would the world's largest tobacco manufacturer also qualify as a social enterprise if it donated funds to a non-profit to help feed the needy elderly in a major city? Or perhaps a big European state-owned energy company that mines huge reserves of brown coal for its operations abroad and manages nuclear plants both in- and outside its national borders? Could it also be considered a social enterprise if it regularly arranged a marathon or other sporting events in a major EU capital? Might the term *social enterprise* also be applied to a global electronics company that claims to be 'the number one social business enterprise in the world' simply because it improved its capacity for corporate social responsibility? Questions about the nature of social enterprise are not always easy to answer, especially without clear standards or guidelines; however, these examples illustrate the market capture of a central academic concept. Moreover, some neoliberal EU governments also embrace a very broad definition of social enterprise in their efforts to privatize the provision of social services (Pestoff & Hulgård, 2015), which suggests political capture.

In the second case, some public bureaucrats, academics and even representatives of the social enterprise community itself can promote an agenda that employs a very narrow focus on a certain kind of social enterprise, to the exclusion of many others. For example, public bureaucrats can seize a new, popular academic term like social enterprise in an attempt to promote their own policy aims. Thus, the European Social Fund and public labour market agencies in several European countries have coupled the term social enterprise with policy aims of job creation, particularly for persons with a physical, social or psychological handicaps. Naturally, such public bureaucracies are interested in promoting work-integration social enterprises (WISEs), since they appear to offer new and innovative ways to promote employment and job training among their target populations. Therefore, some public bureaucrats define social enterprise so narrowly that it excludes most other types of cooperative social services, like childcare, elder care etc., or services of general interest and collectively managed enterprises serving a specific community. So, in the public debate in some, if not most, EU countries, social enterprise has become synonymous with 'work-integration social enterprise'. The Finnish Act on Social Enterprises introduced in 2004 has a specific focus on WISEs. A similar development can be observed in Denmark (Socialstyrelsen, 2014), Poland (Pestoff, 2011) and Sweden (Levander, 2011). Thus, WISEs have become equivalent to and sometimes even the official definition of social enterprise in certain EU countries. However, this excludes other phenomena that closely fit European academic approaches to the study of social enterprises, like cooperative social services. Thus, some observers even suggest that the European bureaucrats have 'hijacked' the concept of social enterprise for their narrow policy goals, to the detriment of the public debate and development of the sector itself (Moulaert, Jessop, Hulgård & Hamdouch, 2013; Pestoff & Hulgård, 2015). This is an example of bureaucratic capture of a central academic concept.

The Academic Discourse

The terms *social entrepreneurship* and *social enterprise* are sometimes used interchangeably, but they should nevertheless be distinguished from each other. Academic definitions of social entrepreneurship can range from narrow to broad (Galera & Borzaga, 2009). According to the narrow definition, social entrepreneurship is clearly located in the non-profit sector and refers to the adoption of entrepreneurial approaches by non-profit organizations in order to earn income. This presumes that the social mission remains explicit and central to non-profit organization activities. By contrast, broad definitions refer to a conception where this phenomenon can be found anywhere and in any business or setting, for-profit, non-profit, public sector or any mix thereof (Galera & Borzaga, 2009, p. 212).

In continental Europe, the term social enterprise refers to an organizational unit or enterprise (Borzaga & Defourny, 2001; Defourny & Nyssens, 2014; Hulgård, 2014). This understanding stems from strong collective traditions found in cooperatives, mutuals and associations in Europe (Defourny & Nyssens, 2006). Thus, the main feature of the European social enterprise tradition is setting up autonomous institutional structures specifically designed to pursue social goals in a stable and continuous way through the production of goods or services of general interest (Defourny & Nyssens, 2006, p. 213). The USA, by contrast, has shown a preference for the term *social entrepreneurship* and adopted a broader understanding of the term that includes the idea of 'market-based approaches to social issues' (Kerlin, 2006) which can be undertaken by any organization or firm in any sector of the economy. This broad definition focuses more on the phenomena of entrepreneurship and individual entrepreneurs than the organizations or enterprises involved in them, and more on the existence of a 'social mission' as a major or minor element of a corporate strategy than the process and governance dimension generating the social value (Moulaert, et al., 2013; Pestoff & Hulgård, 2015).

Moreover, much of the American debate on social enterprise appears dominated by economists, with little input from other disciplines, and it often promotes vaguely universal definitions. Thus, social enterprise is considered an activity that is "intended to address social goals through the operation of private organizations in the marketplace" (Young, 2008, p. 23), or it "involves the engagement of private sector forms of enterprise and market based activity in the achievement of social purpose" (Young, 2009, p. 175). However, such broad, market-oriented attempts to define social enterprise provide little guidance for distinguishing between what to include or not to include in the term *social enterprise*.

Evolution of the European Perspective

In Europe, by contrast, the policy and legal context appears much more conducive to the development of social enterprises as welfare actors, and European legal frameworks reflect specific legal traditions, welfare regimes and economic issues dealt with at the national level. Thus, we find a greater diversity of approaches and solutions in Europe. (Defourny &

Nyssens, 2014, p. 218). This can take two expressions. On the one hand, in order to understand this gradual change in the third sector, the EMES scholars promoted a common definition of social enterprise, based on multiple and diverse indicators of social enterprises in various EU countries (Defourny & Nyssens, 2014). On the other hand, the EMES network's efforts are based on an extensive dialogue between and among several disciplines, including economics, sociology, political science and management. They also take into account the various national traditions present in the EU. Thus, the EMES network emphasises three main dimensions of social enterprises: their economic, social, and governance dimensions (Pestoff & Hulgård, 2015).

According to EMES, a social enterprise's *economic project* is comprised of a continuous production of a good or service, based on some paid work, and it takes an economic risk. Its *social dimension* relies on pursuing an explicit social aim that is usually launched by a group of citizens or a third-sector organization and that has clear limits on the distribution of its surplus or profit. Moreover, what makes the EMES approach truly unique is the existence of a third dimension: *participatory governance*. Here, we find issues related to an organization's autonomy from both the state and market, its participatory nature of involving the major parties or stakeholders affected by its activities and the exercise of democratic decision-making, based on the idea of one member, one vote, rather than capital ownership or shareholders.

The EMES network has extensively explored and developed nine ideal-type criteria for defining and delimiting social enterprises that are comprised of three economic, three political and three social criteria. However, it is important to note that all three dimensions are necessary and none of them is sufficient alone. Only when combined or taken together can they help define and delimit social enterprise. Thus, the EMES approach clearly goes beyond the simple zero-sum perception of a continuum ranging from purely economic to purely social pursuits that dominates the American debate. Moreover, the interrelated nature of the EMES criteria helps reinforce them, making for a more robust sustainable phenomenon than if a single criterion was adopted or applied to the study of social enterprise. Thus, the more complex multi-dimensional approach of EMES has clear advantages over using a single dimension or criterion for defining social enterprises or relying on key concepts from a single discipline.

Public Sector Innovation: Traditional, Social and/or Governance?

Scholars define innovation in many different ways; however, most of them emphasise a newness aspect, primarily in terms of being new to the organization that adopts it. However, these divergent definitions of innovation offer little consensus about what it is, what aspects to include and how it is best achieved. For example, some authors equate innovation in public services with entrepreneurship or being proactive and taking risks in providing health care (Wood, Bhuian & Kiecker, 2000; Salge & Vera, 2009; Hinz & Ingerfurth, 2013). Product and process innovations are commonly distinguished (Rogers, 1995). Product innovations can be understood as what is produced or, more appropriately in public sector settings, what kind of service is delivered. Process innovations pertain to how a service is provided (Walker, 2014, p. 23). Moreover, process innovations can affect both the management and the organization, since they change relationships among organizational members and affect rules, roles, procedures and structures etc. (Walker, 2014).

Social innovation is an ambiguous term, with many and often contending definitions. A key objective of the WILCO Project—Welfare Innovations at the Local Level in Favour of Social Cohesion (www.wilcoproject.eu)— was to contextualize the social innovations and to understand them from the wider social and political context where they originate. There is a growing realisation of the difference between various types of innovation and the need to explore the uniqueness of social innovation. The latter is much more complex than simply applying standard business or market techniques to social issues. Social innovations neither stem from the R&D centres of big business nor the bureaucracies of central government. The origin of social innovations can vary widely, as noted by many authors. For example, Johnson (2010) suggests that there are four different sources or environments that facilitate the creation of new ideas, processes and things. They can be divided into two main categories: market-networked and non-market networked innovations. Fuglsand and Sundbo (2009) distinguish between entrepreneurial or technology-based innovations on the one hand and value-based or reflexive innovations on the other. Brandsen, Evers, Cattacin and Zimmer (2015) compare and contrast two main types of innovations, market or R&D innovations, like the iPhone, which are intentionally non-contextual and therefore designed to sell in different markets around the world, and social innovations, like the numerous local solutions to homelessness, unemployment etc. illustrated in their new book (Brandsen et al., 2015).

The Bureau of European Policy Advisors (BEPA), defines social innovation as "innovations that are social both in their ends and means . . . that simultaneously meet social needs (more effectively than alternatives) and create new social relationships or collaborations" (BEPA, 2010, p. 7). Beckers, Tummers and Voorberg (2013) argue that social innovations in public services have four distinct elements. First, they aim to achieve long-term outcomes that are relevant for society. Second, they go beyond technical changes by promoting fundamental changes in social relationships. Third, most of the important stakeholders, especially the end users, should be involved in the design, development and implementation of new goods and services. Finally, social innovation not only refers to the achievement of new outcomes, but also to the very processes of innovation. Thus, they are usually open to, but also embedded in, a specific local and institutional context, something that may make it harder to replicate or scale them up (Brandsen, 2014, pp. 3–4; Brandsen, et al., 2015).

Governance innovation is a specific category or type of social innovation, since it involves changes in the relationship between service providers and their clients in ways that imply new forms of citizen engagement and new democratic institutions (Hartley, 2005). Rather than being limited to changes within a single organization, most public sector innovation takes place above the level of a given organization and transforms the social structures and processes that deal with a problem (Moore & Hartley, 2012, p. 55). They propose four inter-related criteria to distinguish public sector innovations from private sector product and process innovations. Governance innovation should: 1) Create network-based production systems; 2) Mobilize new pools of resources that can extend or improve the performance of such services; 3) Change the instruments that governments use to steer the production system for achieving social goals; and 4) Alter the configuration of decision-making. Furthermore, this can raise important questions about the distribution of rights and responsibilities in society and how best to evaluate them (Moore & Hartley, 2012, pp. 68–69). Thus, in addition to economic or financial aspects, social innovations in the public sector can have clear social and political implications.

Moreover, it is important to distinguish between the outcome of a social innovation, achieving all or some of its goals and the very processes involved in achieving it/them. The latter can provide added value in terms of promoting collaboration between various participants and generating social capital. Thus, the participation process of social innovations is very important in itself. The open participation of various stakeholders gives each of them a stake in the innovation. Moreover, it also provides the glue that creates connections and relations between various stakeholders and links between the different levels of the innovations process that help them to survive and eventually succeed in the local context.

Results from two separate studies of alternative providers of publicly financed childcare in Europe and Sweden, found below, help illustrate the processes in social enterprises that promote more client/citizen participation, namely greater co-production. Parents in social enterprises not only have a choice about which service to use, they also have a voice in their management through direct representation on the board of such services. This results in much greater influence for both the clients and staff of social enterprises than is possible in public or private for-profit services.

Co-Production

As noted earlier, the OECD argues that co-production is social innovation in public services, since it promotes a partnership that governments form with citizens and civil society organizations in order to innovate and deliver improved public service outcomes. Moreover, such partnerships offer creative policy responses that enable governments to provide better public services in times of fiscal constraints; thus, governments consider citizen input as a source of innovation and change (OECD, 2011). Furthermore, compared with existing solutions of private sector involvement, the emerging focus on greater citizen participation transforms the relationship between service users and providers, ensuring more user control and ownership (OECD, 2011). However, co-production involves more than merely consulting with clients. In addition, citizen participation is more important in the delivery phase of social services than in general services, where citizens are more active in service design. This has some major economic implications, since social services are more labour intensive than general services. However, the OECD noted that government motives for embracing co-production put greater weight on considerations of strengthening user and citizen involvement per se, improving service quality and improving effectiveness and service outcome than on increasing productivity or cutting costs (OECD, 2011).

Co-Production: Some Conceptual Issues

Nobel Laureate Elinor Ostrom and her colleagues analysed the role of citizens in the provision of public services in terms of co-production (Parks et al., 1981, 1999). The concept of co-production was originally developed by Ostrom and the Workshop in Political Theory and Policy Analysis at Indiana University during the 1970s to describe and delimit the involvement of ordinary citizens in the production of public services (Ostrom, 1999). They struggled with the dominant theories of urban governance, whose underlying policies recommended massive centralisation of public services, but they found no support for claims of the benefits of large bureaucracies. They also realised that the production of services, in contrast to goods, was difficult without the active participation of those persons receiving the service (Ostrom, 1999).

Thus, they developed the term *co-production* to describe the potential relationship that could exist between the 'regular producer', like street-level police officers, schoolteachers or health workers, and their clients, who wanted to be transformed by the service into safer, better-educated or healthier persons (see Parks et al., 1981, 1999). Initially, co-production had a clear focus on the role of individuals or groups of citizens in the production of public services. Co-production is, therefore, noted by "the mix of activities that both public service agents and citizens contribute to the provision of public services. The former are involved as professionals or 'regular producers', while 'citizen production' is based on voluntary efforts of individuals or groups to enhance the quality and/or quantity of services they receive" (Parks et al., 1981, 1999).

More recently, Bovaird (2007) proposed another definition of co-production: "[user] and community co-production is the provision of services through regular, long-term relationships between professionalized service providers (in any sector) and service users and/or other members of the community, where all parties make substantial resource contributions." (Bovaird, 2007, p. 847). This definition focuses not only on users, but also includes volunteers and community groups as co-producers, recognising that each of these groups can have a quite different relationship to public sector organizations.

The Three Main Dimensions of Co-Production

The TSFEPS Project[1] examined the relationship between parent participation in the provision and governance of childcare in eight EU countries (Pestoff, 2006, 2008). It found different levels of parent participation in different countries and in different forms of provision, such as public, private for-profit and third-sector childcare. The highest levels of parent participation were found in third-sector providers, like parent associations in France, parent initiatives in Germany and parent cooperatives in Sweden. It also noted the existence of different kinds of parent participation, i.e., economic, political and social. All three kinds of participation were readily evident in third-sector providers of childcare services, whereas both economic and political participation were much more restricted in municipal and private for-profit services.

Vamstad's follow-up study (2007) focuses on the politics of diversity, parent participation and service quality in Swedish childcare. It compared parent and worker co-ops, municipal services and small for-profit firms providing childcare in two regions of Sweden: Stockholm and Östersund. His study not only confirms the existence of the three main dimensions of co-production, but also underlines the difference between various providers concerning the saliency of these dimensions. Both these studies demonstrate that parent co-ops in Sweden promote all three kinds of user participation: economic, social and political. Thus, they provide parents with unique possibilities for active participation in the management and running of their child(ren)'s childcare facility and for unique opportunities to become active co-producers of high-quality childcare services for their own and others' children. It is also clear that other forms of childcare allow for some limited forms of co-production in publicly financed childcare, but parents' possibilities for influencing the management of such services remains rather limited.

Parent and Staff Influence

Participation and influence do not necessarily mean the same thing. So, the difference noted above for different providers may or may not promote greater client and/or staff influence in the provision and governance of social services. Therefore, Vamstad (2007) asked parents and staff at childcare facilities how much influence they currently had and whether they wanted more. The results presented here only report the most frequent categories, those at the high end of the scale of influence. Parent influence is greatest in parent co-ops and least in small for-profit firms. This is an expected result, and nearly nine out of ten parents in parent co-ops claim much influence. However, this is twice as many as in municipal services. Half of the parents in worker co-ops also claim much influence, which is also greater than the proportion in municipal childcare. Finally, only one of eight parents claims much influence in small for-profit firms. The differences in influence between types of providers appear substantial.

Turning to their desire for more influence, again we find the expected pattern of answers, which inversely reflects how much influence they currently experience. Very few parents in parent co-ops want more influence, whereas nearly three in five do so in small for-profit firms. In between these two types come the worker co-ops, where more than one in four wants more influence, and municipal childcare, where more than one in three parents wants more influence. There appears to be widespread expectations of being able to participate in important decisions concerning their daughter's or son's childcare among parents in all types of providers. So, public and for-profit services appear to be missing the boat in terms of promoting greater parent participation and increasing their representation in decision-making.

Shifting to the staff of childcare facilities, once again the logically expected pattern of influence can be noted here, where the staff in worker co-ops claims the most influence and the staff in municipal facilities claims the least influence. Nearly nine out of ten staff members claim large or very large influence in worker co-op childcare, whereas only a third do so in municipal facilities. Nearly three out of five members of staff claim much influence in parent co-ops, whereas half of them do so in small for-profit firms. Again, the proportion of the staff desiring more influence inversely reflects the proportion claiming much influence. Few want more influence in either the worker or parent co-ops, whereas the opposite is true of the staff in the other two types of childcare providers. Nearly three out of five want more influence in municipal childcare and three out of four do so in small for-profit firms. Thus, there appears to be significant room for greater staff influence in both the latter types of childcare providers. Greater staff influence could also contribute significantly to improving the work environment in both of these two types of childcare providers (Pestoff & Vamstad, 2014).

The Existence of a 'Glass Ceiling' in Public Childcare?

Public policies can either crowd in or crowd out desired behaviour by citizens. Co-production is not an exception to this rule. The findings noted above lead to three clear conclusions. First, there are different forms of citizen participation in the provision of publicly financed social services like childcare: economic, social and political participation. Second, a higher level of citizen participation is noted for third-sector providers of publicly financed social services, since it is based on collective action and direct client participation. Parent co-op childcare in France, Germany and Sweden illustrates this. Third, more limited citizen participation is noted for public provision of enduring welfare services, where citizens are allowed to participate sporadically or in a limited fashion, like parents contributing to the Christmas or Spring Party in municipal childcare. But, they are seldom given the opportunity to play a major role in, to take charge of the service provision or given decision-making rights and responsibilities for the economy of the service provision.

This creates a 'glass ceiling' for citizen participation in public services and limits them to playing a passive role as service users who can make demands on the public sector, but make no decisions or take any responsibility in implementing public policy. There are few possibilities for parents to directly influence decision-making in either municipal or for-profit childcare services. The space allotted to citizens in public services is too restricted to make their participation either meaningful or democratic. Perhaps this is logical from the perspective of municipal governments; they are, after all, representative institutions, chosen by the voters in elections every third, fourth or fifth year. They might consider direct client or user participation in the running of public services for a particular group, like parents, as a threat both to the representative democracy that they institutionalize and to their own power. It could also be argued that direct participation for a particular group would thereby provide the latter with a veto right or a 'second vote' at the service level. There may also be professional considerations for resisting parent involvement and participation. A similar argument can be made concerning user participation in for-profit firms providing welfare services, where the logic of direct user participation is also foreign. Exit, rather than voice, provides the medium of communication in markets, where parents are seen as consumers. This logic excludes any form of direct or indirect representation. Thus, we found the existence of a 'glass ceiling' for citizen participation in the provision of public services in the municipal and for-profit providers.

This section explored co-production by social enterprises as social and governance innovations in the provision of public services. Co-production of social services offers new opportunities as well as challenges for collective solutions to growing problems facing the public provision of social services in Europe. It gives citizens both more choice and more voice, as well as allowing and encouraging them to play a more active role in the decision-making processes surrounding the design and delivery of public services. Yet, co-production is a new concept that remains relatively unknown and mostly absent from the academic and political debates about reforming public services in many European countries.

Co-production is a new and relatively unknown concept in the political and academic discourses of the Nordic countries, and it is not nearly as established or used as widely as those of social enterprise and social innovation. Co-production has gained some recognition in Finland, both in the political and academic debates (Botero, Gryf Paterson & Saad-Sulomon, 2012; Pekkola, Tuurnas, Stenvall & Hakari, 2015; Tuurnas, 2015), and it is occasionally mentioned in the academic debate in Norway (Larsgaard, Hauge & Ek, 2015). But, it is almost totally absent from the Swedish debate about reforming public services, except for a few internationally oriented academics mentioned earlier. In Denmark, by contrast, it has gained considerable traction in recent years and has become quite well established in both the political and academic debates (Hald Larsen, 2015; Kjærgaard Thomsen & Jakobsen, 2015; Tortzen, 2015). Perhaps Nordic cooperation in the academic and policy fields will eventually promote a greater understanding and appreciation of this conceptual 'new kid on the block'.

Summary and Conclusions

The concept of democratic governance shares much in common with three other post-NPM concepts—social enterprise, social innovation and co-production. This chapter considered their three main dimensions, i.e., their economic, political and social dimensions. We noted the importance of all three dimensions in all three of these key concepts. We argued that recognising their separate dimensions as well as understanding the similarity between them facilitates forging links between them and also emphasises the mutuality or synergy of the goals they promote. We also maintain that a multi-dimensional understanding of the concept of democratic governance is equally important. Similar to the other three post-NPM concepts, it too requires a multi-disciplinary approach to thoroughly understand its potential contribution to renewing the public sector and public services in the twenty-first century.

The EMES network developed nine ideal-type criteria for defining and delimiting social enterprise that were later combined into three economic, three political and three social criteria. According to this approach, a social enterprise's *economic project* is comprised of continuous production of a good or service, based on some paid work, and it takes an economic risk. Its *social dimension* relies on pursuing an explicit social aim, it is usually launched by a group of citizens or a third-sector organization and it has clear limits on the distribution of its surplus or profit. A truly unique aspect of the EMES approach is the third dimension, *participatory governance*. Here, we find issues related to an organization's autonomy from both the state and market, its participatory nature of involving the major parties or stakeholders affected by its activities and the exercise of democratic decision-making, based on the idea of one member, one vote, rather than capital ownership or shareholders. However, it is important to note that all three dimensions are necessary and none of them is sufficient alone. Only when combined or taken together can they help define and delimit social enterprise.

Social innovation is an ambiguous term, with many and often contending definitions. BEPA defines it as "innovations that are social both in their ends and means . . . that simultaneously meet social needs (more effectively than alternatives) and create new social relationships or collaborations" (BEPA, 2010: 7). Brandsen suggests that social innovations in the public sector promote closer collaboration between professional providers and their clients (2012). Moreover, governance innovation is a specific category or type of social innovation, since it involves changes in the relationship between service providers and their clients in ways that imply new forms of citizen engagement and new democratic institutions (Hartley, 2005). Thus, in addition to economic or financial aspects, social innovations in the public sector have clear social and political implications. Moreover, it is important to distinguish between the outcome of a social innovation and the very processes involved in achieving it. The latter can provide added value in terms of promoting collaboration between various participants and generating social capital.

Co-production focuses on the collaboration between professional providers and their clients. Ostrom and her colleagues developed the term in the late 1970s to describe the potential relationship that could exist between the 'regular producer', like street-level police officers, schoolteachers or health workers, and their clients, who wanted to be transformed by the service into safer, better-educated or healthier persons (see Parks et al., 1981, 1999). The OECD regards co-production as an important social innovation in public services that promotes a partnership between governments and citizens/civil society organizations in order to deliver improved public service outcomes (2011). This emphasises the potential to be a significant social and governance innovation, since co-production implies new forms of citizen engagement and the development of new participative democratic institutions in the public sector.

Empirical evidence from two comparative studies of childcare demonstrates the unique capacity of small social services co-ops to promote all three dimensions (economic, social and governance) of the three main concepts (social enterprise, social innovation and co-production) in the renewal of public services. This unique constellation of concepts and the great similarity between their three central dimensions underlines their mutual contribution to renewing public service. Moreover, the empirical evidence demonstrates that they can clearly deliver on their promise to curtail costs while also promoting and developing social and democratic goals in the public sector.

Thus, we need to forge closer links between key post-NPM concepts like social enterprise, social innovation and co-production in order to fully understand their potential contribution to renewing the public sector and the delivery of public services. We also need to make links between the multiple dimensions involved in these complex and interrelated concepts and forge closer links between the various disciplines interested in studying these phenomena. Focusing on a single dimension or employing the approach of a single academic discipline will not prove sufficient to fully understand them. So, we need to avoid vain searches for simple solutions to complex matters. Moreover, if we want to explore ways to diminish the growing democracy deficit in most European welfare states, it is important to understand the overlap between the political dimensions of social enterprise, social innovation and co-production, particularly given their high degree of similarity. Moreover, there are clear similarities between them and democratic governance. The latter is not just new voter techniques or some new ITC approach. It needs to focus on changing the social relations between the professional providers of public services and its users, involving new groups in decision-making and promoting new ways of including the end users of public services in both their design and delivery.

Can social enterprise, social innovations and co-production eventually lead to a more democratic regime of governance? Hirst (1994) underlines the need to rethink democracy and find new methods of control and regulation of the big public and private organizations that dominate the public and private sectors. Accordingly, 'civil democracy' was defined as "citizen empowerment through self-management of personal social services, where citizens become members of a social enterprise, where they participate directly in the production of local services they demand, as users and producers of such services, and where they therefore become co-producers of these services." (Pestoff, 1998, p. 25). Democratic governance can therefore be defined as "a policy that promotes significantly greater welfare pluralism and substantially greater citizen participation in the provision of welfare services. It can only be achieved by promoting citizen participation in co-production and third sector provision of welfare services that citizens are dependent on in their daily lives" (Pestoff, 2009, p. 199).

However, it is also important to realise that democratic governance, social enterprise, social innovation and co-production do not comprise a panacea for the problems facing the provision of public services, since there is no 'one size fits all' solution for the great variety of services provided by governments in Europe today (Brandsen et al., 2015). Therefore, it appears urgent for governments to develop the necessary policies and strategies that take differences in size, ownership and other important structural variables into account. In their ongoing efforts to modernise, improve and innovate public services, governments will need to weigh both the advantages and disadvantages of engaging social enterprises in co-producing different types of services and different phases of service design and delivery. Government policies can both crowd in and crowd out social enterprise, social innovation and co-production (Ostrom, 2000). Failing to recognise the benefits of promoting social enterprises that provide enduring social services can result in a major hurdle to the expansion of co-production and greater citizen participation in the delivery of public services (Osborne et al., 2013).

Thus, if governments intend to facilitate more democratic governance and citizen co-production in the provision of enduring social services, they will need to devise ways of promoting self-help groups, social service co-ops and other forms of third-sector provision of enduring welfare services that tend to be small scale and facilitate formal, collective interaction among well-defined groups of service users. But, mechanistic attempts to replicate or scale-up successful small scale experiments appear to be based on a flawed understanding of public service provision.

Finally, co-production is a new research field compared with social enterprise and social innovation, and little systematic comparative research is yet available (Verschuere et al., 2012). Recognising their common dimensions and traits could help to put co-production research in the proper perspective. Comparative research is necessary to understand citizen/user participation in various types of service providers for different types of welfare services and also in different countries. In particular, it would be interesting to compare small service co-ops with small and medium-size enterprises and other small social enterprises providing similar services. Research on social enterprises and social innovation should be encouraged in order to promote more sustainable co-production.

Note

1. The TSFEPS Project, Changing Family Structures and Social Policy: Childcare services as sources of social cohesion took place in eight European countries between 2002–04. They were: Belgium, Bulgaria, England, France, Germany, Italy, Spain and Sweden. See www.emes.net for more details and the reports.

References

Beckers, V., Tummers, L. & Voorberg, W. (2013). *From Public Innovation to Social Innovation: A Literature Review of Relevant Drivers and Barriers.* Rotterdam: Erasmus University Rotterdam.

BEPA. (2010). *Empowering People, Driving Change: Social Innovation in the European Union.* Bruxelles: Bureau of European Policy Advisors, European Commission.Borzaga, C. & Defourny, J. (2001). *The Emergence of Social Enterprise.* London & New York: Routledge.

Botero, A., Gryf Paterson, A. & Saad-Sulomon, J. (2012). *Towards Peer Production in Public Services: Cases from Finland.* Helsinki: Aalto University.

Bovaird, T. (2007). Beyond Engagement & Participation: User & Community Co-Production of Public Services. *Public Administration Review*, 67(5), 846–860.

Brandsen, T. (2012). *Social Innovation.* Power Point Presentation at the 3rd EMES Ph.D. Summer School, Trento, Italy.

Brandsen, T. (2014). *The WILCO Project: A Summary of the Findings, 2010–2014.* Available at www.wilcoproject.eu, accessed 15 October 2015.

Brandsen, T., Evers, A., Cattacin, S. & Zimmer, A. (2015). *Social Innovation: A Sympathetic and Critical Interpretation*. In—unpublished WILCO manuscript, www.wilcoproject.eu, accessed 15 October 2015.

Defourny, J. & Nyssens, M. (2006). Defining Social Enterprise. In M. Nyssens (Ed.), *Social Enterprise: At the Crossroads of Market, Public Policies & Civil Society*. London & New York: Routledge.

Defourny, J. & Nyssens, M. (2014). The EMES Approach of Social Enterprise in a Comparative Perspective. In J. Defourny, L. Hulgård & V. Pestoff (Eds.), *Social Enterprise and the Third Sector—Changing European Landscapes in a Comparative Perspective*. London & New York: Routledge.

Fuglsang, L. & Sundbo, J. (2009). The Organizational Innovation System: There Modes. *Journal of Change Management*, 5(3), 329–344.

Galera, G. & Borzaga, C. (2009), Social Enterprise: An International Overview of Its Conceptual Evolution and Legal Implication. *Social Enterprise Journal*, 5(3), 210–228.Hald Larsen, S. (2015). *The Relatives as Co-producers in the Danish Context of Eldercare*. Paper presented to the IIAS Study Group on Co-production, Nijmegen, Holland.

Hartley, J. (2005). Innovation in Governance and Public Services: Past and Present. *Public Money & Management*, 25(1), 27–34.

Hinz, V. & Ingerfurth, S. (2013). Does Ownership Matter under Challenging Conditions? On the Relationship Between Organizational Entrepreneurship and Performance in the Health Care Sector. *Public Management Review*, 15(7), 969–991.

Hirst, P. (1994). Associative democracy. *DISSENT-NEW YORK*- 241–241.

Hirst, P. (2000). Models of Democratic Governance in a Post-Liberal Society. In B. Greve (Ed.), *What Constitutes a Good Society?* London & New York: Macmillan Press & St. Martins' Press.

Hulgård, L. (2014). Social Enterprise and the Third Sector—Innovative Service Delivery or a Non-capitalist Economy? In J. Defourny, L. Hulgård & V. Pestoff (Eds.), *Social Enterprise and the Third Sector—Changing European Landscapes in a Comparative Perspective*. London & New York: Routledge.

Johnson, S. (2010). *Where Good Ideas Come From: The Natural History of Innovation*. London & New York: Penguin.

Kerlin, J. (2006). Social Enterprise in the United States and Abroad: Learning from Our Differences. In R. Mosher-Williams (Ed.), *Research on Social Entrepreneurship*. ARNOVA Occasional Paper Series, 1(3), 105–125.

Kjærgaard Thomsen, M. & Jakobsen, M. (2015). Influencing Citizen Coproduction by Sending Encouragement and Advice: A Field Experiment. *International Public Management Journal*, 18(2), 286–303.

Larsgaard, A.-K., Hauge, H. & Eide, K. (2015). *Improving Children's Participation in Child Welfare Services through Social Enterprise*. Paper presented at EMES conference in Helsinki, Finland.

Levander, U. (2011). *Utanförskap på entreprenad: Diskurser om sociala företag i Sverige*. Göteborg: Daidalos Förlag.

Moore, M. & Hartley, J. (2012). Innovations in Governance: Introduction to *the New Public Governance?* In S. P. Osborne (Ed.), *Emerging Perspectives on the Theory and Practice of Public Governance*. London & New York: Routledge.

Moulaert, F., Jessop, B., Hulgård, L. & Hamdouch, A. (2013). Social Innovation: A New Stage in Innovation Process Analysis? In F. Moulaert, D. MacCallum, A. Mehmood & A. Hamdouch (Eds.), *Handbook on Social Innovation: Collective*

Action, Social Learning and Transdisciplinary Research. Cheltenham, UK & Northampton, MA: Edward Elgar.

OECD. (2011). *Together for Better Public Services: Partnering with Citizens and Civil Society.* Paris: Public Governance Reviews, OECD.

Osborne, S. P. (2010). The (New) Public Governance: A Suitable Case for Treatment? In S. P. Osborne (Ed.), *The New Public Governance? Emerging Perspectives on the Theory and Practice of Public Governance.* London & New York: Routledge.

Osborne, S. P., Radnor, Z. & Nasi, G. (2013). A New Theory for Public Service Management? Towards a (Public) Service Dominant Approach. *American Review of Public Administration Review,* 43(2), 135–158.

Ostrom, E. (1996/1999). Crossing the Great Divide: Coproduction, Synergy, and Development. *World Development,* 24(6), 1073–1087. Reprinted (1999) in M. D. McGinnis (Ed.), *Polycentric Governance and Development: Readings from the Workshop in Political Theory and Policy Analysis.* Ann Arbor, MI: University of Michigan Press.

Ostrom, E. (2000). Crowding Out Citizenship. *Scandinavian Political Studies,* 23(1), 1–16.

Parks, R. B., Baker, P. C., Kiser, L., Oakerson, R., Ostrom, E., Ostrom, V., Perry, S. L., Vandivort, M. B. & Whitaker, G. P. (1981/1999). Consumers as Co-Producers of Public Services: Some Economic and Institutional Considerations. *Policy Studies Journal,* 9, 1001–1011. Reprinted (1999) in M. D. McGinnis (Ed.), *Local Public Economies: Readings from the Workshop in Political Theory and Policy Analysis.* Ann Arbor, MI: University of Michigan Press.

Pekkola, E., Tuurnas, S., Stenvall, J. & Hakari, K. (2015). *Implementing Top-Down Localization Policies—Creation of Local Public Value?* Paper presented at IIAS Study Group on Co-production, Nijmegen, Holland.

Pestoff, V. (1998). *Beyond the Market & State: Civil Democracy & Social Enterprises in a Welfare Society.* Aldershot, Brookfield, Singapore, & Sydney: Ashgate.

Pestoff, V. (2006/2009). Citizens as Co-Producers of Welfare Services: Preschool Services in Eight European Countries. *Public Management Review,* 8(4), 503–520. Reprinted (2009) in V. Pestoff & T. Brandsen (Eds.), *Co-Production, the Third Sector and the Delivery of Public Services.* London & New York: Routledge.

Pestoff, V. (2009). Towards a Paradigm of Democratic Governance: Citizen Participation and Co-Production of Personal Social Services in Sweden. *Annals of Public and Cooperative Economy,* 80(2), 197–224.

Pestoff, V. (2011). *Lost in Translation or What's Not Included in the Polish Social Economy?* Paper presented at the ISTR International Conference, Siena, Italy.

Pestoff, V. & Hulgård, L. (2015). Participatory Governance in Social Enterprise. *VOLUNTAS: International Journal of Voluntary and Nonprofit Organizations:* 1–18.

Pestoff, V. & Vamstad, J. (2014). Enriching Work Environment in the Welfare Service Sector: The Case of Social Enterprises in Swedish Childcare. *Annals of Public & Co-Operative Economics,* 85(3), 353–370.

Rogers, E. M. (1995). *Diffusion of Innovation.* New York: Free Press.

Salge, T. & Vera, A. (2009). Hospital Innovativeness and Organizational Performance: Evidence from English Public Acute Care. *Health Care Management Review,* 34(1), 54–67.

Socialstyrelsen. (2014). *Flere og stærkere socialøkonomiske virksomheder i Danmark*. København: Ministeriet for børn, ligestilling, integration og sociale forhold. Copenhagen: Socialstyrelsen.

Tortzen, A. (2015). *Leading Co-production—Building a Conceptual Framework*. Paper presented at the IIAS Study Group on Co-production, Nijmegen, Holland.

Tuurnas, S. (2015). *The Professional Co-producer: Implications from Four Case Studies*. Paper presented at IIAS Study Group on Co-production in Nijmegen, Holland.

Vamstad, J. (2007). *Governing Welfare: The Third Sector and the Challenges to the Swedish Welfare State*. Östersund: Mid-Sweden University Press.

Verschuere, B., Brandsen, T. & Pestoff, V. (2012). Co-production: The State of the Art in Research and the Future Agenda. *VOLUNTAS: International Journal of Voluntary and Nonprofit Organizations*, 23(4), 1083–1101.

Walker, R. M. (2014). Internal and External Antecedents of Process Innovation: A Review and Extension. *Public Management Review*, 16(1), 21–44.

Wood, V. R., Bhuian, S. & Kiecker, P. (2000). Market Orientation and Organizational Performance in Not-for-Profit Hospitals. *Journal of Business Research*, 48(3), 213–226.

Young, D. (2008). Alternative Perspectives on Social Enterprise. In J. J. Cordes & C. E. Steuerle (Eds.), *Nonprofits & Business*. Washington, DC: The Urban Institute.

Young, D. (2009). A Unified Theory of Social Enterprise. In G. E. Shockley, G. P. Frank & R. Stough (Eds.), *Non-Market Entrepreneurship: Interdisciplinary Approaches*. Cheltenham, UK & Northampton, MA: Edward Elgar.

About the Authors

Linda Lundgaard Andersen is a Professor at Roskilde University in Denmark and the Co-Director of the Centre of Social Entrepreneurship. Her research focuses on theoretical and empirical work in learning, social entrepreneurship and social innovation in welfare services, democratic forms of governance and hybridity, life history and ethnographies, and she has contributed to national and Nordic reports on social enterprises. lla@ruc.dk

Jonas Asheim is the Co-Founder of the design agency Nice and a Lecturer in the Department of Engineering Design and Materials at the Norwegian University of Science and Technology. Jonas has extensive practical experience working as a social entrepreneur and designer in Port Au Prince, Haiti, framing his research interests in social sustainability and design education. jonas@wearenice.com

Fredrik Björk is a Lecturer in the Department of Urban Studies at Malmö University. His research interests include the general areas of environmental history, urban studies and social-ecological innovations, with a special focus on cross-sector collaboration and the role of third-sector organizations in sustainable urban development. fredrik.bork@mah.se

Anders Edvik is a Senior Lecturer and Faculty Programme Director in the Department of Urban Studies at Malmö University. His research focuses on temporary organizations and cross-boundary collaboration in terms of organizing and leading organizational development. His research interests include social innovation and social entrepreneurship within the field of third-sector organizations. anders.edvik@mah.se

Daniel Ericsson is an Associate Professor at Linnaéus University in Sweden. He is particularly interested in understanding how creativity and entrepreneurship are constructed and organized in society and in different ways of rethinking organization and leadership. daniel.ericsson@lnu.se

Yvonne von Friedrichs is a Professor at Mid Sweden University. She has devoted her research to the understanding of the significance of individual and collective entrepreneurship for regional and local development.

Her research interests include social entrepreneurship and social enterprises, gender equality in entrepreneurship, entrepreneurial networks and tourism destination development. yvonne.vonfriedrichs@miun.se

Malin Gawell is an Associated Professor at Södertörn University in Stockholm and has for years been engaged in the research institute ESBRI. Her research on social entrepreneurship, social enterprises and activist entrepreneurship is related to individuals' engagement in such activities and how this shapes and is shaped by organizations, civil society and welfare structures. She addresses these topics also at the policy level. malin.gawell@sh.se

Hans Abraham Hauge is an Associate Professor in the Department of Social Studies at University College of Southeast Norway. His research focuses on empowerment processes in the provision of social services, leadership in public and voluntary organizations and the tailoring of educational programmes to organizational development in social services. hans.a.hauge@hit.no

Lars Hulgård is a Professor at Roskilde University in Denmark and at University College South East Norway. He is the co-founder and president of the EMES International Research Network (2010–2016) and the co-director of the Centre for Social Entrepreneurship at Roskilde University. His research interests are related to civil society, social innovation, solidarity economy and social entrepreneurship. hulg@ruc.dk

Bengt Johannisson is a senior Professor of Entrepreneurship at Linnaeus University in Sweden, and a former editor of *Entrepreneurship & Regional Development*. He has published widely on entrepreneurship, personal networking and on local/regional development. His present interests are process and practice theories and enactive methodology as applied to, for example, soci(et)al entrepreneurship. bengt.johannisson@lnu.se

Harri Kostilainen is a PhD Candidate and senior advisor (RDI) at the Diaconia University of Applied Sciences in Helsinki. He has 20 years of experience developing social enterprises. He is the executive director of FinSERN (the Finnish Social Enterprise Network). His main research interests are social innovations and social enterprises in the context of the renewal of welfare services. harri.kostilainen@diak.fi.

Catharina Juul Kristensen is a Senior Lecturer in social sciences (sociology) in the Department of Social Sciences and Business at Roskilde University in Denmark. Her research interests include social intrapreneurship and social innovation in street-level organizations, employee-driven innovation, organizational ethnography and social exclusion and marginality. Her recent work includes articles on social innovation in social work and employee-driven innovation. cjk@ruc.dk

Ulrika Levander is a Lecturer in the School of Social Work at Lund University in Sweden. Her research focuses on the role of civil society, social economy and social entrepreneurship in ongoing welfare transitions in Sweden. In 2011, she defended her PhD thesis in social work, in which discourses of work-integrating social enterprises in Sweden were examined and critically discussed. ulrika.levander@soch.lu.se

Anders Lundström is a Professor Emeritus at Mälardalens University in Sweden and the Managing Director of the Institute of Innovative Entrepreneurship (IPREG). He has mainly researched developments and effects of entrepreneurship and SME policy programmes nationally and internationally. During recent years, the development of a broad perspective on entrepreneurship, especially in sparsely populated areas, has been the focus of his interest. anders.lundstrom@mdh.se

Brita Fladvad Nielsen is a recent PhD graduate from the Norwegian University of Science and Technology. She has worked as industrial design engineer for the UN and in Norwegian industry. Her research focus has been to apply design thinking as an approach to understand complex stakeholder systems and how to integrate end-user needs into design. In her thesis, design in humanitarian relief markets was highlighted. brita.nielsen@ntnu.no

Victor Pestoff is a Professor Emeritus at Ersta-Sköndal University College in Sweden and a Guest Professor at Osaka University, Japan, and at Roskilde University, Denmark. His research focuses on the role of non-profit organizations, co-operatives and social enterprises in the (re)democratization of the welfare state. He has published more than 100 articles/chapters and 20 books. His current research explores the co-production of health and elder care in Japan. victor.pestoff@esh.se.

Pekka Pättiniemi, PhD, is the President of the Finnish Social Enterprise Network (FinSERN). He has conducted research on social enterprises and co-operatives for many years, mostly in European research and development projects. He has participated also in practical work supporting social enterprises nationwide, for example, the Sortso Co-operative. pekka.pattiniemi@sortso.fi

Unni Beate Sekkesæter is a PhD Fellow affiliated with Roskilde University in the Centre for Social Entrepreneurship. She is also a pioneering practitioner in social entrepreneurship in Norway. In 1996, she founded and has since then been managing a microfinance programme for financially excluded persons in Norway, such as immigrants and those excluded from the labour market. She is also involved in the social business and microfinance sector internationally. unbeate@online.no

Roger Spear is a Professor of Social Entrepreneurship at the Open University UK, where he teaches about organizations and innovation. He is also a guest professor at the University of Roskilde's Centre for Social Entrepreneurship. He conducts research on social entrepreneurship and social enterprise typically through European research projects. r.g.spear@open.ac.uk

Elisabeth Sundin is a Professor in Business Administration in the Department of Economic and Industrial Development and a Research Leader at the Helix Vinn Excellence Centre at Linköping University, Sweden. Her research interests have developed over time—from self-employment and regional development to entrepreneurship, technology, gender and age. Currently, she focuses on entrepreneurship, organizational change and mainly public and social organizations. elisabeth.sundin@liu.se

Malin Tillmar is a Professor in Business Administration in the Department of Management and Engineering and the Deputy Director of the Helix Vinn Excellence Centre at Linköping University in Sweden. Her research deals with organizational change in various contexts, from public, private and social organizations in Sweden to SMEs in East Africa. Theoretically, entrepreneurship, trust and gender are among the key words. malin.tillmar@liu.se

Tora Mathea Wasvik is a PhD student in the Department of Social Studies at University College of Southeast Norway. Her research focuses on the relationships between social entrepreneurship and labour market integration for disabled people in the context of the Norwegian welfare state. tora.m.wasvik@hit.no

Index

of European perspective 255–6; financial instruments for 70; in Finland 58–73; four-dimensional model 10–11; identification criteria 27; as institutional form created by social entrepreneurs 28; institutionalization of Finnish social enterprise concept 68–73; as labour market measure 65–6; local councils on meaning of 87; major approaches to 8–10; meanings of 2–4, 45, 220; narratives of 232–48; precursors of emergence of social enterprise in Norway 80–2; public debate on 253–4; relationship between social entrepreneurship and 26–8; research community 69–70; research on social enterprise in Norway 78–80; as rhetorical device 88; scope and scale 12–14; seed funding 78, 85–7, 88; seed funding institutions on meaning of 85–6; social entrepreneurs on the meaning of 83–4; social value creation in 26; training and education 69–70; university studies 11–12; as vehicle for renewing welfare state service provision 66–7; voluntary organizations on meaning of 84–5; work-integrating social enterprises 239–47

social entrepreneuring: challenges in enactment 108–10; knowledge creation in 93–4; as practice 95–6

social entrepreneurs: characteristics of 128, 135–8; employees as 113–22; on meaning of social enterprise 83–4; meeting points 135–8; motivations of 89; roles of 24–5; social enterprise and 26, 28, 52–3; sources of inspiration for 151

social entrepreneurship: calls for a critical analysis of 54; characteristics of 1–2; in City of Malmö 141–3, 151–6; as collaborative processes in rural Sweden 165–75; community development role 50; conditions for 228–9; in contemporary social design in Norway 126–38; cultural and geographic context of 135; current expressions of 45–9; in Denmark 8, 22–3, 29–34; development of 12, 22–4; development of social activities role 50; discourse 143–4; ecosystems of support for 10–12; emerging institutional structures 10–12;

examining from critical perspective 235–6; forms of 24–6; four-dimensional model 10–11; historical phases in Sweden 42–5; major approaches to 8–10; market-based solutions and 51–2; meanings of 2–4, 23–4, 41–2, 220; non-profit sector and 16, 45, 117, 255; in the Nordic Countries 6–14; origins of 12; as panacea of 'social ills' 232–5; as part of welfare discourse 33–4; policies 10–12; reality of 141–4; relationship between social enterprise and 26–8; roles of 49–52; roots and horizon 23–4; scope and scale 12–14; social design and 126–7; social issues role 50–1; state regulation of 33; in transformed welfare society 215–17; university studies 11–12; value-creating and/or innovative role of 49–50; as vehicle for powerful and conflicting values 22–3; versions of 9

Social Entrepreneurship Research Network for the Nordic Countries 128

Social Entrepreneurship: What Everyone Needs to Know (Bornstein & Davis) 143, 149–51

'social exclusion' 236–40

social impact 85, 129, 138, 162

social innovation: categories of 257; in City of Malmö 151–3; co-production as 253; definition of 23, 114–15, 121, 257–8; democratic regime of governance and 253, 265–6; developing regional ecosystem for 204–9; governance innovation 258, 264; outcome of 258; potential in Nordic countries 128; projects and 198–200; public sector innovation 256–8; role of legitimacy in organizing 198–211; variety of approaches related to 3

social innovation initiatives 12

social innovation theory 23

social innovator 137

social intrapreneurs 117–19, 121

social intrapreneurship 114, 116

'social inventions' 31

social inventions 31–2

social model design 129

social networking 172

Social Network Innovation (SNI) 101–3

social origins theory 5, 12

social policy paradigms 35